The Last Years of Saint Thérèse

The Last Years of Saint Thérèse

Doubt and Darkness, 1895–1897

THOMAS R. NEVIN

OXFORD
UNIVERSITY PRESS

OXFORD
UNIVERSITY PRESS

Oxford University Press is a department of the University of Oxford.
It furthers the University's objective of excellence in research, scholarship,
and education by publishing worldwide.

Oxford   New York
Auckland   Cape Town   Dar es Salaam   Hong Kong   Karachi
Kuala Lumpur   Madrid   Melbourne   Mexico City   Nairobi
New Delhi   Shanghai   Taipei   Toronto

With offices in
Argentina   Austria   Brazil   Chile   Czech Republic   France   Greece
Guatemala   Hungary   Italy   Japan   Poland   Portugal   Singapore
South Korea   Switzerland   Thailand   Turkey   Ukraine   Vietnam

Oxford is a registered trademark of Oxford University Press in the UK and certain other countries.

Published in the United States of America by
Oxford University Press
198 Madison Avenue, New York, NY 10016

© Oxford University Press 2013

All rights reserved. No part of this publication may be reproduced, stored in
a retrieval system, or transmitted, in any form or by any means, without the prior
permission in writing of Oxford University Press, or as expressly permitted by law,
by license, or under terms agreed with the appropriate reproduction rights organization.
Inquiries concerning reproduction outside the scope of the above should be sent to the
Rights Department, Oxford University Press, at the address above.

You must not circulate this work in any other form
and you must impose this same condition on any acquirer.

Library of Congress Cataloging-in-Publication Data
Nevin, Thomas R., 1944–
The last years of Saint Thérèse : doubt and darkness, 1895–1897 / by Thomas R. Nevin.
pages cm
Includes bibliographical references and index.
ISBN 978-0-19-998766-5 (cloth : alk. paper)
1. Thérèse, de Lisieux, Saint, 1873–1897.   I. Title.
BX4700.T5N475 2013
282.092—dc23
[B]
2012043169

3 5 7 9 8 6 4 2
Printed in the United States of America
on acid-free paper

Uxori meae

Contents

Preface: Dwelling Upon Darkness	ix
Introduction	xv
Abbreviations	xix
1. Her Spanish Masters in Darkness: Teresa of Ávila and John of the Cross	1
2. Seeking Light in the Bible	37
3. Bearing the Cross of Community	79
4. Her Spiritual Brothers Guide Her Down: Père Hyacinthe Loyson and Léo Taxil	123
5. Final Charity: The Last Autobiography	147
Conclusion: A Human Passion	197
Appendix 1: The Text of Thérèse Witnessing to Her Doubt: Manuscript C 5v–6v	201
Appendix 2: On Another Darkness: Once More, Teresa of Ávila	205
Notes	211
A Selective Bibliography	259
Index	285

Preface: Dwelling upon Darkness

ACCORDING TO THE Carmel prioress who knew her best, Thérèse, universally known as The Little Flower, spent most of her mature life in darkness. That darkness is not suggested by prayer cards, nor is it associated with the pilgrimages to Lisieux and numerous hagiographies. This book is about that continuous darkness, its sources within and beyond her, in her writings and in her severe education by saints and contemporaries.

The very brief life of this very beloved woman is richly documented by her own abundant writings; by a host of images of her, both photographic and inspirational; by the testimonies of those who knew her; by the ancillary texts of Carmel and of Catholic tradition—one might pause a while before undertaking a journey in her arduous direction toward the truth.

This book, caveat lector, is not a saint's life but the study of a Carmelite sister ordered by her prioresses to bring her life into coherence with the world she knew. She did so as a writer. What makes her recounted life intriguing for any reader who sincerely cares to approach her is that she worked toward that coherence by an irreducible amalgam of reminiscence and self-exhortation. Near death, she confessed she was writing not what she believed but what she wanted to believe. That confession serves as a touchstone for all of her writing life.

To many Christians and perhaps to most of her devotees, Thérèse is the saint of the Little Way of confidence, the sainthood of the ordinary, daily life of small deeds and gifts. She confounds the centuries-old view of sainthood as a remote and lofty attainment of the extraordinary and few. She brings a democratic sweetness and light. This book, however, focuses upon the counterpoint to her confidence: the darkness of doubt, extended to atheism, gathered within her in her last years. I am not arguing that under an almost overwhelming spiritual menace "the real" Thérèse appears; only that the turbulence she had to deal with deeply informs her spirituality and enriches her teaching. Indeed, many Christians know that the darkness she faced is part of their own ordinary, daily life amid benevolence and benefaction.

As a saint, Thérèse, no matter her popular appeal, seems hermetically sealed, like her dust in the gold cask by which she travels yearly around the globe. As a

Carmelite, she was immured from the world for the last nine of her twenty-four years. Hagiographies further seal her off. Yet she came from the wider world, and her vulnerability owes much to it. Short of a detailed, multi-volume biography such as she, along with her family, deserves, we have invaluable archival testimony summoning back that pre-Carmel life and showing how it portended the darkness which engulfed her.

Here are three brief instances. Marie Martin, Thérèse's eldest sister, writing her deposition for the beatification hearings, recalled the ramrod proprieties of their father, Louis. She remembered him leading her and her sisters home from the 7 A.M. mass at the Cathedral of Saint-Pierre in Lisieux: "At this morning hour the occupants of the Galerie de Navarin were getting dressed and we amused ourselves watching them as we passed. One day, my father said to us, 'Pay attention, my children, to all that could tarnish the purity of your heart and don't be looking indiscreetly right and left.'"[1]

Another story from Marie: "Next to our house, Les Buissonnets, lived an officer, whose wife, a rather loose woman, used to laugh and run in the garden with his aide-de-camp and that did not escape our notice. Sometimes we watched through the trees. Our father saw it and told us to stop because it was a danger."[2] Was the surveillance itself a danger, or was Louis referring to the antics of that couple straight out of Zola in the next garden? And was Thérèse present among the "we" on one or another of those "sometimes," as she surely was on the daily strolls home from church?

What is the published hagiographic account given by Marie? Only this summing up about Louis: "He took extreme care to distance us from everything that seemed to him an occasion for temptation."[3] But those vivid particulars, which Marie was bold enough to record (only to have them censored by someone's blue marker), say so much more than the monochromatic affirmation of her father's protectiveness. They suggest that the Martin sisters were normal girls, embarrassed into giggles at the sight of nudity and titillated by what they sensed was a lively scandal next door. These are the behaviors of an ordinary adolescence, but not what the panel at the hearings cared to know about. And not what Thérèse chose to tell us about her childhood.

Céline, the sister closest to Thérèse, also speaks from the archive. She recalls a laundress, openly a nonbeliever, who came to their house. Early in 1888, when she was fifteen, Thérèse tried to instruct and persuade this woman about Catholic doctrine but was answered only with mocking jokes. Then Thérèse took from her neck a medallion of the Virgin and gave it to the woman, telling her "I'm going to enter the Carmel. I want to leave you this memory. Promise me that you'll keep it always." Moved, the woman promised. Years later, when Céline saw her, she asked about "the little Carmelite" and showed the medallion around her neck: "I'm keeping my word to her and I'll die with this."[4] Céline never saw her again.

In that episode Thérèse had recognized and confronted a nonbeliever in the hope of winning her to the Christian faith, a maneuver which seldom succeeds. Frustrated, she resorted to an "act of love." She does not record it in her first manuscript, but it indicates that she knew firsthand of the world which at her life's close she situated at a banquet table, in her darkness.

This book begins with a narrative on the first saints of Carmel. Thérèse's life was powerfully informed by Teresa de Jesús, founder of the Discalced Order of Carmel, and Juan de la Cruz, to whose mystical verse and commentaries Thérèse owed a little, but richly. I refer to them as Teresa and Juan. Although Thérèse is a saint of folk Catholicism, they, with their heady visions, baroque elevations and (above all) centuries of distance, cannot ever be, but both of them introduced her to love's darkness. They are her spiritual parents, but she learned at great cost that she could not live up to their spirituality. Through them she took her first of many faltering steps.

In the second chapter, I take up the Bible, with Thérèse a keenly selective reader trying to understand the affliction, the cross of doubt given to her. I profile her rapport with Jesus, her would-be mystical spouse. (She remained a novice to her last day.) Over the past few generations, Jesus and God the Father have been depicted as all-merciful and loving. Punitive, terroristic, extortionist Jehovah has been shortchanged, save in the vengeful fantasies of apocalypticism. Jesus the wrathful and judgmental has also been obscured. Thérèse has done perhaps more than any other saint to promote the notion of a divine love that overrides divine justice and subsumes it, but her Jesus is the Suffering Servant heralded by Isaiah: abused, misunderstood, tormented, persecuted, annihilated—all of that depicted in the Holy Face she bore as her own denomination. The Suffering Servant wills that she go to what she called the table of sorrow so that, in true imitation, she too may be a suffering servant.

The third chapter looks at Thérèse's painful service to the Carmel community, which gave her a first version of the table of suffering, a gospel of darkness shown in her correspondence with Céline. Other young sisters afford no less important, if less extensive witnessing. I draw heavily from their testimonies at the two beatification hearings (1911, 1916). These relationships reveal how imperfectly Thérèse struggled toward the impossible perfection of doing God's will and how she learned to make her very imperfect self exemplary for other women. Posing their several tests the novices helped her to see, far more discerningly than she had been able to before, the community in a luminous desolation. A new understanding of charity, informed by a loss of faith, forms the mainspring of her last autobiography, Manuscript C.

Two vivid derelicts, highly publicized in their day, occupy the fourth chapter: Fr. Hyacinthe Loyson, an ex-Carmelite friar, and Léo Taxil, a notorious con man. They helped her downward to the table of sorrow; both scandalized her profoundly and personally. I refer to them as her "spiritual brothers," as they occupy the dismal community outside of Catholicism, the community where she finally located her doubting and herself.

The final chapter commences with an archaeology of Manuscript C, its burial within the strata of editing Mère Marie de Gonzague and Père Godefroid Madelaine undertook after Thérèse's death: the product, *The Story of a Soul*, was a benevolent, not altogether beneficent re-casting of Thérèse's writing. Her sister, Pauline, to whose judgment she had always deferred, wrote the palimpsest. This reworking created a misperception that lasted for over fifty years.

Manuscript C marks the culmination of Thérèse's reflections on her place in Christian life and community. It was written literally at fever pitch and with the author's awareness of death's long and desultory encroachment upon her. It is studded with revelatory passages, yet its importance has been sedulously ignored by establishment writers on Thérèse. I look upon its chiaroscuro of lessons, those of frailty and of strength, of perception and confusion, in which she reaches toward humanity in the stumbling way of the cross she was bearing.

All translations from the French and Spanish have been my own. For the convenience of readers, I have placed the translations within the chapters and have cited the complete original passages in the notes along with the identification of their texts. As in my previous book, *Thérèse of Lisieux: God's Gentle Warrior*, I have drawn upon two French lexicons that date from her time, Émile Littré's *Dictionnaire de la langue française* (the edition of 1883–1884) and Louis-Nicholas Bescherelle's *Nouveau dictionnaire classique de la langue française* of 1897. Because this book, distinct from its predecessor, concentrates upon the prolonged struggle Thérèse undertook against doubt and despair, the annotated bibliography identifies only the works, books and films that address that struggle from different vantages. I call them Theresian because of the candor in their confrontations with precisely those steep and menacing challenges that do not offer Christians sustenance and consolation.

I have happily accumulated many debts through helpful and attentive friends and colleagues. Dr. Doris Donnelly, Director of the Cardinal Suenens Center in Theology and Church Life, John Carroll University, kindly gave me time to air in a public lecture some of my rethinking on Thérèse, as of January 30, 2007.

I wish to thank Dr. Nadia Lokma, General Director of Conservation, who facilitated an address on Thérèse and Islam, which I delivered on December 31, 2007, at the Egyptian Ministry of Culture, Cairo. I thank my sponsor there, Dr Abdelrazer, for his generous hospitality and many tours of Islamic sites during the two weeks of my stay in Egypt. Other very helpful readers, to whom I gave individual chapters, include Dr. Sharon Voros, Dr. Zeki Saritoprek, Fr. Donald Cozzens, and Fr. John McNamee.

For their help in securing inter-library loan materials thanks to Bridget Borato and Ellen Valentine of the Grasselli Library, John Carroll University. For technological help I am grateful to Carrie Huszczo, Joann Lentine and Norma Piccirillo. For assistance with the photographs I cordially thank Austin Nevin and Serena Martucci.

I am especially grateful to my wife, Caroline Zilboorg, for her time, patience and sharp eye during her reading of each chapter's final draft.

For a summer research grant that allowed me to explore the Carmelitana holdings of the Joachim Smet Library at Whitefriars, in Washington, D.C., I owe much thanks to the John Carroll University Committee on Research and Faculty Development. The Whitefriars have been models of charitable hosting in an optimal setting of quiet and texts. I am grateful to the library's secretary, Patricia O"Callaghan, for opening the library to me and to Duncan, her amiable golden retriever. My thanks go to the prior, Fr. Quinn Connors, and the community of Carmes. I also thank another community, warm and lively, the Society of Saint Joseph and its rector, Fr. Brian Fox, for housing and feeding me during my weeks of research.

The greatest debt I owe to the present community of Carmel at Lisieux, especially to the archival staff who responded to my inquiries and requests with unstinting patience and efficiency. Two of them read my manuscript, not without objections but never without charity. To the community I remain grateful for every opening of their monastic door. I am happy to add that since the completion of this book, the Carmel of Lisieux has all of Thérèse's documentation now online, and a complete English translation will soon be available.

Finally, I wish to thank Cynthia Read and the editorial staff at Oxford University Press, especially Marcela Maxfield and Sravanthi Sridharan, for their steadfast patience with me and Thérèse.

However many errors and acts of folly the reader might discover in this book, they have all been my doing.

Introduction

IN *THÉRÈSE OF LISIEUX: God's Gentle Warrior* I set Thérèse's last years in the broad context of her familial and Carmelite lives. The present study focuses on a corridor of darkening rooms: in the first of these, we look upon the high and daunting vaults of the Spanish Carmel she faced, the foundational house of her spiritual life; in another, we find her struggling with fellow novices replete in worldly failings; in another, she pores over the Bible in an effort to bolster herself; in the last, she barely survives the month of her final, sustained writing (June 1897) as her sorely tried spirit matures into the second title of her name, the Holy, hidden Face of the Suffering Servant. There, we reach the last of her three "autobiographical" manuscripts, known simply as C.

During these years Thérèse struggles with numerous questions. What happens when the anticipatory virtues, faith and hope, are subtracted from one's life so that only the practice of charity, the Christian meaning of love, remains? How can this charity suffice? Is the soul, no matter how charitable, not inevitably faced with a doubt threatening to destroy it? How can such a condition be sustained as a distinctly Christian life? Is it a dire aberration that one must shun and pray to be spared—"lead us not into temptation but deliver us from evil"—or are there doors opening to a deeper spirituality than can be realized without such a stripping down to nakedness like Job's?

This book thus addresses the doubt within the life and writing of a saint who is best known for the opposite of doubt, confidence. Thérèse's symbolic terms for doubt were "tunnel," "fog," and "vault," each of them suggesting darkness, dimness, enclosure, and a failure or lack of vision. In this spiritual confinement, she spoke of herself as weak and little, helpless in finding a way through and out. But what did doubt mean to her? What was its source and nature? What was its object—herself, Jesus, God, her chosen life in Carmel? Was it wholly a negative force, or in part a healthy skepticism? What syndrome of factors distinguished it from melancholy, boredom, listlessness?

Was this syndrome the product of her environments, secular and contemplative, and thus assimilated, or was it created within and by her fragile "little" self as a protection? Did she enlist "the world" and the Carmel into an alliance with her susceptibilities, all directed against herself? Was her resolve to stay within the novitiate a refusal to face spiritual maturity?

The catch-all term that the Church had long used for doubt was *acedia*, but that word had and still enjoys a wide valence.[1] Thérèse's doubt was not the *acedia* of anger expressed or repressed; not the *acedia* of sloth nor aversion; not its dejection nor the tedium that says nothing is worth doing; not a paralysis of the will and emphatically not a refusal of love by willful separation from others.

Thérèse's writing illuminates her special variety of doubt. Her account of herself is not only descriptive, of places, of people, of events. It is also desiderative. Despite her sometimes treacly style, an impassioned and vulnerable sensibility is within it. As a writer she struggled in psalmic language; she hungered and thirsted. Her sister Pauline, a spiritual mother who knew her very well, attested that Thérèse spent most of her Carmel years in a condition Carmelites then called *sécheresse*, a dryness that sentenced its victim to a masked, performing life.

This term, like doubt, requires close examining. In nineteenth-century French dictionaries *sécheresse* denotes the state of a soul that feels no consolation in practicing piety. Paradoxically, it is a drama in which God is impresario. Eminent seventeenth-century divines reveal some directions in the script, such as "You'll pluck all the fruit God wants from your aridities," and "God delivers those he tests to all the dryness of a mournful and bitter virtue."[2]

From the Church's perspective, doubt and dryness were not about hypocrisy but testing and endurance. The daily sequences of monastic life proved a torture for the tested soul, but they were also a stay. Thérèse had to look up to as well as live up to the life of Carmel, but she remained self-convinced she was too inadequate to do so. Then, grey turned to black and helplessness toward despair. What makes her story exceptional is that she reflected, thought, prayed, and, most important, wrote in the midst of losing the center and focus upon which all of her life had been concentrated, the celestial life with God. The Christian paradox is that such a loss was also a process of finding, and she believed her downward path had been set for her by Jesus. It was a path she could never have anticipated and would never have prayed to be given.

Thérèse gives what the theologian Rowan Williams has called a "touchstone of integrity" in witnessing to "so broad and comprehensive an access to the 'sacred source' of Christian commitment."[3] Williams's agents for this integrity—Edith Stein, Thomas Merton, and Dorothy Day—all admired and celebrated Thérèse but took their own distinctive ways, as life and adversity assigned them. Unlike the hypertrophically intellectual Stein, Thérèse was not martyred. Unlike Merton, she did not realize a career in writing and its peculiar dangers in celebrity. Unlike Day, she had no politics to negotiate in the face of an obtusely uncomprehending world. What she did have, however, was a tutelage in twofold dying, physically and spiritually and on both counts terribly, at an age when she was still green, questing, and naive. Dying stripped her down mercilessly and ripened her fast.

Her third manuscript becomes a riposte to the hazards of doubt. Only by engaging the world in all its horribleness can Christian love have any meaning, but that engagement is risky. Sitting finally with those to whom Christ was wholly unknown, or, if known, despised, Thérèse had to accept Christ as himself a mystery to her; she, in taking his place at the table, could no longer see him within the consoling vantage of her convent life, where he was communally loved and adored.

Thérèse discovered that what at first seemed alienation for her became instead a communion with God at a level deeper than she had known prior to her final testing. She passed into what she called "the abyss of love." Finally, her life finds completion in her internalizing the Christian story of descent into the lowest stratum of human life. Ironically, she is closest to God when outwardly she seems to us most remote from God, because in the lowest stratum the reach of her charity becomes all-inclusive.

She was fearless, not in the sense of a headstrong, reckless defiance of doubt's darkness, but in her sustained awareness that it was the ground for a divine testing of her. All of her life had prepared her for the inner certainty that Jesus had allowed the darkness to come upon her. Jesus had been asleep to her and her longing for most of her twenty-four years, even though, as she fondly put it, his heart remained awake. At times, like the beloved young man in the Song of Solomon, he had been altogether absent, and she, like the beloved young woman of that canticle, had to go in search of him. At no time was Thérèse free of this intimate politics with Jesus. Because Jesus was the center of her spiritual and emotive life, he had to figure in the descent, the dramaturgy of her darkness. He was its agent.

This certainty did not entail a cocksure triumphalism, a presumption that she was due to be rescued from or relieved of the darkness. If she had been kept forever waiting for his awakening to her, why should she not have to remain forever awaiting his return? There is no specious victory here, no bogus uplift, no roseate dénouement. Thy will be done.

Thérèse in her darkness led an unexceptional, if not altogether normative Christian life. Doubt within her claims its integral due as the underside of trust, exerting its tug against the will by a hardy and peculiar resistance to all energies beyond prayer. Doubt forms a rite of passage. One of Thérèse's indispensable lessons is the unperturbed acceptance of helplessness. With acceptance comes imperturbability. Prayer is not helpless, but prayer is a grace, one of the divine abundances, as St. Paul would put it, not of human doing but in it.

Indeed, Thérèse's darkness puts her within a grand, substantially modern continuum of Christian struggle. That struggle derives from the gospels themselves: the Our Father cries out against demonic wiles. This study shows supplications before darkness and temptation were well posted throughout Thérèse's years in Carmel. Every night, when monastic life was acutely still, became devil-ridden territory in which a nun might stray in confusion and anxiety. Sisters were alone with sometimes morbid fears. In one of the *circulaires* (the Carmel's obituary), a sister confessed to her ongoing dread of rotting away in her grave; others were prey to the certainty of their damnation. The continuous darkness Thérèse experienced would have justified some psychopathic release. Her unfailing lucidity is one of the treasures left to us.

Thérèse, although living within the gospels in this book, is a modern. Like her mighty spiritual brother, Dostoevsky, she came to realize she was a child of her age, subject to the suasions of those she knew of only in privatives: non-Catholics, nonbelievers, materialists, or those whom Feuerbach, anticipating crowers against God in the early twenty-first century, denominated anti-theists. Dostoevsky, after his four years of imprisonment, wrote of his discovery that nothing was so beautiful, so true, so good as Christ. Then, he adds, were it demonstrable by modern science that Christ was not the truth or that the truth was somehow beyond Christ, he would stand with Christ, opposite the truth. That assertion seems histrionically extreme, but there is no reason to believe that Dostoyevsky was simply posturing, nor that, like characters in his novels, he had become overly enamored of an idea, rhetorically thriving upon its absurdity.

The point in summoning him here is that truth and truth-wanting were so unshakably vital to Thérèse that we may wonder: How would she have responded to Dostoyevsky's eristic challenge, Christ *or* the truth? Would she have stood with her beloved Jesus if she regarded him as a cherished illusion? One of the chief intents of this book is to indicate why she was not driven to the chasm of either/or into which Dostoevsky gazed.

Abbreviations

A	The first autobiographical manuscript, 1895
AC	Archives of Carmel, Lisieux
B	The second autobiographical manuscript, September 1896
C	The third autobiographical manuscript, June 1897
CG	*Correspondance génèrale* of Thérèse of Lisieux (Paris: Cerf, Desclée de Brouwer, 1974)
CS	*Conseils et souvenirs* of Thérèse by her sister, Céline (Paris: Cerf, Desclée de Brouwer, 1973)
DE	*Derniers entretiens* of Thérèse of Lisieux (Paris: Cerf, Desclée de Brouwer, 1971)
LT	Letters of Thérèse, numbered and published in CG
NEC	*Nouvelle edition du centenaire,* an 8-volume edition of Thérèse's complete writings (Paris: Cerf, Desclée de Brouwer, 1992)
NPPO	Notes prepared by Carmelites for the *Procès ordinaire,* 1911
NPPA	Notes prepared by Carmelites for the *Procès apostolique,* 1916
OC	*Oeuvres completes,* a one-volume edition of Thérèse's complete works (Paris: Cerf, Desclée de Brouwer, 1992)
PA	*Procés de béatification et canonisation: Apostolique,* hearings conducted in 1915–1917 for Thérèse's beatification and canonization (Rome: Teresianum, 1976)
PE	*Pensées sur la charge de Maitresse des Novices dans l'order de Notre-Dame du Mont-Carmel* (Aix: Nicot, 1873)
PN	*Poésies* (Paris: Cerf, Desclée de Brouwer, 1992)
PO	*Procès de béatification et canonisation: Ordinaire,* hearings conducted in Bayeux, 1910–1911 for Thérèse's beatification and canonization (Rome: Teresianum, 1973)
Pri	*Prières* (Paris: Cerf, Desclée de Brouwer, 1992)
RP	*Récréations pieuses* (Paris: Cerf, Desclée de Brouwer, 1992)
VT	*Vie thérésienne,* trimestral review published since 1961

The Last Years of Saint Thérèse

I

Her Spanish Masters in Darkness: Teresa of Ávila and John of the Cross

TERESA (1515–1582)

Llega a Su Majestad me dé gracia para que no esté siempre en principios. Amen.
[May His Majesty be pleased to give me grace that I not always be at the beginning. Amen.]
LIBRO DE LA VIDA, 31:25

Pensáis que son pocos los trabajos que padecen los que el Señor hace estas mercedes?
No, sino grandísimos y de muchas maneras. Qué sabéis vos si seríais para sufrirlos?
[Do you think those to whom the Lord gives graces have light tribulations? No, they're enormous and of many sorts. How do you know you'll be up to suffering them?]
MORADAS, VI, 1577

Que propria de vieja poco humilde va ésta llena de consejos!
[How fitting that a scarcely humble old woman be full of advice!]
LETTER TO NICHOLÁS DORIA, February 10, 1579

Porque toda mi vida se me ha ido en deseos, y las obras no las hago.
[BecauseI have passed all my life in desires I have not made them into works.]
FUNDACIONES, XXVIII, 1580

THE FOUNDATIONAL HISTORY of the Carmel provides the first step to understanding Thérèse's descent into doubt. To know something of the founders, Teresa of Ávila and John of the Cross, is to know her by half. They set the high bar of perfectability toward which she struggled in vain. Each prescribed a spiritual path she presumed would be hers. It is they with whom she had to contend and from whom she had to depart.

I. "Our Saintly Mother" and Those Times in That Land

The first and arguably the best portrait of Thérèse was made three hundred years before she was born and comes from Spain, not France. It is presented during a tour of the fifth, sixth, and seventh of the dwellings (*moradas*) making up the *Castillo Interior* (1577), an edifice whose guide had founded the reformed order of Our Lady of Mount Carmel in 1562. The guide and portraitist, Teresa de Jesús, known as Teresa of Ávila, revered from the first and for several centuries, has become a favorite of feminists, a model of assertion and triumph in the face of the most substantial and enduring male hierarchy in Western history, "O thou undaunted daughter of desires!" in Richard Crashaw's famous apostrophe.

Every sister of the Reformed Carmel throughout its history has had an implicit bond with this woman, its founder. It could not be otherwise, as she determined the course of its life of prayer and left behind an enormous trove of literal signposts: her autobiography, which enjoys repute well beyond the Carmel and Catholicism. Complementing it are the *Castillo interior* (usually known as *Moradas*) and the *Camino de perfección*, the way to spiritual perfection through contemplative prayer.

Beyond these three central texts, however, come several others: a commentary on the *Song of Songs*, the only writing that Teresa was not ordered (that is, sanctioned) to undertake and that she was obliged to burn (copies had been made); next, the record of her founding Reformed Carmel monasteries throughout Spain, *Fundaciones*; then, the *Cuentas de conciencia*, a miscellany of "accounts of conscience," and another miscellany of *dichos*, sayings attributed to her from others' recollections; some poems and some prayers; and last yet foremost in catching her day by day, the twenty years' span of *cartas* known as the *Epistolario*, letters she wrote to people within and without her foundations, from anonymous young women to Philip II, king of Spain, her trusted protector. Among those letters she is at her most relaxed and intimate with the love of her life, Jerónimo de la Madre de Dios, better known as Gracián.

It is not easy to establish common ground between Teresa and Thérèse, her obscure little daughter so far from her in time and place. Thérèse refers to the foundress of the Reformed Carmel surprisingly seldom: only six times in all of her writing does she mention the *Vida* and another six, the *Castillo*. The *Camino de perfección*, at thirteen allusions, seems to have been her preference. Indeed, it cued her at age thirteen to her mission: Teresa had written that she would give a thousand lives to save one soul. In that statement, we find the first shared characteristic of mother and daughter, a penchant for dramatic excess, for a grandiloquent *I*. (See Figure 1.1)

Thérèse refers to other works in the Mother's canon: the prayers known as *Exclamaciones del alma a Dios* and some poetry. A reference to the commentary on the *Song of Songs* occurs toward the very end of Manuscript C. Thérèse herself wished to write a commentary on the same text, but neither her physical debility nor her sister Pauline allowed it. The citations and allusions remain few enough to call into question an affinity between these women, but it is more substantial than has been recognized. Teresa informs Thérèse in ways that signify much beyond the osmosis any sister of the Reformed Carmel would experience. Indeed, Teresa's high-flying spiritual agenda remained well above Thérèse's

FIGURE 1.1 The Reformed Carmel of Saint Joseph, Ávila, founded in 1562. The present convent is situated atop Teresa's family residence. Photograph taken by the author.

capacity to respond. Initially unaware that she would have to find her own way, she responded to Teresan injunctions with a helpless groping. It dismayed her that she would never be able to live up to the demands of Carmelite life.

Teresa made occasional forays into poetry, but her whole being argued the diurnal ruggedness of prose.[1] One of her best known passages in the *Fundaciones* says that God moves among kitchen pots.[2] Her salient feature as a writer is this steady attention to the ground levels of ordinary life. Her *dichos* abound in this rootedness. Sometimes they are vulgar, but she knew better than ever to lose touch with the many women who were struggling to attain the life she wanted for them in the houses she founded, a life of poverty and joy.[3]

Teresa is best known for her autobiographical accounts of visitations. She enjoyed frequent consultations with the creator of the universe and faithfully transcribes them, underscoring how astonishing these experiences could be; they overwhelmed her with instruction more than with uplift. Her famous ecstasies and levitations, observed and recorded by sisters close to her, embarrassed her. Thérèse gave them no heed.[4]

What was Christian Spain as Teresa knew it? Midway through the sixteenth century of Christianity, Spain was teeming with diverse persuasions of spirit, and not merely within the several orders, Cistercian, Dominican, Franciscan, Jesuit, Augustinian, Carmelite. The Catholic Reformation had begun two generations earlier, before Teresa's birth (1512), when the Cardinal of Toledo, Ximénez Cisneros, a Franciscan, confessor of Queen Isabella, founder of the University of Alcalá, and Grand Inquisitor, promoted the first edition of a polyglot Bible: texts in Aramaic, Hebrew, Greek, and Latin. Some four hundred and fifty years before the Second Vatican Council, Cisneros anticipated its call for a universal advance of Christian souls, laity no less than clergy, toward God through learning. Cisneros had books on devotional prayer translated into Spanish and disseminated in convents and monasteries from where the laity in turn was educated. A four-volume compilation of gospel passages and patristic writings known as the *Vita Christi* attained wide and lasting popularity among the literate.

Publishing houses in Salamanca, Alcalá (that one established by Cisneros), Montserrat, and Seville churned out instructive books on the varieties of prayer and how to practice them for the inner life. Made in the divine image, every soul could reach God through contemplative endeavor. The better educated dared to form Bible study groups independent of clerical control. Foreign influences gradually obtruded, including the forbidden works of Luther,[5] the *Enchiridion* of Erasmus (dear to Cisneros), works of neoplatonism[6] and a humanism named for Socrates. (See Figure 1.2.)

With the ignominious expulsion of Jews and Muslims in Spain, a new class arose, the *conversos*. They were members of Islamic and Judaic families who accepted the Church's offer of baptism as an alternative to exile and agreed to

FIGURE 1.2 Alcalá de Henares, the square facing the University founded by Cisneros (1499). In this town, the birthplace of Cervantes (1547), Teresa established a school for Reformed Carmelites (1570), with Juan de la Cruz as its rector. Photograph taken by the author.

practice the Christian faith. The term *marrano* emerged as a popular derogation of these converts whom the Church continued to suspect of the hypocrisy which its own program of an accommodating conversion necessarily implied. *Marrano* was synonymous with brute and traitor.

Many converts embraced Christianity sincerely as though in spite of an official expediency and its extortionist decrees. But a closed domestic culture of Jewish and Muslim practices and rituals continued. Jewish and Islamic Spain thus contributed their substantial, if hidden share (so hidden as to be rarely remarked even today) to the words and thoughts of both Teresa and Juan.

An age so vigorous in both piety and literacy could not thrive without hazard. Thanks to Jan Hus and Martin Luther, churchmen were well aware of the contagion of heterodoxy. That time is caricatured in the agency by which the Church sought to defend itself against Satan and all his works, the Inquisition.[7] It is facile to assume that this agency served some sinister end, Orwellian *avant la lettre*, to control thought and repress any gesture toward freedom. Rather, in the challenge of such a private enthusiasm as the *alumbrados* posed, the Inquisition was up against spiritual chaos, as early as the 1520s.

Alumbradismo took its impetus from Franciscan teachings about mental or inner prayer, known as *recogimiento*, and invested authenticity within individuals. They claimed divine inspiration via prayer entirely independent of Church tradition and its guiding norms. Spiritual directors and theologians were no longer necessary. The telltale sign for the Inquisition was arrogant defiance from *alumbrados*, including some women who attained repute and then notoriety when they instructing men, even Franciscan friars.[8] The Church had no way to determine which inner paths of prayer were genuine, but a conspicuous pride imputed to *alumbrados* said enough. The *alumbrados*' protestation of a love for God, even to the rejection or abandonment of individual will, offered no extenuation. Worst of all, they denied the humanity of Christ. They had a singular devotion to the Eucharist, but that could not redress their derelictions regarding elementary Christian doctrine. Inquisitors believed that such a movement could only be demonic.

Although the Inquisition moved against them in the 1520s and 1530s, their example was so powerful as to cast a lasting discredit upon any pursuit of inner or mental prayer that was not firmly adherent to the guidance of spiritual directors and theologians. That is why Teresa's autobiography gives so much space to witnessing her humility before learned authority. Yet she spends hardly less time in stating her constant need, often frustrated, of authoritative guidance from confessors.

In her story, the real tensions have nothing to do with the flood of importations such as Savanorola's works, which reshaped Spain's Dominicans, or the *Enchiridion* of Erasmus, which heaped scorn on ecclesiastical rituals, the veneration of images, and vocal prayer. There is no evidence that Teresa read Savonarola, Erasmus, or Luther. Rather, those tensions were determined by an ongoing struggle between two states of mind within the Spanish Church's hierarchies over the issue that the *alumbrados* had brought forward and that required juridical mediation.

One group was composed of men who studied and interpreted scripture: the theologians, or those whom Teresa called "people of the book, of learning and understanding."[9] The other group, *espirituales* or *experimentados*, took the inner life and its potential light to degrees of private vision generally known as quietism and pietism. Implicitly, as mystics they were antinomian, a present danger to Tradition and its guardians, the theologians. A notorious, monitory instance of the aberration latent within a feminine sensibility had once come in the mental vagaries of a Dominican nun, Maria de Santo Domingo, known as the Blessed Woman of Piedrahita, presumed to be blessed for having received visions and even the stigmata, until she was put away and corrected. She could well have gone up in smoke. Such a dangerous example obliged Teresa's Jesuit confessors to be skeptical, at times punitive toward her.

Teresa achieved a delicate peace for herself between both camps. She wrote and lived as one of the spirituals. Her *Castillo interior* abides as a masterwork from their quarter. It is not only a celebration of the contemplative life Christians might seek for a journey toward God. It also achieves equipoise between the heights and depths within that journey, the gradual ever prayerful proximity to God by a divine and wholly unmerited favor, and the perils that could at any time or station (*morada*) confound a soul and send it back down to the nullity from which the journey commenced. Teresa had an acute, almost over-ripened awareness of human foibles, those of women in particular. Her *Castillo* reads as a kind of literary and spiritual makeover of Chutes and Ladders.

Her cautions were informed by theologians she tactfully courted for advice and guidance. These very men could have put her life at risk or required that her manuscripts be destroyed. (When she died, in 1582, she did not know whether the Inquisition would permit the publication of her *Vida*, written almost twenty years before.) Some of them had been suspicious of her, and yet she sometimes disarmed them, even brought a few, such as Ibañez and Garcia de Toledo, round to the mystical life. It is difficult to overestimate the agility of her charm or her earnest sincerity in her consultations with the erudite *hombres de tomo*, for such agility, charm, and sincerity are qualities apparent in her writing. In her autobiography she speaks of theologians as servants of God and makes clear that she does not regard them as adversaries to the *experimentados*: "Let us not deceive ourselves by saying that learned men who do not practice prayer cannot be suitable directors for those who do.... [T]hey are not enemies of the spirit or ignorant of its nature, for they are familiar with the Holy Scripture, where the truth about it can always be found."[10]

That is adept diplomacy, the fruit of her having moved among eminences in the orders (not to mention her many connections with the Spanish nobility) and having secured from them some lasting friends: the Jesuits, Borgia and Alvarez; the

Dominicans, Bertrand and Granada; the Franciscans, Alcántara and Laredo. Such diplomacy she performed before some who would not have scrupled to pounce upon defamatory reports of her or her Carmelite sisters. She had to protect both herself and those sisters, but the assiduous solicitude she showed them in advancing them along the road to God, the *Camino de perfección* (1566), does not go to the heart of her life's story.

In her writing, she loaded herself down with negatives. She believed herself a lowly creature (yet she was born into the minor aristocracy of *hidalguía*), ignorant (she was educated in religious life at a convent school), worthy of damnation (a possible destiny for any soul), and foolish (which meant she knew she was a woman). She sounds these notes of self-recrimination and self-deprecation repeatedly in her *Vida* and elsewhere.[11] As they are so frequently bound into a theistic context which indicates that God is blessing her with divine assignments, some modern critics have seen her confession as a coy rhetorical angling against the ecclesiastical authority she was addressing.[12] Hagiographers see only Teresa and God; moderns see only a Teresa in an imbroglio of ecclesiastical power challenged and subverted a generation after the *alumbrado* interrogations. Embedded inextricably as she was in the Church's politics and yet having to struggle as a woman for authentication within it, she fought back with self-empowering doses of ironic and polemic savvy.[13] As Teresa was canonized within a generation after her death, her life and work read as a stupendous triumph against the odds. (See Figure 1.3.)

Like that other masterly self-deprecator, Augustine of Hippo, whose *Confessiones* she knew well,[14] Teresa addresses herself almost entirely to God. Her chief avenue to authentication of herself as a *mujercita* or little woman (a tautology, as she knew) was to invoke the example of women in the company of Jesus himself, as in this bracing passage from the *Camino*, damaged in manuscript by official erasure: "O, my Creator, you are not ungrateful, for when you were in the world, Lord, you did not loathe women but, on the contrary, you always favored them with much compassion *and you found in them as much love and more trust than in men, as your most saintly Mother was there, by whose*

FIGURE 1.3 From Therese's large collection of prayer cards. She never experienced a mystical ecstasy such as Teresa's, who felt Christ piercing her heart with a spear. Copyright Archives du Carmel de Lisieux

merits—and because of our wearing her habit—we deserve that of which our failings make us undeserving."[5] Closing her *Vida*, when discussing how souls may experience union with God, she leaves this parting shot from her beloved Franciscan: "The Lord grants such graces to many more women than men, I have heard the saintly friar, Pedro de Alcántara say (and I have seen it myself)...."[16]

Such is her kind of omega, earthly and tenuous, a brief on behalf of the women sequestered in the cenacles she had founded. But the alpha, the struggle of beginnings, was never absent from her consciousness. It is that susceptibility that endears her perhaps most of all to her readers, the steady absence of self-righteousness or any smug sense of arrival. Yet the sources for her fit-for-hell self-estimate cannot be located precisely. It is not enough to say that it had been nourished in a culture of fear: fear of God's wrath, fear of damnation, fear of authority. She tells us that before she discovered Francesco de Osuna's *Tercer abecedario* (1527), a book she clung to for over twenty years in the absence of a proper spiritual director, her religion was egocentric. She also says she was tormented not by God's silence and apparent absence but by the abundance of graces (*mercedes*) to her. Even so, she could not shake free of her need for human amity, no matter her desire to be solely God's; hence, a recurring dread of offending divine love. Behind these limits and failings is the message that God is the source of all virtues, including her desire for service to God. She admits that she took a long time to learn that all human efforts are futile until we banish reliance upon ourselves and find rest wholly in God.[17]

That is no sappy concession to piety. Teresa, unlike Thérèse, did not live in an age of sentimentality. In acknowledging God's primacy, she undercut whatever voluntarism threatened her *camino*, for such an emphasis upon the human will, common in Franciscan and Jesuit spirituality, held as great a danger as its opposite, abandon, in the *alumbrado* persuasion. Teresa had to mediate cautiously, not only between theologians and spirituals but between extremes in her own sensibility. She had to develop a robust sense of self-criticism, a steady vigilance upon herself.

Her keenest phrasings in self-reproach served a double means to a single end: by remembering her adolescent foibles and exaggerating their gravity, not to mention her attachments to friends in adulthood, she was humbling herself in the initial, purgative stage of prayer. She was also following the injunction of Osuna who had described humility as a trench to be dug to lay the foundation for a dwelling in prayerful life. He spoke of humility as a dunghill, and she made it a word describing herself.[18]

How did she arrive at such an accomplished self-scorn? The account of her childhood holds barely a clue. She had been blessed with a saintly Jewish Christian father, Alonso Sanchez (her paternal grandfather, Juan Sanchez, a wealthy linen merchant of Toledo, was a converted Jew).[19] She had a formal upbringing in the Catholic faith and the stimulation her father provided by reading to her throughout her childhood. He instilled in her a keen love of books, which means he remained a Jew and she was raised one. In a Jewish household, intellectual curiosity was matured in the posing of questions. Teresa grew up as a very bright and decided girl.

Was she, then, educated into self-reproach and self-debasement? Theological training was, of course, denied her as a woman. In 1531, at sixteen, Doña Teresa de Ahumada, as she was then known (Ahumada was her mother's family name), was sent by her father to the Augustinians but was put off by their austerities in piety and penance. She returned home ill. Her *Vida* indicates that she never experienced any of the positive signs pointing to conventual life: a vision or a summoning voice, an experience of unearthly joy, the tell-tale sense that she would love God more than family. What decided her was thoroughly negative, that she perceived the brevity and vanity of mortal life. Whatever her faults or misdemeanors, she believed they would dispatch her to hell. She saw the convent as a kind of substitute for purgatory. It would rescue her from a morbid fear of damnation.

Why did she not enter one of the other orders, the Cistercian (which locally subsumed four Benedictine monasteries) or Dominican or Franciscan? All of these were acutely strict. Her entry into the Carmel of the Incarnation seems to have been prompted by a banal but important factor, the presence there of her friend, Doña Juana Suarez. From her, the adolescent Teresa learned of the Carmelite spirituality of that time. Doña Juana convinced her that the Carmel offered a purgatory as good as any. (See Figure 1.4.)

Irony plays thick here. One of the foremost saints of Christian mysticism began her spiritual life on craven grounds, a fear of hell, and it was only through the example of a friend (hardly a reliable basis for action and one in risk of attachment) that she was brought into the order that she was to transform magnificently. For much of her life she suffered from an inclination to human attachments. She knew from scripture that a true follower of Christ forsakes the earthly bonds of

FIGURE 1.4 The Carmel of the Incarnation, outside of Ávila. Teresa entered it when she was 20, in 1535, and returned as its reforming prioress, in 1571. Photograph taken by the author.

family and friends, that a Christian is called to act and feel unnaturally. Yet her choice of Carmel was almost intuitively the right one, as though she personified a syllogism with faulty premises that comes nonetheless to a sound conclusion.

The ferment that literate Spain had been enjoying in the diffusion of all those manuals on spirituality, especially on the inner life of prayer, became finally insupportable for the Church's hierarchy. In 1559, the Grand Inquisitor, Fernando Valdès issued from a press in Vallidolid the *Cathalogus Librorum,* better known as the Index, a list of all books which could not be read by any of the faithful.[20] The number of objectionable texts came to 253, including 14 editions of the Bible and 9 of the New Testament.[21] Most of the then circulating books on prayer were proscribed; anyone possessing such books was subject to severe discipline, including imprisonment or excommunication.

Teresa was forty-four years old in that dire year. The formal beginning of her writing life was three years distant but the publication of the latest Index (there had been others, in 1551 and 1554) was no warrant in that direction. Without hesitation she cast her library of books on prayer into a fire—or were they confiscated? Her *Vida* tells us, in disingenuous overdrive, how she felt in facing that loss: "When many books in Spanish were removed, which weren't to be read, I felt it a lot, because some gave me pleasure in reading them and now I couldn't, for those remaining were in Latin."[22] Books on a life of prayer gave pleasure—not instruction or enlightenment? She did not dare to say so.

Characteristically, she makes an incident momentous, and from disaster she foresees triumph. The Valdès Index, sinister in intent, turned out to be a grace. The passage just quoted on the great censorship signals at once her new life in writing and the authorization for it. God consoled her, she writes, for the loss of her books on prayer. He told her she would be given a living book. This alludes to Christ's offer of "living waters" to the Samarian woman.[23] Teresa tells us that she came to realize the book was Christ himself "read" in her visions of his sufferings. But the *libro vivo* was also the recording of those visions: *she* was composing this book. God was giving her as a writer to herself. Brava!

The Index necessitated and God validated her new life as a writer concurrent with her new vocation, unclaimed, as a *fundadora* of houses for the Reform of the Carmel.[24] The stylization of her life by writing, the enlistment of God as CEO of the Reform, and her efforts to create the houses from without and guide their spirituality from within were all of a piece.

II. The Houses She Built

On October 6, 1571, Teresa, then fifty-six, began to carry out on orders from the Carmel's provincial an assignment she dreaded. She was to assume the priorate of the Incarnation, the very house she had left a decade before when she set out to found convents in reform of the order. It had been her intent to create a house-community of no more than thirteen sisters pledged to Jesus by a rigorous poverty and an asceticism the Mitigated Carmel had long forgotten. Precisely to what primitive condition she was seeking a return remains a question, but her hagiographer, Marcelle Auclair puts the matter succinctly. For the Mitigated sisters at the Incarnation, all 130 of them, "no more visits, no more going out, an end to gossiping in each other's cells, a frightful fast, penances enough to make one shudder, the discipline till the blood comes through the broken skin, dry bread or the prison cell for the least disobedience, the slightest lateness in chapel, the least inattention, the least infraction of the Rule—that Rule that was originally meant for hermits in the desert and not for poor girls many of whom would have preferred marriage to the convent, if so many young men had not gone overseas with Cortés, Pizarro, or Almagro."[25]

Teresa came unwillingly. Her sudden priorate had been forced upon the Mitigated sisters by the Apostolic Commissary, Pedro Fernández, with no subtlety in the design. The Carmel's general in Rome, Cardinal Rossi, known to Spaniards as Rubeo, had permitted Teresa to found as many Discalced Carmel houses as she could, even as many, he said, as she had hairs on her head.[26] But his permission was now countermanded in her appointment to the Incarnation, where Teresa was to spend three years.[27] By the time she returned to the Carmel of the Incarnation in Ávila, God had founded eight houses of the Reform.[28]

The address that October day was a genial mix of candor, diplomacy, and spiritual endeavor. Calling them *señoras* she told the sisters of her pain in knowing they had not elected her, that she had been appointed against her will and pleasure as well as their own. She came solely to serve them and give them all she could, hoping for God's help to such ends, even to the offering of her blood and life. No need that anyone fear dispossession: "...although till now I've lived and managed among the Discalced, I know well, by God's goodness, how to manage those who are not.... I am quite familiar with our weakness, which is great, but now what we are not achieving in works let us arrive at with desires, for God is merciful and shall little by little bring it about that the works catch up with the intent and desire."[29]

This Mitigated house six years later to the day voted by 55 to 44 to bring Teresa back as prioress, even though the provincial had forbidden them to do so. That minor ruckus in October 1577 precipitated what Teresa called the years of persecutions: the arrests, imprisonments, and hidings out of Discalced friars and the danger that all the houses Teresa had worked to establish would be dissolved. The nuns who had voted for Teresa were denied mass, confession, and all contact with the outside. Two months later, King Philip ordered that the rebellious nuns be absolved but the friars remained at hazard.

In fairness to her fearsome enemies, it bears emphasis that her enterprise was redolent of subversion and rebellion against central Church doctrine. St. Paul had famously forbidden women to open their mouths: no preaching, no teaching. Here was a woman presuming to instruct others, and her many friends in the orders, especially those of Augustine and Ignatius Loyola, were willing to have her instruct them. Far worse, her mysticism smelled of heresy, all too private and uncontrollable. How could it be distinguished from the *alumbrado* fantasies of only two generations before? Did it not distract the Church and its sheep from the needed daily practices, sacraments, penances, good works, vocal (collective) prayer? How could churchmen know she was not malevolent, an agent of Satan? Was it for her to deny that she was either deluded or mischievous?

So there were legitimate grounds for apprehension. It would be mistaken to follow her own cue and to charge her critics with devilish or conspiratorial intents. They were too many and too various (some were her friends) to settle for an inclusive condemnation. Teresa admits in her *Vida* that nothing was so difficult for her as the opposition she faced from good people. Perhaps that was the chief reason for her keeping one eye upon her critics and detractors when the other was on the page she was writing. Yet she was unshakably convinced that her work for the Reform was divinely inspired, directed, even commanded when she grew weary of it. Besides, she underwent the travails (*trabajos*) with an arcane joy, for she knew that with the opposition to her she was attaining a genuine *imitatio Christi*.

She owed a very great deal to her pharisees, scribes, and high priests. As she was up against the Establishment of her day, even as Jesus had been in his, how could she not be confident in the divine rightness of her course? It is an irony that when the Inquisition came to review her works subsequent to her death, there was general accord that the Reform houses she had founded were of due and lasting merit. It was her writings and teachings that proved questionable. She herself was objectionable. Her teachings, however, had been directed to houses where the Inquisition's officers realized, to their relief, that most or possibly all the sisters fell short of her spiritual fervor. The Reform's sisters were permitted to read nothing from Teresa when she was alive. Oddly, the strongest case made for how she had suffered at the churchmen's hands came in a deposition from a sister who had herself suffered much from Teresa's suspicions and reproaches, Sevilla's prioress, Maria de San José.[30]

Teresa's autobiography consists of the *Vida* and the *Fundaciones*. The principal texts of the Reformed Carmel's inner life are also two: the *Camino de perfección*, which Teresa commenced soon after completing the *Vida* (1565–1566), and the *Moradas*, the beginning of which Teresa precisely indicates, June 2, 1577. She finished it six months later, on November 29, amid the turmoil that had begun at the Incarnation Carmel of Ávila.

For Teresa the great paradox of Saint Paul, that weakness is Christian strength, meant that "little women," so long as they remained little and humble(d), occupied a peculiarly advantageous position within a supposedly Christian society.

They were closer to God than were the male hierarchs. They were the unlearned whom Jesus himself privileged over the apparently wise. Arguably as helpless as little children, they were far nearer to the kingdom of heaven than the Church's theologians. Without training in nor even acquaintance with Thomism, Teresa grasped intuitively one of its central tenets, that spiritual freedom lies in dependence upon God—and that God was within her, to be sought and found through prayer. Jesus's blistering charge against the Establishment, that it had hidden away the key of knowledge, was answered by his saying that the kingdom of heaven was within oneself.[31]

The Reform's *fundaciones* had created small houses where women, preferably entering poor, could become Marias of contemplation, sequestered for their own glory (*honra* was a very weighty matter to the Spanish but Teresa's references to it tend to ambivalence) by men who felt obliged to monitor and censure, whenever necessary, their potentially dangerous spirituality. Teresa's *Camino* and *Moradas* (a route and a residence) show her ripening awareness that God's authority was insuperably above and beyond all ecclesiastical manipulations. She shows how she accommodated the churchmen so tactfully and how she faced candidly the many hazards that her sisters en route to God were likely to encounter. Contrary to some recent interpretations, the texts show that she subverted no one and nothing. She found in the Church the foil necessary to her own spiritual development. By its bracing challenges, she learned through unobstreperous diplomacy to station herself and her well-wishers, brave souls like Gracián and Ambrosio Mariano.

The *Camino* was written at the request of Teresa's sisters at the first of the Reformed Carmels, St Joseph's in Ávila. They had known of her *Vida*, but her life's story, however luminous, was not what they needed; rather, her written counsel on how to lead a prayerful life would surely inform the new communal ascetic for which she was working. Her confessor and censor, Domingo Bañez, gave the necessary order for her to write.

She is famous for injunctions to her sisters to be masculine and martial. In a characteristically vivid passage, she adds that they must not be like those who drink on their bellies before entering battle.[32] As a military business, her spirituality could be cast in tactical and strategic terms.[33] The strategy pointed to union with God through contemplation, known as unitive prayer. Experience of this visionary life was usually brief—minutes, hours—and yet a guarantor of peace and strength to whomever God graced with it. Even so, it was no promise of the saintliness to which Christians aspire. Teresa distances herself from the haughtiness imputed to the *alumbrados*, saying that she has known many souls who have never had prayer's visions but were saintly, and many who had but were not.[34]

The tactics became the staple of the Discalced Carmel and its retrieval of the old Rule: a rigorous yet genuine humility, detachment from the world, and love of each other.[35] These are the three desiderata she set down. In pursuing humility, the most advanced of sisters was the one who held herself in lowest esteem, was silent even when unjustly condemned, and would accept her sinfulness and stumbling. To her life's end Teresa was alert to human inadequacy, wrong-headedness, and ignorance—not least her own[36]—and her sisters' steady alertness to such negatives in their own selves would, she trusted, prepare them for their way godward.[37] Self-examination, candid and thorough, would enforce humility. The koan of Carmel's spirituality matches the koans of the gospels: the only merit is the self-conviction, without the slightest dissembling, that one has no merit.

By detachment (*desasimiento*) Teresa meant primarily the absence of close personal ties, whether with members of one's family or with friends. Bonds within a community of sisters could be a poison (*ponzona*). If the bond within the convent were between natural sisters, it would be, she said, much worse, a kind of pestilence.[38] Did Lisieux's Mère Gonzague weigh Teresa's words when she ingathered three of the four natural sisters of the Martin family? What Teresa would have said about the "Martin clan" needs no guess: can we say that we have left the world and everything for God if we do not separate ourselves from what counts first, our relatives?[39]

Her concerns in this matter were twofold. First, she recognized the hazard in allowing any factionalisms (*bandillos*) to crystalize within a community. Her intent that the Reform's new houses not exceed thirteen sisters was informed by the turmoils she had observed among free-ranging sisters ten times that number in the Incarnation convent of Ávila, where she had spent the first twenty years of her spiritual life. The other consideration went deeper, against the grain of self. It is hard to oppose self, she says, given that we love ourselves dearly.[40] Teresa knew her own preferences, suffered the awareness of this imperfection in her, and never overcame it.

What of the third requirement of Carmel life, love for one another? How could it even be possible amidst everyone's due feelings of worthlessness on one hand and the penchant for selfish intimacies on the other? Teresa's way was to cultivate a solidarity of perception, beginning with her audacious claim that the Carmel's every house was celestial. If there could be a heaven on earth, it was there.[41] She appealed to her sisters as a community of women who knew the score in a mannish world. We women, she told them, are not clever nor learned but we have God within us, just as Jesus dwelt within Mary.[42] No theologian could make such a maternal claim, and she knew it. She knew as well that she was standing at the precipice of *alumbradismo*. Yet as these women were by nature weak, they depended more upon God, even for the trust they needed to feel in him.[43] In cautiously veiled language, she claimed that as women were weak and needy, each one certain she was the basest of all ("la más ruin de todas"), God through Christ would come for them, not for the upright, the men.[44] The righteous have no need of Jesus. Had not Jesus himself said as much?[45]

Martial metaphors served Teresa well, for the sisters lived in an age of wars, both at home and in the Americas, but she also drew one from chess, which was then becoming a popular pastime in affluent Spanish culture. It appeared in the Escurial text, but she herself tore it out; it must have been too unseemly and worldly for the sisters to digest. The Reformed Carmel had recreational hours, a necessary daily pause from the austerities, when inspirational plays were performed as well as improvisatory songs, known as *coplas*. Teresa herself composed some. But games as such? Chess? Not for a moment. Yet she introduces a chessboard in remarking wryly, "Here you'll see the mother God gave you and how far her knowledge of vanity reaches!"[46] First, she advises, you must know how to set up all the pieces. Among those pieces, it is the queen who rallies them all against the king. This queen is humility informed by love. Through her the king shall be brought down—from heaven, that is. We have from this extraordinary lesson one of many Carmelite koans, that the king is defeated by an aggressive submission. Three centuries after this writing, Thérèse spoke of storming heaven so as to surrender upon taking it.

Even bolder is another metaphor she suppressed, this one from bullfighting. She urges her sisters to be like those who, safe in the grandstand, watch the bulls (the dangerous temptations in the world) and not like those who risk impaling themselves on the bulls' horns. Few go astray from the higher vantage, and when they do, everyone is astonished, as spectators would be if someone fell from the grandstand into the arena. The life of contemplative prayer is the sole safety, so what, then, of those practicing only vocal prayer? And what of the theologians, whom the saintly Franciscan, Alcántara, urged her to ignore? Are they not toreadors? As she claims that she has heard of the bullfight image and finds it apt, perhaps Alcántara suggested the comparison.[47]

In the *Camino* Teresa teaches her sisters that their virtues are not their own. They are loans from God. Besides, a sister truly humble sees those virtues resident only in other sisters, never in herself—a deft reverse of Jesus's lesson about the mote and the beam in people's eyes.[48] In the continuous, never wholly successful attempt to kill the self, there is suffering aplenty, but Teresa views suffering positively: tribulations, imperfections, sins—they all provide occasions for needing God—but suffering them also brings the sister's soul closer to Christ and the remembrance of his far greater suffering. Given that most-to-be-desired proximity, she insists, the genuinely humble soul will feel the peace and joy that come only from trust in God. If self-knowledge keeps a sister focused on her unworthiness, her essential lowliness (*bajeza*), she also knows that God transforms that condition into union with himself through Christ. Suffering is the lot of those whom God loves.[49] A Carmelite welcomes suffering only because it brings her closer to union with Christ. Joy comes in that closing, not because of suffering itself and not despite that suffering, but with it.

These summary remarks derive entirely from the *Camino*, which, following close upon the *Vida*, was literally a midway in Teresa's matured spirituality. The iterative notes of self-reproach closing this work, including the disconcerting admission that she is not certain that she loves God nor that her desires are acceptable to God, suggest she was subject to undue fretfulness. She is weary of life and of her intolerable wickedness. But she had answered, at least for the while, her sisters' need for guidance. The *Camino* became what one critic has called the Magna Carta of the Reformed Carmel.[50]

III. Each Sister Guided Within

If the *Camino*, cast and re-cast from 1566, profiles the communal life of the Reform's sisters, the *Moradas* of 1577 gives us a portrait of and for the sister within, in her ripening through prayer. The intrigue around this work begins with its year, one of Teresa's richest in correspondence: she dealt at length with such issues as the diplomacy by which the Reform could overcome suspicion and hostility; melancholia in the houses and how to deal with its victims; bringing children to live in the houses; the conduct of priests with sisters; and the hazards of gossip. The autumn brought to a calamitous pitch the tensions between the Reform movement and the Mitigated Carmel friars, those Teresa sometimes caricatured as "all the devils" and knew for their "fake amity."[51]

Four days after Teresa completed the *Moradas*, Juan de la Cruz and another friar of the Reform, both confessors at the Incarnation, were arrested. Juan was incarcerated in the Mitigated Carmel's monastery in Toledo; for eight months, Teresa had no news of his whereabouts, not even that he was still alive. Then he escaped.

Composing the *Moradas* in the midst of tense and dangerous circumstances,[52] Madre Teresa seems to have taken sustenance from her own writing. Pressing adversities inspired her. She told Mariano early in that fateful year that she was happier in bad times than in good.[53] When Gracián, anxious about facing the Inquisition with her, rushed to console her and to be consoled, he recounted all the wicked things being said of her and then was horrified to notice that she was rubbing her hands in glee.[54] Provided God be praised and glorified through her writing, she insisted that she did not care if all the world were to shout at her, especially as she did not expect to live to see her writings in print, anyway.[55] Nor did she.

What was her interior castle? A splendid metaphor; perhaps a remembrance of the palatial apartments of Madre Teresa's friend, the Duchess of Alba, in Segovia, whom she visited in 1574. She tells us expressly that the castle is God, for sinners commit their worst offenses within God, and she counted herself in their number.[56]

This castle with its seven levels of dwellings takes the soul initiated in mental prayer through the gradations of the godward life. She warns that in no matter which of these the soul may be spending its prayerful time, even the seventh and most magnificent, it will never lose sight of what it is nor become what it wants to be. In a sense, the soul must always remain captive to its own humility and settle for seeking to know God without ever presuming to have reached such knowledge. Instead, that seeking is a way to self-knowledge. Even receipt of graces is no surety, since the soul can always slip back and down into sinfulness. God shall even try the seeking soul with demonic tribulations from time to time, as in the drama of Job. If all this makes the itinerary seem not worth the candle, the deceits of the world are far worse, as happiness on temporal terms is doomed to evanescence. Moreover, the soul has the nourishment of both humility and suffering. The more there is of each at work within the soul, the more one's meager little will is conformed to God's.

The bleakness of this interior design mercifully includes delightful zoological resting places. Teresa likens the soul at work in its humility to a bee laboring in a hive over its honey. If God allows reptilian fears to slither about and even bite, they serve a better vision of one's limits and offensiveness. We would like to withdraw from the world into ourselves as the tortoise into his shell, but can do so only if God wills it. When she speaks of the marvels of God's creation to be found in so tiny a creature as an ant, she could be William Blake speaking. Her favorite image, drawn from Spain's Islamic textile industry, is of the silkworm (*gusano*) which, large and ugly, feeds on mulberry leaves.[57] From a shroud-like cocoon it fashions comes an amusing little butterfly.[58] She admits she's never seen, only heard (from her Jewish father?) about this lepidopteran process, but she spins from it a joy that the human soul can give of itself, as does the silkworm.

As she traverses the castle, she returns again and again to the worm-butterfly: its life and death conform to the extremes of Carmel's mystical penchant. On one hand, we should not try to comprehend God's secrets, given that we are mere worms; on the other, God wishes to communicate with such worms and to reveal himself.[59] The worm for its part goes about creating its shroud and is mystically transformed from something gross and hideous into a new creature, small and angelic white.

In the final plateau of *moradas*, where the mind of the soul becomes one with God, Teresa claims a lasting union: "siempre queda el alma con su Dios."[60] This completion of the soul and its journey means death, but the butterfly dies happily because now Christ has at last become its life. The real sense of death is, however, not physical but spiritual, a total occlusion of self: the soul forgetful of self seems no longer to exist; there are not even thoughts nor imaginings of heaven but a dwelling solely upon God. In a particularly inspired moment, Teresa likens the quietude and peace within the arrived soul to the silent building of Solomon's temple: all the stones had been hewn fine before they were brought, so not a noise was heard in their fitting.[61] The hewing had been the testing and sufferings of the sister that she might be like Christ. Now, with Christ in place of self, the sister would be made a slave of all others.

Through this last of the *moradas* a transparent affinity between Teresa and Thérèse emerges. Teresa says that those who have undergone the greatest testing are closest to Jesus. That signifies to readers of Thérèse the crucial importance of Manuscript C and the Christocentric weight of her presence at the table of suffering: her identification with helpless souls, her petition that the divine light of faith be given to them—and to herself. Second, the sister who from the seventh *morada* becomes the slave of Christian community must also seek to become tiny, "the least of all and their slave...setting stones so firm that the castle not fall upon you."[62]

Thérèse made littleness her chief predication. Corollary to that littleness is weakness, a tacit inefficacy that leads to the third of Teresa's lights: that God looks not to the scale of one's works, but to the love in their performance. Thérèse drew upon this lesson in benevolence twice, in an early letter to her sister, Céline, and in the midst of her last days with Manuscript C.[63] Suffering in the place of Jesus so as to be one with him (the mystical quest in Solomon's Song), perpetual shrinking of self in littleness, serving others through love alone—Thérèse did not learn these cross-bound burdens; rather, she daily lived them out.

IV. Family Notes on Teresa and Thérèse

Two books and numerous discussions have been given to the influence that Juan de la Cruz exerted upon Thérèse. No such attention has been given to Teresa's influence upon her. Thérèse herself is the chief reason: she waxes eloquently to fellow novices over Juan and his inflamed notion of love for God. She makes only five references to Teresa's *Vida*, the same number she makes to Juan's *Subida del Monte Carmelo*, a book she never read. The *Camino*, a summa of Discalced Carmel spirituality, gets no more than eight references and the *Castillo* a meager four. Thérèse cites Teresa's best known poem with its oxymoronic refrain, "I am dying because I am not dying," only to remark that she herself would not say any such thing. She wants only what God wants. It is a curious, trump card line.[64]

Was Thérèse emulous of her Mother? (Teresa had been so in her time, toward the most reputedly lofty of sister souls.[65]) Or was Thérèse put off by the central fact of the *Vida*, that throughout it Teresa is sustained in all her qualms and anxieties by continual visitations from God, visions and voices, in which she puts total and unshakeable fidelity? Thérèse enjoyed no such excitement; she lived in a pedestrian age. For her audacities, she had no censure to fear from an Inquisition. Neither did she have to fear that her writings would not survive her, that a body of men would consign what she wrote to flame. Thérèse had the consolation of knowing that she would leave this life with a veritable book industry at work on her behalf. She had started contributing to it herself in her last months by honing her poems.

These considerations raise the question of how appealing an age so distant (by more than three centuries) and its alien culture could have been to Thérèse. In school, she showed interest in history: the martyred Christian virgins of Rome, the great French worthies, Geneviève and Jeanne d'Arc, but could she immerse herself in the turbulent Church politics glimpsed in the *Vida*? It is unlikely that the *Vida*, the record of a baroque mysticism and the survival of its thoroughly politicized expositor, spoke to Thérèse's particular needs. It is also unlikely that she could respond to the rhetoric of self-abjection that abounds in the *Vida*. Would Thérèse, a little bird, a tiny flower of Normandy, ever be proximate to "so foul and stinking a dungheap" as Teresa?[66] A piously educated bourgeoise, Thérèse must have been daunted by such phrasing. Substance figures here as much as style. An edgy sense of sinfulness, of wickedness, the generic burden of being ontologically worthless as a woman do not comport easily with a diminutive, passive sense of weakness. The first cries out in strident shame and self-horror, while the other barely raises its voice. The first seems lunatic and the other, sickly. Teresa writes as a sober and seasoned adult who has staggered through adversity and been tested again and again, a failure rescued again and again by divine mercies. Thérèse's strategic resort to a seeming infantilism, in which she presents and simultaneously protects herself as a child, suggests she was unable or unwilling to brave storms, that she could suffer only by staying little and hidden. Yet her story, too, is of graces abounding, and not without fierce weather. At the end of Manuscript B, she combines an emblem of adversity with her weakness, calling herself a little bird (the *avecita* of the soul, borrowed from the *Vida*) hovering low and lowly in a storm.[67]

Lexical differences, or rather, preferences bring mother and daughter aside one another. A thorough survey would require much more space and effort than this essay can sustain, but a few terms deserve highlighting. If Teresa sees herself as *ruin*, base and contemptible, that conviction prompts *lágrimas*. Tears flow as a thematic estuary throughout the *Vida*. Those prayer books she had been compelled to burn had taught her that tears, whether issued spontaneously in remorse or drawn out by God or both, were reliable signs of self-cleansing, contrition for sins and the resolve to overcome them. She says that by the time she picked up Osuna's *Abecedario*, God had already given her "the gift of tears."[68]

Tears serve the Vida's most famous metaphor, the soul as garden. Tears of contrition, the *via purgativa*, supply the water in the well for the watering of the soul's flowerings. They become plentiful in joy as the soul moves along the *via meditativa*. Teresa admits that a time of dryness (*sequedad*) might ensue. She does not claim that the well goes dry; we are left to infer it. At that well's dry bottom, I would suggest, Thérèse found herself: yet another setting of darkness and enclosure in the *attente de Dieu*, which she describes at the table of sorrow in Manuscript C. Teresa tells us that if God withholds the waters of grace, the soul must be content with its nothingness and by such humility the garden's flowers shall grow again.[69]

It is at such a point that Thérèse surpasses herself and her famous *offrande* of June 1895 and composes her most lowly and most sublime prayer, the one she utters from the table of sorrow.

Proximate to the tears of joy in Teresa's mystical garden is the divine spark (*centellica*) that kindles the soul struggling in love of God to a greater flame. The humble soul, however, can offer only its measly straw (*pajitas puestas*) toward this conflagration.[70] Thérèse drew upon this image at several turns. Jesus sewed "the sparks of love with his hands full into our souls" (A 48r). In her poem to Céline, "Rappele-toi," she claims that a feeble spark suffices to light an immense fire (PN 24.17). In a letter to Céline, she comforts them both for not having the great faggots of the well-educated to contribute to the fire (the kindling wood of erudition which Madre Teresa was too discreet to mention), given that they are both in darkness and dryness: "Aren't we obliged to throw there some little straws?...Jesus is happy to see us putting a bit of fuel there..."] (LT 143).[71]

Neither Teresa nor Thérèse was so unlettered as either of them makes out. Both knew the Bible and drew upon it amply; that book alone would have sufficed each of them. But they had also read deeply and thoroughly. If Teresa kept the *Abecedario* with her as steady companion, Thérèse had done something fantastically more: in the years before she entered Carmel, roughly her twelfth to fifteenth year, she had committed to memory the book Teresa had known as *Contemptus Mundi* (Scorn of the World) and that she herself knew as the *Imitatio Christi*. It would be impossible to overestimate the importance of this mnemonic effort by an impetuous adolescent; she had assimilated a major text in monastic spirituality as part of her quite private preparation for Carmel. This extraordinary osmosis has yet to be amply appreciated in studies of Thérèse. Even superficially considered, she showed her fierce resolve to dedicate herself to conventual life and to prepare to follow Jesus in the most exacting terms. What would Teresa have said of this amazing girl?

Mother and daughter have a great deal in common at the disciplinary levels of action: suffering, self-humbling, love's service, but there are other patches of shared ground. Both exemplify affective theology, an investment of the whole self in seeking God. Practical experience counts for much more than intellectual knowledge.[72] The intimate, anecdotal first person attests a keen awareness of how divine graces inform living and does so far more convincingly than the detachment of faceless discourse about the soul. As an historic response to the intellectualism of the scholastic tradition, a province restricted to the Latinate and learned, the affective way said that one must seek to follow Christ with heart and mind, no less than with soul. Only such a full commitment can count for anything. Teresa became a master of the affective because she had to live it out with the sisters in her charge, think it out and write it out for the learnèd and disciplinary churchmen judging her efforts. The affective way was instrumental for spiritual directors because it served as a register of how legitimate one's confessions of visions and other epiphenomena were: peace, joy, and especially a deeper humility were deemed reliable hallmarks of a progression toward divine union. The devil could never deliver serenity, and any contrived version of peace or joy would soon be exposed.

Thérèse, unlike Teresa, never found steady and reliable spiritual direction, and that is why her *audace* was able to take wing. How well she might have fared had Almire Pichon, her Jesuit confidant, directed her cannot be guessed; his positively hortatory way might not have put due constraints upon her.[73] She wanted to hear what she wanted to hear. The Franciscan Alexis Prou, who preached a retreat at the Lisieux Carmel in October, 1891, uncritically validated her in the confessional and all but launched her on her way "on the tides of *trusting* and of *love*," as she put it, four years after the treasured fact (A 80v). He was, in effect, undoing the hurt that the Jesuit, Laurent Blino, had caused her the year before, when he scolded her for saying "I want to love God as much as Saint Teresa."[74] What brazen pride and presumption! She should look to correcting her faults, said he, and to controlling her outlandish desires. In a remonstrance such as Teresa would never have granted herself—talking back to a priest!—Thérèse told Blino that her desires were *not* outlandish: "I can well aspire to sainthood, even to a sainthood higher than that of Saint Teresa, if I wish, since Our Lord said, 'Be perfect, as your heavenly Father is perfect.'"[75] Teresa would probably have been delighted with this outrageous riposte and actually inspired it via Thérèse's reading of the *Vida*. Both women could have pointed straight to the Sermon on the Mount.[76]

Both delight in Christ's telling his followers to ask. It means that there is no such thing for them as impossibilities; he has given a kind of "Open, sesame!" to otherwise marginal and helpless souls—women's, especially. We have just heard Thérèse enlightening a priest about possibility. Teresa writes that as God's will is done on earth as in heaven, then the earth has become her heaven: and hence the divine will can be performed in her.[77] Was that passage in Thérèse's mind when she wanted to spend "her" heaven doing good upon an illimitable earth?

This feminine expansiveness, the colonial staking out of the world itself under the divine imprimatur of love, hardly constitutes the whole of these women's enterprise. Converse to the centrifugality of desire is the centripety of penance; the shrinking of self alone justifies desire. Both take the *Our Father* in full earnest, not least the petition for the forgiveness of sins. It has to be pondered carefully: better slowly said once than hurried through by rote and routine, the *Camino de Perfección* advised, and Thérèse, struggling with formal prayer, listened, at the last.[78] Addressing the innate folly, blindness, and final helplessness of sin, Teresa asserts that "the soul's sins and self-awareness are the bread" with which all the main courses of prayer are to be eaten.[79] Did Thérèse draw from these words when she prayed over *le pain de douleur* with her brother sinners? For Teresa, that bread is the first course. For Thérèse, it is the only fare at the table.

Both women discovered themselves as writers, so far as writing always occasions self-address and self-examination. Implicitly, it also brings self-authentication, not least in "confession," for the author becomes the confessor to the confessing self. These women were steeped in the experiential and the diurnal, as Teresa reminds us with her kitchen pots and chessboard, with her eye appreciatively cast upon some of nature's smaller creatures, and Thérèse with her attention to flora and her dreamy conveyances, the famous elevator and the little boat. As women, they see God initiating a love in which they become actively passive. They dote on the suffering Jesus, the wholly human and wholly vulnerable savior. They both find his image within the sororal soul that loves him: the divine image is sculpted in Teresa's view, painted in Thérèse's. Their finding that image implicates the claim in the *moradas*, that the sister who attains the highest summit of prayer gives way to the Christ who has been within her.[80]

The *Camino* says that such a perfect soul desires the trials of this life and never turns the back to devils bringing those trials.[81] Devils are only God's stooges, and it is God who sends trials, as to Jesus in Gethsemane's garden. Confronting evil Thérèse offers a weighty counterpoint, telling her prioress that in facing the fog of doubt for over a year, she declines to engage the voices that doubt created. They tell her that her expectation of escaping from this spiritual prison and of possessing her God, creator of all wonders, is pointless, that she shall be enveloped in black nothingness. She says she pays the voices no heed and runs to Jesus instead, but in writing so vividly what the voices say, she *is* confronting the demons of her severest trial.

The final testing and final confrontation for Thérèse is at the table of sorrow. Teresa for once declines the combat. In the *Vida* she says that her only relief was in conversation with the friends of God, to the extent that she could have no friendship nor love for any people lacking love for God and the desire to serve him.[82] In the defensively aggressive climate of her time, when the Church was having to confound and sometimes burn up suspects, such a statement might be excused as part of a loyalty oath. Still, it remains painful to read because it argues a rather drastic limit on her understanding of charity. At the table of sorrow, Thérèse knew better and grew better. In the end, the daughter had one thing necessary to teach her mother.

JUAN (1542–1591)

"lo que se espera es de la que no se posee"
["One hopes for what one does not possess."]
SUBIDA DEL MONTE CARMELO, III. 15
"Porque no hay peor ladrón que el de dentro de casa. Dios nos libre de nosotros."

> *["For there's no worse thief than the one from within the house.
> God frees us of ourselves."]*
> CARTAS, XXIII (no date)

> *"Señor, lo que quiero es que me deis trabajos que padecer por Vos
> y que sea yo menospreciado y tenido en pocos."*
> *["Lord, I wish you to give me labors to suffer for You, to be despised
> and reckoned for little."]*
> SEGOVIA, 1591

I. Juan in Those Same Times

In turning from the mother of many sisters to the poet and mystical guide whom Thérèse most cherished, what differences we find! Juan's writing life comes to a small number of poems, very lengthy commentaries upon them, and a mere three dozen letters. The loftiness of vision, the ardor of a night endured with crying out to the hidden God, the drama of consuming fire—all this suggests that the air has become thin. An overwhelming solitude of self and God could force one to a sheer longing for the vileness of Teresa's terrain, the political intrigues surfacing in the *cartas* and the *Fundaciones*, the awkward, hardy struggles toward a hallowing life for little groups of women, from Castille and its unsparing winters to torrid Andalusia.

It is a pity that Juan de la Cruz left no autobiography. His reticence and option for silence most of the time were ineradicable parts of his temperament, deeply informed by his domestic background. It would be helpful to know his family in a depth comparable to what is known of the Sanchez and Cepeda branches of Teresa's tree. Juan's father, Gonzalo de Yepes, was *judeo-converso*. That means that no less than three of the four Carmel greats come from an Hebraic lineage, Edith Stein being the third. Thérèse is the sole Gentile.

He was born in the Castilian town of Fontiveros, sometime in 1542, one of the years of bad harvests, of famine and epidemic. His father came from a noble line but lost his inheritance when he, who had been orphaned himself, married an orphan, Catalina Alvarez. The Yepes family might have feared more than the poverty Catalina brought as her dowry: some Hispanic scholars of the Golden Age contend that she was of an *islamo-converso* family, the daughter of a Moorish slave. Juan likely got his Moorish complexion from her.[83] Public documentation of their backgrounds would have "blown the cover" protecting both lines. However romantic this "all for love" story began, the consequences were grim. Gonzalo, who practiced the then Jewish craft of weaving, died of malnutrition, when Juan was only two years old.

He bore for life the infirmities of rachitis, an inflammatory disease of the vertebral column, also known as rickets: a shorter than the then average stature (he was 4' 10"), an enlarged cranium, and unrecorded particulars that could have been part of the syndrome, such as a tendency to bowlegs, spinal curvature, muscular pains, an enlarged liver and spleen, sweating, an acute sensitivity to touch. Fire and light form the metaphoric staples of mystical traditions generally, but for Juan they in their immediate, physical way might have been palliative: sunlight and vitamin D would have mitigated the pains he bore to his life's end. To that condition he added the substantial pains of self-abnegation and poverty. From a positive side, his simple, sparing diet (usually, greens prepared with garlic and vinegar) and his many long journeys on foot (he managed as much as thirty miles in a day) offered an amelioration about which he know nothing. Had he known it was an amelioration, he would not have accepted it. Vegetarian fare and strenuous walks were merely the practices of poverty and mortification of the soul in that age.

Teresa's father by his military service to the crown had successfully applied to become a *hidalgo* or nobleman, thus securing his family's assimilation into propertied Christian culture. That fact resonates in her often quoted words about dying a daughter of the Church, as though emphasis or a reminder were needed. But no assimilation was ever possible for Juan's impoverished parents. A poor weaver's son, he grew up in the warp and woof of two underground cultures. It would be impossible to overstate this fact. I believe that Juan remained an outsider by fate and temperament; the synthetic nature of his genius ("genius" as Schopenhauer puts it: Juan hit a target that others could not see) sealed both temperament and fate.

Because his Jewish and Moorish backgrounds shaped Juan's early life and even his mature writing (his debt to Sufi mystical poetry is well documented),[84] it is important to review the hazardous positions that both Muslims and Jews occupied throughout sixteenth-century Spain. Although demographies remain approximate at best, it is certain that since the so-called *Reconquista*, the emergence of a predominant Christian Spain, Muslims continued vastly to outnumber Jews. Having arrived in 711, Muslims had held much of Spain, then known as al-Andalus, for nearly eight hundred years. Although viewed as a distant outpost by Eastern Islamic cultures, Iberian Islam engendered one of the richest civilizations in European history. The same could be said of Sephardic Judaism in the first century of its *converso* subjugation. Under the emirates of the Islamic centuries, many Christian and Jewish communities spoke Arabic. The emirs taxed them as infidels but did not attempt conversions. The *Qur'an* taught that Jews and Christians were in a prophetic succession and had to be respected as part of the tradition of which Islam itself was the culmination.

Gradually and by lurches (Córdoba fell to a Christian attack in 1236), the emirates lost ground to Christian armies from the north, until Islamic Granada, the nucleus of Muslim culture, capitulated in 1492. Although initially granted religious tolerance, the Muslims of Granada (those who had not emigrated to Islamic North Africa) were within a decade forced into conversion, which meant that the Church was obliging them to accept polytheism (as the Trinity was viewed), the abomination the *Qur'an* most vigorously denounced. Foremost in this ill-considered effort was Queen Isabella's confessor, Cardinal Cisneros, the sophisticated educator.

Compulsory measures against Islam brought a rebellion that ran from November 1499 to March, 1500. Muslims were then forced to choose emigration or conversion. Muslims who chose not to leave Spain came to be known as *mudéjar*, the Spanish for *al-mudajjar*, meaning "those remaining." Mosques were closed, and in 1501 Islamic books were publicly burned. The *mudéjar* saw through the distasteful hypocrisy of which they were made both victims and participants, for the chrism of compulsory baptisms was washed off at home immediately after the rite, but for the Church the assumption of baptism's efficacy sufficed, *ex opere operato*, which made for an uneasy peace. If baptized, one could not become a non-Christian again, only a heretic. At the popular level, however, Spain's Christians continued to denominate Muslims as *moriscos*, a tag roughly equivalent to *niggers*, even as the country prospered by the Muslims' silk industry. Persecution of Muslims was limited by the fact that taxes on this industry were indispensable to funding armies within Spain and beyond, but the Inquisition of the 1550s confiscated the property of alleged heretics. The Inquisition had no authority over Muslims and Jews as such; hence, the convenience of assuming they had become Christians, at least until someone conveniently denounced them.

After the third session of the Council of Trent (1559–1563), Spain's churchmen attempted to purge the outward signs of a continuous Muslim culture. King Philip feared collusion between Spain's Moors and the dreaded Turkish fleet then active in the western Mediterranean. On January 1, 1567, Arabic was formally prohibited and *moriscos* were ordered to abandon their own dress and assume Castilian style. Enforcement of this profound silliness, coming after several years of steeply increased taxes on the silk industry, brought the second major revolt of Spain's Muslims. In its two years, 1568–1570, the revolt was co-incident with Juan's founding of the first Reformed houses for Carmel friars, at Duruelo and Mancera. Far more important, however, was King Philip's post-revolt policy of internal emigration, which was intended to depopulate Islamic Granada. Tens of thousands of Muslims were compelled to settle far to the north, in Castilian towns and villages. Juan in his many travels likely had contact with these impoverished exiles within their own country.

Quite different, if hardly less painful was the common fate of Hispanic Jews. During the expansion of Christian kingdoms, some Jews had ascended to powerful professional positions, most prominently as financiers and tax collectors to the royal court, also as moneylenders in the economies of haciendas, but Jews generally remained despised, suspect, and ever likely to be scapegoated.[85] By a decree in 1313, they were obliged to pay tithes to the Church and to wear an insignia identifying them as Jews. Court intrigues caught them in cross fires, which meant that aristocrats could instigate rounds of overt anti-Semitism, as under Sancho IV and Alfonso X. Pogroms were intermittent, the worst occurring in 1391, when hundreds of Jews were killed in Spain's largest cities. Many Jews became *conversos* in the wake of those murderous riots. The great expulsion of 1492 briefly marked the triumph of the Church's iterated preference that Jews be kept segregated from Christians and excluded from the professions.

The *conversos* continued to pose a problem, however. Some baptized Jews, necessarily acceptable as Christians, regained the professions, Teresa's grandfather being among the converts of Toledo, one of the largest Jewish communities. Though scant, there is evidence that these communities were bitterly divided between the assimilationists who wanted to keep their professions and secure their property, and the *cryptojudíos* who continued Judaic practices behind closed doors. The sequestered culture of observant Jews was a kind of greenhouse, in which Judaism was sustained by renewed awareness of its distinctive and lamentable history: pharaonic persecutions, diaspora, pogroms. The danger of their exposure was clear from such exterminations as the one brought upon a hidden community of practicing Jews in Quintanar, a small town in Mancha de Aragón, in 1588. All of its Jews were incarcerated; the holdouts were burned alive; the rest were put through the ritual humiliations and brought back to the Faith.[86] For the greater part, both cryptojudaic and Moorish culture continued to thrive in confinement, the oppressive policies of state and Church reinforcing what they had been meant to obliterate.

It is easy to simplify these bleak stories unduly. Sensible men within the Church, such as the archbishops of Granada, Hernando de Talavera (1492–1507) and Pedro Guerrero (1546–1576), favored a moderate gradualist policy of assimilation because they perceived that compulsory measures were futile. As Talavera remarked of Granada's Muslims, "We must adopt their works of charity and they of Faith."[87] As to Jews, some *conversos* had risen within the Church's hierarchy and there were Moorish converts in the priesthood as well. That does not undervalue the contribution of innumerable clergy too indifferent to enforce Church doctrine.

Two Dominican friars of the mid-century merit special attention. Francisco de Vitoria and Bartolomé de las Casas wrote tracts on the necessity to convert "by means of argumentation, invitation, and the gentle movement of the will" but both men were addressing conversion as practiced upon vast numbers of heathenish tribes subjugated by *conquistadores* in the Americas.[88] From Aquinas they knew that forced baptism was *eo ipso* invalidated. Why that lesson was not extended to Spain's Jews is not clear. As for the *moriscos*, they were given theological attention as early as 1523, when it was determined that although baptism had been forced upon them, it was not "exact and absolute"—a critical departure from *ex opere operato*.[89]

On the peripheries marked by Judaism, Islam, and poverty, Juan never attempted to overcome his origins with the fustian of *honra*, the cultural additive indispensable to Iberian pride. He, his mother and his brothers Francisco and Luis (twelve and ten years his seniors) lived on public charity. Encouraged by his mother toward learning, Juan attended a *colegio de la doctrina* for orphans and then worked in Medina del Campo as a nurse at a hospital for syphilitics, veterans of Spanish sexual "conquests" in the Americas. He begged alms publicly for these wretches.

Little is known about Juan's education in Medina del Campo (from 1551 to 1558) under Jesuits,[90] his subsequent instruction, mostly unsuccessful, in artisan's skills such as carpentry and stone masonry (from 1559 to 1563), his four years' training in Thomism at the celebrated University of Salamanca (1564–1568).[91] Already in Medina he had drawn inspiration from the humanist theologian there, Gómez Pereira, who vigorously defended introspection. In Salamanca, although no documentation exists on what courses Juan pursued under whose instruction, he learned "skills in the numerous dialectical jousts" and the scholasticism that facilitated his synthesis of philosophy and theology, including the expository method used in his commentaries.[92] Noteworthy, too, in Salamanca's lecture halls was the Renaissance humanists' attention to Platonism, a route that mystics tended to prefer to the standard Aristotelian gravity burdening most of the curricula. (See Figure 1.5)

Throughout his education Juan was exposed to the contrary currents of scholastics and *"espiritualistas,"* to the breadth of assiduous learning, and to the lure of illuminative vision. The age was fervent in awakenings—Spain's Siglo de Oro had the highest percentage of universities in Europe—and the widest sense of

FIGURE 1.5 Salamanca, the University. Here, Juan studied rhetoric and scholastic philosophy, 1564–1568. Photograph taken by the author.

mission. Juan's generation "was that of pacification projects in Europe, in America and in man with God."[93]

What of his subsequent journey from Aquinas and scholasticism, a journey none of the Carmel sisters he knew could have taken? The more intriguing question remains: where, when, how, from whom did he learn of the Sufi mystical poetry that came to inform his own verse? From his mother? In Salamanca? From both her and it?

The sordid course of his infamous persecution—from December of 1577 into August of 1578 a severe confinement and daily lashings from each of his Carmel brethren in Toledo—gives counterpoint to his ethereal flights of verse dating from those months and that place. How might his *converso* origins have figured in this brutal mistreatment? What was the source of the apparently pathological hatred visited upon him so brutally and collectively? Had he not escaped, abetted by the jailor, he would probably have died, and that was perhaps the real intent. (See Figure 1.6.) This matter goes deeper than doctrine or even incidental clashes of personality. Juan was not confrontational or provocative by nature. If he was in fact tormented on other grounds, ferociously irrational ones, we might see the bizarre inflictions in a new light.

Slight in stature, amenable in manner, Juan had been a conspicuous target for envy and worse. As the first Reformed Carmel friar he worked in tandem with Teresa in creating new Reformed houses, a procedure inevitably stirring resentments. Teresa, whose family had by military service won entitlement to the *hidalguía* (an honor they could legally enjoy only within their own towns), was relatively safe from harm; it would have been unchivalric to persecute a woman. Juan enjoyed no such protection and was vulnerable as a *marrano*, that word synonymous for traitor or heretic. It would be naive to suppose his tormentors were ignorant of that status or resisted taking advantage of it.

In the generation after the expulsions of 1492, some Jews had risen as Christians into high governmental offices and

FIGURE 1.6 Toledo's city wall, at the precipice where Juan risked his life. The quatercentenary plaque quotes his words on the dark night of anxiety and love when he left the house, unobserved. Photograph taken by the author.

economic posts formerly held by Christian nobles. It was easy for the more anxious members of the aristocracy to stir up lower-order hatreds against ascendant Jews and to purvey myths of their domination of Hispanic society. Juan came from a beggarly home, but to prejudicial minds that fact would not have weighed much against his being a Jew. That is not to mention his Islamic background. In 1582, the year of Teresa's death, a lexicon known as *La Picara Justina* was being edited; it included the term *morisqueta*, a trick or ruse practiced by a *moro* or Muslim. Today, Juan is known only as a saint (and Doctor of the Church) of a very high order, but then he was regarded as other than a gentle, humble, patient soul inflamed with love for God. He seemed devious, subversive, a danger to authority and order. His *converso* status may hold a key to his role in the drama of the cross as he was forced to live it, to be despised not because he was a Christian but because he was believed to be something else: like Jesus, a criminal to be gotten rid of.

Unfortunately, little is known of his relationship to Teresa, who induced him to join the Reform in 1567. She chose him to serve as confessor to the Carmelite sisters of the Incarnation in Ávila, not long after her unwelcome appointment there. He served in that position for five years. That she esteemed him highly is evident in the *cartas*, when she writes to King Philip just two days after Juan's arrest (December 2, 1577) saying of the sisters he confessed, "They take him for a saint and in my opinion he is one and has been one all his life."[94] Elsewhere, she had admitted that he could be exasperating. There is no evidence between them of the close, sometimes fretful amity so readily observed in her relations with Gracián or others to whom she showed warmth and sometimes heat, such as her brother Lorenzo de Cepeda or Maria de San José or even the contrarian Ambrosio Mariano.

Yet Juan's writings provide an immediate succession to Teresa's. At least some of his poems date from his incarceration, and Teresa later enjoyed them with her community as they were widely distributed and set to music. Juan began his great prose commentaries in 1579. As Teresa's writings had been ordered, Juan's prose works had been solicited, primarily from sisters seeking to know more about what enthralled them in his verse. He wrote and completed his chief commentaries, on the *Subida del Monte Carmelo* and the *Noche Oscura*, in the year of Teresa's death, 1582. The books that exclusively informed Thérèse's understanding of him came closely after: the commentaries on his *Cantico Espiritual* in 1584, and on the *Llama de Amor Viva* in the spring of 1587, but the second versions he composed to both of those works, now known each as B, are the ones Thérèse cites. In her day, Carmel's sisters were not permitted to read the *Subida* nor the *Noche Oscura*, works considered hazardous for impressionable women, especially young ones. That is regrettable, at least Thérèse's case, as she had the wit to draw profit from them. In the event, what she was permitted to read, the *Cantico*, the *Llama de Amor* and the *Dichos*, provided a sufficiently inebriant tonic.

It was a wonder that Juan's B commentaries came at all, as he was burdened with disagreeable administrative tasks, the worst being that of a *definitor* or disciplinary officer of the Carmel's chapter. He also had a falling out with the vicar-general, an Italian aristocrat, and went so far as to volunteer for a mission to Mexico. Foes in his own house sought his expulsion from the Reform he himself had established. In December 1591, when he was 49, Juan died of staphylococcic erysipelas and contempt. Like Teresa's, his body was subjected to ghoulish visits and pious dismemberments, his limbs and trunk discreetly apportioned between Ubeda, where he had died, and Segovia, where he had served as its Carmel's superior.

The writing lives of Teresa and Juan together form a continuum of about twenty-five years. The best documentary tie between Juan and Teresa comes in her *vejamen* cited earlier, where she recoils from Juan's dead-to-the-world aiming at perfect contemplation in all things and at all cost. This response sounds like a Martha reproaching a Mary, but here it is Martha who has chosen the better part: with all her worries there are songs, with all the awareness of sins there is laughter. When down to earth as she was, one is closer to the gospels' dark world.

Evidence abounds that Juan, too, lived in the world. He loved its beauties, especially natural ones grand and small, and music: his poetry offers the proof on these counts. Like Madre Teresa, he could never overcome preferential love for his natural family, Catalina and Francisco. His asceticism was no hedge against life's ordinary ugliness; he had to proceed through the vulgar necessities of setting up new Carmel houses for friars. As the Incarnation's confessor, he lived nearby the convent in a poor neighborhood and was at ease and familiar with its inhabitants, even instructing their children. He happily engaged in heavy manual labor within the monastery. He cooked meals for the ill and infirm, and he swept floors. He was well known for his fastidious cleanliness, which was perhaps informed by his time at the hospital in Medina del Campo but more substantially by the Jewish and Islamic sanitary practices he learned at home.

All that being so, Juan's comportment was not of the world: his unearthly detachment and well-attested serenity mark his apartness from the rather thespian and forward Teresa. There is something eerie, if not altogether off-putting, about a genuinely saintly person, but Juan apparently never cultivated a starring role. He himself eschewed the sanctimony of cultism, refusing repeated invitations to visit the most popular celebrity of the day, the visionary and stigmatic Dominican prioress, María de la Visitacíon.

II. Thérèse's Juan

From the Hispanic Carmels and their unhappy politics let us look to the Juan Thérèse knew. The obvious needs remarking: she was ignorant of the virulent antagonisms attending Teresa's Reform, the bemusing strata of ecclesiastical titles and jurisdictions, the sundry plotting and solemn deliberations, the bewildering cast of characters, Italian as well as Spanish, close and distant. She would not have known what *converso, morisco, marrano,* or *morisqueta* meant.

Studies of her by eminent Carmel friars suggest that Thérèse in her first years within the convent needed and found in Juan a release from both profound anxieties about herself and the stiff, even oppressive atmosphere of the house, where she was by several years the youngest.[95] The extremes of Juan's divine *tout* and human *rien* offered a heady complement to her own heady extremes, her immeasurable desires ever in tandem with her absolute helplessness. Juan's notion that a soul could lose itself wholly to God in a dramatically self-incendiary way fired the adolescent craving of this lonely, very young and altogether impetuous woman. Indeed, she never grew beyond Juan: in her last years she cited him frequently to the novices she was training, and in the last months she made veiled references to him when talking with Pauline. This inclusion of others in her enthusiasm for Juan carries irony, as she was especially fond of his figurative abandonment of his priestly office, a shepherd leaving the flock to pursue God's love.[96]

Were there one dictum from Juan which Thérèse could have chosen for herself, it would undoubtedly come from the second (B) version of his *Cantico Espiritual*, the one she consistently used. The canticle, departing from the *Song of Songs*, affords an exchange of *coplas* between a bride and her initially vanished and then recovered groom. The 194 lines consist of mostly alternating rhymes. This work became popular among the Reform's convents and perhaps as early as 1578 (within Teresa's lifetime) the sisters made many copies. They importuned Juan to provide commentaries (*declaraciones*) on it. It became the most popular of all his writings in his lifetime and was alleged to be his own favorite.

In the nineteenth strophe, the bride pledges her soul and all her largesse in service to her groom. She shall no longer guard her flock nor perform any other charge, "For now in loving alone is my action."[97] In his commentary Juan speaks in mild deprecation of external works and services in love for God. He claims that "a little bit of this pure love does more benefit to the Church, though it seems to do nothing, than all the other works combined." He next commends the example of Mary Magdalen, alleged to have spent thirty years in the desert realizing that pure contemplative love.

If we juxtapose this passage with Teresa's *vejamen* chiding Juan for his otherworldliness, the two of them seem to give their allegiance to Martha and Mary respectively, in all but exclusion of one another. That, however, would be unfair to Teresa, who had a thorough devotion to Mary (albeit a Mary confused with the Magdalen).[98] Juan for his part has cast his lot with the contemplative life.

And Thérèse? The passage cited above reads this way in the French translation known to her: "the slightest *movement* of pure love is more useful to the Church than all the other works combined together."[99] She brings it into her own writing four times: in opening her prayer of consecration to the Holy Face (August 6, 1896), in her letters to Adolphe Roulland of March 19, 1897 (LT 221), and to her natural sisters in the summer of that year (LT 245). Like other Juanist pronouncements, this one exerted a kind of mantric force upon her.

Thérèse was also fond of a corollary to the "little bit of pure love," that a soul's love can ensnare God. Introducing his Canticle's thirty-second strophe, Juan claims: "Great is love's power and its stubbornness.... Blessed is the soul that loves for it holds God prisoner, subject to all it may desire."[100] Such is his gloss on the lover's exclamation in Solomon's *Song of Songs*, that the beloved has ravished his heart with a single look or a lock of her hair. Thérèse fairly runs away with this image of captivation, but alters the key action of the beloved's wounding the lover in this way (the Vulgate's "vulnerasti cor meum" and Juan's "llagaste") to an innocuous and rather deflationary charming, *charmer* and *charmant* being among her favorite words. Beside the edgy eroticism of the Solomonic wounding, *charmer* seems pallid. Fortunately, she arrived at her own tactic for ensnarement, claiming to her sister Marie that genuine poverty of spirit renders their souls so lowly that Jesus will come in search of them. This brilliant variant on the lost lamb story includes Juan's fiery dénouement, *"howsoever distant* we are, he'll transform us into flames of love."[101]

In Manuscript B 4v she cites "the slightest movement of pure love" but adds the sobering and salvific question, "But is *pure love* really in my heart?"[102] That is the commendable accent: had she presumed that her love was pure, she would have diminished herself to a littleness other than that for which she is known. But Juan's "a little" set beside "all works," (those that pure love surpasses) seems alluringly hyperbolical, the teasing rhetoric of paradox. It is questionable on the very grounds Thérèse in her brutal honesty adduces: *how* does one know that one's love is pure? *How* does it benefit the Church more than concrete acts of charity? In Christian benefactions does not the benefactor face Jesus himself? Are Christians not to be known by their fruits? Or was Thérèse perhaps troubled that Jesus himself foretells rejecting those who have preached, performed exorcisms, and worked miracles in his name?[103] These most high profiled works may become suspect as mere public shows. By contrast with these works of faith, love in the New Testament is never suspect. Jesus offers and commands it without any qualifying.

That offering and that commanding form a nexus between Thérèse and her dear Juan. They are both exultantly voluntarist in their response to Christ's call for love. If there is any one compacted expression of the vibrant loving in Thérèse, it is her *offrande* of June 9, 1895, her self-consecration to the immolating fire of divine love. In this solemn pledge of herself as a victim of, for, and to Love, she surpasses the mythic feminine victims of antiquity such as Jephtha and Iphigenia, both of whom were sacrificed to the rashness and folly of their earthly fathers. In the *offrande* Thérèse's audacity goes to the limit. The prayer from Juan that complements it, his *Oración de alma enamorada*, does not have the incandescence of the *offrande*, but does have its propulsive vim, registered in a heaping succession of psalmic questions—where are You? What are You waiting for? Won't you accept my mite?—as it proclaims this loving soul's desire for an immediate and intimate response.

Even this excited, exacting, extortionist pleading from the two of them does not bring full accord. At one crucial juncture, they move at odds to one another: why does Thérèse see fit to alter the relationship of love between Christ and the Christian, which Juan de la Cruz himself sets down in the *Cantico*? In the trope he takes from the *Song of Songs*, Juan's bridal soul is sickened with longing for the divine lover. Wounded and abandoned, the soul wants an epiphany that will end its suffering, indeed kill it.[104] In Thérèse's view, however, *Jesus himself* is sick with longing for the bridal soul, famished for human love. The thirst Jesus felt on the cross, a physical one, she extends by a magnanimous but entirely imaginative breadth into a figurative thirst for the unredeemed, as though it were not enough that Jesus sought God's forgiveness for human culpability. In Jesus's thirst for souls Thérèse invents parity for herself with Jesus as she thirsts for those souls, too, in her Carmelite mission. But this motif falls away after Manuscript B and September 1896 as she gradually intuited a far more subtle and elusive thirst, the unconscious longing for spiritual light in souls who sit in darkness.

Her steady dwelling upon love for and from Jesus as the central motif of her life and spirituality, points to another of Juan's potent utterances in his *Cantico*. Writing of the loving soul's desire that its heart be stolen by God, Juan urges that the soul seek no payment nor reward for its love, "for love is not paid save by itself."[105] Love, instilled in the soul by God, is working its way toward its perfection, rather as Teresa's silkworm worked in its shroud-cocoon to become a butterfly. But Thérèse, misled by the French translation, "l'amour ne se paie que par l'amour" "love is paid only by love," construed a reciprocity that Juan did not intend.[106] Did she finally realize her mistake, or did this reciprocity fade from her consciousness? Like the divine thirsting, it disappears after September 1896. Why?

She gave up on the perfectability of her love, the very thing that Juan expressly states to be the loving soul's desideratum: "the loved cannot be satisfied if he does not feel he loves as he is loved."[107] Such is his itch for parity. Instead, she resorts to what her humility in all its helplessness and littleness required of her: a borrowing of divine love itself. In the last pages of Manuscript C, she speaks of Jesus's love drawing her to him, *attirer*, one of her favorite words.[108] It became definitive of the prevenient grace safe-guarding her from sin in her childhood. But then, imagining Jesus's love for her as an abyss that she would like to fill, she admits that she is not even a dewdrop lost in the ocean of divine love. That acute ontological meagerness is the reason she needs to borrow divine love and give it back.

This concession of root inadequacy marks a substantial move away from the loving and hence transformative arrival Juan denotes in his *Cantico* and in his *Llama de Amor Viva* [*The Living Flame of Love*], Thérèse's other favored text from him. Although Thérèse follows his lead and takes inspiration from "All that is mine is yours," as the Prodigal Son's father says to the begrudging brother, she does not closely heed Juan's vigorous insistence upon illumination, purification, and union in the loving soul. That does not mean she did not experience the testing identified with purgations: her recording of her inner adversities, as far back as 1889, show that she was being tested by "the soul's pains, its drynesses, its anguish, its evident coldnesses."[109] She writes of these daunting, terrible privatives firsthand. Upon making her profession in September 1890, she conceded to Pauline that she might be passing "all my life on the dark road."[110] A prophetic remark, an extraordinary admission.

Even more extraordinary is her simultaneous desire that her own shadows serve to enlighten others. As early as 1890, she intimated her mission at the table of sorrow. By the time of her final writing, her darkness had arrested her and taken her to its own nadir, and that is why the borrowing of God's love, inspired in its way, became necessary. She wanted to follow Juan's itinerary and savored his signposting language, but she was honest with herself and took the obligatory detour marked by her own hard-won experience.

Juan himself showed her the trajectory of this way as its darkness overwhelmed her in the spring of 1896. His *Dichos de luz y amor* [Sayings about light and love], known to Thérèse as *Maximes* because of their aphoristic brevity, figure several times in her writings. She may have drawn instruction from many she does not cite, as they proffer guidance in darkness: best not to see at all in matters of God, best not to trust one's own self and claims to knowing, best not to seek revelations but to let the gospels and natural reason suffice—as Luther and Erasmus would have agreed! In the *entretiens* of her last summer, 1897, she seems to be speaking her own sorts of maxim to her bemused sisters. When Pauline remarked a thought she had about heaven, Thérèse replied, "Me, I have eyes only to see my little nothingness. That does me more good than [having] eyes for faith." When Marie anticipated angels accompanying Jesus upon Thérèse's death in a vision of light and beauty, Thérèse deflated this baroque fantasy: "All these images do me no good, I can nourish myself only by the truth. That's why I have never desired visions."[111] These responses are vintage Juan, and she made many of the same sort over that summer. Alas for her sisters, puzzled and left behind—with the rest of us.

Such gravity recurs in Thérèse's paraphrase of a strophe from the *Llama viva de Amor*, which she composed for the profession of the novice, Marie de la Trinité, April 30, 1896, only days after the descent of final inner darkness. There she sets out in verse the injunction that Carmelites seek no consolation, only the cross in all its bitterness. God brings outer and inner suffering to all the souls He desires to perfect and finally deifies them by union with the Holy Spirit. Thus, Juan showed Thérèse how to see her suffering as it became most intense, a life in shadows and with no hope of light.

She confided to Marie de la Trinité that when she read Juan's gloss on his poem, it took her breath away, as it was exactly what she needed to read as a revelation of what she had come to.[112] Her own gloss on Juan is breathtaking in its rare admission of evil within herself: "Love, I have realized, knows how to take profit from the good and the evil in me (such power!)...." This passage adverts to Juan's commentary on his words "Love pays every debt," the debts being "your sins and imperfections, which are your bad habits."[113] Thérèse goes along with this notion of Love making use of both good and evil in the soul: there has to be something to be purified, does there not? Finally, however, Juan's notion of purification does not have a high profile in the Theresian lexicon, no more than does the contaminant of sinfulness upon which it depends.

When she writes about purifying (only a dozen times), it is about hearts and souls, without any mystical union as the terminus. Two instances deserve heeding. In a late letter to her "spiritual brother," Adolphe Roulland in China (LT 226) on May 9, 1897, she asks how Jesus can purify in purgatory the souls that have already been consumed by the fire of divine love. That she meant herself among such an exalted band is evident from the second passage, in Manuscript C: "Oh, Jesus, if it is necessary that the table soiled by non-believers be purified by a soul that loves you, I truly wish to eat there alone the bread of testing till it please you to bring me into your luminous realm."[114] That is not by any reckoning Juan's sort of unitive purification, which is never social nor otherwise collective. Instead, these prayerful words hearken to Isaiah's injunction (58:10) to "satisfy the afflicted soul: then shall thy light rise in obscurity, and thy darkness be as the noon day." Thérèse, had she known the phrase, might have spoken of Juan's "fuego oscuro" or dark fire as the cleanser of that table.[115]

It would be wrong to assume that Thérèse, by her enthrallment to Juan and her use of his works in instructing the novices in her charge, became his mimetic votary. She remains her own person, uplifted by Juan's rhetoric but not in any final absorbing conformity to it; no more, indeed, than Teresa herself could have been. All three of these personalities were, despite their admissions of anxieties, lassitudes, or other weaknesses, resolute. They knew that they had to go their own way, not because of furtive egotism but because their crosses bore them that way. Teresa became fond of Gracián because he was wholly conformable to her wishes; he served as a foil to the autonomous Mariano and others who challenged her. Juan, frail and emaciated, knew how to exert conferred authority—he called Teresa, twenty-seven years his senior, his daughter, *mi hija*—and his exercise of it, especially when he was *definitor*, brought him bitter enmities.

For all of her adolescent and post-adolescent susceptibilities, Thérèse was a decided girl. Juan did not so much guide her as speak to her deeply rooted needs and urges, thus enabling rather than disciplining her. He corroborated with her an awareness of love's primacy in Christian life. Thérèse discovered and pored over him at a crucial time, during her seventeenth and eighteenth years, in the midst of her painful acceptance of the Carmel's life after her initial fervor had reached its inevitable tempering. Thérèse found affinity with Juan and rescue. He is not an older brother to Thérèse; much rather, a companion.

In his helpful study of Juan and Thérèse, Guy Gaucher remarks that "she is truly a daughter of him for whom faith is habitually 'night,' dark and certain."[116] I suggest that she be regarded as Juan's equal; she, like him, gives primacy to love over faith. True, she employs the phrase "nuit de la foi" when she tells Pauline she would rather remain in darkness and not see God and the saints as others desire, but "foi" is so feeble in her lexicon (used only twelve times in all her writings) that she all but cues us to her word of choice. When she says, "In Heaven, I'll see the good Lord, that's true! But to be with him, I'm already there right on earth,"[117] she is at one with the immortal Bernanos asserting that there is only God's kingdom and we are in it. I urge amendment of Gaucher's "absolute" identification of her "foi et vision" to "amour et vision."[118] That change underscores the immediate and possessive nature of love in Thérèse's sensibility. The anticipatory, distant-looking nature of faith proved inadequate for her, an insufferable retardation of her guiding impetus.

Here, to underscore the point, is a remembrance of Thérèse which Céline discreetly omitted from her official deposition at the beatification hearings. "During her illness, reduced to a frightening thinness she always kept calm and a joking word was on her lips. Without fear she saw death coming. One of her novices having admitted a personal fear of Purgatory, she answered: 'Oh, how you hurt me! You greatly insult the Good Lord in fatalistically believing you're going to purgatory. When one loves with a pure love, there is no purgatory.'"[119]

Only someone akin to Juan could say such words. But she does not mean that supreme Juanist moment when the loving soul is unified with God, the veil between them having been rent. She speaks of the soul still loving God. Céline's remembrance makes evident that unto her sister's last days, Juan's unitive vision, like Teresa's way of perfection a version of spiritual completion, could not be Thérèse's way of helpless, blind love as trust in God. Against the Iberian impossibilities, she had to stay with the cross of imperfectability and remain upon it.

2

Seeking Light in the Bible

*Montre-moi les secrets cachés dans l'Evangile.
Ah! que ce Livre d'or est mon plus cher trésor.
[Show me the secrets hidden in the gospels. Oh, how
this golden Book is my dearest treasure.]*
PN 24, "Jésus, mon bien-aimé, rappelle-toi."
["Jesus, my beloved, remember."]

IN MAKING HERSELF "of the Book" by reading it and by claiming Jesus as her spiritual advisor, implicitly her only one, Thérèse cut herself loose from an instilled passive receptivity and wandered into her own wilderness of temptations. Presented here as a New Testament figure, she confronts Jesus with her acute perceptions and her inexhaustible needs.

As Jesus was within the heart of Thérèse's Carmelite spirituality, indeed the heart itself and her very denomination as a sister, so the gospels provide the one sure entry into her life and writing. All she wrote and all she was, were to find their interpretive breadth and depth in the New Testament and the life of Jesus within it. Of course, the same could be said of any Christian—each Christian's life is a fifth gospel, as the exalting cliché has it—but in the case of this young woman the articulations of solicitude, longing, and joy in her life with and for Jesus reach a singular intensity. That proves true when he is absent and she at last discovers him where she had not looked. His withdrawal and her recovery of him mark the particular witnessing in her life and writing. Along the way, she found what Kierkegaard calls the dizzying freedom of anxiety.

Her relationship to Scripture is one of creative tension, a dynamic determined by the fact that she did not, could not read either Hebrew or Greek; she had only the French translations afforded to her within Carmel. Her deficiency, the inevitable concomitant of education for girls in her day, turned out to be positive. It required that she remain continually on her own to reflect, wonder and imagine her way through the biblical passages she knew from the *Breviare romaine* (1893) and the *Manuel du chrétien*. Like many or even most Christians, she found that her surest guide was her own intuitive and deeply affective rapport with Jesus, a bond that had grown in and from her childhood and that took on the needed scope of suffering and affliction that came with her senescent father's debilities and death

In passing from reflecting and praying to writing, that is to the written life of her prayers and reflections, Thérèse became a psalmist. As a reader of the Old and New Testaments she became a singer who dramatized her own life through and into the texts at hand. Her Christian life was effectively nothing else than that, a lived and keenly experienced appropriation of scriptures and a recasting of them via her singular sensibility, into letters and the daily lessons for the novices she was training.

Because she was blessed with a meager education, she had no avenue toward exegesis, the scrupulous attention to context and the sometimes wide semantic range within words such as "righteousness" or phrases such as "the Son of Man." She had neither the training nor the time (the Carmel's day allowed her only two hours to herself) nor the inclination to entertain and record a range of possible meanings or interpretations. Without knowing it, she was the ideal foil to Renan, the formidably learned professor of Semitic languages who had everything save Thérèse's unflagging love of the gospels and the avidity for sacrifice of self that they summoned. Without Renan's linguistic mediations, she had the far more vibrant immediacy of her personal response, her instinctive placement of herself within a text to the point where she could identify herself with the speaker, including Jesus himself. If her identification with him seems impiety, she could answer that by her Carmelite vows she had given her life to imitation of him through her obedience and through the redemptive suffering she had assumed, particularly in her *offrande* of June 9, 1895.

It cannot be said that she offers a hermeneutics, a way of interpreting scriptures. The word *hermeneutics* would perhaps have seemed devious to her, and *interpretation* would have been likewise worth shunning. She would not have understood any sort of partisanship, as for a feminist or a deconstructive reading. The very notion of reading seems inadequate, if not misleading in a Theresian context because her bent was upon assimilation of the text. Passages she particularly cherished she made her own.

For example, she frequently turns to Psalm 89, "I shall sing forever the mercies of the Lord"; to the lilies of the field (in both the *Song of Songs* and the gospels); and to the sufferings of the servant, prefiguring those of Jesus, in Isaiah 53. The first of these amounts to the briefest possible statement of her Carmelite mission and, no less, the substance of her autobiography as a record of mercies given to herself. The second provides one of the most imaginative instances of her Christology, in which she makes Jesus into a lily of the field and herself a drop of dew to appease a divine thirsting. The passage from Isaiah calls up her father's earthly destiny and denotes the second (and usually neglected) epithet of her name, Thérèse de la Sainte-Face. It also points to her own destiny in acute physical and spiritual suffering. All three passages, in sum, are compacted commentaries on her own life and spirit.

But frequency or infrequency of reference cannot be conclusive in assessing Thérèse's use of the Bible. Not every allusion she makes to the same passage matches the sense or breadth of the other allusions. It is not only the biblical context that matters but the context Thérèse is supplying from her side. The central questions become: whom is she addressing, and when and to what purpose?

At times she lets her imagination go astray. She says of Jesus that at the Last Supper "He knows that the heart of his disciples burns with a most ardent love for Him"[1] but there is no gospel account that attests any such fire. She seems unduly generous to the disciples at the table. As they eat, they learn that Jesus shall soon be leaving them and that there is a traitor in their midst. How, given this dismal news, could their hearts be burning with love for him? The answer comes from Luke's account, the only one, of the resurrected Jesus teaching a couple of his gloomy and ignorant apostles on the way to Emmaus, where he eats with them.[2] After *that* supper, the apostles recognize Jesus but he disappears. They say to one another, "Did not our heart burn within us while he talked with us by the way, and while he opened to us the scriptures?"[3] The single heart burning gives us the clue that Thérèse has either confused the supper at Emmaus with the Last Supper or—and this is an enchanting possibility—she has consciously retrojected the burning heart, which could only have meant love to her, into the account of Jesus's last words to his disciples.

This mistake (or novel recasting) is instructive. Whichever route she takes, errant or fantastic, it is exemplary of how Thérèse puts herself into the story. It is *she* who is at the Last Supper, burning with love for Jesus. This was the only way she could conceive of responding to Jesus in the ritual of utmost self-sacrifice. This extraordinary venture has gone without attention from her hagiographers but it says much about her; she had to bring herself up close to Jesus or bring him by dramatic fiat to her.

She carried on her person a very little book, which had initially been 4.5 × 3 inches, and over 500 pages in depth. This *Manuel du chrétien*, published in 1864 by Alfred Mame of Tours, contained the Psalms, the New Testament, and the *Imitatio Christi*, the latter a work that she had memorized in the Lamennais translation in the last years before she entered the Carmel. It also held the Ordinary of the Mass, Vespers, and Compline. In an act that one does not read about in hagiographical studies, she removed (scissored?) the four gospels (they amounted to well under half the book, at 216 pages) and sent them to Céline, her sometimes confederate in audacity, who was still at home in their father's house, Les Buissonnets. Céline had the gospels bound anew and gave the text to Thérèse. She carried it on her person to the end of her life; it served as a talisman against despair, a life-jacket in her sea of doubt, and an attempt to co-opt Jesus, at least in his story and words.

The *Manuel*'s translation of the New Testament was the one from which she most often drew, sometimes from memory, in her writings, and it is the one used in the gospel citations of this chapter. The translator is anonymous, but recent research has identified two early eighteenth-century Jesuit fathers, Bouhours and Lallement, as the authors.[4] Their quaintly dated yet literal renderings, over six generations distant from the language of her day, were exactly what she needed.

The multiplicity of biblical translations intrigued Thérèse, for she had several sources on which to draw beyond the *Manuel*. She had grown up hearing her father read citations from both Testaments in Dom Guéranger's multivolume series, *l'Année liturgique*. She heard other readings daily in Carmel from the *Bréviaire romain*. She read still more in the French translation of Juan de la Cruz, whose commentary on his own poem celebrating the "living flame of love" abounds in biblical quotation. Whether it ever bothered her that she did not have the Spanish to embrace Juan on his own terms remains a mute question, but the differences among translated versions of the Bible did trouble her. As Céline recalls in her memoir, these variants "afflicted" Thérèse, who owned that "If I had been a priest, I would have studied Hebrew and Greek so as to be able to read the word of God as he deigned to express it in human language."[5]

In Thérèse's biblical citations, four topics predominate: love, humility, a testing of the soul (*éprouve*), and glory.[6] Yet only three of these rubrics engaged her. Glory, something not at all prominent in her mature spirituality, figures for nearly half of its instances in her letters to Céline. Was the promise of celestial glory the most powerful antidote she could offer to her sister against the suasions of the vain worldly life that was tugging at her? Thérèse, who, for her sister's sake, was downplaying the necessary cross, invoked heavenly reward, the most commonplace of inducements for Christians.

In this discussion I look at three texts of the Old Testament: Trito-Isaiah, The Song of Songs, and Psalms.[7] These are the Hebraic sources that most deeply informed Thérèse's Christology, both the person of Jesus and her relationship to him. Altogether they provide the twin poles of her Carmelite vision of Jesus: his suffering in service to humanity and the intimacy within which she could express a compassionate devotion to him. The important questions seem to me to be: just who is this Jesus she loved? How did she craft from the scriptures her portrait of him, and is it an adequate one? Why did he allow her to descend into a darkness bereft of him? As that darkness brought from her a prayer, is it finally a prayer of lamentation in exile, or does it require some other identification?

I then turn to the gospels and look at passages especially appealing to Thérèse, as she repeatedly mentions them in paraphrase or verbatim, along with others that help in interpreting her. It is my contention that, treated as a character one might find in the gospels, a dramatic sort of person, she was given to or pushed toward extremes. The code word for that extremity she herself provided in each of her autobiographical stories, *audace*, sheer boldness.

I. Thérèse on the Old Testament

Of the more than one thousand biblical allusions and quotations in Thérèse's writings, more than four hundred concern the Old Testament. The preponderant number centers upon Trito-Isaiah's Suffering Servant and, in complement to that figure, the ethics of service and of justice assumed by the penitent soul. The fifty-third chapter offers what the Church takes as a proleptic view of Jesus, a prophecy of his rejection and death: "He was despised and rejected of men; a man of sorrows, and acquainted with grief:... But he was wounded for our transgressions, he was bruised for our iniquities: the chastisement of our peace was upon him; and with his stripes we are healed" (53: 3,5). In Protestant translations such as the Geneva and King James versions, the iniquitous hide their faces from the sufferer whom they reject, but the translations Thérèse knew follow the Vulgate's "et quasi absconditus vultus eius et despectus" ["his face was as though concealed and despised'], meaning that it is the sufferer's face, Christ's, which, remaining hidden, keeps him a secret only for the called and chosen to know and savor.

For Thérèse that hiddenness was an all-important matter because the obscurity of Jesus from the world was hers as a Carmelite. It was an obscurity shared within the community but also shared with God and the chosen devout. As she told Céline in a letter of August 1893, "To find something hidden, one must oneself be hidden, our life must then be a mystery, we must resemble Jesus, Jesus whose face was hidden."[8] She was aware, as she notes elsewhere in this letter, of Jesus's teachings "in regard to the *crowd* of Jews," but it was the silence of Jesus to which she was drawn, his silence before Herod and Pilate, who condemned him. On the wall of the *dortoir*, Pauline had painted the message that silence is the language of angels, but it is the unheard melodiousness of Jesus's silence that appealed to Thérèse and tickled her sense of the paradoxical.[9]

In effect, Jesus is more a presence for Thérèse than a lesson giver. Her remark about the crowd of Jews is deprecatory, given that its collective numbers sway with the winds, now heeding Jesus and stampeding to him for miraculous cures, now calling for his crucifixion. What she called treasures hidden in the Holy Face (her imaginative conflation of Isaiah 45:3 and 53:3) could be accessible only to the initiated few. Yet, if the world's contempt for Jesus comes from not recognizing his divinity, that is exactly the way Thérèse wants it: hidden, he cannot be known, and being mis-known, he is abused, suffering in such a way that she can console him. In one of her boldest prayers she writes that "Our sole longing is to beguile your divine Eyes in hiding our face as well, down here on earth, so that no one can recognize us."[10]

Most intriguing about this notion are its transparent incongruities and hence, its incompleteness—Jesus, unrecognized, was not only abused; he was killed. The Carmelites were hidden, but they were not persecuted unto death, at least not in

Third Republican times. They were, in their way, forgotten, but Jesus could not be, as such was not his mission. Quite the reverse, the resurrection was a supreme heralding. He foresaw fake versions of him, power seekers who would try to manipulate the Christian community to their own ends. In sum, the hiddenness figures only as the shared aspect of Jesus and his sister followers. Thérèse had to go deeper into the mystery of the Holy Face, until she became hidden even from herself.

She might well have intuited that she needed an anti-epistemology of mystery. If Jesus remains hidden, he is unknown, but he must remain so even to the initiates, the devout Christians, who seek to achieve their own hiddenness. Their remaining unknown even to themselves and their acceptance of that ignorance are vital because such humility forms the only stay against discipular presumption, the pre-emptive claims that Jesus's students make repeatedly. Such unhappy and false turns come because Christians cannot know the ways of God. That ignorance, sometimes proceeding to foolishness and cruelty, is succinctly observed not in the gospels but in Isaiah: "as the heavens are higher than the earth," God's ways and thoughts are not our ways and thoughts (55:8–9). The conclusion is humbling, but for Thérèse it was joyful as well, a corollary to one's being hidden, unknown, implicitly despised.

One of her most important expositions of Isaiah 55 comes in the first of a series of five letters to Céline composed over the summer of 1893. Céline had been caring for their father for nearly a year after his release from Bon Sauveur, the sanatorium at Caen. He had become a suffering servant *par excellence*, afflicted with illness and ignominy, secreted away in his helplessness and gradually sinking toward death. The pressure upon Céline, alone with Louis, had been mounting from eligible beaux; the possibility of a career in painting; the prospect of working as a laywoman for the Church in Canada; and the Carmel. She defended herself with the "consolation" that God expected far more of her convent sisters than of herself. She protested that she did not have their strength: "I do so little for God and you, you give him so much. I find you so good and myself so wicked!..."[11]

These were exactly the necessary words to sound in preparation for a spiritual calling, the conviction of a profound unworthiness and inadequacy of self, and perhaps covertly a cry for direction. In her first letter Thérèse applied pressure with unequivocal force: "'My thoughts are not your thoughts,' (says the Lord). Merit does not consist in doing and giving much, but rather in receiving and loving much."[12] Thérèse is hinting that the contemplative prayerful Carmel should be her sister's preference over a life such as she had been leading, sacrificing herself for her father. Mary's way is the better part, Jesus says, but Martha's is still a part. Thérèse seems to deprecate a spirituality of practical work and endeavor and to commend instead a recumbency for receiving God's word.

Céline's sacrifices for Louis were hardly in vain, but they were entirely conventional. Thérèse in effect seizes upon Isaiah 55 to warrant an emotive and imaginative depth within oneself greater than social and even verbal constraints can sustain. She presumes that God's ways, as they are not ours, must therefore be all but diametric to the human. Jesus's own teachings, that the last shall be first, for instance, encourage, if they do not altogether justify, this presumption. Isaiah 55 proves to be a kind of secret, as was 53, a promissory note that everything is controvertible. To so audacious a temperament as Thérèse's, this divine axiom was fetchingly antinomian, and she noted its pertinence to herself and other women when she was writing her autobiography.[13] In heaven, she hints, women shall be first and men last.

Her last recorded understanding of Isaiah 55 went to Père Adolphe Roulland, her missionary brother in China, on May 9, 1897, a month before she began Ms C. In this letter she takes the unfathomability of God as a conclusion rather than a premise. How is it that God affirms the divine kingdom within souls by the persecution and suffering they are forced to undergo rather than by any of their preaching? How can submission to evil bring a soul closer to God? Having begun to savor this paradox, she unfortunately discards it by celebrating martyrdom as the way to celestial recompense. This mercantile view Roulland perhaps needed to sustain him as he anticipated his imminent death in the Sechuan province of China. In his first years there, that province was alive with brigandage; Thérèse's injunction to martyrdom he had long been primed to hear.

Another passage from Isaiah 58: 5–12 is of particular moment because, although Thérèse never cites it within any of her writing, she copied part of it into her little *carnet* in November 1896. Céline recalled at the hearings the use Thérèse made of it in instructing the novices. It concerns charity to the suffering. As the passage is too lengthy for citation here, I shall cite only the verse, the tenth, which Thérèse herself wrote down: "And if thou draw out thy soul to the hungry, and satisfy the afflicted soul; then shall thy light rise in obscurity, and thy darkness be as the noon day."[14]

Here is compacted the twofold mission Thérèse set herself in Ms C, to succor the marginal within the Carmel's walls and to relieve suffering well beyond them, by the missionary act of prayer. "What a mystery! By our little virtues, our charity practiced in the shadow, we convert souls *far off*."[15] Céline claims that her sister glossed the *effusion* of that first passage in this way: "...that is, with heart, with love, with disinterestedness, if you console those who are suffering, *you'll recover your spiritual well-being*, your soul shall not languish."[16] She found especially attractive the paradox that spiritual shadows would become sources of light, put to use, as it were. And the concluding promise, that God would fill the charitable soul with splendor, was irresistible: "he shall make fat thy bones and thou shalt be like a watered garden." It is not difficult to imagine the force of such eloquence upon a young woman whose body was being wasted away. It bore the metaphor Teresa of Ávila loved, the soul as a garden to be watered.

Isaiah exerted another prophetic power upon Thérèse's sensibility by identifying the Suffering Servant who in that suffering would provide a luminous mercy to the lost and hurt. This prophetic text spoke at once to her deep and abiding need of mission. More, it spoke to the sore tribulation of body and spirit that threatened to render everything in her into a void. Isaiah did not, however, offer her a model of feminine enterprise and endurance. Only the *Song of Songs* was able to do that. It became so much a part of her self-perception as Jesus's spouse that it deserves introduction.

"An Excellent Song Which Was Salomons," so the Puritans' Geneva Bible of 1560 described what is known in the Vulgate as *Canticum Canticorum, Song of Songs*. Excellently sensuous in spices and spicily sensual, the *Canticum* has long stood as a parable of Christ's perfect love for the chaste soul of his Church, the bridegroom offering to the bride "benefites," to recall those Puritans of 1560 for a moment, "wherewith he doeth enrich her of his pure bountie and grace without any of her deservings."[17] That scheme goes back as far as Origen (early third century, A.D.), when the Church was in polemical exchange with the Jewish community over the interpretation of Old Testament texts. The Targumic or Aramaic paraphrase of the *Canticum* read the verses as an exchange between God and an Israel fallen in sin, punished, and brought to atonement.

From another vantage, such readings, exalted and anagogic, seem a cheat. They leave aside so much that makes this lyrical exchange of two lovers exquisite and earthly. The so-called naturalistic approach has won the upper hand in recent generations; it smells myrrh as myrrh, a fragrance off of a spiny shrub, and when the young woman, having "opened" to her lover, speaks of her hands dripping with myrrh, the beauty of eroticism appears untrammeled by mere lust. Censure of or aversion to the vibrant sexuality in this work rests on the tacit assumption that such love cannot be anything other than vile and unwholesome, even though the first and last impression of this *Song* is that it celebrates nothing other than the goodness of such love, something akin to the divine in its ardor, bliss and longing. Besides, it was included within sacred scriptures well before it was transmuted into the God-and-Israel or the Christ-and-Church constructs.

A concession to the opulent immediacy of images is not enough, however. Although the *Song* is an exchange of lovers celebrating each other's comeliness, a narrative creeps through in often menacing tones. For the *Canticum* is girded with a fairy tale's ambiance; the young beloved is abused by her mother's angry (and wicked?) daughters who oblige her to tend their sun-baked vineyards. When the lover, having consummated their love, leaves her, she is abused by watchmen while she searches for him through the city. Her outdoor complexion (not to mention her wandering about town) has made her seem to others a slave-woman, perhaps a prostitute. She is challenged by the "daughters of Jerusalem" to proclaim the grounds of her love, as they taunt her with a question and an ironic salute,

"What is thy beloved more than another beloved, O thou fairest among women?"[18] That she is despised and oppressed, privately and publicly, gives the beloved a Cinderella air, to which the dereliction of the lover contributes. He is a fairy tale prince who comes, then goes, and with his sudden going comes all the cruel, inexplicable causality that every childhood is forced helplessly to ingest in such tales.

Far from some cheap ecstasy of the pornographic, this poem celebrates the fierce but transient bliss in humanity's nature at a point where it seems to disclose the divine. It is about the joy of union and the woe of losing it. There is simply nothing in the gospels about sexual love per se, and there is simply nothing in the *Song* about marriage, familial proprieties of any sort, or even God. Eros and agape are a forced marriage, at best. Best, too, that this story concludes with the fond sentiment that love is as strong as death, a motif that belongs only with the doomed, fleeting nature of eros itself, not with agape. It is the story of Pyramus and Thisbe, Tristan and Iseult, Romeo and Juliet.

Given all this, it is not surprising that Thérèse, seeing in the lover only Jesus, de-eroticizes him. Passing by the kissing that fascinated Teresa of Ávila, Thérèse dwells upon the perfumed Jesus. Like a character in Ovid, he is turned into a flower, the lily of the valley at the beginning of Solomon's Chapter 2, even though the text makes clear that this metaphor belongs to the beloved young woman by self-identification, not to her lover.

That is not the only instance of misplaced gender. Thérèse longed to know Hebrew and Greek because she knew they would have brought her closer to what she called the "secrets" of Scripture. These languages were effectively themselves secrets to her, but she made do with what she had, and that was enough. The *Song of Songs* figures in a long letter to the postulant Céline, preparatory to her profession of vows on the following day (February 24, 1896), when Thérèse choreographed her restive sister's approaching wedding to Jesus. As it was not unusual for a young woman entering the novitiate to recoil in sudden trepidation and self-doubt, and as Céline had effectively been drawn into the Carmel by her sisters, this letter has an exhaustive gravity, part exhortation and part consolation.

It is charitably effortful. Thérèse draws upon Solomon for inspiration, imagining Jesus the groom saying to a well-meaning angelic choir poised to start a matrimonial concert: "Do not awaken my Beloved, leave me alone with her, for I would not be apart from her a single instant."[19] Thérèse knew about the lover-Jesus's inclination to take leave, but such alluring words as those she wrote were what her sister needed, and she knew that, too. Even so, her recast of the *Canticum* (she has borrowed only the first clause) stands rather too distant from the Vulgate's "Ne suscitetis, neque evigilare faciatis dilectam, quoadusque ipsa velit." ["Do not rouse nor stir the beloved until she herself be willing."] The Hebrew indicates, however, that this verse is an injunction against external interference, as by the use of incantational magic or ritual spells. It is a plea to let love, powerful and fickle as it is, have its own way in its own time.[20] It is not either of the lovers who is asleep here but love itself.

That reading would have proved a stumbling stone for Thérèse. So earnest was she in her own love of Jesus that she could not accept the dormancy of such love in Céline. As Thérèse was dismayed to realize, her sister had been drawn to ordinary, earthly sorts of love. Céline at her own level grasped the *Canticum* better than Thérèse did or could. She in the outer world was closer than her cloistered sister to the language of erotic transport that Teresa herself used in writing of Solomon's poetry.[21] But did Céline truly love *Jesus*? Was her love only a consenting, willing love? No matter, tomorrow she would *have to* take her nuptial vows, accepting that her will finally did not count. It was there only to be given away.

As a Carmelite, Thérèse in reading the *Canticum* sees herself as only one of many young virgins following Jesus, drawn by the savor of his ointments. Toward the end of her life, she wrote (C 33v) that Jesus's scent would draw all those she loved along with her to him. The exclusive I-Thou drama of the *Canticum* does not finally impose itself upon her, except that the lover when mysteriously absent is patently the Jesus she had known to be hidden (or asleep) to her through most of her life.[22] Yet she puts some of Solomon's verses to singular good use: Jesus, she tells herself, hid her, a dove, in the rock clefts and hollows of 2.14, for these recesses could only be the Carmel. He had compassion upon her weakness, she says in her first manuscript (A 44r).

Mentioning another of Solomon's passages, 1.11, one of the novices, Marie de la Trinité, recalls Thérèse puzzling over why a gold border is there studded with silver. It seemed absurd that an inferior metal would overlay a more valuable one. Thérèse concluded that the silver signified humility, which must first present itself in order to make the gold of love agreeable to Jesus. She notes how she arrived at this conclusion: "During prayer, Jesus gave me the key to the mystery."[23] This little episode affords an exquisite instance of Thérèse's resourceful wit and what prompted it, the need to help herself as well as her fellow sisters in the novitiate to make sense of scripture, to search for a daily access to its realm so as to inform and nourish their lives and hearts.

In that pursuit, she managed to go beyond the *Canticum* even while abiding within it. She takes up the central drama, the hidden awayness of the lover, and answers the question that Solomon's beloved might have asked: not "Where is my lover gone?" but the anxious "*Why* is he gone?" The Carmel context requires brief noting as it brings the reminder that Thérèse's readings of Scripture are more often than not *in situ*. They are feeding a situation, sometimes enlightening it.

In one dramatic example of enlightenment, Thérèse had lost control of herself. She was human enough to become irritated, angry, perhaps even to lash out. On May 28, 1897, Sr. St. Jean-Baptiste had approached her, asking for help with a painting. At about this time, Thérèse had undergone a hurt that is not usually registered in the biographies: she had been relieved of her work with the four novices she had been training. She nowhere remarks this change, one she accepted in obedience, of course, and with an appreciation of her increasing debility, which necessitated the prioress's decision. She could no longer perform any task nor even attend the daily Office. Illness physically and psychologically sequestered her from the community, even though she did not go down to the infirmary until July 8. But she suffered bereavement in losing the precious ties she had established with her four charges. In the midst of losing that singular motherhood, she wrote her valedictory verse, a celebration of the first of mothers to Christians, "Pourquoi je t'aime, O Marie!"

Pauline, present when Sr. St. Jean-Baptiste importuned Thérèse, had attempted to excuse her sister, then feverish and weak. Sr. St. Jean-Baptiste later admitted that she was wrong to make the request and asked forgiveness. Whatever biting words Thérèse may have said, whatever sharp look she may have given, it produced tears of self-reproach later. That she wrote to Pauline about it suggests she was, even consciously, providing evidence of her fallibility, as though it might be yet another lesson for the novices: "This evening, I showed you my *virtue*, my TREASURE of *patience*! Yes, me, who preach so well to the others!!!!!!!!!!!!!!!.."[24] (LT 230).

Characteristically she mined the unhappy occasion for some rich metal. She told Pauline she was glad to have revealed how imperfect she was; it was even better than being ever the model of gentleness, which only a divine grace could sustain in her. With no less characteristic extravagance, she reminds herself of the woman caught in adultery whom Jesus rescues (John 8:1–8). An offender, here in an extreme instance for monitory purposes, can be sure of mercy from him. It was well that Jesus was so often absent from Thérèse, or so she claims, showing himself, as Solomon says in 2.9, only through the lattice "...indeed, I realize I could not bear [his presence], my heart would break, being helpless to contain so much happiness."[25] That claim even Solomon's beloved had not made, and it is a brilliant gloss upon his vivacious poetry.

Both the Solomonic poem of love and this response from Thérèse point to a chasm of difference between the ways the genders respond to scripture, especially to Jesus. Men tend to read in terms of domination and control, including adventure and risk. Women tend to read for the emotive and affective life they feel strongly within themselves. Such are the two principals of the *Canticum*. He is a military figure in the midst of a campaign; he comes and goes, while she is stationed in recumbent but expectant longing. She ventures out to find him and cannot wait to get him back within close quarters.

Here in this action lies one basis of Thérèse's tsunami-like popularity within the first generation after her death, that she feminized Catholic spirituality as no one else had ever done. That it was a kind of international populism that drove forward her canonization has long been evident, but I believe there was an urgent vulnerability of the feminine within that populism, a vulnerability Thérèse so exquisitely embodied, and it was beneficent and mighty. She rehearses the vulnerability in her own feminine sensibility, so earnest and welcoming before an overwhelming yet also elusive masculine (or masculinized) power. By gender, Catholic women could readily identify themselves with Thérèse, but Catholic men—there would be millions of them during the First World War—found in her a sororal accessibility alive within their own generation. As the Virgin was and remains mother to the Church, which is itself known as maternal, so Thérèse brings the irresistible proximity of a little sister.

While the *Song of Songs* furnishes a little banquet richly laden by Eros, a hymn to conjunctive love, the Psalms dwell in a world far apart from such bliss. It is hard to proceed very far through them without dismay and even repugnance. Their keynote is hostility, and one's politics with God has much to do with the afflictions suffered or threatened at the hands of "mine enemies." The appeal to a divine justice is fueled by a punitive righteousness, one lamentably all too familiar in today's landscape of global vexations. After just a few of these "songs," it is a relief to turn to Christ's provocative injunction to love one's foes. Such a command, however steep or even inconceivable it appears, at once clears the air of the sordid, at-bay disposition of the psalmist. The decisive disjunction that the New Testament marks from the Old lies here, in the attitude one assumes toward one's neighbors. To put not too fine a point on the matter: Christ's story of the "Good" Samaritan (Luke 10:30–36), someone a Jerusalem Jew would have despised as lower than a dog, is told in counterpoint to the examples of those who refuse to show the Samaritan's elementary charity to the bandits' victim: a priest and a Levite, the most righteous and official breed in the Jewish community. Evidently, Jesus pondered the vindictiveness in the Psalms and perceived it was a dead end.

These remarks may seem a warping caricature of the Psalms. It is true that the three kinds of psalms must be distinguished: lamentations, supplications, thanksgivings. It is true that some are ennobled with poetry and a charitable regard for others, the poor and afflicted, while yet others ring out in grandly major keys, as at the close in the last of them, Psalm 150. It is also true that Thérèse in no way partakes of the reprisal mentality that argues itself as unwholesome fare, the very substance, psychologically considered, of Voltaire's dig at the Old Testament as a "tissue of horrors."

Yet Thérèse made substantial use of some psalms, and, as with the *Song*, she tended toward iterations of favorite passages; sometimes, as with Psalms 30:21 and 83:7, to as many as eight instances. In all, she cites fifty-two psalms; twenty-seven of them only once.[26]

An intriguing instance of rejoicing, death, celebration of God, and abandonment by God comes in June 1897 when she refers to Psalm 88 (89) whose opening, "I shall sing of the mercies of the Lord for ever" she had cited several times in

Ms A. Here she alters it for the first time with "Me, I want to sing your mercies," inviting conjecture that she cannot, even as she wrote that she *wanted* to believe (C 7v), implying she could no longer do so. That supposition can be resisted in this psalmic context, as Thérèse has just alluded to the elevator that shall exalt her to Jesus, a motion and a direction that at this time counted for her as more than heaven. She thanks God for bringing her to realize that she needed only to remain small; indeed, that she should seek to become ever smaller, as though in her diminution she may be borne upward the sooner by this newly discovered divine physics and into the arms of Jesus.

In another instance she suggests that her death may be imminent and passes directly to a psalm she quotes only once: "Thou hast taught me from my youth: and hitherto have I declared thy wondrous works, I shall continue to proclaim them in advanced age," says Psalm 70 (71): 17.[27] She asks herself and the prioress, Marie de Gonzague: "What will this advanced age mean for me? I think it might be now."[28] The intrigue deepens as she does not cite the next line: "O God, forsake me not, until I have proclaimed thine arm to all the coming generation." In fact, she had cause to cry out that God *had* forsaken her—it was now fourteen months since her Easter conversion—but she had also discovered Jesus's elevating arm. She could well have proclaimed that discovery as the mission of her "advanced age." But she could not fathom how Jesus was to lift her up into a celestial realm she no longer believed in. That was, I believe, what perplexed her—Jesus without heaven.

Thinking only to please Jesus, Thérèse concludes, "The good Lord needs nobody (me even less than others) to do good upon the earth."[29] These words anticipate those famously associated with her, what might be called the very ground of her saintliness. She told Pauline only six weeks later that earthly benefaction was what she wanted, but her struggling toward it is evident here. The psalmist of white hair would proclaim God's justice, magnificence, and so on, but she had only weeks, days, or hours to live. As though to defeat a pointless emulation, she dismisses the psalmist's pledge, for God does not need anyone's proclamation. There could be no such need, as it is smallness, weakness, and helplessness that He wants. That is what the elevator meant. Such was her first movement toward realizing her mission—its initial negation.

Psalm 70 has further pertinence within the first pages of C. Before singing the Lord's mercies, the psalmist remarks the foes who lie in wait for his soul, saying, "God hath forsaken him: persecute and take him; for there is none to deliver him." Thérèse drew inspiration from this passage some five days and as many pages after she had sung the Lord's mercies when she gave voice to her interior enemies who told her that she, too, was without divine protection, that divinity itself was an illusion: "rejoice that death shall give you not what you hope for but a night yet more profound, the night of nothingness"[30] An accomplished dramatist, she astutely makes the inimical remarks effective by using the second person, rather than the psalmist's distancing third. It becomes a sinister taunt, a collective menace such as she had not heard since her lonely, vulnerable days at the Benedictine school.

Thérèse does not respond to this enmity in the psalmist's fashion. She does not call upon God to wreak vengeance upon others and lay them waste, as though God could be co-opted to satisfy anyone's puny fretfulness. The enemies she faces are deeply embedded within her, as though a fever were running through her soul. The *Concordance Thérèsienne* indicates that the very word *ennemi* recurs substantially in only three texts: the second of two plays on her beloved Jeanne, *Jeanne d'Arc Accomplissant sa Mission* (nine instances); her play on the hoax figure, Diana Vaughan, *Le Triomphe de l'Humilité* (five instances); and C (another five). Their common denomination is clear, three young women facing imperilment of their souls' salvation.

In *Jeanne d'Arc accomplissant sa Mission*, the Bishop of Beauvais, Pierre Cauchon, condemns her with a laundry list of ecclesial infractions: "...you are a heretic, a relapser, an apostate, an idolater; by your witchcraft you've had an heretical king crowned, waving your magical standard over his head during the ceremony.... now you can go in peace, the Church to which you have refused submission can no longer defend you. Every dead branch must be separated from the vine and cast into the fire."[31] For Jeanne, as for her admiring Carmelite, these words supplied the worst possible censure. The Church through one of its consecrated voices was declaring her damned in the very words Jesus used, the cutting away of the dead branch (John 15:6). Jeanne was cruelly mocked, besides, in the gratuitous use of the Nunc dimittis, "Now let thy servant depart in peace" (Luke 2:29).

Cauchon's terrifying words are relevant to the psalmic context of this discussion because they enact in vivid particulars the pronouncements of the psalmist's enemies in 70: the abandonment of the soul, the persecution, that no one shall deliver this soul. But Thérèse's Jeanne, chained and about to be immolated, defies Cauchon. She knows it is he, not the Church nor God, who condemns her. Could she go to Rome, she knows the pope would find her innocent (a claim recorded at the trial). But that is incidental. What matters far more is that Thérèse's Jeanne attains an *imitatio Christi* by asking God *not to punish* her enemies, and she forgives all those who have brought about her death.

Enmity, then, has no political substance for Thérèse. It does not stick to her, nor would she have been able to grasp it in any social context. Even those who might have slighted her or put her down within Carmel's walls, those who disliked her and her natural sisters—all of them remained her sisters in Christ who were daily called to prayerful charity. Besides, she had learned to recognize reproof from anyone, especially from the prioress, as benevolent and beneficent. Thérèse could not have comprehended Jesus's injunction to love one's enemies since she herself had no immediate experience of them, the psalmic enemies in a neighborhood desert. But enmity from her shadowy voices was something else, a deadly challenge to her spiritual well-being, a power diametric to the charity that had sustained her in the Carmel and that she in turn had imparted to the four novices in her charge. If Thérèse, unreflecting in her loyalty to the Church, could not have fathomed Jesus's opposition to and enmity from the hierarchs of his day, the scribes, Pharisees, high priests, and elders, she did perceive the far deeper spiritual enmity that Satan posed to Jesus in the great temptations of miracle, mystery, and authority, as recorded by Saint Matthew (4: 1–11). And yet she not once alludes to those temptations in all her writings, including C.

In C, Psalm 118 closely follows 70 as though coming to her rescue. Within a few lines, she fuses no less than four discrete passages from this, the longest of the psalms (176 verses). When set out in her sequence, they look higgledy-piggledy: 141, 100, 105, 60, but she has gathered them into a clear, progressive coherence: "I am young and despised," says David, "but in seeking the divine will I have become wiser than the aged. God's word has enlightened my way so that my soul, untroubled, can now fulfill God's commands." This is deft editing.

"Thy word is a lamp unto my feet, and a light unto my path," says verse 105. It would seem that that lamplight has led Thérèse to the inspired image of the elevator, an ingenious bypassing of what Thérèse called Teresa's "coarse stairway of perfection,"[32] the arduous stairway to the same goal. But her compaction of passages from Psalm 118 comes *after* Thérèse mentions the elevator. She is still searching out a way for congruence with what Psalm 118 makes explicit, God's arrangements. Alternating with a need for re-assurance, as she found in the youthful wisdom of David, comes a resolve to push further, with prayer, pen, and just enough respite to move toward the passion she knew was awaiting her, as it had Jeanne.

She begins that account with a reference to her succession of testings about which Gonzague knew but with what Gonzague perhaps did not know and could not have intuited, that Thérèse was now meeting her suffering with joy and peace. Thérèse would abide in this conundrum until the end. It is a phenomenon wholly absent from the Psalms, where joy and gladness are moods entirely separate from the whining and wailing of the soul fastened upon its possible annihilation.

Having established that mysterious fact about herself, she passes to the first of her great and final afflictions, the discovery that she would die soon. The first hemoptysis, which she underwent in darkness during Holy Week of 1896, brought her an eerie exhilaration, as she could now hope shortly to be with Jesus. She does not remark that that had now been fifteen months earlier, and effectively her hope had been cheated. Instead, in that Easter season she was set at once upon an epistemological journey. With the elevator she had presumed that Jesus would bear her up. She did not foresee that he intended to set her down. Deeming herself little and weak, she did not entertain the possibility that she could be made yet more weak and littler.

If the elevator figures as the chief metaphoric prop for Theresian Christology, gracious love coming to meet a consented littleness—Jesus, she writes, raises the soul to him as a loving parent would raise up a child—her terminal image is not one of an elevator door opening onto a paradise. Rather, it comes from Psalm 126 (127) and is inspired by the perception, a kind of clairvoyance, which she says Jesus gave her: "Jesus made me aware that there are truly souls that do not have trust in God, who by the abuse of graces lose this precious treasure, source of the only pure and real joys."[33]

This abuse figures implicitly in Psalm 126, which takes as its theme the vanity of all human endeavor made without God. God's presence in the constancy of human need is that "precious treasure" to which the faithless and untrusting have turned their backs. Rising early and staying up late, says the psalmist, will be pointless shows of their industry, and the bread they eat can only be grievous because it, too, is pointless.[34] With the psalmist Thérèse knew that this *pain de douleur* could not be otherwise because it is a godless bread, but neither she nor he makes clear when and how or even if the untrusting shall come to such an awareness. It might well be initially and for an indefinite time sweet-tasting bread, made savory by a heady triumphalism in the self.

Bread itself was the essential sustenance at the Carmel. The real life of the community subsisted upon the mystical bread called *Pain Vivant,* the eucharistic bread for those still exiled from heaven, the bread in which Christ is hidden. But there was earthly, fattening bread, too. During Lent, it was the only food apart from fruit that the sisters ate. For those forty days in the wilderness of modern life, they denied themselves even the aliment of bouillon and soup, thus imposing considerable digestive pains. They were obliged to eat all the bread set before them, a force feeding of self. Such bread was a penitential diet, but it is the absence of penitence that sets apart those in Psalm 126. They have thrown away the graces of God.

Other psalms can be adduced in setting the table for the bread. Thérèse writes an intercessory prayer from darkness: "…she asks your forgiveness for her brothers, she agrees to eat for as long as you wish it the bread of sorrow, and she does not wish to rise from this table filled with bitterness where poor sinners eat before the day you have determined."[35] It is illuminating to contrast the words, sequence, and tone of this prayer with the near psychosis in the most familiar of all the psalms, the twenty-third. While this psalm is free of the persecution mania that mars many others, it is not free of the calamitous I-them. "Thou preparest a table before me in the presence of mine enemies." Only there within the six verses are other people, but it is this passage in this psalm that comes to the mind of a Christian reading Thérèse's prayer at the prepared table of sorrow. The differences are telling and define what is Christian.

First, the table at which Thérèse comes to sit has not been set solely for her; she makes it clear that "poor sinners" have been there before her. She might consider herself an uninvited guest or a latecomer,[36] but she makes nothing of the sinners' disposition toward her—she does not regard them as "enemies." The adversarial tone is absent here as from every page of C, for it is the work of a mature person who had struggled toward selflessness, not someone who takes definition from people he fears and despises, as they do him in turn. The table is not anyone's possession, either; it belongs to the sorrow of the world into which Christ came and lived. "The King of the country of the resplendent sun came to live for 33 years in the land of shadows, alas! The shadows did not grasp that this Divine King was the light of the world."[37] From behind this fairy-story phrasing, it emerges that Thérèse's backdrop for the table is the grim, suspirious realm of the gospels, a shadowy world imbued with menace.

While for her as a lover of Christ, the table had eucharistic association, another psalmic table bears directly upon Christ's passion. In Matthew 27:34, he is given vinegar mixed with gall before the crucifixion. He tastes and rejects it. In Psalm 68 (69), these ingredients are given to the psalmist by the usual host of enemies on all sides; as in Psalm 23 they are in God's presence as well as his own. "May their table become before them a snare, and the punishment they deserve, a stumbling block." What that meant to Thérèse remains obscure; it is not one of the psalms she quotes but she knew well the me-them syndrome it exemplifies. The psalmist's notion that someone must sit and eat while others starve, or that a dining table might trap the seated—none of this figures in Thérèse's tableau. The pummeling self-righteousness of the psalmist is not needed in order to see what Thérèse makes clear in her prayer, that sorrow itself is, when deep enough, a great leveler, overriding all occasions, all partisanship of spite and rancor.

The most fetching of all tables laid in the Psalms comes from another, 77 (78), which Thérèse does not cite but which seems to have informed her understanding of the table she came to by Christ's leave. That psalm rehearses the Hebrews' straying from God since their deliverance from Egyptian slavery. As in their wanderings they do not trust in God's care, they turn against him: "And they spoke ill of God and said 'Can God furnish a table in the wilderness?'" (v.19) God answers by sending them more than enough: manna, corn, angel's food, and meat to the full, yet even that abundance does not curb them. After some monitory killings, they turn to flattery and lies, finally securing God's compassionate forgiveness of their evil hearts. Thérèse transposes this drama into her own story of the table; the sinners are fed even in their void of trust, as though they were consuming manna from a heaven they could not see. They do not even know it is manna. Spiritually, they are in the wilderness of an atrocious life that would be altogether random, were they not now centered and seated in this strange communion.[38]

This conjunction of Psalm 77 and C's prayer provides the lesson that even as many of Thérèse's biblical citations are iterative and thus may not always deepen the context in which they are recorded, so there are many she undoubtedly drew richly from without citation or even paraphrase. That signifies a wide open field for examination of her biblical theology. If such a possibility smacks of adventurism, she probably would not want anyone to be discouraged from it.

II. Thérèse on the New Testament

That extraordinary excising and rebinding of the gospels from the *Manuel du chrétien* so that she could carry them on her seems an adolescent sort of gesture but would in any case have required the prioress's permission. As a bold and original thing to do, it is characteristically Thérèse. The epistles of Saint Paul and the Johannine texts were of comparatively little importance to her, but she does quote from St. Paul's letters and from the Apocalypse of John in both her late letters and in the last manuscript. She was the spouse of Jesus, however, not of Paul or John. They had taken Jesus their way, and she had one no less singularly her own.

Her life before Carmel had spells of turbulence for which Jesus was the sole navigator and compass she could trust. There were times when she had to see and hear him speaking from the open page itself. This practice betokens an acknowledged inadequacy of self. She knew the gospels by heart but reading and rereading afforded her a sustenance that eludes reasoning. Perhaps it was not Jesus alone she was seeking. In starkest contrast to the communal leadership of Jesus's day, positive characters in the gospels emerge as antiheroes, people burdened with exceptional loneliness and affliction. They appear in the parables and the narrated encounters. Jesus seems to have had a particular fondness or at least a ready attentiveness to these strays as they seek him out, even through the demons that possess some of them. It is not hard to imagine how Thérèse delighted in such audacious characters as Zachaeus, who climbed a tree in order to be able to see Jesus in a crowd or the woman who had for nearly twelve years an ailment that doctors had vainly treated and who dared to touch Jesus's robe in the midst of another crowd, that she might at last be healed. Thérèse could not have read such a story without thinking of her mother anguished and vulnerable before the perfunctory treatment of doctors when she was dying of cancer. These exceptional people of the gospels are like Thérèse herself: insistent, persistent, a curious mix of helplessness and boldness.

While the Prodigal Son in Luke 15 seems exemplary of this sort of deviant,[39] and one to whom Thérèse gave attention, even to the last page of her final manuscript, on that page two other characters exemplary of contrition and humility appear, a tax collector and a prostitute. The first provides the best introduction into the meaning of the table of bitterness and Thérèse's place there, while the other is the one biblical person toward whom she felt a nagging emulation.

I shall address the prostitute first. In Luke 7, she enters a Pharisee's house where Jesus is dining, weeps tears over his feet as he lies reclining at table, wipes his feet with her tears, and anoints them with precious perfumed oils from an alabaster vase. Her impromptu appearance and her loving attention to him—a gesture of funereal anointing before the fact—provide contrast to the stuffy host, Simon (specified as a former leper in Matthew 26) who can only grumble at her presence and dismiss Jesus himself, the guest, as no prophet, else he would have recognized the woman as a sinner and refused to let her touch him.

The condemnation of this bold woman matters not at all to Thérèse. She gives no heed in her writings to the politics that engulfs Jesus, including the centripetal pull of Jerusalem, the templar city where prophets were destined to be killed. She passes by the issues of Hebraic propriety, the hate-filled teasing interrogations of Jesus by the defenders of that propriety. Her optic, focused solely upon Jesus, is so close up that only those who are in some way intimate with him fall within range of her own notice. They have left a record of a sudden, fleeting rapport with him such as she wanted for herself, not in a passing occasion but as a bond. They come and go. Had Thérèse been in their position and had Jesus tried to reject her importunate pleas to stay with him, she would have worn him down until he relented.

The woman of tears and alabaster was commonly assumed in Thérèse's day to be Mary of Magdala, a woman from whom Jesus exorcised several demons. That is just half of what is known of this woman specifically. She re-appears in the garden of Joseph of Arimathea where Jesus has been entombed, and she is the first to witness the Resurrection. Catholicism in Thérèse's day also identified Mary of Magdala with Mary, the sister of Martha and Lazarus, even though that second Mary is from Bethany, the town in which the penitent woman washes Jesus's feet. The Mary of Bethany chooses, as Jesus says, the worthy portion, contemplation over activity (Luke 10: 41.). Tacitly, she is one of Jesus's disciples. For Thérèse, then, there was a single Mary who was first possessed, then healed, then made an eager and attentive student, an all-but-disciple, and finally a co-equal of the eleven disciples who fled when Jesus was arrested. It is she who brings to them the miraculous news. To have just one Mary (other than Jesus's mother) affords a convenient, if not quite convincing synthesis.

Meager though this profile proves, Thérèse dwells only on its first portion, the scene at Simon's dinner. Having remarked the humble prayer of Luke's publican as a model for her own, she goes on: "... but above all I imitate the conduct of Mary Magdalen; her astonishing or rather her amorous daring which charmed the heart of Jesus, seduced mine."[40] Thérèse's assertion is the real daring. It would probably be hard, if not absurd, to look for charm in the gospels, but charm figures with high frequency in her writing, as substantive, verb, and adjective. The total in her concordance comes to 147 instances. It denotes a substantial appeal and attraction that she acknowledged in the fallen, secular, earthly life but which she had no real trouble resisting since she never had the occasion, opportunity, or complicity—the appeal of a young man, for instance—to lure her into it. As a Christian, she grew up convinced that the joys and happiness of this world are phony and shallow; real joys are only in the celestial life.

The real *charme* in the present instance lies in Thérèse's confident ascription of it to "Madeleine" in relation to Jesus. Not a ravishment, a delight, nor anything else that might suggest a superficial eroticism, it is a pleased fascination that Jesus might be showing, altogether understandably, since the extraordinary initiative of a marginal, despised person substantially suggests his own life's course. Here, as elsewhere, a word from Thérèse that might seem sugary or superficial has a deeper valence than a reader, whether of French or English, might suppose.

"Seduced"? That is a strange word for a dying nun to speak, yet it exemplifies Thérèse's ironic wit. Seductiveness belonged to "Madeleine" if she is regarded as a Parisian courtesan of *la belle epoche* rather than as a prostitute, but it is her audacity in entering a Jewish supper for men only that allured Thérèse. Whither, if not to the table of sinners? Her joining them at that table of bitterness, uninvited, complements the story in Luke. It is her most dramatic *audace*, an unexpected tableau. That she would be reviled and mocked by the sinners at that table is altogether probable. She tactfully leaves it to her readers to make this supposition. Ex-leper Simon's contempt for the woman at his banquet, his inability to read her loving gratitude, his blindness to her humility—not to mention her courage—all these negatives figure twofold in the missionary setting Thérèse gives herself in C. Those alien to her spirituality can only dismiss her, even as she prays for them. To cherish only a rosewatery image of her from such texts as B is to recoil from a Thérèse keeping company with atheists, a Thérèse identifying herself as one of them, their sister. In ending as "Madeleine" had begun, with sinners, and in commencing her mission as "Madeleine" had concluded hers, with love, Thérèse invites (seduces?) the dubious to consider her action, which is something more than sincerity, and she invites Christians to remember the snare of the pharisaical. Her *audace* entails an implicit, even a certain rejection from both sides, leaving her supremely alone, even as Jesus was, at the end. Is this not her *imitatio Christi* in its final expression, her version of Carmelite perfection?

Even so, the nub of this story comes only after Jesus contrasts the tearful woman's conduct with his starchy host's. Simon has stayed in an immobile complacency from which to condemn other people. Unlike Simon, Jesus speaks here not about sorts of people but of individual actions and the woman's unabashed, sacrificial action—anointing him with the oil she would have carried in her business—betokens the depth of her love for him, one of gratitude. Jesus draws the lesson: "Many sins are forgiven her because she has loved much. But he to whom one forgives less, loves less."

It is a disconcerting lesson that to pious people Jesus has all but nothing to give. Sinners have need of Jesus and love him in the depth of their need. They alone, including those sequestered from community by diseases such as leprosy, can establish an emotive rapport with him. Them alone Jesus acknowledges, not as types but as loners, distinctive in their exigency. Behind the appeal of "Madeleine" in all her *audace*, Thérèse felt the tug of paradox, that the more fallen one is, and hence isolated, the more dependent and potentially responsive to Jesus one shall be. "Madeleine," alone of all the wayward in the New Testament, receives Jesus's compassion in two discreet statements. He tells her that her sins are forgiven. Then, to reflexive objections from stage left and right, he tells her, "Your trust has saved you; go in peace."

The Madeleine story took another turn when, on July 11, 1897, Thérèse instructed Pauline to include in the publication of the manuscripts a passage from a book on the Desert Fathers, "The Story of a Sinful Woman Converted and Dead of Love."[41] As it is not appended in modern translations of Thérèse's autobiography, it deserves the special attention Thérèse requested for it. In brief, a young woman, having lost her parents, establishes a hospice to receive go-betweens from a monastery that sells the friars' manufactures. Perceiving the costliness of her charity, she turns from that work to a life of sin, urged on by evil counselors to lose all taste for virtue. The friars dispatch one of their own who confronts her gently with the question, did she have a complaint against Jesus for having abandoned her, for having reduced her to the piteous state she is now in? Once she is moved by that question, he breaks down in tears. When she asks him why he is weeping, he says the devil has deceived and mocked her. She asks if penance is possible, and he leads her out of her dissolute life. En route to a convent, she dies in the desert, and the monk sees her in a vision, borne by angels into heaven. Finding her dead, he hears a miraculous voice telling him that "her penitence in an hour was more agreeable to God than what others make over a long time because they do not do so with so much fervor as she did."[42]

It is, of course, the penitent's fervor that so appealed to Thérèse. The impressionability of this young woman mattered not at all, her rather precipitous turn from virtue to vice and then back again. Her rapture into heaven—what Thérèse herself might have longed for, had she not made peace with her darkness—exceeds in drama even Jesus's compassionate response to "Madeleine."

With the penitent's fervor exerting ineluctable pull, another dynamic of Thérèse's *audace* comes to the fore: vigorously editorial, selective, even rapacious. She seized upon anything that bore directly upon her own temperament. Everything else receded so that what was especially or exclusively pertinent would have its primacy. Without its fervor, this story might well have proved unappealing to her. She drew upon it several times. She alludes to it in two of her more important poems, "Vivre d'Amour" (February 1895), one of the few she wrote for herself, and "Comment je veux aimer," composed late in 1896 for one of the more withdrawn Carmelites, Sr. St. Jean de la Croix. In the latter poem, Jesus pardons the suppliant on the ground that she has loved *him*, but the passage from Luke does not make it explicit that Jesus was meant at all. Rather, in saying that "Magdelen's" many sins are forgiven because she loved much, Luke shows that a certain arduous generosity even within carnal life argues a loving soul, and that Jesus, contrary to the presumptions of dull censure, knew it.

The "Magdalen" arrives in another, extraordinary context. A mystical union of souls figures in a letter Thérèse wrote to her first "spiritual brother," Maurice Bellière, April 25, 1897. In that fourth letter to him, she for the first time addresses him as "my dear little brother" (a promotion to littleness, Theresian style) and tells him that contrary to his fond estimate of her, she is not one of the great souls of Carmel. Rather, she is *"absolutely little* and very imperfect."[43] Then, in a bold self-portrait she joins the Virgin's *magnificat* to Jesus's celebration of the "fallen Mary" in Luke 7: 47: "I know that He has done great things in me, and I sing that every day with happiness. I recall that he must love more who has been forgiven more, so I try to make my life be an act of love and no longer bother myself about being a *little* soul..."

Obviously, Thérèse was emulous of the Virgin herself and emulous of this fallen Magdalen, even as she had been of Teresa on entering the Carmel. The proof of her loving much would not be in particular acts, as Magdalen's had been, but in her life itself. *It* would become an ongoing act of love. Her essential littleness would then matter not at all, or, rather, it would become great. Her discovery of this oxymoron, a magnificent inconsequence, was perhaps *the* great thing that God was working within her.[44] To be lowly and loving like Mary and Magdalen became the little way by which she survived the worst of her spiritual darkness.

That letter to Bellière goes far to illuminate the uncanny equanimity in the style of C, not least when Thérèse is reporting her darkness to Gonzague. Yet more illuminating is another letter to Bellière, June 21, 1897 (LT 247), when Thérèse was already two weeks within the writing of C. He had written to her of all the saints from whom he had asked assistance, including St. Paul and Teresa,[45] but in her response, Thérèse acknowledges only Augustine and Magdalen. She, too, loves them, she assures Bellière, not only for their repentant turn from a sinful life but for their "loving boldness."[46] It was audacious of Magdalen to have passed before the other banqueters and to have moistened Christ's feet with her tears: "I'm aware that *her heart* has comprehended the abysses of love and compassion in *the Heart of Jesus*, and that wholly sinful as she is, this Heart of love is not only disposed to forgive her but even to offer her the benefits of its divine intimacy, to raise her to the highest summits of contemplation." Magdalen, on her way to becoming the Mary too rapt in Jesus's words to help Martha, has found her own elevator, one in which she, too, is raised up by Jesus to his mystical level. The denominator Thérèse establishes here between herself and Magdalen is helplessness; her own is an ontic weakness (a character defect) and Magdalen's, a moral weakness, which makes each the more receptive and sure of Jesus's compassionate reaching down to them.

Magdalen as the Mary who subsequently "has chosen the better part" or contemplation (Luke 10:40) is more assertive than a loving yet weak passivity would suggest, but that bothers Thérèse not in the slightest. Mary's listening to Jesus is greater than any outward giving, she says towards the very last of C (36r). So her Magdalen comes full circle in bounty, first with the audacity of her tears and last, with her attentive fixing upon the "divine intimacy" of a contemplative life with Jesus. Thérèse could not tell Bellière that her own intimacy with Jesus was far otherwise, as Jesus had left her alone and was silent.

Now to the figure who complements Mary Magdalen, a publican at prayer in the temple. His foil, a Pharisee, prays in thanks that he himself is not like other people, thievish, unjust, adulterous, and he compliments himself for fasting and tithing. He does everything that law and convention prescribe, and he keeps an appreciative eye on the monitory failings of others. The publican, a collector of taxes, is disgraceful by profession: thievish, unjust, and as a lackey of the Roman occupational authority, a kind of cultural adulterer. He is exactly the sort of person the Pharisee is proud not to be. He stations himself at a good distance from the righteous Pharisee—and from God. He does not even wish to raise his eyes to heaven and instead strikes his chest, calling upon God's mercy: "O Lord, have pity on me, a sinner."[47]

Jesus says that the publican went down from the temple to his house justified in having lowered himself in his prayer. The genius in this little story is that the publican returns home beyond, apart from, and quite different from the Pharisee *in his own eyes*, all of that compressed into the Greek, *par' ekeinon*. He is worthy in Jesus's eyes because he humbled himself but to himself he remains unworthy in comparison to the Pharisee. There is no payoff for humility. It is not play-acted for recompense. Its only predicate shared with the divine is illimitability.

Thérèse responds to this remarkably economical narrative in her own remarkable way. She takes Jesus's words on self-humbling and conflates the lesson (also Luke, 14: 7–14) with that of the first and last place at the divine banquet. The Pharisee would have presumed he had the right to first place, chief guest, and the publican the last, at the farthest remove from the host. The publican is so humbled he would not have presumed himself entitled to any place at all. Unlike the publican, Thérèse has the benefit of Jesus' teaching. The publican does not know his prayer of contrition has given him the uplifting righteousness the Pharisee had arrogated to himself. Thérèse steals the confidence of the Pharisee and gives it to the publican in herself: "rather than promoting myself with the Pharisee, I repeat, filled with trust, the publican's lowly prayer."[48] That is a bit coy and might seem disingenuous without her admission of feeling herself truly lowest of the low. She can be subtle as a serpent.

But did she truly understand the publican? Seven weeks before her sister's death, Pauline recorded Thérèse's reflection on one of her last communions, August 12,

1897. "I felt like the publican, a great sinner. I found the good Lord so compassionate! Oh, how impossible it is to give such feelings to oneself. Only the Holy Spirit can produce them in one's soul."[49] Such was one of the many graces for which she was thankful, an acute consciousness of sin within her and yet without the substantiation of that consciousness in particular acts. The publican, like another tax collector, Zacchaeus in Luke 19, had extorted money from many people. His sense of sinfulness, of injustice, is focused in acute grief, as Thérèse's is not.

Her sense of sinfulness comes, however odd it may seem, with joyous confidence in God because God's compassion is predicated upon that sinfulness. Thus she sweeps away all morbid preoccupation with one's grievous shortcomings: sins, faults, strayings, stumblings. Drawing inspiration from John 14:2, where Jesus tells his followers that there are many dwellings within God's house, she tells Bellière in the letter of June 21, 1897, that because of Jesus's words "I'm following the way that Jesus is tracing for me. I try to no longer be preoccupied with myself about anything and what Jesus deigns to do in my soul I leave to him, as I did not choose an austere life to expiate my own faults but those of others."[50] When she entered Carmel, she had priests in mind, but now she has atheists as well.

If she could have said more to Bellière, she might have told him what her impromptu hermeneutical skills in reading the gospels had revealed to her, that she had achieved an imaginative synthesis from Luke 18:9–14. In her prayer at the table, she took the Pharisee's attention to others' faults and saw them from within the publican's grief. The grief, the *douleur* of the table, wondrously effaces the particularities of sin, even as the publican, beating his chest, had cried out only that he was a sinner. He furnishes no inventory of his sins. Thérèse's intuition that sinners are at the table by their abuse of divine grace provides a capacious but not specific term. She does not ask what that abuse consists of, nor is there any point in making guesses about it. In the synthesis she discovers what John Donne called "the society and fellowship of sin," a shared helplessness and *a fortiori* a common need for confession and contrition.

What of Jesus himself? As befitted the full name she assumed at Carmel, Thérèse gave her meditative, writing life primarily to the beginning and the end of his mission: the infant Jesus helpless in Bethlehem and Jesus in his last hours of prayer, in the agony at Gethsemane, on the way to Calvary. In this alpha and this omega, he faces indifference, contempt, and murderous hatreds from a dark world. He begins life hunted by the soldiers of fearful Herod and ends it tormented by a harsh imperial machinery. (See Figure 2.1.) Thérèse makes what seems a strange use of these grim tableaux: she wipes them clean of their sordid politics and mannish violence by focusing entirely upon Jesus himself, his vulnerability and suffering. It is as though she were one of the gospels' attendant women who stayed with him to the end, giving him unsolicited and unheralded trust and succor. For her, Jesus's mission is the search for a requital of God's love. Almost

FIGURE 2.1 Delacroix, "Christ in the Garden of Olives," declining angelic solace. Church of Saint Paul and Saint Louis, Paris. In her last month, Therese said, "I have no need of consolation." Copyright Bridgeman Art Collection

all of her writing expresses in one dimension or another the bounteousness of this love and the urgency she felt in meeting it, embracing it, celebrating it, despite and yet through her own feeble self. That self was all she could work with. It was her only possession.

That seems a sanguine business, the proclamation of divinely merciful love, but in Thérèse's instance it falls necessarily short of triumph and triumphalism by the suffering that makes of Jesus's mission a kind of encoded failure. Jesus *must* be mocked, derided, despised, murdered because in that way the Hebraic scriptures of prophecy are fulfilled, but for Thérèse all of these things must happen in order that Jesus be accessible. His vulnerability suffices as his humanity. Because her vantage is by choice and by gender one of intimacy with Jesus, Thérèse does not heed Jesus the public figure who draws the suspicion and then the conspiratorial hostility of the Jewish elders. Jesus is betrayed and traduced, but she is not attentive to the machinations of malice and its agents, the issues of the Law's interpretation, even the often raised issue of Jesus's identity and authority. The many confrontations (traps) set for him by the scribes, the elders, and high priests belong to a brutish world Thérèse could have only guessed at.

Because the accounts of his miracles demonstrate his recondite power, they, too, do not matter to the Theresian perspective. Those accounts include both the populist miracles (feeding of loaves and fishes to thousands) and the private healings. Jesus's cures, in some instances achieved spontaneously by the seeker (the shrewd Phoenician woman, the woman who had been hemorrhaging), also do not matter to Thérèse and for noteworthy reasons. First, the Jesus of power and healing relieves suffering. The Carmelite ethic itself enjoined the practice of suffering because it provided both self-mortification and implicitly a bond with Jesus, a fragile response to his own suffering, psychological and physical. A further and perhaps no less weighty factor was the history of affliction within the Martin family.

Both of Thérèse's parents had suffered horribly from terminal illnesses. Zélie had been left ignorant and helpless with a breast cancer that metastasized in its merciless way and left her exhausted with pain, crying out in her last days with supplications to all the saints and especially to the Virgin—all to no avail. Louis had been broken down by strokes and a steady dementia, all of which humiliated him and his family when he had to be consigned for his own safety and steady care to a sanatorium. After more than three years of that virtual imprisonment, during which he could see family members only thirty minutes per week, he was released, too enfeebled by strokes to be ambulatory. His last two years and three months were spent in a pathetic invalidism under the care of his in-laws, the Guérins. The wheelchair in which he was moved about became Thérèse's in the last weeks of her life. She lies in it in the last photo taken of her living.

These ravagings and humiliations the Martin family accepted in the traditional Catholic way, as part of the divine will, a severe testing not unlike Job's, but the deep bitterness in this testing cannot be gainsaid. It was not a poison for Thérèse but rather a truth serum, an enforced, steady look at the horror within some forms of grace. It is *not* to be supposed that God wills suffering upon anyone, but God wills that Christians bear crosses, be the pain ontic, as in hideous diseases, or psychological, as in disgraces and scandals or afflictions entailing lasting sorrow. Without Thérèse's sharp initiations into the sufferings of others close and dear to her, sufferings preliminary to her own, she would not have been able to arrive at her charitable estimate of suffering in distant others. That estimate informs her sitting at the table. And she would not have ripened in her skepticism about the shallow benefits of consolation, well-meant but inept comforting. She learned to read shrewdly and well the stark evidence that God's will is not our will. A lesson from Gethsemane.

Christ, however, cures many, and so do his disciples (sometimes) when dispatched to spread the gospel. Thérèse knew from Mark 9 that what she called *confiance*, an unreflected and unwavering trust in Jesus, was requisite in those seeking healing. In that chapter, a distraught father calls upon Jesus to cure a youth who has been throwing himself into fire and water; a demoniac in biblical terms, an epileptic in modern terms, as Mark records gnashing of teeth, foaming at the mouth, and the body's stiffening. When the father begs Jesus to cure the boy if he can, Jesus puts the burden of trust upon the father, who exclaims, "Lord, I believe. Help thou mine unbelief." Here, what is usually translated as faith, *pistis*, is revealed in its proper Theresian sense: it is not belief in any propositional sense, but instead an entrusting of oneself in absolute confidence to someone else. The father admits to holding back from Jesus, his unwillingness to trust Jesus's power to heal the tormented boy.

Thérèse was aware of the pitfalls in even the most devout when challenged as Jesus had challenged this father. Her mother, en route to Lourdes for a miraculous cure of her cancer (she did not know it as such), suffered from her quite natural fear and knew that that meant she could not summon the trust in the Virgin she needed to effect a remedy. Instead, she leaned heavily upon Pauline, who was already turned toward a religious life. If only Pauline had trust, then Zélie's own debilities would be compensated. It was a terrible and unfair burden to put upon an adolescent girl, but unsympathetic readers might charge that Jesus was unfair in burdening Mark's anguished father. It is human to recoil in apprehension even before something keenly wished and known to be beneficent. Misgiving is embedded in human weakness, and Thérèse learned to become an astute student of weakness, beginning within herself.

If both the healings and the political exchanges might be called occasions of authentication, when Jesus is brought to pity of Jewish community life, they remain historical incidents woven as narrative threads. His teachings, both by injunction and by parable, are of a different order. The parables may leave a reader wondering how to resolve them, as they tend to remain open-ended, even suspenseful. What, for example, happened to the prodigal son (Luke 15:11–32), whose resentful brother has inherited all of their father's property and can subsequently treat his recovered brother with spite, even as the lowliest servant the prodigal had returned home to become? Are they ever reconciled? Or what of that most troublesome figure, the unjust and disloyal steward (Luke 16:1–9), who defrauds his master to the benefit of the debtors? Jesus commends not the cunning itself but the resourcefulness it shows as a lesson to the stolidly pious, who tend to be prudent, timid souls. In reading the key parable of the sowing of spiritual seeds (Mark 4:1–9), one is left to wonder what one's own seeds might prove to be: exposed, desiccated, consumed, or fruitful. A mixture of all of them, perhaps.

Even more challenging are the two door-slamming parables, bitter lessons of human inadequacy (Matthew 25:1–30). Of the ten virgins who go to meet the bridegroom five foolishly neglect to carry oil for their night lamps. When, on the announced arrival of the bridegroom, they importune the other five, who wisely brought enough oil for themselves, they are denied any sharing of the oil. After the foolish five go off to buy oil, the bridegroom shuts the door to them and will not listen to their entreaties. They did not have the alacrity of the other five, not to mention the wits of the unjust steward, but the groom's absolute rejection of them seems cruel and cold. Poor girls.

Thérèse responded to this disconcerting story in one of her written prayers, "Fleurs Mystiques,"[51] when one of the *converse* sisters, Marie-Madeleine, was about to profess her vows, November 20, 1894. The sixteen "mystical" flowers, each voiced by a choir sister, form the wedding basket for the bride.[52] The Carmelites are of a kind with those wise virgins who brought oil with their lamps. They remain securely within the chamber door that the groom has shut. Thérèse's Jeanne d'Arc, the moment before the Bishop of Beauvais condemns her as a heretic and an apostate, puts on the robe of "a virgin going forth to meet her bridegroom"[53] and the announcement of her own groom's arrival came to Thérèse when she suffered her first hemoptysis, April 3, 1896 (between 2 and 3 A.M.) and rejoiced that Jesus had come in Eastertide, the season of his own death.

Thérèse never mentions the hapless, foolish virgins shut out. By foaming blood she had been awakened, watchful as the virgins' story urges, so that she was ready when the night and the hour of the bridegroom was announced. Yet her destiny obliged her to share the company of those others, the excluded women. She writes of the vault that sealed her off from celestial life. That was but another version, on a cosmic scale, of the door slammed shut. And as that admission comes only five pages after the remembrance of the first bloody coughing, it is fair to suppose that Jesus's failure to arrive with the expected and longed for death had now, after fourteen months, ripened her to an unspoken and unwritten acknowledgment that her own fate was no different from that of the foolish virgins. A most bitter turn: she had had the lamp lit, she was ready and eager, and she was sent away into darkness. The light had gone out, for there was too little oil to sustain it.

She ended her life bereft of the lamp and the light. Even as she had told herself the story of the Pharisee and the publican in a novel synthesis, so she had to read and live out another synthesis, of the wise virgin who was shut out from the groom's paradise. As though taking her perspective of spiritual exile from this parable, she makes of Jesus an activist, a teacher and director in her exclusion: "Jesus made me realize that there truly are souls who do not have faith.... He allowed my soul to be invaded by the thickest shadows."[54] Jesus was allowing the shadows, voiced with nihilistic threats, to test Thérèse sorely, even as God allowed Satan to test Job.

Her darkness belongs within the contexts of her gospel reading because in them she attains an intimacy with Jesus distinctive and far more imposing than Carmelite conventions of betrothal to him could be. Her syntheses create an imaginative company for her—she understands both the publican and the Pharisee, both the wise virgins and the foolish—and bid comparison with the intimacy Martha and Mary enjoy with Jesus in the house of Lazarus. Martha is busy with her chores, Mary is busy listening to Jesus, as Jesus is sending Thérèse on an extraordinary mission, not to preach the gospel but to join the unredeemed world as one of its own. Here for once, Jesus is not the helpless child nor the despised and rejected rescuer and chosen lover but a taskmaster with a dire summons.

Immediately succeeding the wise and foolish virgins is another parable to which Thérèse refers, that of the three servants. Their master, about to leave on

Seeking Light in the Bible

a journey, deposits with them disparate amounts of money. The two with larger shares perform as finance capitalists and have doubled their investment upon the master's return, but the third buries his deposit and yields it to the master as he received it. The master gratefully rewards the investors, "good and faithful servants," by putting them in charge of larger sums. The third then dares to stand up to his master and explain why he has not played the investment game, "Lord, I knew thee that thou art an hard man, reaping where thou hast not sown, and gathering where thou hast not strawed." In his fear he has left the money inert. The master reproaches him for wickedness and sloth but does not deny that he reaps where he has not sown. He then throws the unprofitable servant into the darkness of wailing and teeth-gnashing.

This story is about heaven and hell, a terrifying judgment that identifies and pays out both haves and have-nots. Thérèse in her references to it (four, all in Ms A) focuses solely upon the loyal servants rewarded for working. In each instance she is referring to her father, the munificent and ever charitable Louis, who gave to beggars and churchmen alike, and whose own suffering made him Christ-like to his adoring daughter.[55] If she does not mention the plaintive, fearful, self-excusing servant, it is because he suffers the same wretched fate as the foolish virgins suffered. It is a fate from which any Christian would draw back in dread, but for Thérèse it was indigestible. The tormented Jesus seeking meager human love does not jibe with a master who punishes abruptly, severely, unforgivingly, irreversibly.

Exegetes of this story emphasize the trust the master shows in his servants by leaving them his wealth, which represents divine love freely bestowed. They see the decisive importance of the testing, what the servants will literally make of this love. The love proves its own reward as it grows greater when magnified. The parable becomes an index of Christian activism and its particular physics, expressed in the koan-like conclusion that to those that have, more shall be given and from those who have not, even that shall be taken away. The inert and therefore loveless servant could not fathom this physics, only complain of its unfairness.

In Theresian terms, it is easy to read both the foolish virgins and the unenterprising servant as derelict in trust. Theirs are exemplary failures. They do not rely upon given means of showing their loyalty to the groom, Jesus, and to God, the distant lord. At the same time, their falling short argues, though it does not justify, their inadequacy, their weakness, and in the servant's case, fear and furtiveness (the hiding of the deposit). By all accounts, Thérèse would have had compassion upon such wretches, not for their failures but for the profound weakness in them that those failures manifested, the girls so careless with their lamps, the man so timid with the money. They are the sort she finds at the table of sorrows, even as they are left in a hideous grieving and exclusion at the end of their gospel stories.[56]

What Thérèse does *not* cite from the gospels by no means argues a negligence or slighting on her part. Quite the opposite, in such passages as these thirty verses from Matthew 25 she found messages she had to ponder as she came to a mature realization of her own weakness and inadequacy and the implications of such deficiency for her relationship with Jesus. The passages she does cite, here in approbation of the wise virgins and the loyal servants, provide hortatory strength to her narratives, both for herself and her sisters, but they do not help her to reach the darkness and bitterness to which Jesus finally sends her. There remain many passages of the gospels that, in their great junctures of mystery, afford a kind of subliminal commentary upon Thérèse's spirituality. Matthew 25 is one of them.

Although or because Thérèse had grown up always within the gospels' story, she did not develop prior to April, 1896 the deepening that came only with an awareness of how violently that story challenged her life. She had accepted the narratives in a kind of conventional stupor, an acceptance more reflexive than reflective. She had always known that it was not her business to interpret any scriptures on her own. That task the Church gave to priests exclusively. She must, then, have surprised her first readers—Pauline, Marie, and Gonzague—with the daring of her allusions within the context of what she was writing. It became no small part of her *audace* that without permission she undertook to probe the gospels. Implicitly, she was assuming the authority to teach the Bible.[57] As Gaucher has observed, her readings and interpretations of the Bible were extraordinary for her time, and the efforts and insights she gave them were exceptional for someone in her early twenties.[58] It could be added that they were hard won and remained extraordinary well beyond that time.

The insights Thérèse gained in reading Jesus's story meant she was beginning, ever beginning, to become a Christian. She had not lived out any sure trajectory of faith, no linear progression, try though she had to adhere fast to all the strictures of the Rule, the Constitutions, and the *Direction spirituelle*. She had kept close the memory of Mère Geneviève, the founding prioress of the Lisieux Carmel, who in her eighties had lived as simply and as compliantly as the youngest novice. The consequence of Thérèse's realization that she had to remain forever little, to be childlike for Christ's sake, was that she did not claim expository mastery of what she read. It was an epistemological humility. She did not expound the text; she faced it.

Here is her way of putting it: "Oh, how opposite the teachings of Jesus are to our natural feelings! Without the help of grace it would be impossible not only to put them into practice but even to understand them."[59] Thérèse's exclamation is closer to delight than to dismay, because she knows that Jesus is challenging her and that by grace she might understand and thus implement what he requires of her. As to that understanding, she is punctilious in giving Jesus the credit for whatever she claims she has grasped: "that which Jesus has *made me to understand* on the subject of charity" means that Jesus has been her instructor for virtually the whole of C.⁶⁰ For C is Thérèse's letter on charity, the summary to that date of her understanding of what she longed to pursue, a science of Christian love. Citing Jesus as her teacher ratifies the claim she makes for her writing, as though she has become an amanuensis for him. In listening to Jesus, she is a Mary; in taking time and making effort to write about that listening, she is a Martha.

The Sermon on the Mount provides a summa of Jesus's guidance. What did Thérèse draw from it in writing C and why? Almost all of her citations of it occur at least once in her writings in addition to their reference in C. Some appear in her *entretiens* or in the late letters. Those that appear for the first and only time deserve identification and special heed. Beyond C, the occasion, the recipient, and the context for the citation claim their due of recognition, but they remain ancillary to the great confessional effort Thérèse was making for Gonzague, her addressee.

She first mentions the Sermon on the Mount in reflecting upon the Our Father. For her "Thy will be done" means a sacrifice of her self. This is no abstract intent. It comes within a criticism that she has been eased at the Carmel, loved but too well and without the travails of the cross, of a genuine *exil du coeur*, the heart's exile. Mordantly she observes, "I don't perceive that the poverty is ever lacking anything."⁶¹ It is even a criticism of her writing yet another manuscript, "the nice and easy task you've entrusted to me," she tells Gonzague.

Impatient with herself, she was not reviving the masculinizing fantasies she had reviewed in Ms B—her desire to be a priest, a soldier, a missionary—but it is plausible that in reading letters from Fr. Roulland at his dangerous missionary post in China and from Bellière preparing for a similar enterprise in Africa, she could not help recalling her hope of going to the Carmel in Saigon, there to receive the obscurity and hardship she, by a higher Christian instinct, craved. A cruel pulmonary disease could have sufficed this need of exile as it brought her alone to the infirmary; the loss of heaven for over a year brought an adequate darkness—what greater privations could she have asked? Her answer in a letter to Roulland cites the same phrase from the Our Father: "apart from this loving *will* [God's] we shall accomplish *nothing*, neither for Jesus nor for souls."⁶².

Here she is protesting far more than the cosseting given in her years at Carmel, even as its unprecedented writer in residence. Deprived of her fellow novices after she became too ill to sustain the office of *compagne*, she lost the quiet activism for them which had buoyed her with its manifold challenges. Her fellow novices had been daily dependent upon her, but only now did she realize how dependent she had become upon them. In a sense she was writing C on their behalf, as though she was telling Gonzague, "Do not deny my sisters their poverty. How will they be able to do God's will unless they feel the burden of exile?" And the activist's accent: what if they have done nothing for Jesus, nothing for souls other than their own and each other's?

Thérèse seems beset by the feeling of having lived inauthentically, of not truly having borne the cross and done God's will. It was a feeling requisite to final humility, a necessary concession of inadequacy. Her central self-revelation that she was inherently weak, little, a *néant*, she accepted as a grace because these were indispensable qualities of the child-self she wanted to remain in order to be worthy of Jesus. But there had to be a tension in that inadequacy lest it settle into complacent self-regard. Those bemusing injunctions of Jesus on the Mount provided the vital tension of a worthiness other than that of a safely little child.

Subsequently in C, Thérèse says that Jesus makes God's will known on virtually every page of the gospels, in all he does and says, but she is keen to distinguish doing from saying. She cites Matthew 7:21: "It's not those who say Lord, Lord! Who shall enter the Kingdom of Heaven but those who do the will of God."[63] This is a puzzling text, as Jesus goes on to exclude people who on the latter day shall claim to have prophesied, exorcized, and accomplished many works. They have demonstrably done the will of God. Thérèse's answer is that the only activism sure to count is love. She imports into the context of Matthew a passage from John 13: 34–35, Jesus's injunction at the Last Supper that the disciples love one another.

Loving one another, the sign by which they shall be known as Christ's followers, amounts to doing the heavenly will and therefore constitutes doing good. But Thérèse enlarges the notion of Christian loving by moving past the eachotherishness of discipular bonds. In alluding to John's teaching (15:13), ""greater love hath no man," she alters the succeeding phrasing from life given for one's friends to life given for those one loves, a much more inclusive phrasing than the biblical wording itself, if enemies are indeed among those one loves.

In the most audacious, if not unsettling passage in the Sermon on the Mount (Matthew 5:40–44) Jesus confounds the old Jewish injunctions to vengeful retribution[64] by urging nonresistance, even compliance with troublesome people, culminating in the oxymoronic love for one's enemies. Pray for those who persecute you! This impossibly tall order Thérèse takes on with relish; it appeals to her own *audace*. Within Carmel, she notes, there could be no enmities for reconciliation; all matters of discord would be resolved regularly in chapel, where faults would be aired and resolved with humility and penance. Even so, natural human affections could, by being preferential, isolate one sister or another, and such neglect would constitute persecution.[65]

Thérèse's perceptions argue unusual sensitivity to human feelings, even in so hermetic a world as the Carmel. (The memory of schoolyard hardships stayed with her.) Yet she is not addressing the harsh outer world just beyond the convent's door where, for example, her Uncle Isidore and other royalists and loyal churchmen were feeling hounded by local antiecclesiastical adversaries. The Church was at bay, both locally and nationally, and so Catholics could readily feel themselves the objects of scorn and antagonism. But Thérèse was not walking the streets nor reading the journals where such hostilities were sometimes manifest. She had to go some distance to find those who might be qualified as foes to her. In a final sense, her going to the table of sorrow was her little weak soul's movement of life-giving by love to the anonymous, those indifferent or hostile to her Christian life. As the community's marginal Carmelites whom she sought to help were not her friends (Teresa had forbidden friendships), so too neither were nor could they be her friends who rejected God, despised believers, and stewed in self. She knew she had to love them, anyway.

If Ms C is read as a journey in evangelical logic, a concatenation of Jesus's commands toward what Thérèse called the science of love, there is a noticeable progression. Johannine love of friends turns into love that does not name friends and thus opens the way to foes. How that is possible Thérèse has already indicated; it can come, both in understanding and in practice, only by grace, but as the Church teaches, one can pray to become receptive to that grace. It is a request that God prepare a table in the presence of one's enemies so that one may sit with them as a family of sinners and eat.

That receptivity comes only through a thorough humility. Thérèse remarks on the beatitude of humility: "Oh, what peace floods the soul when it is raised above natural feelings.... No, there's no joy comparable to what one truly poor in spirit savors."[66] With this statement she breaks away from a long succession of first-person remarks, as though the generality does not or cannot apply to her. Indeed, she then admits as much: "My dear Mother, I'm quite far from practicing what I understand, and yet the mere desire that I have for it gives me peace." Humility poses a challenge to which she responds with an odd mix of self-disqualification and eagerness: it is something she wants to attain and yet feels too imperfect to attain.

She next tells of the most difficult work Gonzague assigned her, the direction of her fellow novices: "My Mother, since I understood it was impossible for me to achieve anything by myself, the task you imposed upon me no longer seemed difficult. I realized the one thing necessary was to unite myself more and more with Jesus, and then the rest would be given me in addition."[67] She remarks to Gonzague that God had filled her little hand whenever she needed to nourish the novices' souls. Had she depended upon her own strength, which was not there, she would have had to give up. The lesson entails what doing good was coming to signify to her: "doing good is as impossible without God's help as making the sun shine in the night."[68] It is also, however, a conscious subtraction of self, as though one could get in the way between God and other souls: "it's absolutely necessary to forget one's tastes and personal ideas and to guide souls by the path which Jesus has set for them, without trying to make them march by one's own way."

All of this benefaction to the novices she loved, inspired by Matthew 6:33, seems a detour from the humble loving of enemies prescribed by Matthew 5:44. Her common denomination in that benefaction and that loving is a radical attenuation of self and a total reliance upon Jesus. In recognizing that Jesus sets a different path for every person to travel, Thérèse is reminding Gonzague of the path that Jesus had set herself, leading her to the table of sorrow where she did not expect any of her sisters to follow her. She was also saying that *la petite voie*, the Little Way was either not hers alone (she could scarcely have been possessive of it) or that there were other ways for other people, ways known only to Jesus.[69]

One final instance in C of the Sermon on the Mount comes through a back door, when Jesus says of benefaction (Matthew 6:4) that "your Father who sees what is hidden shall recompense you for it." Thérèse cites this passage after alluding to another, Luke 14:12–14, in which Jesus urges that relatives and friends not be invited to table, because they can return the favor; instead, invite poor and disabled people, the lame and the blind, who cannot. This citation is significant on two counts: Thérèse introduces it expressly in a paraphrase, an unusual qualifier, and at the close she omits Luke's key phrase, "you shall receive your due at the resurrection of the just." It is hard to believe that she had forgotten about Luke's resurrection of the just. What matters, by her own account, is that she no longer believed in this resurrection.[70]

Here is a major advance toward the table of sorrow and its bitter bread to which Thérèse sat down uninvited. That table had been set not for the physically but the spiritually incapacitated, emphatically people who, being without real charity, would not return any favor. "Sinners" of this sort appear at the banquet to which Jesus himself has welcomed them, just beyond the Sermon on the Mount, Matthew 9:10–13. It is yet another occasion for the officially righteous, the Pharisees, to reproach Jesus by asking, Why is he eating with sinners and publicans? His answer is reasonably devastating: he prefers mercy to sacrifice and has come for sinners, not for the righteous. He all but says he *prefers* the sinners, as the banquet episode with "Magdalen" suggested. People who have nothing to be forgiven implicitly have no need of (nothing to do with) Jesus.

The occasion for this mercy affords the real meaning of doing good. It is not "works" as generally understood but primarily a loving that seeks nothing in return. Jesus does not say that his mercy to the objectionable sinners will gain him any reward. It is completely gratuitous and without any merit sought or required of those benefitted. It is not even clear that those who appear at his house have come in conscious need or that they are relying upon him for help of any sort. What *is* clear via the metaphor he uses, a physician come for the sick, is that they are ailing in a profound way. This vagueness figures at the table where Thérèse has taken her place. Her writing does not make clear whether those sitting by her *know* of their wretchedness. Neither does she hint that any among them are seeking to overcome it.

Thérèse says is that she is praying on their behalf for the illumination of faith to come to them, but it might be argued that they would reject it or at least be unlikely to understand it. That is not her concern. What matters is that in this obscure banquet she assumes the celebrant's, the priest's role. She implicitly occupies a unique station at the table, for she alone is the benefactor of all the others seated there. She alone is godward, which means that she alone is doing good. This passage marks a prolegomenon to her famous words on how she would "spend her heaven."

Not only the gospels illuminate this drive to benefaction. In Acts 10:38 Luke records Peter's words to the pious Roman centurion, Cornelius, at Caesarea, speaking of "how God anointed Jesus of Nazareth with the Holy Spirit and with power, who went about doing good, and healing all that were oppressed of the devil, for God was with him." Thérèse is sparing of Acts, citing passages from it only three times, and 10:38 is not one of them.[71] It deserves remarking, nonetheless, because it identifies Jesus's mission in terms that make sense of the table of sorrow and Thérèse's presence there. She might well have concurred that those seated by her were "oppressed of the devil," and that her prayer was a call for the healing power of the Holy Spirit.

Acts 10:38 has further pneumatological significance for understanding Thérèse at the table. Jesus was cast into the wilderness by the power of the Holy Spirit and cast forth again by the Spirit into the company of the demonically oppressed. Jesus never speaks of the Spirit at work upon him. Thérèse, for her part, claimed toward the close of Ms A that Jesus instructed her without words: "Never have I heard him speak, but I realize He is in me, at every moment, He is guiding me, inspiring in me what I should say or do."[72]

This extravagant assertion bends toward the private privilege known as Illuminism (a boon her sisters vigorously denied she ever had), but it suffices to establish a parallel with Jesus's benefactions in Acts. Thérèse would not have been able to utter her prayer at the table of sorrow unless prompted to do so. The passage just cited from A would justify the inference that for her the power to pray at the table came from Jesus himself, he who had sent her there, yet she does not iterate that claim from the table. Thus, Acts 10:38 gives another instance of a New Testament passage rich in interpretive depth for Thérèse's life and work, even though she had no explicit recourse to it.

What she *does* cite regarding benefactions comes from Luke 6:35, Jesus's command, "love ye your enemies and do good and lend, hoping for nothing again." This passage is a special one among those Thérèse quotes, as she takes the outlandish step of challenging Jesus's word on lending. To lend without hope of getting anything back seems contrary to nature, she observes; better to give outright since a gift is by definition something that becomes no longer one's own. "That would agree with one's self-esteem, since giving is a more generous act than loaning."[73] She all but says that she would like to emend this passage. Jesus surely could not prefer lending over the more generous act of giving! Knowledge of the

Greek, which she so much desired, would have told her that it is exactly the giving that Jesus is commending.[74]

More striking than even her urge to emend, however, is her mention of doing good without her noting that the passage refers to one's enemies. The business of lending evidently distracted her. Yet she has to sit with enemies even if she disarms them by charitably calling them her kin. The fact that Jesus tells how to deal with one's enemies is an acknowledgment that one has them. He goes even further when instructing his followers on how to face official enemies who shall summon them to answer for their fellowship with him.

Not one of the versions of this last instruction—Matthew 10:19–20, Mark 13:11, Luke 12:11–12, and 21:14–15—figures anywhere in Thérèse's writings, even though she was living in an age lively with anticlerical sentiment and governmental actions against the Church. Such absences are remarkable, given that Jesus says the Holy Spirit shall be speaking through his followers. They need rehearse nothing in their defense. Thérèse makes clear why these lessons on political confrontation do not apply to her, even at the table of sorrows. She does not regard those who are hostile or indifferent to the Church and its God as enemies at all. Although other Christians might presume them such, and they themselves might wish to be so accounted, she feels compassion for them as sinners. They are *not* set to persecute her, since she has taken her place with and among them; sitting there makes her one of them. In Carmelite fashion, were she asked to identify the table, she would not call it theirs nor hers but "ours."

This "ours" makes the point. In the Psalms, two kinds of table are set, that of the psalmist and that (or those) of his alleged enemies. God has prepared both tables. But in Thérèse's view, there is only one table, prepared by God, at which her compassion reaches into the suffering of others. Their facelessness and their lack of denomination beyond her mercifully vague and universally loving reference to them as her kin show how she transcends the bitterness that pervades even the evangelical letters of Saints Paul and John. She does not rail about nor against "children of darkness." She does not nurse fantasies of revenge at the expense of others.

Perhaps hers is a womanly antidote to male peevishness and spite. Perhaps she is betraying a pointless naïveté. In joining the sinners at the table, she may be thinking of the voiceless "Magdalen" in the house of Simon. If so, then the equity she claims with kindred sinners in eating with them marks at last the longing for the roles of male empowerment she had reviewed in Ms B, the apostle, priest, missionary, doctor of the church—all that put aside so that now she could step into an egalitarian post she had never dreamt of, one of sinners. As Jesus preferred mercy to sacrifice, Thérèse prefers mercy to politics. That is why her proleptic gesture of spending her heaven upon earth indicates a real doing of good.

Her prayer at the table might justly be called Thérèse's supreme biblical moment, the point in which at the seemingly farthest remove from her Christian community and from God, she was carrying out Christ's will. All the better that she does not claim to do so, which means she does not presume she is acting under grace. All the touching egotism of Ms B has fallen away from a young, dying woman helpless and yet loving of others. Her table's prayer is a psalm of lamentation, solicitude, and thanksgiving, all in one. Had she written nothing but the fifth sheet of Ms C, she would have found her sainthood of the little way. The table is where that way took her.

Before a close to these notes on Thérèse's life in the Bible, the most weighty criticism of her deserves noting. It comes from the formidable Hans Urs von Balthasar, Jesuit and Cardinal. Observant of her adhesion to certain passages in the Old and New Testaments, citations to which she often returned in her writings, he charges that she did not read the Bible properly, with the aim toward a "depersonalization" of the self. He suggests that she was a selective reader, picking and choosing according to the needs of her temperament. The particular gravity within this charge is that Thérèse was looking for and finding confirmations of herself or, to put it in a minor key, consolations, rather than letting herself be shaped and disciplined by a meditative reading of scripture, as would befit any religious. Or any Christian, for that matter.

The fact that wide patches of the gospels, those involving miracles and even the resurrection of Jesus, go almost wholly unremarked anywhere in her works lends weight to Balthasar's case. The radically unpleasant Jesus, the fulminator according to Matthew, the Jesus of a furious righteousness cursing his securely entrenched foes, does not comport with Thérèse's beloved Suffering Servant fetched from Isaiah, and yet this railing Jesus is too prominent to ignore. He is not begging for human love, either. It is possible that this Jesus's rhetorical terrorism, with iterated threats of wailing and gnashing of teeth forever in an outer darkness, a terrorism insupportable to some people in recent times ("not really to my mind quite the best tone" complained Bertrand Russell),[75] was too heavy and acerbic for Thérèse as well. It cannot be doubted that she read and perhaps knew from memory much or even all of the scriptural passages that play no part in her writing. She read such vitriol as "Generation of vipers!" and "Hypocrites!" but she evidently had no use for them.

That difference between the written and the unwritten may afford an answer to Balthasar's charge of selectivity; the scriptures she quotes she uses for the homiletic purpose at hand. It can hardly be justified to conclude *ex silentio* that what she does not quote meant little or nothing to her. Rather, she came back to certain passages because they continued to have application to herself and to her sisters; that is clear from her letters, poems and *recréations*. Conversely, what she does not cite could well have contributed to the spiritual trials she went through intermittently from 1890 until her death. The angry, minatory Jesus, heard in homilies and read from the *Breviaire*, might have been too dismaying for her to dwell upon. Did her fastening upon love, love given and received, blind and deafen her to much else?

The frightening, punitive Jesus obliged her to take a kind of refuge in the Jesus of tears and blood she knew to be awaiting her on the Via Dolorosa, the Jesus wounded and forsaken. The harsh and censorious Jesus, the one who speaks of everlasting fire and outermost darkness, reminded her all too well of the harsh, censorious confessors and retreat directors of her childhood and early adolescence. Pauline recalled that such priests "paralyzed" Thérèse with fear. The only way to overcome paralysis from the menacing Jesus of the gospels was to contrive or stylize a Jesus who is *only* loving, merciful, and mild. By extension comes the covert campaign against hell signified in the now almost slogan-like "God is love."

Embracing that Johannine claim of love too closely, however, ignores too much in the gospels. In effect, the modification of Jesus, one radically less than comprehensive of the scriptures, brings the very denominations of him that Thérèse carried literally in her person, Jesus the small child and Jesus whose bloody face is portrayed on the so-called Veronica cloth. The absolute helplessness of both these Jesuses conforms precisely with the only kind of Jesus Thérèse could love: on the one hand, little and therefore needy; on the other, suffering and therefore needy. This is a Jesus much like herself. Balthasar's charge seems well-grounded; it says that Thérèse got round what she claimed to value above everything else, the truth.

But one answer to Balthasar would be concessive: that of course everyone reads scriptures aslant, preferring some passages or narratives to others. It is human to suppress, more or less wittingly, some distinctly unpleasant or unsettling ones. It may be enough to fall back upon the Johannine injunction not to be troubled, since God's house has many resting places, enough for everyone. Or the Johannine assertion that God so loved the world that Jesus was the incarnate promise of deliverance for anyone who believes in him. The gospels dispense many promissory notes of this sort. Only a few dwell upon "If thy right eye offend thee, pluck it forth," an admonition that occurs three times in two gospels, just so it will be kept it in mind. If promises abound, so do scares, impossible orders—be perfect as God is perfect—and threats.

Thérèse might have heard the dark, invective notes that Jesus sounds as evidence that he felt unloved. Human ingratitude toward God stung and exasperated him. But such a rationale does not cover the whole ground. She might have admitted to a limited, preferential reading of the gospels and other biblical passages for the very solid reason that she was weak and inadequate; that she could not help being partial; that as Jesus's love or her love for Jesus was all that mattered to her, she remained purblind to the Jesus of nasty, unsparing moods and words. To summon the cliché that to the pure, all things are pure would be to speak too defensively, needlessly on her behalf. Besides, she rejoiced in her limits, and lamenting her inability to understand the biblical texts on their own linguistic terms was one of them.

She was not ignorant of what occupies the epicenter of Jesus's wrath; his anger unequivocally concerns human failings in matters of justice. While he shows compassion for the needy, even extended to multitudes as in the story of the loaves and fishes, violation of justice truly rouses him. His fearsome eloquence against the ecclesiastical authorities stands as proof. This public, political Jesus was not so much intimidating as too remote from Thérèse's world, too alien to her experiential grasp. Love was her only ambit. Sequestered as she was within her first and final homes, she did not know the wider reaches of the world and its daily violence to justice.

The Theresian account of Jesus is thus nonhistorical, perhaps even antihistorical, in subtracting the lively and not merely local issues of righteousness that Jesus takes up, chiefly in the Sermon on the Mount but also in many confrontations with his foes, scribes, Pharisees, archpriests—"Hypocrites!" Ignoring them, she has ignored the charges Jesus makes against them. She did not, apparently, intuit that Jesus was attacking the Church hierarchy of his day; that he was anything but obedient to the sorts of conventions and dogmas to which she gave daily, unquestioning deference. In sum: Jesus set himself against the ecclesiastical authority of his day, and Rome was such in her own day, but Thérèse ignored these salient facts. Such politics was alien to her disposition and her needs.

Her suffering Jesus, abused and misunderstood and longing to be loved, cuts a sorry figure. Worse, such a Jesus could never have been hated by his high priestly rivals. They would merely have laughed at him and passed him by with contempt. He would never have been so great a threat to them as the gospels' confrontational and witty Jesus who repeatedly beards and humiliates the powerful—seldom a strategy for self-advancement—and is never left wanting for a riposte. Thérèse's tearful Jesus would never have earned the Cross, but it is the Cross that forms the alpha and omega of any Christology. She was fascinated with the pursuit of what she called a science of love, but how would she have fared with her belovèd Juan's science of the Cross?

All of these considerations are germane because the modern representations of Jesus, especially in cinematic epics, are too sentimental to do him the justice that the gospel texts demand. They show where the God-is-love message goes when absent of the unsettling, savage and insupportable scenarios of both Testaments: Abraham obliged to cut his son's throat; upright Job tormented with deaths in his family and sore boils; Jesus forced to accept betrayals, desertions, and the hideous ignominy of crucifixion. What kind of loving God oversees such a world as these brutalities afford? One of the terrible lessons Thérèse teaches, unwittingly, is the peril of slighting the old issues of theodicy. It is necessary to be scandalized by Jesus. Thérèse all but forces a flight to honesty in the bosom of that keen ironist, Kierkegaard.

All that said, studying her as a reader of the Bible prompts an awareness of much more than the spirituality that takes direct inspiration from her favorite passages. Those are easy to trace and lace together; they arrive directly at the loving and compassionate God who decrees child-like littleness to all believers so they may enter the heavenly realm. Best to be obedient, unquestioning, self-effacing. That is the sure and only way to make vested authorities pleased with you. But more may be learnt in the meaty portions of text to which Thérèse has *not* given attention. It is more likely that a Christian who meditates upon them and seeks to live through them shall be staggering under a heavy cross than shall the Christian who pursues a timidity that is much like humility and gets through life with as little offensiveness as possible. (See Figure 2.2.)

Thérèse by example alerts us to possible hazards and snares in a too personal reading of the Bible, one that does not accommodate the scandal, the offensiveness of Jesus. She would almost certainly have felt dismay at Balthasar's plea for a depersonalized approach to the gospels. A not personally invested sense of the gospels could have made no sense to her. She, for one, had to respond to Jesus on an intensely intuitive level of affirmation. What she brought to the gospels was and could be only herself, imperfect and therefore acutely needy. That is why she writes with an at times suppliant fervor, especially in the prayers but also in the poems. Her reading itself and her use of biblical allusions suggests this loving obstinacy.

FIGURE 2.2 "Thy Will Be Done," a panel from an icon illustrating the Our Father, late seventeenth century, the Russian Museum, Saint Petersburg. "God prefers to see us stumbling upon a stony path in the night, not walking an enameled path in bright daylight through a flower garden," Therese wrote, December 24, 1896. Photograph taken by the author.

Implicitly, the writer of the *offrande* of June 1895 can be glimpsed in every gospel reference, as though it were the all-sufficient response to Jesus's bidding. It can legitimately be charged that she shaped her perception of Christianity according to the needs of her own temperament; that she failed to discover any other way; that she failed to maintain herself on Teresa's way of perfection. She would have gladly acknowledged all of these shortcomings. They give her writing a vibrant, almost thespian life, as though she were finally enclosed in a little theater of her own, confronting Jesus with all the longing of her indigent heart.

3
Bearing the Cross of Community[1]

> *"Ne crains rien, ici tu trouveras plus que partout ailleurs la croix et le martyre!"*
> *[Don't be afraid, here you'll find better than anywhere else the cross and martyrdom!"]*
> TO CÉLINE, July 18, 1894

> *"[Thérèse] était heureuse de me voir lutter pied à pied avec des défauts qui me tenaient constamment dans l'humiliation, car avec mon caractère impétueux il m'arrivait souvent de petites sorties avec les soeurs. Sorties qui m'affligeaient beaucoup à cause de mon grand amour-propre.... Paraître imparfaite aux yeux des créatures, me semblait une montagne à avaler."*
> *["Thérèse was happy to see me struggle step by step with my failings, which kept me in constant humiliation. Indeed, given my impetuous personality I was often in little sallies with the sisters, sallies which afflicted me greatly because of my selfishness.... To appear imperfect to others' eyes seemed to me a mountain to swallow."]*
> CÉLINE, Souvenirs autobiographiques, 1909

> *"Quand nous reprenons les fautes, il faut aussy parler à nous mesme plustot qu'à celle quy a failly, et en cette sorte nos avertissements fonts de bons effects, parce qu'ils sont acompagnés d'humilité."*
> *["When we reprehend faults, it's necessary to speak to ourselves rather than to the novice who has committed them, and in that way our warnings are to good effect, because they are accompanied by humility."]*
> MÈRE MADELEINE DE SAINT-JOSEPH TO SR. MARIE DE SAINTE-ÉLIE, sous-prieure of the Carmel of Lyon, ca. 1631

THE ARGUMENT OF this chapter is that well before she came to the table of sorrow that she identifies in Manuscript C, Thérèse had found one within her spiritual community. Disciplined as well as disposed to see all of her sisters as exemplars of a piety far greater and deeper than her own, she discovered within and beyond her natural family many instances of the stumbling and falling that she made part of her own spirituality. The Carmel became for her a laboratory of human frailties, failings, and faults. Her pastoral praxis of caring for profoundly troubled sisters helped her to understand her spiritual darkness as collective, the burden common to many and yet experienced by them in isolation from one another. The Carmel prepared her for her arrival at the crowded table of unbelief and its bitter bread, a new kind of communion.

I. In a Boat without a Pilot

The third manuscript records Thérèse's ripening into an awareness of the dark world of sinners situated at a vast table of grief. It reveals her matured perception of other Carmelite sisters, those she had known, for the greater part, over her more than nine years in Carmel. It is surprising that only in that ninth year did she discover people she had known for long and so closely, but the discovery was made only because of the dark table and the tremendous advance in her Christology that it marked. In C an apparent absence, Christ's, is a presence, hidden in the Carmelite way, but there. Thérèse puts it succinctly, telling us she had discovered charity.[2] This does not mean she became consistently charitable, no more than that it would mean she had not been charitable before. She told on herself to her prioress mothers, Gonzague and Pauline, and to her readers.

Her somber community of sinners aside, Thérèse lived her last eighteen months in an acute apartness. The onset of her final illness sequestered her from her sisters. She was to die, and they were to live. Pleased with what she believed to be death's imminence, she nonetheless had to come to terms with her life in community, to give it a final Christian sense as a way of saying farewell. That process, emerging as from a chrysalis in C, was outwardly accelerated by her enforced move to the Carmel's infirmary on Thursday, July 8, 1897.

The far graver apartness was spiritual and derived immediately from the onset of darkness during Holy Week, 1896. It had several dimensions. First, it silently set her apart from the community of believers. In writing poems upon request and in writing the last of her recreational dramas, Thérèse had received an unsolicited access to several of her sisters, a confidentiality they bestowed that gave her some intimation of how they were progressing along Teresa's *camino* toward spiritual perfection. She, however, had come to realize that she was destined for the way of imperfection, of spiritual stumbling and groping. If others were moving ever toward light, no matter how fitfully, she was set apart within a mighty dark all her own.

In Manuscript B she had likened herself to a small bird, barely able to take wing in a storm, whereas her sisters were greater, stronger birds, confident of soaring flight. This position was the obligatory stance of genuine humility Teresa had signaled, in which everyone would appear worthier than oneself, in which one would be lowest, least, last of all. Thérèse saw herself as last but moving in a direction wholly contrary to what Teresa prescribed, downward and beyond Carmel to her fellow sinners at the table. With that movement came an imposing helplessness, as one might feel in a moving elevator while one stands still. Thérèse's late insights, dearly won, come from this lowly vantage of weakness, of littleness, of inadequacy, with darkness ever surrounding.

Beyond the isolation from community, an isolation intensified by daily but limited contact with more or less shadow-free sisters in the offices, the refectory, and the recreational hours, was the absence of a perceptive and helpful spiritual director. A poignant proof of that absence was the industrious letter writing that Thérèse sustained with the one cleric she had trusted since childhood, the Jesuit father Almire Pichon. He had settled permanently in Canada in 1888, the year of Thérèse's entry into the convent. His extant letters to her are too few and too skimpy to establish anything other than what is well known, that as he was engulfed in an exhausting schedule of retreats and received innumerable letters from communicants, he did not maintain a correspondence adequate to Thérèse's needs.

Her situation was thus altogether different from Teresa's in Spain. Although living in an age of extraordinary turmoil, political and spiritual, Teresa enjoyed from her adolescence a strong and stabilizing, thoroughly masculine society of support. She was unusually fortunate in coming into her spiritual maturity and adulthood in a close, steady rapport with both religious and secular fathers. That sustenance began with her widower uncle, who gave up all his property and became a friar. After her father's death, it continued with his confessor, the Dominican Vincente Barrón. Later, she met Don Francisco de Salcedo, a lay theologian to whom she confided her fears about internal voices she had been hearing and who put her in touch with the then budding Jesuit community. The Society of Jesus offered her continual assistance when she faced formidable opponents within the Church hierarchy as she was undertaking her Reform. The Jesuit Baltasar Alvarez was another confidant, as was the venerable Franciscan Peter of Alcántara, and so were the Dominicans Pedro Ibáñez and Domingo Báñez. That is not to mention her filial supporters, Gracian and Juan de la Cruz.

In stark contrast Thérèse had not one man she could depend upon to direct her as she needed.[3] Teresa had needed the ballast of her male friendships and confidants in order to carry out her exceptional mission of establishing a new order of Carmel. The wee, insignificant, entirely unpolitical and very young novice in another age, tucked away in Lisieux, had no such itinerary. Yet in her autobiography Teresa frequently shows herself as confused and helpless as the greenest of novices. She considered her young charges saintly and herself sinful, but that might be maternal vanity peeking through, for what mother would not rejoice in the glory of her children? They were giving up their young lives to the austerities she had fashioned for them, but she herself had come to that same goal only quite late. So many years wasted and so much to confess! Thérèse did have a confessor, Abbé Louis Youf, the chaplain or aumonier (literally, alms giver) of the Carmel, to whom she admitted the doubt within her. Her remarks to Pauline (June 6, 1897) do not suggest that he offered her a depth of insight as fathoms down as her own: "Monsieur Youf spoke to me about my temptations against the faith: 'Don't dwell on it, it's very dangerous.' That's hardly reassuring to hear, but happily I'm not distressed. Don't worry, I'm not going to break my 'little' head with self-torment. Also, he asked me: 'Are you resigned to death?' I told him, 'Oh, Father! I find that there's only a need to be resigned to living. As to dying, it's joy I feel.'"[4] Manifestly, Youf fell short before this hardy young sister, and his terse injunction seems to indicate that he knew as much.

The same may have been true of Pichon. His hortatory skills could reach only so far, and Thérèse may not have realized nor wanted to face the possibility of his disappointing her. All too aware of one's shortcomings, it is not always a simple matter to acknowledge them charitably in others. Thérèse came to a mature perception of limits in others by her work as de facto mistress of novices, but it seems improbable that she could have accepted limits in someone so treasured and esteemed as Pichon had once been. The letters to him facilitated an illusion that he was "there" for her and that she for her part was carrying the same need. Surrogate of Jesus as he was, Pichon kept the distance and silence that Thérèse had long identified with Jesus: he was the absent beloved, the one to be ever longed for. Her lost monthly correspondence with him dates from her early years; there were none after she learned of how he had attempted to lure Céline to Canada, without the Martin family's awareness.

Thérèse also had the superficial handicap of her youthfulness, which would have been a snare for anyone, such as Youf, who did not know her well. She had remained in the novitiate when after two years she reached the normative terminus of that stage in her conventual life. Such an unusual ongoing state of preparation, outwardly a kind of protracted adolescence, would have argued to a spiritual director an immaturity, which her dual burden of adversity, the tuberculosis and the onset of shadows, had been forcing her to shed. From the community's viewpoint, this perpetual novitiate obviated a concern that many of the sisters might have felt but did not articulate, that there could and should be no more than two natural sisters in full status. Would not Teresa have been outraged that there were no less than five women from the same family, the Martin-Guérin "clan," in a community of just two dozen? Apart from such delicate procedural considerations, it deserves emphasis that to the end of her life Thérèse was voluntarily liminal, on a threshold that allowed her to occupy two positions, that she was in the Carmel but never entirely of it. Besides, being a novice meant that she still needed to grow, and she did not want to do so. She preferred to remain a fledgling.

Having to manage without a solidly reliable director did not seem to trouble her. As though in compensation, her favorite text from Spain, Juan's *Llama de amor viva* [*The Living Flame of Love*], gave numerous cautions about the perils of a spiritual direction that might be well meant but could prove inadequate. Juan refers to stages from which some directors themselves cannot and should not as directors advance; in their proper station they may serve well, but with higher exigencies in the progressing soul, they fall disastrously short. As Juan bluntly observes, when a blind man needs guidance, it must be God alone who directs him, not another blind man.[5] Teresa said as much from another perspective. She had known a sister whose director had kept her in self-examination for years, well beyond the time when she had been made fit for the prayer of quietude.[6]

Spiritual direction, however, involved chiefly a developed life of prayer, a soul's progress toward transformation into God, but Thérèse had put some constraints upon herself in that regard by admitting that formal prayer, and *a fortiori* directed prayer, was far less effective for her than the spontaneity of prayers she said in her own unreflected language. She learned to trust the impromptu over the rehearsed because the impromptu, by speech and pen, came from her, a self whose shortcomings she knew authentically. Coming from her own sensibility a prayer had an immediately ratified sincerity that a missal, in effect speaking to as well as for her, could not afford. Such spontaneity seemed a legitimate first step toward truthfulness, and the more needy its expression, the better. The best proof comes from the late prayers and C itself, which is an extended prayer.

The first of these prayers was composed within the darkness, August 6, 1896, on the Feast of the Transfiguration. For herself and two fellow novices, Marie de la Trinité and Céline, she wrote on a small card that bore "the Holy Face" of Tours, a widely circulated painting of Jesus in the Passion.[7] She asked that the sisters' souls might exert themselves toward the divine love, that they might be consumed and come directly to see Jesus face to face. This prayer complements the magnificent *offrande* of June 9, 1895. But now, in her darkness, Thérèse looks past the Transfiguration on Mt. Tabor. Allusions to Juan de la Cruz in this brief text indicate that she is praying for a Christian death as soon as possible.

In his commentary on *Llama de amor viva*, Juan explains that by consuming the veils of the natural, temporal and even sensitive life (the soul joined still with the body), the living flame of divine love produces a most exquisite death in those who have prepared themselves for it "And thus the death of such souls is most sweet and gentle, more than was all of their spiritual life, since they are dying with love's most sublime impetus and savory encounters, even as the swan sings most sweetly when dying."[8]

It is easy to imagine the intoxicating headiness of such language upon the young and now dying Thérèse. How could she have resisted it or have wanted to? She had re-discovered Juan now as a spiritual director giving her the focus and élan by which to endure a truly high cost of living.[9] Having fleetingly alluded to this passage at the close of her first manuscript (A 84r), she returned to it again and again in her writings and her *entretiens*. The prayer marks also the first time she uses one of Juan's annotations to his *Cantico Espiritual*, that the littlest movement of a pure love for God is more useful to the Church than all other works combined.[10] The littleness and the love were all-important for her, for they were all she had.

In this consecration to the Holy Face, Thérèse writes also of the sisters' need of souls, "especially souls of apostles and martyrs so that by them we may embrace with your Love the multitude of poor sinners."[11] This is a striking passage. Thérèse uses *embraser*, to embrace, here and there when writing about the divine Love that takes hold of souls, but in this exceptional instance she seeks the divine Love so that she and her sisters may in-gather with it all poor sinners.[12] That last phrase anticipates the table of sorrow, where Thérèse again perceives the piteousness of those whose lives face away from God.

By gradual and minuscule hints, she moves toward a mission that puts to exalted use the time she had not expected to have, as she was obliged to live on and on. She had been cheated of the promise of an early death; the first hemoptysis (coughing blood) failed to deliver on the joy she had taken from it. Instead, left more and more alone with the burden of time and slow debilitation, she began to compact the two selves of her vocables, the Infant and the Holy Face, into one. She became a suffering child compelled to walk the Via Dolorosa, with her Beloved ever distant.

What did her confessor see in her imminent death? On July 6, Thérèse remarked to Pauline: "Monsieur the Abbé told me, 'You're going to have a great sacrifice to make in leaving your sisters.' I said to him, 'But, my Father, I find that I'm not going to be leaving them. On the contrary, I'll be still nearer to them after my death.'"[13] Here, in tandem with the shadows, was her nascent awareness of a mission to do good on earth. Earth became the heaven she chose for herself, an election made within and for the darkness and among and for all who might be in it.

Two days later, July 8, when she was carried to the infirmary, she heard Abbé Youf and Carmel's physician, Dr. Alexandre de Cornière, discussing whether she should be given extreme unction. (It was not in fact given until July 30.) For the while, though, "I seem to be dreaming. At last, they aren't fools."[14] Alas, they were, the poor cleric and the poor doctor, as death was playing at their expense. And when it finally came to Thérèse, it tarried awhile and then took Youf, too, only a few days later. He was 55.

The twofold isolation benefited Thérèse in accelerating the sense of mission she intuited from her writing and from her natural sisters' response to that writing. That mission began on April 6, 1897, when Pauline began to record her conversations with Thérèse. Ironically, the first of these celebrates the blessing of silence instead of speech, but the *entretiens* are casual, even offhand in their tone, offering a warp to the woof of C. In a virtually pretechnological age, they furnish proximity to an audio recording.

After Thérèse went to the infirmary, her other natural sisters began to record their own series of remarks from her. Death's looming, in ghastly blood-spitting spasms, had forced upon them an acceptance of their sister as far more than the runt they had always known. For Céline there was yet another adjustment. In the novitiate, she had to learn to accept her little sister in the role of a guide, wiser in Carmelite years than she, but now she had to face the inevitability of being left behind by the sister who had importuned her to enter the Carmel so that they might spend the rest of their lives together there. Less than three years after Céline's entrance, Thérèse was cheating her of that togetherness. At the same time, the Martin sisters' note-taking tacitly recognized her distance from them, that she had moved well ahead of them in her grasp of the realities of Christian life, thanks to the adverse bonds in which she was being held.

It had long been the convention in the Carmel, and in the secular world as well, to gather a dying person's last words. They were presumed to carry a special power, as though death were conceding revelations to someone it was about to claim. But the Martin sisters, particularly Pauline, were industriously passing well beyond that convention as they intuited that Thérèse had been on a journey that, well short of the dying, afforded much more than gnomic last words. If, as I am arguing, C is the alembic in which her spirituality is distilled, the three series of *entretiens* are like elements floating about in a fluid awaiting centrifuge. The sisters did not know how to analyze the precipitate, no more than did Gonzague in reading C, nor even, in all likelihood, did Thérèse herself. She kept on writing, speaking—when she was able—in full awareness that death might end her next breath.

Thérèse, however, had plenty of time to bring her spiritual journey to elective closure. She wrote so as to make sense of her life for Jesus. She did so in such a way that the darkness within her and the immanent, abiding community of her two dozen sisters around her occluded at last the terrible burden of selfhood.

II. With Christ Painting Souls

According to Juan de la Cruz, the soul's preparation for what St. Paul called putting on the new man in Christ involves an exacting, tormenting process of *desnudar* or undressing. It begins with the ascetic rigors of penitential prayer and corporal self-punishment. It then advances toward a contemplative passivity that detaches the soul from all that is sensory and imperfect. Juan likens the soul's perfectability to the making of a sculpture: first, the stone must be hewn, then carved, then polished. Each of these tasks must be kept discretely within the hands of its artisan, "for each of them cannot make of it more than he knows, and should he seek to go beyond [his competence], he would ruin it."[15]

For Thérèse, imperfection sufficed. It was also necessary in protecting her as a woman. In the Carmel of her day, Juan's texts on the denuding of the soul and its preparation for a new life in God were forbidden territory to the sisters. From the seventeenth century a residue of suspicion remained about feminine susceptibilities to transport of any kind. Teresa's writings had shown keen, olfactory alertness for any scent of fraud and deception practiced by and upon the self and others. A woman might become an accomplice of Juan, carried off by the buoyancy of her own susceptibilities. An excess of emotive power or sheer intellect in a woman meant disruption or subversion.[16]

The *Subida del Monte Carmelo* and the *Noche oscura* enjoy only infrequent mention in Thérèse's writing; and she cites only the verses, never the protracted commentaries upon them.[17] The passage just cited on artisanship comes from the *Llama de amor viva*, a work she read extensively, both for the poetry and its expositions. Given the strenuous, perilous reach of Juan's itinerary, Thérèse chooses not so forbiddingly masculine an exercise as sculpting, but the gentler, less athletic art of painting,[18] long a hobby-life for her and her sisters, Pauline and Céline.

The theme, however, is the same: the artisanship required for shaping a novice's spiritual life. Where Juan positioned three workmen to prepare the sculpture, each in a discrete skill, Thérèse had two, complementing her position as *compagne de novices* with Gonzague's as *maîtresse de novices*. Here is how she articulates and differentiates their tasks: "I'm a little brush that Jesus has selected to paint his image in the souls you've entrusted to me. An artist doesn't make do with just one brush; he needs at least two of them. The first is the more useful as he provides the general color scheme with it, covering the canvas completely in a very short time. The other, the smaller, he uses for details. My Mother, you are to me the valuable brush that Jesus's hand lays hold of with love when he wants to make a great work in the soul of your children, while I am the very small one he deigns to make use of afterward for the slightest details."[19]

Trivial though this language seems, the notion within it is complex. First, Thérèse, for all her love of Juan de la Cruz, is declaring her independence from him on several counts. She makes it clear that there is no risk that one artisan might overstep a function and ruin the job. The small brush could not possibly serve for the grand portrait; it remains subordinate and subsequent to the greater. More important, the two sororal brushes are only the efficient means, not the truly creative agent. As Jesus is the artist, there can be no danger of a botched effort. Further, the love with which Jesus chooses the greater instrument binds him both to it (Gonzague) and to the subject he is in effect re-creating through it.

The natural self that so exercised the severe and anguished Juan is not to be submitted to a nocturnal anguish of imperfections chastened into non-entity; rather, such imperfections are being painted over. That painting does not denote superficiality but its very opposite. Jesus is making this great work within the soul of every novice sister. The inward painting conforms with the Carmelites' ethos of the hidden. At the same time, the dynamic of love is manifest; Jesus loves Gonzague in choosing her to depict his love for her sister. Gonzague's love for that sister and for Jesus is expressed in this task. And the sister's love for her and for Jesus lies in the depiction. It amounts to a communal dynamic, an arch for which Christ and his vicar within the Carmel, the prioress, supply the keystone.[20]

Thérèse is careful to underscore the secondary nature of her own effort. Jesus takes up the Gonzague brush lovingly but merely "deigns" to use the small Thérèse brush, serviceable only for small matters. It might seem a disingenuous way of putting herself in the last position, which is spiritually assured of being the first, but Thérèse was also tactfully deferring to Gonzague as her superior in age, in experience and wisdom, even as Gonzague was also the spiritual mother of her charges as both *prieure* and *maîtresse*. At the same time, what Thérèse calls "the least details" comes through in the following admission: "With certain souls, I realize I must make myself small, not fear to humble myself in acknowledging my struggles and defeats. Seeing I have the same weaknesses as they do, my little sisters admit in their turn the faults for which they reproach themselves and rejoice that I understand them by experience."[21]

This passage opens a small window onto the help that novices gave Thérèse in making herself humble. Through her life in Carmel, as her writings attest, her endeavor had consistently been to *rester petite*, to remain little. Her fellow novices gave her the vital lesson that one can become littler not only before figures of authority such as the confessor or the prioress but, and perhaps best, before those wholly without authority who can be edified by the example of lowering the self. Thérèse savored this lesson and came to enjoy occasions that exposed her weaknesses.[22] Her natural sister gave her many such occasions.

III. Céline Enters the Carmel

It is reasonably certain that when she was appointed companion of novices (formally, *maîtresse auxiliaire*) and became in effect their *maîtresse*, Thérèse was given a small volume, published in 1873, the year of her birth, which Gonzague had used when she had served in that position. *Pensées sur la charge de Maîtresse des Novices dans l'Ordre de Notre-Dame du Mont Carmel* remains suitably anonymous, but it establishes from the first the spirit of the order's founder, as the following injunction for the *maîtresse* makes clear: "May she count neither upon her own efforts nor her own talents; but may she, ever persuaded of her personal uselessness, plant and water and wait upon God alone."[23]

This directive draws, of course, upon Teresa's serviceable gardening metaphor, here expanded to include planting. It poses, however, a conundrum. How in planting and watering could one be convinced of one's uselessness? How could Thérèse, earnestly bent upon remaining little and weak, take her charges upon her knees, like the consolatory mother in one of her favorite Isaiah passages (66:12–13)? She could adduce an answer from Teresa herself, that the humbling that makes one see others' virtues and one's own "great sins" is a grace; God reaches others through the humbled person, that smaller brush.

This bidding provides a hortatory loftiness, which, as often in Teresa's *Vida*, argues the capacity in human beings to achieve a selfless dignity. Even so, in the daily praxis it was hard going. The Carmel *Pensées* prove invaluable, full of caveats in dealing with the inscrutability of human personality, including its possibly sinister turns. "One must also keep from believing that one knows a novice straight off or in a short time, except for certain decided sorts so obviously dangerous for a religious house."[24] For Thérèse such stipulations posed a profound challenge in the case of the one novice she could well presume to know inside and out, her sister, Céline, who came into the Carmel under tremendous pressure exerted by Pauline and Thérèse, immediately upon the death of their father.

It is not well known that the Martins' cousin Jeanne La Néele and possibly her parents resented Céline's precipitous departure from their home, where she had been taking care of Louis. In effect, she rejected the models of marital domesticity in the Guérin and the La Néele families. It seemed rank ingratitude. But extant family correspondence establishes that all three conventual Martins, not Thérèse alone, had long treated Céline with the pious assumption that she was on her way to becoming one of them, de facto if not de iure. As Céline become the caretaker of their stricken father, her eldest sister and adopted mother, Marie, could tell her, "For you, my dear little sister, your role has been and always will be to sacrifice yourself." And this, a month later "For you Jesus is continually gathering roses aloft in Heaven's gardens. There's not a thorn which pierces your heart that he will not change soon into an everlasting rose, into a joy which shall NEVER pass!"[25]

It is probable that Céline heard such fulsome nonsense many times. The Martins' correspondence is surfeited with pious, consolatory phrases that they rolled off for one another. A medium that could have provided these women with a profound and buoyant intimacy strictly *inter se* remained in the shallows of linguistic conventions they had been trained to affirm, platitudinous echoes of their parents' unreflective exchanges. Ironically, Louis himself became the prime reason for and focus of the women's lamentations and their attendant need of mutual sustenance.

As Louis had called her "Paul" in childhood, Pauline often addressed her sister in a masculine form, "Mon petit Célin chéri" only to tell her, as Marie had, about her heart. Looking to the vow of chastity Céline made (December 8, 1889) Pauline wrote, "Your heart is a sanctified little flower, belonging to Jesus forever!"[26] But she rarely failed to supply more dramatic metaphors: "It's the target where Jesus directs all his arrows. But as the rock struck with force throws off sparks, so your shattered heart shall become all flame."[27] Céline had to read and accept confident pronouncements and predictions about what was going on within her.

The degree of her complicity with her Carmel sisters can be inferred from remarks by Marie which suggest that Céline as early as 1891 had told them either that she had no intention of marrying or that she would enter an order: "Oh, Céline! You, too, will not belong to the world! Not one of our family will contract an alliance here below! I think that in heaven our dear Mother must be very happy to see her wishes so completely realized."[28] Had she been permitted to enter the Carmel at twenty, perhaps her story would not be so fetching and complicated. She had had to learn patience with her own indecisiveness and to accept what that said about her otherwise headstrong character. She emerges as the most interesting of the five Martin sisters, not because she had options never dreamt of by her sisters, but because she chose after their fashion and became a Carmelite in spite of herself. (Figure 3.1.)

FIGURE 3.1 Céline, known as Sister Geneviève of Saint Teresa and of the Holy Face, in her bridal dress at the Carmel, February 24, 1896. Copyright Archives du Carmel de Lisieux

Céline exemplified a challenge the Carmel and a *maîtresse* had to face with women who came in later than the usual ages (between 16 and 20, Céline being 25) and who were accustomed to degrees of autonomy and worldly adjustments that had to be undone by a strict life in community. Such women were mature but on their own terms. What is unique in this instance is Thérèse's covert preparation of her sister for Carmel years in advance of Céline's entry on September 14, 1894. Thérèse sent to her many letters from her own first months in Carmel up to the autumn of 1894. Céline was by far her most important correspondent, not only a sympathetic reader who had enjoyed lifelong affinities with her but also a valued recipient of what might be called Thérèse's apologia, a defense and rationale of the life she had chosen and which thereby separated them indefinitely. Thérèse hoped all along that her sister would someday enter the Carmel and thus reconstitute the family that began to scatter when Pauline left home in October 1882. Céline meanwhile gave her invaluable occasions for articulating the Carmelite life with Jesus. More than two dozen letters read as luring little homilies, which, as Thérèse's "letter to the world," count among her most important writing. They also constituted a preparation for her work as a *maîtresse auxiliaire.*

The letters to Céline resumed early adolescent dialogues. The most cherished of those conversations Thérèse records in Manuscript A. She recalls a summer evening when they engaged in a kind of mystical lift-off while contemplating the natural beauties from the belvedere window of their father's house. The "mystical" tagging of this innocuous pretentiousness was conferred in hallowing fashion long afterward, when both sisters exalted their chatting by likening it to the exchanges between Monica and her son, Augustine, at the window in Ostia when Monica was about to depart for her African home but then died. Thérèse mentions only Monica by name and does not indicate which of the two sisters occupied her solicitous maternal role. Céline was the older by more than three years, but it was Thérèse who had performed the protective Monica part to the wayward, worldly Céline. Céline had to fight the Augustinian attachment to a pagan world over and over again; it was she who was long kicking against the pricks by even considering that she might make her way in the secular life: marriage or a career in painting; perhaps both.

Céline was the perfect correspondent because of these tugs; she was leaning toward a life other than the one Thérèse had unswervingly chosen for herself. Implicitly, Céline was challenging Thérèse, not to join her on some other path, which would have been completely contrary to Thérèse's disposition, but to articulate how she saw the Christian life, a life no longer outside and under common worldly constraints but thoroughly well defined within a Christian community. Where was it leading her?

Céline had thus long ceased to play only a collusive role in her sister's life. She had become a kind of antagonist.[29] Her entry into Carmel had been concessive, without the normative sign of a true calling that shut the world out from any consideration. The bracing, inspiring inevitability of a genuine destiny for Carmel was absent—a calamitous sign. Did she feel that her sisters were pushing her to perpetrate a fraud? Fortunately, Thérèse did what she could to fashion her sister anew, and the correspondence reveals that process along its subtle way. Unfortunately, Céline, late in her life, decided to destroy a substantial portion of her correspondence in Thérèse's first Carmelite years: all of her letters between March 13 and December 24, 1889, and between July 22, 1890 and August 17, 1892, a total of well over two-and-a-half years.

At no time did Thérèse reach the sibylline altitude ascribed to her by her hagiographic admirers. Her letters mark ongoing struggles with herself, especially when she is being urgent and hortatory with Céline. When Céline seems to flag, Thérèse indicates her own susceptibilities, her sharing in that faltering. She remarks only two weeks into her novitiate (she had just turned sixteen), that as Jesus had fallen three times on the way to Calvary, she and her sister are to fall a hundred times over in their own journeying.[30] The steady proof of their weakness would manifest love for Jesus, but "What ineffable joy, to carry our cross WEAKLY." She speaks to Céline as though she, Céline, were herself a Carmelite, having her own "novitiate of grief."[31]

This coining and that dwelling upon the cross along the Via Dolorosa were cued by Louis Martin's hallucinatory collapse into dementia and his removal to Bon Sauveur, the sanatorium in Caen, where he spent more than three years. This familial catastrophe obliged both young women to be tested and ripened under the same burden, but one that each bore differently from the other. Louis had already been undergoing spells when Thérèse, leaving her postulancy, added "de la Sainte Face" to her name.[32] Their father, now the living emblem of the stricken soul within the Holy Face, became the catalyst by which they were suddenly forced to stumble further along the Calvary route in a togetherness that neither could have imagined when Thérèse entered the Carmel in April, 1888.

They had sustained one another with reasonably girlish talk about their hearts ever beating as one, about their golden days and fond nights dreaming of sainthood in the belvedere, and about their virginal loyalty to Jesus who, like an importunate lover, now as ever required of them "tout Tout TOUT"(everything times three) as Thérèse put it with her hyperbolic vigor.[33] They managed the anxieties attending their separation by propping up each other. To Céline's plaints about being left behind, about the joylessness of life with their cousins, the Guérins, Thérèse, free of such tedium, could respond only that she wished Jesus would send herself all of her sister's chagrin, melancholy, and ennui, but would it not be egotistic, she adds, to ask as much? Instead, she imparts the Carmelite ethos of suffering for Christ; all the world's treasures are as nothing to the smallest suffering for him. Even if one feels no love for Jesus, it wipes away the tears that the wicked cause him to shed. But Thérèse herself gives way and admits she needs to talk with Céline as of old, in the belvedere's way.[34]

On occasion, Thérèse chides her, as when Céline claims she wants to be a flame rising up to Jesus: beware, "self-love quickly comes like a fatal wind and extinguishes everything."[35] Thérèse was particularly alert to egotism and anything that smacked of ingratitude. She put Céline down for both, well after Céline entered the Carmel. In those same early years of the novitiate, to her self-pitying cousin, Marie Guérin, floundering like Céline in boredom, indifferent to the eucharist and refusing herself communion for weeks, Thérèse responded, "Thank the good Lord for all the graces he has done you and don't be so ungrateful not to acknowledge them."[36] She likened Marie to a peasant girl whom a mighty king comes to ask in marriage and who refuses him because she's not wealthy and does not know the ways of the court, but he knows her poverty and weakness better than she.

Already, Thérèse had found a central motif in her spirituality, a rejoicing in her weakness, derived from St. Paul's glorying in his own (II Cor. 2:5). To Marie she adds a further note on the courting monarch: Jesus is everything, we are nothing. These dumbfounding words came from Juan de la Cruz and his *Subida* (Ascent of Mount Carmel), but Thérèse received them indirectly, from the mistress of novices, Marie des Anges. Indeed, a good deal of what she imparted to her sister and her cousin she herself had been given, sometimes in reprimand. She herself asserted a flame-flying exuberance, the longing to rise up to Jesus.[37] She found herself guilty of ingratitude to Louis. Her very weakness obliged her to leave him behind at Les Buissonnets and enter the Carmel. That was the way she explained to Céline her departure from home. Céline, the apparently stronger, had to remain with Louis.

Being a novice, Thérèse herself needed guidance, sometimes in strong doses. Gonzague reproached her generously for her slightest lapses and failings. But the prioress also gave sound and sober advice. In that first autumn, she wrote to Thérèse "It's suffering, and even more it's sacrifice that will make you a great saint."[38] In the beginning Thérèse, like any number of other postulants and novices, had ambition (that noun is a verb in French) to go to the top. Whether she realized so early that going to the top meant, by the paradox firm and central to Christian life, going to rock bottom may be doubted, though her intuition was leaving her glances in this direction when she dwelt upon weakness.[39]

In her first year she was starting to pass toward the darkness that eventually engulfed her. The fall of 1889 provided a rehearsal for the Easter darkness of 1896, but much of what she was having to endure within herself has to be inferred from her correspondents. Chief of these was her Jesuit confessor, Pichon. His imperative tone afforded the tonic she needed. She had taken a vow of obedience, and he had the powerful perquisite of the masculine, priestly voice she had long trusted: "I forbid you in God's name to put in question your state of grace. The devil's cackling over it. I protest against this base distrust. Believe obstinately that Jesus loves you."[40]

These stunning words reveal Thérèse's most dire fear, that Jesus did not love her. She was too weak, meaning she was not up to trusting him. What hurts Jesus, she had told her fretful cousin, Marie, is our lack of trust in him.[41] The antonym of *confiance* or trust, was *défiance*, the very word with which Pichon had charged her. When to Céline she characterized a desiderated martyrdom as loving Jesus without feeling the sweetness of this love, she was saying that it was not a reciprocal love: love Jesus passionately even though feeling nothing back from him.[42] He doesn't really love us [me], does he?[43] Pichon's remarks show that Thérèse's sometimes strident protests of love for Jesus cover over or compensate for her lack of trust in him. Her writings are sometimes a kind of con job on herself.

All of the Martin sisters struggled with the burden of self. Thérèse's eldest sister, Marie, asked her to pray that she, Marie, would become a saint by her life's end so that there would be no regret for her having suffered what she called "the heart's martyrdom."[44] Then, she said, the family could at last bless the cross borne by their father at Bon Sauveur. Thérèse rose to the challenge and reminded Marie that their father, fearing he had not suffered enough in his life to enter heaven, had asked for something to offer to God. It proved to be himself, broken and helpless. Her words following that sacrifice are portentous: "It was God who brought that about."[45] She later saw her darkness as something Jesus allowed to happen.

Pauline was not immune to profound distress over faith, especially during her private retreats.[46] Sharing her apprehensions with her baby sister she helped Thérèse to admit fear and a sense of sin, exactly what Pichon reproached her for. Sin meant doubting or distrusting Jesus's love. That is why Thérèse wanted Jesus to take her, grain of sand as she was, and conceal her in his countenance[47] where she would be "certain of no longer sinning!"[48] Her iterated desire to be downtrodden, ignored and forgotten derives from this unbearable separation from Jesus caused by her questioning his love for her. She attempts to overcome it with written insistence to Pauline (during Pauline's retreat in the spring of 1890) that she no longer belongs to herself but to Jesus. The rub is that she then asks Pauline to hide her under the veil of the retreat.[49] If she had truly belonged to Jesus, she would not have needed Pauline's protective solicitude. She was hiding as much from her sinful distrust as from Jesus. She presumed that if she could disappear into his sorrowful countenance, she would then no longer have to face him or herself.

On September 5, 1890, Thérèse, preparing to make her profession of vows, had Céline take her crown and crucifix to Bon Sauveur for their father to bless. Both girls hoped Louis could attend the profession on September 8, but their guardian, Uncle Isidore, deemed it imprudent to attempt such an arrangement. From the ceremony came two extraordinary documents. The first is Thérèse's first recorded prayer as a Carmelite, what was known as a *billet de profession*. Conceived as a kind of second baptism, it conventionally contained the novice's prayers for divine favor for herself and others. She carried the billet over her heart when she prostrated herself in the ceremony. It was believed that prayers rendered in that time would be answered.

Thérèse's billet asked that Jesus take her before she committed any faults in the community; that she seek and find only him; that other people (denominated *les créatures*) count for nothing to her nor she to them. Yet she also asked that she be able to save souls and that all those in purgatory be saved. Most striking are her closing words: "Jesus, forgive me if I say things I mustn't, I want only to gladden you and console you."[50]

For Céline it was a jarring note. Thérèse and she had engaged in steady, mutual assurance that nothing had parted them nor ever could. They were one at heart. But now, as Thérèse was taking in full the implication from Juan de la Cruz that as Jesus is everything and we are nothing, there could be no point in any earthly bond, Céline was being dispossessed, poor and miserable creature. Sundered from Thérèse, she could no longer count for anything.

Neither sister could afford to dwell upon this definitive and irreversible parting from one another. But Thérèse found a way round it. Her subterfuge to make Céline a kind of honorary Carmelite (Jesus already fastening the mystical ring on her finger), and to enlist her into the Carmel itself to become another bride of Jesus, was a transparent tactic to make sure there would be no division nor alienation between her and Céline. Only as brides of Jesus could they remain as one. In effect, Thérèse was having it both ways, or, in the famous phrase of her childhood's bout with Céline over some cloth fragments for dolls, she was choosing everything, and everything meant Jesus in the mystical way, but it also meant Céline, too, whenever the two sisters needed each other.

After her profession of vows, Thérèse wrote to Céline[51] that Jesus wanted his bride to be an *orpheline* so as to be alone with him.[52] As to the all-ness of Jesus, Céline took Juan de la Cruz more seriously than Thérèse herself, and could not bear what seriousness unequivocally meant.[53] At some time late in her life, Thérèse carved into the inside of her cell's door the claim of exclusivity, "Jesus is my sole love."[54] After her sister's death, Céline had a board nailed over this carving. It was removed only after Céline's own death, more than sixty years later.

Ever shrewd, Gonzague had it right: "Alas, our nature is always re-connecting us with the matter of this life."[55] And with one another. Thérèse's greatest challenge within Carmel, short of the ultimate darkness, was her keen attachment to Céline. The difference from the darkness is that she did not recognize it as a challenge or a temptation. In trying to console, uplift, and advise her sister, she was, consciously or not, performing the same tasks for herself. She made it harder for herself in continuously insisting that they were, almost mystically, one. The rhetoric of sharing in adolescence passed into a rhetoric of identity for early adulthood or, as Thérèse put it, of unity, something greater than the union of, say, their cousin Jeanne Guérin and her husband, Francis La Néele.[56] She even told Céline that Jesus had prepared for them not two places, only one in heaven, "indeed the same throne is doubtless reserved for those who on earth were never but a single soul."[57] That Thérèse could write such flummery suffices to show her earnestness; she was not only ignoring, or better, flouting Jesus's own injunctions against family ties but Teresa's as well. She could not let go of the deep psychological bond established in her childhood. Céline had unstintingly performed as her confidante at home, her protector at school, her playmate, not one of the maternal guides and sometimes scolds that their older sisters, Pauline and then Marie, had become in place of their departed mother.

Thérèse's bogus mysticizing of this bond took renewed impetus from the tensions Céline underwent when other young women were marrying. Jeanne Guérin's wedding had been close enough to home; she was a virtual sister to the Martin girls. A few weeks later came the wedding of Jeanne's cousin on her mother's side, Marguerite-Marie Maudelonde, to a magistrate, René Tostain, who consternated the Guérins and the Martins with his atheism. But far weightier, I believe, was the marriage of Marie Asseline to Marguerite-Marie's brother, Henry, who had once eagerly courted Céline. "He's mad about you!" Marie Guérin had once reported.[58] The wedding party, April 20, 1892, is well known in Ms A (82r) as the occasion when Thérèse, fearing Céline's sociability, prayed that her sister would not be able to dance. And so it happened, but Céline's version tells more.

At the Carmel reception parlor's grill, Thérèse, somehow apprised of the impending party, was weeping as her sister had never seen her weep. She was also indignant. She asked Céline to think of Shadrach, Meschach, and Abednego, the Jewish bureaucrats of Nebuchadnezzar, who chose to be cast into the fiery furnace (Daniel, chapter 3) rather than to worship the idol their employer king had set up, "And you, the bride of Jesus, do you really want to make a compact with the world and adore its idol by delivering yourself up to its dangerous pleasures?"[59]

Thérèse's near desperate anxiety, muted in her autobiographical account but vivid in Céline's memory, is touchingly ridiculous. Thérèse did not regard their parents' marriage as a compact with the dangerous world, but it would have been terrible if, like them, like her uncle and aunt, like her cousin, Céline married, because Thérèse had convinced herself that Céline was already a Carmelite. That was clear in her dressing down before she could let her sister leave the parlor "See how God recompensed his loyal servants and try to imitate them."[60] Céline resolved not to dance (a resolution perhaps extorted from her before she left the Carmel that day), tucked a crucifix into her pocket, and prayed ardently. Thérèse, in the language of the novice mistress's *Pensées*, was not getting ahead of divine grace but seconding it with "sustained eagerness."[61]

This comic episode reveals Céline's peculiar deference to Thérèse's having passed into a spiritual life with its own special gravity. Céline could not allow herself to get beyond her sister's injunctions and to perceive both Thérèse's cruelty, the sharper for being unconscious, and the fathoms of insecurity beneath that cruelty. In their shared sensitivity and vulnerability, both very young women, Thérèse now nineteen and Céline just short of twenty-three, worked roughly upon each other, or as Bishop Fénelon was fond of putting it, one diamond was polishing the other.

Thérèse borrowed her censoriousness from Pauline. When the allurements of the world exerted themselves, Pauline deprecated Céline's interest in a career, "Give up the pointless effort of painting," but sacrificing her talent was not enough, because the real menace was the lascivious appeal of men which threatened to bear Céline away, "you whose soul is like a cloud.... [D]o not dissipate yourself nor commingle with the world's poisonous breath...." Unlike Thérèse at twenty, Pauline at a much riper thirty could see Céline's world on its terms: "the environment in which you live provides more than one mirage and sometimes you might believe that it is we who are living in shadows."[62] That belief amounted to the world's contempt that Carmelites, following the *Imitatio Christi*, expected and even desired in living each with her cross.

Thérèse told Céline that Jesus wanted her purest joys to become sufferings so that she would turn to him. But she did not identify what were her sister's purest joys. They could not possibly be marital, since "in the moment she was united with a young pagan who breathes only profane love, it seems to me Céline would have to tremble and weep."[63] That poisonous breath! "Pagan" was the code word for any man who might take her away. And yet, there were magnificent examples of women who managed with genuinely pagan husbands: Monica and Cecilia, among the hardiest of saints. The cloistered Martins had little trust in their sister's good judgment because their thorough ignorance of the waltzing world Céline knew made them fearful and helpless. Having turned their backs upon the world even before entering it, Pauline and Thérèse sought to control someone who had learned its appeal to her heart.[64]

Céline, short of entering Carmel, obliged Thérèse to ponder the hardship of her own life's election. Submission to the arbitrary and exacting discipline of the Order could be justified only by the rock-solid conviction in oneself that it had been worth it. What challenged Thérèse was not any phantasy of marital bliss or any life beyond the Order—such imagining never visited her—but her own incapacity to live up to the Order. As she could not, she needed Céline, the supposedly stronger sister, to help her through it. The piquant irony is that when she was dying a few years later, Thérèse had come to accept the uxorious model of Saint Cecilia as fully commendable, and Céline, having left the secretly cherished prospect of marital life forever behind her, faced more than sixty years of a celibacy she had never truly wanted. (Figure 3.2.)

FIGURE 3.2 Céline in her late eighties. She died on February 25, 1959. Copyright Archives du Carmel de Lisieux

It defies epistolary facts to assume a smooth linear progression in which Thérèse came to her saintly imperfection, shaped by the counsel of her trusted and sagacious elders, Gonzague, Pichon, Marie des Anges. Céline shaped her far more effectively than these counselors because she performed a number of roles they could not assume and that had some resonance within Thérèse: the other self, the antagonist, one who could take risks, even the teacher. In the latter role, when listless with boredom at her Uncle Isidore's home, La Musse, Céline wrote that her soul was passing through "a sequence of nothings or rather one mysterious nothing...in shadows...I think of nothing," "propped without a prop," she adds, showing she had read Juan's paradox.[65] Thérèse's summons to her to join in the Carmelite mission of saving souls fell aborning.

Céline was at loose ends, facing a void alone, her sisters all safely accounted for elsewhere.[66] Thérèse read from her that Juan's purgative darkness could be traversed apart from monastic life. In such exalted talk, she was not only speaking Thérèse's language but also claiming parity—and where better to be despised and helpless than in the world. The Carmelites could not feel such contempt; they were hidden within communal walls. Céline in her boredom felt it unlikely she could ever enter Carmel, no matter that her sister was behaving as though she had already arrived there.[67]

Thérèse's injunction that like Zachaeus (Luke 19:4) they should both descend and become themselves a lodging for Jesus was piteous rhetoric.[68] Céline had made herself a lodging for the *Sainte Face* she knew well, her father's, and she could not imagine her soul empty of *"créatures."* For her to save countless souls would be one thing; to wheel her semiparalyzed and babbling father into a garden was another. To make herself a dwelling place for Jesus was one thing; to see at a chapel or in a parlor the man who adored her was another.

IV. Thérèse and Marthe de Jésus

Thérèse was fully aware of her sister's rootedness in the world at large, and her exhortations to Céline, her untiring protestations of their oneness, were tactically posed to counter and confound that alien life from which she herself was forever sundered. At the same time, in Céline she was having to fight her own need of attachment, of bonds that carried over from a former life and became more imposing for having survived the transition. She recognized the problem as the egotism it was. Of her soul she wrote "Alas, I realize that mine is not wholly void of me."[69]

Late in 1892, well before she became *compagne* to the other novices, she had to face a genuine crisis concerning an attachment she saw in another novice, Marthe de Jésus, an attachment not to her but to the prioress, Gonzague. Such an inclination was not uncommon among the younger sisters of Carmelites, who, suddenly without their families, naturally were drawn to the community's maternal guide as a new locus of warmth and comfort. Novices had to learn that the prioress was there chiefly as Christ's substitute, burdening them with Christian obligation to others and even to themselves in not comforting ways. Thérèse herself had been drawn to Gonzague, who was only three years younger than Mme. Martin. How gratifying to be given another mother, truly so called, who had known Thérèse since her tenth year, when Pauline had entered the Carmel. Gonzague had called her Theresita from the start and had kindly supported her application to the Carmel when the Church hierarchy had resisted it.

As when she had reproached her cousin Marie for her attachment to Céline, Thérèse now had to reproach a fellow novice for what she believed was an unwholesome one-way bonding with the prioress. It is not certain why Thérèse felt that Gonzague herself would not correct this potentially grave inclination or that Marie des Anges, as novice mistress, would not do so. In the way of school girls, it seems to have been something only the novices were aware of among themselves. Thérèse makes much of it in recounting in C the decisive episode with Marthe, but she does not say how hazardous it was for her to be interfering where she had no authority.

From notes prepared for the second hearing on her sister's beatification, Pauline has left invaluable testimony indicating that Thérèse was aware she was overstepping and consulted Pauline in the sacristy "'Pray hard for me,' she said in a grave voice. 'The Blessèd Virgin has inspired me to enlighten Sister Marthe. I'm going to tell her tonight what I think of her.' 'But you're risking exposure,' I told her, 'and then Our Mother won't be able to support you any longer and you'll be sent to another convent.' 'I'm quite aware of that,' she answered, 'but since I'm now sure that it's my obligation to speak, I mustn't weigh the consequences.'"[70]

Florence Marthe Cauvin was almost eight years older than Thérèse. From the age of six, she had lived in an orphanage run by the Sisters of St. Vincent de Paul. She entered Lisieux as a *converse*, one of four sisters who served as domestics in the cloister, preparing the food, performing the housekeeping. They were distinctive from the choir sisters by retaining a white veil after the profession of their vows. It may have irked Marthe that although she had entered the Carmel in December 1887, four months before Thérèse, she was finally permitted to profess her vows only after Thérèse had professed hers.[71] Such differences seem stupendously petty but could suffice as occasions for resentment, just as in secular life.

In a profile of the Carmel community in that time, a fellow sister has written of the effects of a harsh childhood on Marthe de Jesus: "Having been deprived of affection, she was excessively attached to her prioress and would show herself rather aggressive all her life.... While admiring Thérèse, she used to suffer from repeated violent attacks of jealousy in her regard."[72] Even so, the extant photos of this small woman (a head shorter than Thérèse) suggest a rugged personality. She sometimes welcomes the vanity of Céline's camera with good humor while other sisters are staring blankly.

The class racket goes unobserved in the remarks just quoted. A *converse* sister could be given tasks (ordered around) by any choir sister, a fixed condition that promoted some *esprit de contradiction*.[73] Marthe de Jesus, like her namesake, the sister of Lazarus who was ever distracted by her chores[74] and had no leisure time to spend with Jesus—only to be gently reproached by him for complaining!— had to defer to a sister much younger than she and who after their nearly five years together in amity was appointed her *maîtresse*. She now had to defer to her friend daily. And Thérèse had half of her family within the walls, an extraordinary privilege sharply apparent to an orphan. Céline, who herself had been considered for what would have been, to her, a degrading position as *converse* and who entertained no high estimate of almost anyone in the Carmel community, characterized Marthe as "hardly intelligent and without a calling to Carmel. She exhausted the diligence and strength of the Servant of God [Thérèse], evidently to no purpose."[75] Pauline's remembrance of Marthe is scarcely more positive.[76]

The hazard Thérèse was running in a confrontation with Marthe is addressed in the fourth chapter of the Constitutions (dating from 1581) warning against particular friendships. Well and good, but Thérèse in speaking alone with Marthe was violating procedures set down in the Carmel Constitutions regarding weekly chapter. It was there and then only, with all the sisters assembled, that one sister could speak of a fault committed by another. By initiating a private exchange, Thérèse was going even further, acting without the prioress's permission. She knew that Gonzague would not have granted it. Instead, she gave herself leave by claiming that the Virgin herself had authorized her talking to Marthe. Had she been ordered to explain herself, recourse to the Virgin would not have helped.

If Marthe was as subject to "repeated violent attacks of jealousy" as alleged, Thérèse was foolhardy in confronting her. Marthe would have only had to report her in the chapter meeting to precipitate a disaster in the community. A sister accused could not contest or retaliate with counter charges, lest she seem to be sowing discord. Pauline foresaw trouble and forewarned Thérèse to no effect. That Thérèse felt it imperative to act seems strange, since Gonzague's term as prioress was to expire in just four months. Such a change in the priorate was, however, not a consideration in this matter. Thérèse indicates in C why she was able to act with some confidence, despite the risk. She recalls her first year at the Carmel and that Marthe's "childlike character effaced the difference in our ages"[77] and then adds words omitted in the *Historie d'une âme*: "Soon, my Mother, you had the joy of seeing your two little postulants understanding one another wondrously and becoming inseparable." Gonzague even allowed them "little spiritual talks" together.[78] As Marthe added, some twenty years later, these talks were "for my soul's profit."[79]

Those words are in print, but in her initial draft for the hearing, Marthe speaks less abstractly and with painful self-deprecation in regard to Thérèse: "...she seemed always happy to receive me, and she smiled amiably at me, something she undoubtedly did out of virtue. Indeed, what pleasure could she find in talking with a poor, little ignoramus like me, who of course must have bored her rather than having engaged her interest." Besides, Thérèse's disarming smile was in its way a grief for others to bear. Marthe, presuming Thérèse had some arcane access to a happiness, which eluded herself, went for help to their *maîtresse*, Marie des Anges. "How I would like to be like Sister Thérèse of the Child [sic], she seems so happy, so consoled. She [Marie des Anges] smiled at my confiding and told me her soul was like mine, in the greatest darkness. That surprised me, persuaded as I was to the contrary."[80] Marthe did not draw the conclusion recorded by Thérèse in C, that appearances are so often false because of one's own imputations that color them.

The depth of Thérèse's commitment to this hapless soul is suggested in an anecdote Marthe records concerning one of the periodic rumblings when the Carmels feared the anticlerical government would expel them from their communities. Marthe claims that Thérèse told her, "Do you realize that if we have to leave, I won't abandon you, you will come with me? But what will your [natural] sisters say, they won't want to accept me into their company? If they don't want you, she replied, I'll rent a little room and we'll live together, the two of us."[81]

The confrontation over Gonzague, precisely dated by Marthe to December 8, 1892, began and ended quite unexpectedly, given all the jealousy. There are no less than four accounts of it: one in C, Marthe's formal, published 1911 and 1916 depositions, and her preparatory notes. To the extent that they can be conflated, here is what happened. Before mass Thérèse called Marthe to her cell, sat her down beside her on the straw bed and embraced her (another contravention of the Constitutions), "something she never did."[82] Marthe rested on her breast and listened to the caveat about her hazardous closeness to Gonzague, that it was painful to God that she should be so self-seeking, all this given "with words so tender, testifying to her such a great affection that soon her tears were mixed with mine."[83] Thérèse seems to have been unaware that in detaching Marthe from Gonzague she risked attaching Marthe to herself. (Figure 3.3.)

FIGURE 3.3 Thérèse and Marthe de Jesus. Copyright Office Central de Lisieux.

Substantial differences in her recollections of Thérèse's words occur between Marthe's 1911 and 1916 testimonies, a fact that raises the question of just what Thérèse did tell her, but the substance of the advice was unequivocal and amounts to the same thing in the two accounts.[84] Marthe attests that she accepted Thérèse's urgent counsel at once. In her preparatory notes, however, she tells a different story, claiming that Thérèse admonished her to see Gonzague only "for truly useful and indispensable matters. Then she confided to me the sacrifices she'd made at the start of her religious life. But not being content with her reflections, however proper, I answered her vigorously. You go there so why can't I do as you do?" As this incident occurred before Thérèse became her overseer, Marthe in her forceful objection was clearly appealing to their equality as novices. In response, Thérèse justified her visits to Gonzague: "I no longer have to deny myself this consolation because my heart has been strengthened in God."[85] Thérèse had to face a remonstration that argued the parity between them which Marthe wanted, a parity conformable to that little room for rent after expulsion. But the four versions of one incident, a miniature *Rashomon*, leave at best an approximation, tears and hugs apart.

These two young women, bereft of their mothers when they were still little children, desperately needing ordinary human affections and affirmations, and feeling them for each other, had to cut themselves off from such warmth and sustenance. Gonzague provided a painful occasion for this surgery upon the friendship that had grown between the two postulants-become-novices. Thérèse obliged Marthe and herself to say goodbye to their own very human hearts. Marthe, an emotionally crippled person, was told suddenly and brutally to walk without crutches, like someone in a gospel story. Thérèse had to stagger on, seeking that void of the self. If, on that tearful and bitter day, she had been thinking of a gospel text other than that of the day's lesson, it might have been Peter's pointed questioning of Jesus (Matt. 19:27): "We have given up everything and have followed you. What shall there be for us?" None of the synoptic narrators indicates that Peter and the other disciples rejoiced in Christ's answer.

V. Reaching Sr. Saint-Joseph

Most of the Carmelites around Thérèse, noticed in Céline's photographs and some of them briefly passing through the writings, remain hazy presences, at best. Her natural sisters have all received book-length attention. At the beatification hearings, only six of the spiritual sisters testified, three of them having been under Thérèse's guidance when she was *compagne de novices*. They predictably corroborated Pauline's advancement of her sister's cause. Then they withdrew, only fleetingly noticed and prayed for at death's occasion, each encased within her obituary, the *circulaire*.[86]

Such abiding obscurity was exactly what Carmel was meant to embrace and to cultivate. If sainthood meant that Thérèse's "little way" was to be illumined with the glaring lights of celebrity, that did not require any one of her sisters to be aglow beside her. And yet, the *circulaires* themselves open a window onto an uncelebrated sort of saintliness, one hinted or implicit, suggested rather than proclaimed. The irony is that these *circulaire* profiles were written by Pauline, who, having been appointed in 1923 to the anomalous title of prioress for life by Pope Pius XI, years later wrote of her realizing that the true saints remain unknown. Perhaps the portraits she made in the *circulaires* brought that insight and she had learned to see Jesus in these women, as Thérèse had learned and taught.

Two women never called to the beatification hearings are ones to miss keenly. The first of these is Marie de Gonzague, the prioress many times over and the addressee of Thérèse's last major writing. By the time of that writing, she had been the formative leader of the Carmel community for twenty-five years. She inherited it from the first generation's Mère Geneviève and lived to see a new, budding generation of Carmel sisters pass through their novitiates before she died of cancer of the tongue in 1904.

When in 1903 a pious visitor to the Carmel, having met the Martin sisters, recalled of Gonzague, "she was colder, less enthusiastic, not so feminine. There were no exclamations in her language," even though she apparently considered Thérèse "an extraordinary soul in the matter of saintliness."[87] Gonzague knew more about saintliness than did this visitor, and he less than she about Carmel and its not so exclamatory life. She might have been enthusiastic about Thérèse, but she had long seen it as her duty to reign in the pushy politics of the Martin sisters, especially Pauline's, about the youngest among them.

In the second round of hearings toward canonization, the *procès apostolique*, Pauline and other sisters spoke out harshly about Gonzague but nothing exceeds the bitterness of what Pauline wrote in preparation for the hearings but did not include. Once, reproaching Pauline for expressing concern about Thérèse's health, Gonzague erupted, allegedly, as follows: "Well! That's what comes from having sisters! Undoubtedly, you want preferment for your sister, but I have to proceed otherwise. She's much prouder than you think. She has to be constantly humbled. Besides, she seems to have come here just for the quiet life, she's a good-for-nothing, and I'm not alone in saying so. If it's her health you've come to beg about, leave that to me, it's not your business."[88]

Complicating that surcharged air, obviously very early on in Thérèse's life at Carmel, is Pauline's confession in her private notes that she had long abused her sister, beginning at home: "...I grumbled at her sometimes and very severely, when I was in a bad mood. I attributed to her some feelings of pride or jealousy, I accused her of something she hadn't done. Later, at the Carmel, she told me I had been mistaken much of the time."[89] But Pauline continued with her domestic severities toward Thérèse even at the Carmel, finding faults in trivialities: "...and the more she wept, the more I faulted her. I refused to pardon her, nothing appeased me, and I stayed angry for a good while. I excused myself in thinking she had to learn discipline....I tormented her for her alleged slowness and her lack of carefulness..."[90] Pauline thus knew quite well how to keep her sister from the preferential treatment Gonzague presumed the Martins sought for her.

Complementing these arts of reproach are a number of notes (*billets*) Gonzague sent her before and during her years in Carmel. Thérèse must have written the prioress upwards of fifteen letters, of which only two survive, one of major significance.[91] As in C she confided to Gonzague the darkest particulars about her final testing, it is a tease to guess what Thérèse might have shared with Gonzague in writing before June, 1897. Those *billets* were either destroyed or suppressed when the *Histoire d'une âme* was published.

The other missing witness for the beatification hearings, Sr. Marie de Saint-Joseph, offers an entirely different profile. Fifteen years older than Thérèse, she entered the Carmel at twenty-three, in 1881. Marie-Joséphine-Lucie Campain thus occupied with a few other sisters, including the two older Martins, the middle generation of the Carmel during Thérèse's decade among them. These middle-agers, outnumbered, were suspended between the authoritative elderly (Mère Geneviève,

Mère Hermance, Mère Marie des Anges, and Mère Gonzague among others) and the youthful generation of postulants and novices. They had neither a claim to the wisdom of the older sisters nor an excuse to assume the wayward exuberance of the younger.

Sr. Saint-Joseph had one of the few beautiful voices in the Carmel. Indeed, she was its nightingale, according to the *sous-prieure*, Marie des Anges.[92] She proved invaluable to the Carmel for her ability to write legibly and quickly in refractory circumstances. It was she who, veiled and in the semidarkness behind the grille, recorded verbatim notes from retreats that Almire Pichon gave to the Carmelites, notes from which Thérèse apparently drew.[93] Yet everyone shunned this woman. (Figure 3.4.)

She was given to sudden swings of mood, including fierce rages. Naturally, this bizarre behavior disconcerted anyone in her vicinity, and no one was disposed to work with her. It might be wondered how someone subject to what is now loosely called mood disorder could have been retained in a spiritual community.[94] Nothing in the Carmelites' Rule or its Constitutions had provided for cases of psychological abnormalities, there being no appreciable clinical recognition of them in Teresa's time. In 1909, after nearly thirty years in the Carmel, Sr. Saint-Joseph was expelled. Back in secular life she corresponded amicably with Pauline. She died in 1936.

FIGURE 3.4 Sister Marie of Saint Joseph, 1903. Gifted with a beautiful voice and a calligraphic hand, she was prone to violent raging, and was forced to leave the Carmel, in 1909, after nearly thirty years within it. Copyright Archives du Carmel de Lisieux

Once again, Pauline's negative portrait of a sister puts Thérèse into the hallowing position when dealing with her. Of Sr. St. Joseph Pauline writes that "The Mother Prioress rightly judged that it was impossible to impose so staggering a burden on anyone," but Gonzague nonetheless allowed Thérèse to work with Sr. St. Joseph in the linen room. Pauline goes on: "...with her poor sick mind, she made her heroic counsellor endure a genuine martyrdom....[Thérèse] had to struggle, wear herself out, and put up with awful scenes some of the time....[S]he was well aware that her exertions were, so to speak, fruitless."[95] Like Pauline's estimates of Marthe and of Gonzague, this one seems dubious. There were outbursts enough, but it is unlikely that Thérèse regarded her own efforts as futile. She did not presume to be able to cure or heal the charge she assumed, only to deal with her as discreetly as she could.

Sr. St. Joseph's expulsion compromised anything she might have recalled at the beatification hearings, but there is sufficient evidence that Thérèse managed to approach her and secure her unusual favor. She volunteered to work with her in the laundry. She also shared some of her poetry, which Sr. Saint-Joseph copied and sent home to her family. (Sr. Saint-Joseph had lost her mother when she was nine years old.) In eight cursory notes to this difficult woman from the fall of 1896 into the summer of 1897, none so substantial as to be called a letter, Thérèse addressed her in the third person as "le petit Enfant," the little child whose task was to cast flowers upon the dormant Jesus or to serve as a private in his army or to be his missionary. In two notes, Thérèse gave herself the unusual denomination of ambassador, but another tag she gave herself, *petit frère*, indicates the gaming, egalitarian nature of this relationship, that she was an adoptive older sibling, rather as in her relationship with another inward and unfortunate soul, Maurice Bellière. Thérèse succeeded in disarming Sr. Saint-Joseph by enlisting her in a privately shared mission, which made this marginal woman feel altogether special.

What emerges most remarkably in this game is Thérèse's appointment, as it were, of Sr. Saint-Joseph to the role that she herself had always embraced, the small child, and with that role its indispensable performance of littleness, scattering flowers before Jesus. She called up that image of innocence and abandon in her first manuscript (A 58v), but it became iterative and almost obsessively present in one of the folios of her September 1896 retreat notes.[96] This striking frequency in Manuscript B suggests its possible concurrence with her first *billets* to Sr. Saint-Joseph, neither of which bears a date. Reinforcing that connection is her referring to Sr. Saint-Joseph as "a child missionary and warrior, what a wonder!"[97] These are two of the masculine titles of authority and empowerment that in B she claims to have put behind her as they were bootless fantasies. Here, covertly, they are re-instated with "the little child" as if Thérèse had realized that her own littleness would suffice as a calling for this adopted sister as well.

Immediate to the Carmel's politics, however, was the possibility that one or another sister would go to Indo-China and serve at one of the daughter Carmels of Vietnam, in Saigon or Hanoi. Gonzague, bruised by the contentiousness of her re-election, had expressed the wish to go there, but she was now prioress, so it was an idle expression of her exasperation. Pauline had also been considered. Had Céline and their cousin, Marie de l'Eucharistie, gone together (for awhile that was a possibility), the pressures of the "Martin clan" would have been relieved. But Thérèse, with her own health in serious doubt, knew that Sr. Saint-Joseph would never be eligible for such a mission. Her including Sr. Saint-Joseph in her missionary fantasy is a singular charity, as she wrote these words of a hidden compact to console them both: "The most painful, the most LOVING martyrdom is ours since Jesus is seeing it. It'll never be revealed to earthly "creatures." But when the Lamb opens the book of life, what astonishment for the Heavenly Court to hear proclaimed with the names of missionaries and martyrs the name of poor little children who never achieved brilliant deeds."[98] Meanwhile, what heady fare for an isolated and unhappy woman to read about herself, and all this from a novice!

The elective affinity went deeper in the last year. Sr. Saint-Joseph did not proceed altogether easily in her close order drill as a soldier, nor was she always as Thérèse once commended her, "courageously earning golden epaulettes."[99] She admitted to not seeing Jesus carrying her in his arms, as Thérèse had told her he would, and she suffered from nocturnal terrors of abandonment. Thérèse urged her to be sacrificial, effectively to let go of any claim on Jesus, to close her eyes until calm, if not joy, ensued. As to chimeras, it was best not to fight them—the sort of counsel Thérèse herself received from her confessor, Abbé Youf.

The last notes to Sr. Saint-Joseph embroider a conceit that had first occurred to Marie des Anges; to her, Sr. Saint-Joseph may have been a nightingale, but for Thérèse the obligatory littleness meant that Sr. Saint-Joseph would have to content herself as a chaffinch. While Sr. Saint-Joseph is singing, "me, like a poor little sparrow, I'm trembling in my corner."[100] Thérèse once imposed upon her older charge a mock penance for importuning her up the stairs of their "barracks" by obliging her to sing in "the prison of love." Toward the end, when daily expecting to die and cut off from any exchanges with Sr. Saint-Joseph, she suggested that as God had chosen to remove the branch on which the chaffinch had been resting, it was time for the bird to take wing.

Sr. Saint-Joseph's importance in the last year's chronicle is easily overlooked. She was not one of the novices, who formally required Thérèse's daily counsel and guidance. She did not enjoy the exceptional prestige of the newly arrived spiritual brothers, Bellière and Roulland. She was obviously not a part of the tight familial circle of Martins, nor did she bear any authority. Isolated psychologically from the community, she attracted Thérèse for exactly that reason. Thérèse had no difficulty recalling how terribly hurtful her own isolation in school had been, especially after Céline was graduated. She knew how easily an isolated person could be misunderstood, the victim of cruel imputations. But Thérèse helped Sr. Saint-Joseph by looking forward with her, rather than back, forward all the way into the next world. The predication of their solidarity was that poor martyrdom of special love, forever—on earth, that is—inconspicuous but given its final account in "the book of life."

Through Sr. Saint-Joseph Thérèse discovered her common lot with the marginal and excluded. That conjunction required an improvisatory daring that her talent for immediate rapport and her imaginative panache concealed. It was a literally extraordinary mission, the rescue of someone within the Carmel and yet, because of Sr. St. Joseph's unsettling handicap, not of its ranks. In guiding the four novice charges, Thérèse took instructional cues from the Carmel's formative texts and the trove of counsel she had herself received from Pauline, from Gonzague and Marie des Anges, and even from the grandmotherly Mère Geneviève. With Sr. Saint-Joseph she was on her own; she had elected to be so. Rather than attempt to bring Sr. Saint-Joseph closer to the community, a task that her psychological imbalance would have made extremely difficult, if not hopeless, Thérèse took the easier expedient of going out to her. This is the "little way" of trustful love in its extrinsic dimension, one that was completed at the table of sinners.

From a clinical viewpoint, Thérèse was ill-equipped to confront a substantial mental disorder. It was not the disorder, however, that she addressed. Rather, it was the suffering that disorder brought, especially the shunning that the victim's raging invited. But Thérèse was not even treating that suffering. Instead, she saw it as a necessary common ground for Sr. Saint-Joseph and for herself to share and to comprehend. As to the sharing, the scriptural warrant she knew well, that wherever two or three were gathered in the name of Jesus, he would be there. It was a tender mercy when Thérèse told Sr. Saint-Joseph that Jesus was looking upon their inconspicuous martyrdom, thus making a gathering of two into three.[101] Pauline ascribed her sister's therapy to a supernatural zeal, but it is enough to assume that Thérèse knew how to paint with both brushes.

It would be a mistake to regard Thérèse's exceptional bond with Sr. Saint-Joseph as sentimental indulgence or hand-holding. It exemplifies a certain fluidity operant within a communal life otherwise strictly regulated. A novice would have no business advising a fully-fledged choir sister, and one fifteen years her senior. Such an audacity was made possible because Sr. Saint-Joseph had a need that, as she had learned from Thérèse's hortatory writings for the community,[102] this novice could meet. Thérèse had been serving as de facto *maitresse de novices* since February, 1893, an office of maternal authority she showed she could exercise conscientiously despite her very young age—she had just turned twenty. In performing that function she answered to Gonzague, who retained the title de iure, and continued to report to Gonzague when she again became prioress. The Carmelites all knew the intrinsic value of confidentiality, where hierarchism was not necessarily the first rule. Gonzague must have heard from Thérèse of Sr. Saint-Joseph's confiding in her, but Gonzague herself confided in Thérèse and Thérèse in her. That mutuality, unfortunately not to the fore among extant documents, is nonetheless the foundation stone for Manuscript C.

VI. *Thérèse Adrift*

Céline again, for a moment. No matter that Thérèse's spirituality finally took her deep down to the common lot of hopeless sinners. Her rhetoric of comfort, as it might be called, she dispensed well short of that initiation into darkness. This rhetoric is redolent with the insipidities of her time, not least in flowery phrases she uttered to Céline and which Céline drank up as a rare liqueur. Florid imagery was commonplace among the Carmelites,[103] but Thérèse embroidered her metaphors with grotesque threads: Jesus, she fancied, did not merely celebrate the flowers of the field, he was one, a lily of the valley, and Céline was a tiny dewdrop (*goulette*) fallen not from clouds but from heaven itself, to be held in the lily's calix. When Jesus came in glory, the dewdrop would reflect him, then be united with him and reign forever.[104]

Céline expressed profound thanks for this precious conceit[105] and went one better, saying that Thérèse and she were two droplets of dew made one, and they would become the ocean for this supreme Lily. This magniloquence deserves some extenuation, for it served as anodyne for the pain from which Céline needed assuagement when she found herself floundering with no clear future. The fact that Christianized flowers provided the solace undoubtedly played a part in her giving way to Carmel after her father's death in July, 1894. Beyond extenuation there is substance: Thérèse was too thoughtful, too reflective of her own Christian mission to be asphyxiated in the embalmery of her own diction. In the letter in which she concurs with Céline that they shall be the "ocean" of Jesus, she records a major advance with her cross, from the impossibility of merit to the balsam of consolation.

Thérèse's need of consolation, the dispensing being also a self-administering, derives from a fact Pauline revealed at the beatification hearings that Thérèse was "tested by almost continual dryness during her time in the Carmel."[106] Pauline adds that her sister met this challenge by finding every possible occasion for doing charitable acts, especially on behalf of those who were marginal within the community due to peculiarities of personality or illness, if not both. This testimony jibes with Thérèse's exceptional letter to Céline in which she admits to her incapacity for prayer or for the practice of "virtue." In a fetching image, she speaks of Christ's fiery love aflame on a woodpile to which she and Céline can toss from their distance only bits of straw "when we're in the shadows, the dryness."[107]

Thérèse could usually convert shortcomings and failings into minor sources of triumph. In that same letter, she confesses fears that she does not have what is required of a Carmelite (perfectability), that she is not always faithful, but she is not disheartened. All she has to do, she claims, is to abandon herself into the arms of Jesus. Yet only five days later her message is altogether different. She writes to Céline about being adrift at sea, all alone in her very little boat. "the land has disappeared from her eyes, she doesn't know where she's going, whether she's moving ahead or backward."[108] The upbeat one might expect is dislocated. Jesus is not in that little boat asleep, but in Céline's. She might feel heavy-hearted and enshrouded with night, but Jesus is resting on her suffering heart. It is she, Thérèse promises, who shall look upon Jesus's divine face, and her soul shall be consoled. That says how very alone Thérèse herself was; Jesus was no longer with her. Céline's boat was nearing safe harbor, wafted by the divine afflatus of love. The inference from these bold assurances is that Thérèse was not only feeling no love for God; neither was she feeling any from God.

All the more strange is the *envoi* to this letter: "Never has Our Lord yet refused to inspire you with what I have prayed that He tell you. Always He does us the same favors together."[109] Such claims contradict what she has just written about her aimless, rudderless boat. If she has intercessory power in prayer, how can she be without a compass? If God grants her and her sister always the same graces, why has Jesus disappeared from her boat? Why does she privilege Céline's darkness but not her own? The only positive reading admissible for the letter is that Thérèse was learning to savor the absence of consolation. The salient words are these: "The night shall become brighter than the day," an uncanny prolepsis toward the last months of her life.[110]

In what seem vagaries of her temperament, now desolate and alone, now intimately confident of Jesus, Thérèse learned to mediate between a tendency toward despair and a tendency toward presumption. Both were dangerous. Pauline cautioned against the lability of one's disposition.[111] Feeling alone and without mooring signaled the threat of far more than a failure to live up to the exactions of Carmelite life; it suggested life might itself become meaningless, that she could lose Jesus. On the other extreme, she could declare that he always conferred on her and Céline the same graces. Either she entirely credited this statement, or she was writing only what she wanted to believe.

It is difficult not to presume the latter was the case. Her confidence-building of her sister was a tonic of which she herself was perhaps too fond. Only toward her life's end did she admit in writing the critical difference between genuinely believing something to be true and wanting it to be so, but the turmoil within her had long necessitated a cultivated delusion. In that late distinction between believing and wishing to believe, her transparency of style in exposing these contradictions and weaknesses facilitates the tracking of her way through deep unrest. In a key text of this process, she refers to her favorite biblical reading beyond the gospels, the *Song of Songs*. She notes with keen delight that, the lover having vanished, the poem's young woman, in searching for him through the city, had to go beyond its gates to find him. Ergo, Jesus wants to remain hidden, even though in his mission he had to confront "the crowd of Jews" which, as Thérèse observes, rose up against him (Luke 19:48). Ergo, aggregates of people are suspect and easily become for her too much a part of the world not to be shunned. "Let's be misers to others but prodigals for Jesus," she urges Céline.[112]

It seems entirely sensible that if one wishes, as Thérèse fervently wished, to pursue the hidden way of Jesus, even as the *Imitatio Christi* enjoined, one cannot be turned attentively toward others. In a variation on the theme, Thérèse wanted to find Jesus himself needy. Hence, "let us be prodigal for him." Into the confines of this shared weakness, others could not penetrate.

At times, Thérèse seems to be an Isolde wanting her Tristan, Jesus, so entirely alone with her that they make up their own world, far from any multitudes. In wanting Jesus so much to and for herself, Thérèse was for a long while blinded to the neediness of others. By ignoring others (the Jewish crowd) she misread Jesus's lesson (Matthew 25:35–40) on how he was fed and taken in by those who do not recall doing such things, as they were feeding and taking in others, without reflecting on their own charitable acts (the original right hand not knowing what the left is doing). This spontaneity of true charity, antonymous to all calculation, Thérèse discovered only in her last years, chiefly through her novices and then, by a kind of rippling, through other sisters as well.

VII. Bearing Pauline

Thérèse carried more than one cross in those last years. The darkness disclosed in C was in some ways the most negotiable of crosses, if only because she was able to grasp it as a divine dispensation, an utmost testing both of her love for God and, at last, for others. The first cross of self was given her by her fashioned other half, Céline. Thérèse learned to bear that cross only by the toughening discipline required of her in instructing other novices. Another cross came when, in the summer of 1897, it was clear to everyone in the community that Thérèse would not live. Oddly, the weighing down of that cross upon her came from someone in whom she had found much strength and guidance, her sister, godmother, and prioress, Pauline. While Céline, well adjusted to the outer world, seems to have come kicking into the Carmel, Pauline had been drawn there by an unswerving sense of vocation, and yet both sisters taught Thérèse how futile and unhappy were the attempts each of them made to satisfy the longings of self.

The nature of that cross Pauline presented her was this: to sustain the importunities of a pious and observant Christian soul who sought an assured scenario of celestial relief, a heavenly reunion of familial souls, an everlasting recompense for all the sacrifice and suffering willingly borne in this unhappy world—this dénouement to be all but pledged, promised, secured by a dying, soon to be angelic woman who had lost the belief in heaven and had even developed a wary distaste for the very bliss, the elusive eternal bliss which Pauline so anxiously needed. (Figure 3.5.)

FIGURE 3.5 Madame Martin's holy card of the soul received into the lap of Jesus, the solace that Pauline longed for. Copyright Archives du Carmel de Lisieux.

The miserable dependence Pauline developed upon her little sister, to whom she had for three years been the Christ of the Carmel and for much longer than that a mother, recalls a no less grievous dependence their mother had weighed upon Pauline in her early teens. Adolescent Pauline, the favorite of Mme. Martin, had to become not only her confidante and closest friend but the surrogate for her mother's disappointed life by entering an order and becoming a saint. Now, Pauline was assuming her mother's needy posture and expecting far more from Thérèse, effectively that she realize the last chapter of the story that Mme. Martin had begun. It is a piteous spectacle come full circle, that Mme. Martin, who had died twenty years before, was envisioned to be waiting for Thérèse on the other end, among angels, saints, and the four little siblings who had early been lost to death.

Pauline lived out to a magnificent degree what Jesuits call a life for others, chiefly as prioress of the Lisieux Carmel for most of her nearly ninety years, but she also lived at the behest of three women in succession from her birth to her death: her importunate and needy mother, Zélie Martin; her immediate predecessor and successor in the priorate, Marie de Gonzague; and last, her adopted daughter and littlest sister, whose cause she promoted with indefatigable devotion. With her older sister, Marie, she was one of the better educated of her family and of her time. She was steeped in the Visitandine spirituality of St. François de Sales. From her parents' thrifty example she learned to be a sound administrator, but unlike her parents she had a flair for the artistic, for writing and painting, two of the few expressive outlets that bourgeois women of late-nineteenth century France enjoyed. She put these talents, as she put herself, into exclusive service to the Church community she knew.

Intelligent though she was, Pauline lived by rules and their tacit constraints upon initiative. That abiding by the book was requisite for administration, but it also exposed her lack of daring and of imagination, which necessarily feeds upon daring. Thérèse's *audace*, a definitive quality she herself acknowledged and seems to have reveled in, emerged as a foil to Pauline's propriety, as though Thérèse knowingly compensated for her sister's penchant for the procedural, the expected, and appropriate. Thus the two sisters complemented one another well: Pauline with the centripetal virtues, ever reliable, prudent, prim; Thérèse with the centrifugal ones, inquisitive, bold, exuberant. The world always needs an abundance of people of Pauline's stamp so as to insure order, regularity, routine, and ritual. Hers was a calendrical sort of temperament. It is not, however, Pauline who prompts one's curiosity about what might she say or do or discover next. Only an ardent and restive truth-seeker affords delight by rewarding that curiosity.

The drama began on May 30, 1897, when Pauline discovered during Compline, that Thérèse had begun coughing up blood well over a year before, in Holy Week of 1896. She wrote to Thérèse at once of "a genuine abyss of bitterness"[113] overwhelming her, not in the revelation of tuberculosis, for she claims to have guessed that disease already, but that Thérèse had concealed so long from her so portentous a fact. She would be devastated, she adds, were she to find out anything else about Thérèse post mortem. Pauline significantly calls this apprehension her "motherly weakness" as though consciously invoking the memory of Mme. Martin, whose letters Thérèse knew intimately. Pauline had felt she could never live up to her mother's glowing expectations. Now, the question was whether Thérèse could die to hers.

Thérèse sought to alleviate Pauline's wounded feelings. Using a trope familiar to the age, she wrote in reply that Jesus himself had torn a small corner of the envelope (her body), within which was the letter (her soul) that Pauline had begun writing twenty-four years before. (This figure plays a nice variant on the Theresian view of Jesus, the interior painter of souls.) Pauline answered that Thérèse, soon to be in heaven, would help to make her a saint. Not only that, "she'll teach her to get control of her desolating sensitivity."[114] Death, in the singular elevation of its victim, was making Thérèse into Pauline's new mother and teacher. No one needed Thérèse's sanctification more than her sister did. (Figure 3.6.)

At this time, the spring of 1897, Pauline had already discussed with Thérèse the possibility that Mère Gonzague would give permission for the resumption of the autobiography. Thérèse's new writing was meant to serve Pauline as a propaedeutic for the heavenly life, or so Pauline may well have hoped, but it was addressed to Gonzague, who, as prioress, had authorized it. As Thérèse had developed a particular bond of understanding and affection with this sometimes difficult and mercurial woman, Manuscript C can be read as a kind of appreciation. Under Gonzague's priorate, resumed shortly before Thérèse's passing into darkness, Thérèse had expanded her horizons, as the multiplicity of letters and the inclusion of new correspondents attest.[115] With the new perspectives Thérèse gained, she achieved charitably critical distance from her natural family, including her "mother" among them.

Pauline's next letter, written and sent the following day, May 31, was perhaps the most astounding that Thérèse ever received. It is about a would-be conversion experience. Her sister began by remarking that the

FIGURE 3.6 Pauline, known as Mother Agnes of Jesus, 1909. Copyright Archives du Carmel de Lisieux

statue of the Virgin had given her a special smile, perhaps akin to the one that released Thérèse from her mysterious illness in childhood. Not a cure this time, but "if you pray for me, I'm truly going to start a new life."[116] Even were Gonzague to tear up the new manuscript, Pauline was confident, "I'll feel nothing but a more powerful attraction to heaven." These were amazing pronouncements: a thirty-five-year-old woman, already seasoned as a prioress, was sounding naïve, helpless, ardent, and as green as the youngest novice.

Just what all this meant she made clear toward the close. Thankful though she was for all her sister's tactfulness (*délicatesses*) toward her, "Even so, I've been quite faithless in my little religious life, but I'm going to start to change myself, to resemble you. The good Lord will pardon me my little sins, I hope." What is most striking in the plaintive, almost adolescent ardor of these words from a woman over ten years senior to Thérèse is that they sound much like the tenor of the ingenuous and fretful Maurice Bellière's letters: the pathos of inadequacy, of straying, balanced by a resolve to hold on to (clutch) the exemplary and dying Thérèse. Pauline, deeply reverent and no less deeply needy, became the first of Thérèse's cultists.

That burden of sororal dependence Thérèse perhaps had no trouble in sustaining, but with it came a celestial script in the form of a poem Pauline had just composed. She imagines Thérèse "above the clouds peacefully at play in the fields of the Heavens." She asks Thérèse to consult the book of life to see whether she, Pauline, is destined to be at her side. Thérèse replied curtly that she found Pauline's verses far too touching and melodious, adding that she would prefer to remain silent rather than to attempt futilely to render into song what was happening within her—a very gentle putdown. Thérèse by now was not one to share others' scenarios, certainly not those of a heavenly life, that tormenting void. She had been given her own scenario by Jesus, and how different her song would have been from Pauline's!

Expressing hope that Thérèse would often come down from celestial bliss to embellish what Pauline called the little world of her heart and soul, she became the first to respond to what became her sister's self-stated universal mission, to do good upon the earth. (Thérèse had vicariously articulated that mission three months before, in her final *récréation*, on the Polish saint, Stanislaus Kostka.[117]) Pauline fancied her revenant sister would bring along the retinue of their four sibling angels; an oneiric company of the heavenly life would be vouched her short of death. (Figure 3.7.)

Faced with this piteous and sentimental longing in her sister, Thérèse was forced to speak and write in a code of equivocation, which subtly betrayed her lack of any feeling or desire for Pauline's envisioned "fields of the Heavens" but which managed an adroit balance between two now apparent contraries, charity and truthfulness. Her own interior experience of God and her family's religious

FIGURE 3.7 Pauline in 1949. She died on July 25, 1951, two months before her ninetieth birthday. Copyright Archives du Carmel de Lisieux.

convictions, mediated by Pauline as its spiritual leader, were at an undeniable variance. The best statement of all in this vein is the definitive one: "I want to spend my Heaven doing good on earth" from an *entretien* with Pauline.[118] It is Thérèse's supreme audacity. She speaks as though her destiny were elective, something she has wished and therefore chosen for herself, signifying that one could be blessed apart from the eternal community of souls with God. That to do so could amount to her heaven—or what she could now in her darkness accept as heaven—is a corollary audacity. Pauline, perhaps blinded by suffering her own anxieties, could not finally grasp Thérèse's ripely joyous predilection for suffering as the ground in which she could realize a bond of love with Jesus.[119] To Bellière a few days later Thérèse wrote with a candor she did not evince for Pauline, telling him she would find heaven all but unbearable if it cut her off from suffering for Jesus.[120] Jesus himself, she adds pointedly, would have to transform her nature if she were to accept a cloud-free heaven. She does not indicate how she would feel about such a transformation.

If she had been pressed to justify her outrageous preference for earth and its guarantee of sorrows over heaven and its imagined raptures, she would have likely answered in words she gave to Bellière: "Jesus has always made me desire what he wants to give me."[121] She was certain that in letting the darkness descend upon her, Jesus wanted her to embrace it, and so she did. Had she been pressed further, as at a heresy trial, to explain just how she knew it was Jesus's will that she enter the darkness, she might have had another Jeanne-like answer, that she was able to match the extremity of the darkness with the extremity of her solicitude for those she found there, that she was praying for them.

She could also have invoked the primary data of her own consciousness, her intuitive charity in response to the darkness, her experience of a loving she had not known before. In Thérèse's last years, with what she called her discovery of charity a trajectory becomes visible, from her unruly and willful novices to the unhappy elders of Carmel directly on to the sinners sitting in darkness. The terminus of this line is her desiderated and celestial benefaction on earth.

Another often-cited utterance, usually construed for uplift, speaks no less forcefully. To Bellière on June 9, 1897, nearly the day when she wrote to Gonzague of her darkness and her fellowship with sinners at the table of grief, she said, "I'm not dying, I'm entering into life."[122] This remark is at giveaway variance from her heroine-martyr Jeanne's "I am entering eternal life!...I see ...the angels, the elect...."[123] As the acutely impressionable, emotionally labile Bellière could not have borne the reality of Thérèse at the table of sorrow, she could not have initiated him into the extraordinary, frontier life where Jesus had taken her, where she had become a missionary of a kind different from that to which Bellière was aspiring. Unlike her Jeanne d'Arc, she was not envisioning angels and the elect but helpless, lost souls. But she did not presume that life with them would be everlasting. She would wait till time's end for "the illumination of faith" and the divine command for her to rise from the table. "I am entering into life" complements "I want to spend my heaven doing good on earth." Each is an embrace of suffering in love for Jesus. As Thérèse was inclined to dramatize life (how better than through suffering?), to transform the slightest incidents into dialogue, to re-create people by her deft mimicry, her election of the darkness given her by Jesus should be called *Thérèse accomplissant sa mission.*

In that letter to Bellière, Thérèse identified what was to her the one thing necessary: to work for God's will, not for oneself, not for *"créatures."* Yet she had no choice but to work hard to sustain Pauline in the illusions Pauline needed in order to go on. In shrewd compassion, she copied out for Pauline some cherished hortatory messages from favorite saints. Thérèse herself had cherished them, but some had become hard for her to savor, such as Théophane Vénard's "One day we'll meet again in Paradise."[124] She writes without comment, but to another sister she provided an unusual gloss on paradise.

This sister was Marie de la Trinité, the only girlish novice of the four who had been in Thérèse's charge. Céline's estimate of her was almost as harsh as the one she dispensed regarding Marthe: "so hard to educate that she should not have remained in the Carmel but for our young mistress's patience."[125] That, however, was not Thérèse's view of the only "little" sister fate chose to give her, and if Marie was not easy to discipline, she had a cheerful disposition which Thérèse knew how to treasure. Now, toward the end of May, illness forced Thérèse to give up her post as *compagne* to Marie and the others. Only her natural sisters were allowed to talk with her. Marie and Marthe felt abandoned and lamented their lot to Pauline.

Notes could still be passed. Marie de la Trinité learned that Thérèse was writing, and her curiosity about what was being written of herself occasioned a hearty laugh from Thérèse in a time otherwise tense and gloomy. Marie's *billet* has been lost but she apparently put a question Thérèse had grown tired of hearing: "You want to know if I'm happy to be going to Paradise? I would be very much so, *if I were going there*, but ..."[126] Her interlocutors did not see how alien such swell-headedness as one's heavenly future was to her. It is not known how she responded to the claim from her own *maîtresse de novices*, Mère Marie des Anges, that Thérèse would not be spending even a moment in Purgatory,[127] a station which, like the table of sorrow, was all about suffering. (Figure 3.8.)

Thérèse shared with Marie de la Trinité her revised views on ingratitude toward God for all the blessings of life given in divine love, chiefly in the sacrificial

FIGURE 3.8 Mother Marie of the Angels, mistress of novices. Therese called her "a saint of boundless kindness" but found it hard to learn from her. Copyright Archives du Carmel de Lisieux.

presence of Jesus. She had written of the ingratitude of the wicked and sinful, which she and her Carmel sisters would overcome by consoling Jesus.[128] But in one of her late prayers she made a significant transition, passing from the wickedness of unbelievers to the wickedness of the righteous. She asks God "to forget the ingratitudes of souls who have been consecrated to you and to forgive poor sinners."[129] In a letter complementary to that prayer, she expresses to Marie the wish that Jesus may still find in her the lamp of fraternal love to rejoice his heart and make him forget "the ingratitude of those who *do not love him enough*."[130] It is as though the radical deficiency in love for God which she had experienced and was then recording from the table of sorrow sharpened her sensitivity to it in a less virulent but still objectionable form among the pious.

Their deficiency in love she scored in the liveliest of her plays. In *Le Triomphe de l'Humilité*, Lucifer, suitably enraged, urges his fellow fiends to invade the monastic society of virgins and "suggest to them above all to be self-centered, for self-love is the weakness of every human being, it's even found in the cloistered communities, and I assure you, my friends, it's my most reliable weapon for slowing down the love of God in the hearts of all his nuns...."[131]

This dramatic passage might be read as Thérèse's homage to Teresa, who ended her *Camino de perfección* with the candid admission that she did not know whether she loved God. That was her way of saying that self kept coming upon her. Thérèse's admonitions via Lucifer say that she, too, was short of love for God, and that was perhaps the very heart of what she had always meant by weakness. If so, then she clung to weakness as an epistemological ballast: what she did know was her inadequacy.

VIII. Seeking Escape from Self

When undertaking to write her last manuscript, she recalled her concerns when she had started the first one, two-and-a-half years before, that her account would "dissipate my heart in pre-occupation with myself."[132] So, she told Bellière, an eloquent and self-confessed victim of egotism, that "I'm trying to be no longer occupied with myself."[133] Thérèse saw her own failings, even her own ingratitudes clearly, at least some of them. Because, as she tells Bellière, she had left everything to Jesus to work upon her soul, she had experienced the joy of starting to get free of self. But she could not claim to have gotten wholly free without finding herself ludicrously proud and self-deceived. The physics of her weakness and inadequacy was to stumble, fall, and pick herself up again. The more helpless one is, she had told Céline, the more loving is God: "He prefers to see you stumble in the night upon the stones of the way than to walk in the full light of day on an enameled path of flowers which might slow you down."[134] Now, Thérèse herself was on that stony nocturnal path, the indispensable counter to her elevator where Jesus raises up the weak, little soul.

Of the evidence of her stumbling and falling off from charity, one instance, prominent in hagiographic accounts, deserves scrutiny. Thérèse, in a vigorously appropriative way, had exerted all of her suasions upon Céline to bring her into the Carmel. I have noted that the loss of Céline's correspondence over long stretches prior to her entry in the late summer of 1894 makes it impossible to detail her feelings about the attractions of ordinary life, including marriage. It is evident that Thérèse could neither be patient nor long suffering with her sister's absence, nor could she even admit that Céline gave no unequivocal sign of a spiritual calling to surmount the many challenges facing both postulant and novice. Thérèse may have supposed that the exceptional reinforcement which Céline could count upon from her natural sisters would get her through the initiatory years. That was a risk; that it was unconscionable of the sisters within the walls to have taken it, is debatable. It is strange that Gonzague, sympathetic to Thérèse in this delicate familial politics, was an enthusiastic advocate of Céline's entry.[135]

Thérèse's rationale for coopting Céline is recorded in her autobiography: "The only thing I couldn't accept was that she not be the bride of Jesus, indeed loving him as much as I. It was impossible for me to see her giving her heart to a mortal. I had already suffered a lot in knowing she was exposed to dangers in the world that had been unknown to me."[136] She was speaking for Pauline as well, her addressee. In their ignorance of the wider world, an ignorance briefly relieved for Thérèse in her journey to Rome in 1887, they naturally feared it and conjured up its dangers. But the real danger for Thérèse was that she might have to give up her possessiveness.

Ex post facto, more than ten years after Thérèse's death, Céline ratified her sister's pushiness by claiming to have had a vocation, even though it had hung so narrowly in the balance before the advances of her second cousin, Henry Maudelonde, that "I would have only had to say one word, [to give] one glance! When I muse about it, I'm seized with amazement. My vocation was so close to eclipse! It seems to me it was hanging by a thread."[137] That admission would have sufficed for any priest to tell her to re-examine herself, that perhaps she had no vocation at all. Céline's choice of a marital partner would have seemed—and therefore would have amounted to—an unbearable rejection of Thérèse, an option for a realm in which everything was supposed to be pointlessness and vanity.

In a less weighty instance of failure in charity, Thérèse tells on herself after an importune visit from Sr. Marie de Jean-Baptiste. This sister, age fifty, was in charge of the linen room, which was near Thérèse's cell. On a few occasions, she had opened without warning the door to the antechamber of the cell, where Thérèse as *compagne* met with her four novices. Pauline later wrote that the novices, observed from the linen room as they came and went, were indignant over this intrusive behavior, "but they were at the same time edified by the behavior and counsel of their prudent mistress [sic] who remained calm."[138] On the occasion at issue, one we have already glimpsed, Thérèse lost patience and somehow showed it—a scowl, maybe, or a sharp word of reproach or refusal, or all of that—enough that it registered. Pauline, present at the time, noted that Sr. Saint Jean-Baptiste had come to ask Thérèse's immediate help with a painting. Pauline objected that her sister was feverish and exhausted but to no avail. "Then an emotion appeared on the face of Sister Thérèse of the Child Jesus, and that evening she wrote me...."[139] Pauline's "an emotion" is unhelpful and evasive of the very facts that prompted Thérèse to reproach herself in a sardonic tone: "Oh, this evening, I've shown you my virtue, my TREASURE CHEST of patience!.. And I'm the one who preaches so well to others!!!!!!!!!!!!!!!!.. I'm glad you've seen my imperfection."[140] The brisk punctuation and the capitals show Thérèse not only derisive of herself but of others such as Pauline and the novices as well, who had already begun to mistake her for a seraph. She knew better and said so without stinting.

Her example, underscoring that humility meant an unending lowering of self, taught that one needs that lowering. She was no Uriah Heep, feigning to be always in that lower position. This incident underscores something Thérèse herself had perceived, that Pauline might have seen her sister's imperfectability but could not accept it. She had started to invest too much of herself in the process of enameling Thérèse with an inviolable piety.

Both sisters say much about themselves within the small compass they occupied that day with Sr. Saint Jean-Baptiste. Pauline's inability to admit fully and openly to her sister's quite human limits became the foundation stone for canonization, but Thérèse's failing was the occasion for showing her ruthless candor, her urge for the truth, even when she found truth turned against herself. This animated *billet*, trivial though the prompting event was, is one of Thérèse's indispensable writings, a vinaigrette to savor.

A more ample testimony of her falling off from patience and charity occurs in the very center of C. Seated in her father's wheelchair at the cloister's northeast end, near the infirmary, Thérèse enjoyed the June sun as she was writing to Gonzague. She was not able to enjoy solitude, however, because other sisters, including the *infirmières*, were coming and going. She says their interruptions were costing her pen its nimbleness, even as it recorded their little kindnesses, their taking, as she writes, two thousand steps where twenty would have sufficed. One of the *converses*, Sr. Marie de l'Incarnation, aged seventy, "believes she's distracting me (from the pains of illness) with a little chatter,"[141] and so Thérèse had to hear about the hay and the poultry. No sooner was this sister gone than another came by and presented Thérèse with some freshly cut flowers, "perhaps believing she's inspiring me with poetic ideas," but Thérèse would have preferred that the flowers had stayed on their stems. "I don't know if I've been able to write ten lines without being disturbed...yet for the love of the Good Lord and of my sisters (so charitable to me), I'm trying to seem content and especially to be so." Finding, in her didactic way, a message in even minor happenings, Thérèse again told on herself. She was peeved at the sisters' disruptions but saw their benign intent, their putting charity into actions, not into fine phrases. Her forced agreeableness weighed on her, as she knew she had to contrive it for her sisters' sake. Although that contrivance was itself a kind of charity, it apparently bothered her that it was a dissembling. Her writing against herself reveals this disquiet.

A few days earlier, she had looked back over all the frets of her early novitiate, and with the ripeness of maturity she accepted her shortcomings, even to laughing at herself that "now I'm not surprised at anything and don't trouble myself in seeing that I am weakness itself. On the contrary, it's that that I boast of and each day I expect to find new imperfections in me."[142] The hens, hay, and flowers obliged her. Thus tucked away in these leisurely remarks, Thérèse's "little way" attains one of its formulations. That "way" has been construed as little daily acts by which one can work toward a cryptic sainthood. What has not been given sufficient emphasis is Thérèse's own model of a studied imperfection, an attention to daily inadequacies and failings. Her way of imperfection marked the path of trustfulness she wished to give to God. Without continuous imperfection and a continuous sense of it, trust could fall into presumption of one's sufficiency. Thérèse is not explicit but she hints at a creeping Arianism, the heresy of self-advancement, wherever a steady conviction of one's inadequacy and weakness may falter.

As her trust necessitated inadequacy, any sign of that weakness caused her joy. Every failing made her more dependent upon divine mercy. It was her way of ensnaring God's compassion. It would be a mistake to neglect or underplay the affirmative tone, almost a triumphant one, when she tells on herself. Her stance is not only contrary to human egotism, which ever seeks to promote and fulfill itself; it is also contrary to the way of perfection, the *camino* Teresa prescribed for all Discalced Carmelites. Thérèse's way controverts Jesus's own imperative that his followers be perfect, even as God is perfect. But Thérèse once drew upon this steep injunction: if Jesus commanded perfectability, she wrote to Céline, it must be possible to attain.[143] According to Pauline, Thérèse accepted Jesus's command and stood up to a priest with it. The priest told her to control her presumption that she could become a saint if, as she claimed, she could love God as much as Teresa had loved him. It sufficed her that Jesus had commanded spiritual completion, and she told the priest she would run about in a wide field towards it.

What happened to make her deviate from perfectability, to all but abandon Teresa's *camino*? She had long tried to hold onto it, but she had done so defensively. Her boldness before that priest was in part a reaction against the terrorism visited upon her for years at the Benedictine school in Lisieux. Confessors and retreat directors alike had been trained in the minatory, punitive styles of earlier generations, and most of them felt awkward and sometimes aggressive to their young female charges. The tormented life in that school came to mind whenever she heard in the reading of the *circulaires* about young sisters excruciated in their novitiate. Many years even beyond the novitiate they had spent struggling to become saintly yet they remained burdened with guilt, even anxiety about damnation. Teresa in her autobiography regularly confessed to her own damnable unworthiness. For many centuries of Christian life, there was no level terrain between the chasm of hell and the lofty peak of completion. Thérèse's wide open field in which to run, stumble, fall and run some more, an image culled from her happy summer days in the rolling country of St. Ouen-le-Pin, is itself a merciful piece of terrain. Yet the abandonment of perfectability was more than a concession to the truth of her inadequacy; it was a requisite of her self-acceptance, and it brought her a particular peace not readily shared by other sisters.

She writes primarily of the helplessness of imperfection to which sinfulness is closely related. In a letter to Céline on June 7, 1897, that Monday of Pentecost immortalized by the camera in three kneeling studies, Thérèse remarks on the envy that Céline's creative efforts (including photography) prompted within the Carmel. She observes that the only thing not envied is the last place, which from Jesus's words should be the most desired. Thérèse then offers her sister the insight that God helps in the certainty of one's nothingness: "Yes, it's one's sheer nothingness enough to humble oneself and sustain one's imperfections gently. There's the real sainthood!"[144] And there is the real audacity of Thérèse, all but claiming to have found what saintliness counts as genuine and where it is found, in last place.

As sinfulness presents the deepest ground of inadequacy, it is fair to ask how far Thérèse plumbed its significance. In her writings she speaks of sinners a total of seventy-five times. She prayed that the Carmel would embrace with divine love their multitudes.[145] But she writes about sin only seventeen times.[146] Her novices seem to have drawn her out to say something. Unlike her, they had not come to an insouciance about human failings, and they were aware of being in the grip of their own. Thérèse saw in their struggles the obverse of the priests' terrorizing, that the effect of such discipline was to instill a kind of negative narcissism, a preoccupation with the misery of self. One such victim was her cousin, Sr. Marie de l'Eucharistie, whose recitations of anxiety ("her boring twaddle about scruples") wore out Pauline.[147] Marie later acknowledged that Thérèse had perceived the dead-endedness of this neurotic behavior and admonished her to think about saving souls.

Sr. Marie de la Trinité has left this enlightening note, written to Pauline two months before Sr. Thérèse became Ste Thérèse: "What canonized saint has ever spoken like this: 'We others,' she told me, 'we're not saints who weep for their sins, we rejoice in them as they serve to glorify the Good Lord's compassion.'"[148] If Thérèse did not reach the bathyspheric perceptions of sin that Dante records in his *Commedia*, she was well informed, by herself and by her sisters, both natural and spiritual, that a futile self-oriented longing, an ever turning of self into Self, moves diametrically against the trust that must always be directed to God. Self also moves against charity, which can only be directed to others.

Thérèse learned to bear her community's cross, but no one made that bearing more burdensome than her own sisters, Céline and Pauline. In a dramatic sense, they were her foils, far more than any others among the troublesome sisters. Their need for consolation and direction undoubtedly taught her much. Perhaps from these two she best learned to smell the cheat of all consolations and the folly of all projected heavens. Choosing to spend her "heaven" on earth was, arguably, a sharp piece of wit.

4

Her Spiritual Brothers Guide Her Down: Père Hyacinthe Loyson and Léo Taxil

"Tu ne soupçonnes même pas la profoundeur effrayante et hideuse des plaies qui rongent l'humanité."
["You've no idea of the frightening and hideous depth of plagues that gnaw upon humanity."]
ISIDORE GUÉRIN to his niece, Sr. Thérèse de l'Enfant Jésus de la Saint-Face, July 24, 1897

THIS STUDY BEGAN with the two immortal Spanish masters of Carmel. It is now the turn of two people a light year from that Carmel who nevertheless decisively shaped Thérèse's life toward its end. In a previous work on Thérèse, I gave each of them brief mention.[1] They matter substantially to the present discussion because they informed her about faces that evil could assume in sovereignty over souls. A renegade priest and a world-class charlatan have that in common. They also have it in common that Thérèse prayed for both of them over her last summer. She never met either of them.

Both were, in their way, exemplary of the souls she found in her time of deepest darkness, those cut off miserably from God and left in the desolation of an atrocious aloneness, no matter their number. The story of each of them, unique, lurid, strangely sad, affords a dramatic engagement. Thérèse had a yellow journalist's view of the world beyond Carmel; she dramatized realities to a certain excess. These stories supply their own theater in abundance. In their day, they reeked of gesture, and they invited outrage. Yet both of them contribute a centripetal weight to the tunnel-and-mist pages of Manuscript C.

If Hyacinthe Loyson turned to apostasy, Thérèse, by the time of writing C, found herself on the precipice of blasphemy, where some of her writing and her offhand remarks have an astoundingly proud ring: she would at last reveal the meaning of charity! She elected to pass her heaven doing good on earth! And if Léo Taxil was a consummate con artist, what about the voices within her to which she gave words out of the gloom of her own doubt, those words that urged the embrace of nothingness? How close might she have felt to each of these men remains an imponderable issue, but she knew both of them were souls in need of retrieval. They were her escorts toward despair.

In the hagiographies, Thérèse has two "spiritual brothers," the young priests, Adolphe Roulland and Maurice Bellière, missionaries to Asia and Africa, respectively. They sustained her as loyal and substantial correspondents in the midst of her temptation, but neither could have guessed she was under that trial. In this study, she gains two other "spiritual brothers" of an entirely different ilk, kin for her within the void she found. Her position might be called her final *imitatio Christi*, as Jesus cried out in abandonment while stationed between two criminals.

What Thérèse knew of Loyson she knew only from Céline, who brought her news clippings and, perhaps, some gossip. How extensive that knowledge was, it would be impossible to determine, but it is safe to assume that it was consistently negative, Loyson being an apostate, and Céline's press sources strictly Catholic. The dramatic question that engaged Thérèse was, Might he return to the fold?

As for Taxil, she knew nothing of him until his self-revelation; she and the Carmel community knew only of Taxil's Trilby, Diana Vaughan, who posed as an escapee from a Satanic cult and was seeking Christian refuge. Her sensational published writings, all dictated by Taxil, were read in the Carmel community.[2] Thérèse was not alone in being duped, but she went to extraordinary lengths that show how engaged she was in Vaughan's rescue and salvation. The dramatic question for Thérèse in this issue was, Might Diana be brought into the Carmel?

I. Praying for Father Hyacinthe

> "Causons un peu de P. Hyacinthe. C'est folichon! chagrin pour les bonnes âmes, réjouissance pour les libres penseurs! Farce! Farce! Le pauvre homme! Il ne sait pas ce qu'il se prépare!"
> ["Let's talk a bit about Father Hyacinth. It's wanton! Grief for good souls, grist for the free-thinkers! A farce, a farce! The poor man! He doesn't know where he's heading!"]
> GUSTAVE FLAUBERT TO EDMA ROGER DES GENETTES, october 5, 1872

> "Décidément, Loyson se contente, purement et simplement, de copier Luther, son prédécesseur dans la révolte: il n'invente rien, absolument rien...."

["Decidedly, Loyson is, purely and simply, happy to ape Luther, his predecessor in revolt: he's inventing nothing, absolutely nothing..."]
LA CROIX DU CALVADOS, July 23–30, 1891, a clipping
kept by Thérèse, now in the Archives du Carmel

Having grown up securely immured within Catholicism, Thérèse remained for most of her life ignorant of atheism. The word, at least, does not figure in her writings. Nor did she write of heresy or apostasy as such, but she knew and acknowledged that the heroine of her childhood had been condemned as both a heretic and an apostate. She included these charges in her play, *Jeanne d'Arc accomplissant sa mission*, even though Jeanne knew herself to be, as Thérèse also makes clear, a loyal child of the Church. As Jeanne protests gently to the offstage voice of Pierre Cauchon, the bishop of Beauvais who performed as a hireling of the victorious English pressing for her death, had she been taken to Rome, the pope would have recognized her innocence. Cauchon took his and the Church's view of apostasy from John 15.6: "If a man abide not in me," says Jesus, "he is cast forth as a branch, and is withered; and men gather them, and cast them into the fire, and they are burned." So was Jeanne.

In an arresting moment of her poem, "My Singing on this day," written for her sister Marie's feast day (June 1, 1894), Thérèse depicts the soul, hers and Marie's alike, as a weak bough seeking to be grafted on to the Sacred Vine, Jesus, so that it might bear fruit: "And I might offer you a cluster golden of grapes, Lord, from this day forth."[3] Implicitly, the petition is saying that the branch, if not cast forth, has either been sundered from or has yet to be grafted to the trunk. The tone, however, remains ardent: the soul-branch is weak, not withered. Its strength and help can come only from Jesus. Marie, as her sister well knew, had entered Carmel less than eagerly; she had not come via the intense inner summons of a true vocation. The dark draw of anxiety remains latent in the commonplace of Christian exile, the obligatory earth-bound apartness from God. Thérèse went back to the grape cluster at the close of her first manuscript, where she included a blazon she had drawn and colored, her own coat of arms in which she, the branch, is offering to Infant Jesus the cluster to squeeze as a child would a ball. She is offering it also to the Holy Face of the tormented Jesus to staunch his thirst during the passion, Jesus's own exile from God and humanity.

For Thérèse as for any Catholic, the worst of earthly exiles was excommunication, the most dire penalty the Church can weigh as it denies an offender the sacramental life. The scandal of the Carmelite Order in her lifetime came from a rebellious priest who had once been the superior of the Carmel in Paris and was later excommunicated. Charles-Jean-Marie-Augustin Loyson, born in Orléans in

1827, had spent his seminary years at Saint-Sulpice in Paris, where he was later curate. After ordination (1851), he taught philosophy in Avignon and theology in Nantes. For five months of 1859 he was a Dominican and then entered the Discalced Order of Carmel. Within each order he was known as Père Hyacinthe. He came to be reputed an effective homilist, drawing ample acclaim for his eloquence in *conférences* at Notre-Dame beginning in 1865. During Advent in 1868 he prompted some anxiety by exceptionable remarks on marriage. To him, still securely celibate, it was "the most complete, most intimate and most holy of all unions that can exist between two people."[4] "Decidedly a dangerous fellow," Flaubert remarked of him to George Sand in that season.[5]

He broke with Rome in 1869 over the issue of papal infallibility, which was then in process of formulation for the First Vatican Council. He was excommunicated the same year. He later wrote to Pope Pius IX of looking forward to the day when a future pope would retract the dogma. Montalembert, whose own criticisms of the Vatican Council would soon win him a very small-scaled funeral, commended Loyson for his open statement of grievances but reproached him for its Protestant accents. John Henry Newman begged him to come back into the Fold.

Loyson's opposition to the decree of infallibility was hardly eccentric (the matter had deeply troubled Montalembert and Newman, too), as an ecclesiastical minority was soon springing up in revolt against the Council. Centered in Germany, opponents of papal infallibility maintained that it was against the teachings of the early Church. Besides, there had been no freedom of discussion by which to contest it. Rebel parishes came to be known as Old Catholics, a splinter sect that originated in Germany and to which Loyson briefly adhered as a pastor in Geneva, that bastion of Protestantism. But even there he proved restless, not least because he had in the meantime come under the spell of a wealthy American widow, Emily Butterfield Meriman, with whom he entered into a civil marriage in 1872. (Figure 4.1.)

It would be an instructive study to observe how profound spiritualities in the history of Catholicism have been shaped by a pairing of opposite sexes: Francesco and Chiara of Assisi, Teresa of Avila and San Juan de la Cruz, François de Sales and Jeanne de Chantal, Fénelon and Mme. Guyon, Thérèse herself and Almire Pichon, S.J., not to forget Dorothy Day and her guru, Peter Marin. Loyson, rejected by the Church, drew inspiration from Emily to found his own, which he did, in 1879. Unlike the saints of Assisi and Sales, Loyson had enjoyed a side career as a ladies' man. Women had been especially attentive to his homilies. He knew that he had no trouble in charming them, and his exalted endorsement of marriage was flattering to them in its tacit plea for parity of the sexes. The Church did not and could not go that far in acknowledging marriage as a sacrament. Besides, it was still a commonplace that a religious vocation was the optimal station in earthly life; marriage was acceptable but of a secondary status. Thérèse's parents had

FIGURE 4.1 Hyacinthe Loyson in his heyday, 1876: a Carmelite priest of great piety and charismatic charm, and founder of the schismatic Gallican Church of France. Thérèse devoted her last communion to him. Copyright The Image Works.

entered into marriage only after their hopes of entering into orders had been disappointed. Madame Martin in becoming a mother hoped that each of her children would become a religious. If her prayers were answered, one of them would even become a saint. As a devout and pious Catholic, she was upholding thoroughly conventional views. Not so subtly Père Hyacinthe outraged the convention.

Loyson single-handedly established l'Église catholique gallicane, the Gallican Catholic Church. The title shrewdly harkened back to Bossuet and, more than a century after him, to the hoary royalist prejudice of the post-Napoleonic generation when the throne was used by churchmen as a stay against Roman authority. Indeed, *gallicanisme* can be traced back into mediaeval times, prior to the ascent of the modern papacy, when the pope was regarded chiefly as the bishop of Rome. It is not incidental that the nascent French nationalism of Philippe le Bel (1285–1314) did physical violence to the papacy and the pope, Boniface VIII, and prepared the way for the so-called Babylonian Captivity of the papacy in Avignon, beginning with Clement V. Thus, while Loyson made himself a sensation, he was also drawing upon a kind of subterranean power of French tradition and pride at the expense of Rome. He himself had no political ambitions. Much to his credit, he declined Gambetta's offer of a parliamentary seat during the first wave of his curious celebrity.

The Emperor Napoléon I had weakened and humiliated papal power, having imprisoned one pope, Pius VI, and dictated terms to his successor, Pius VII. In 1870, Napoléon III deserted Pope Pius IX by withdrawing all French military support from papal territory in order to fight Prussia, with the result that the Italian Republic divested the papacy of all but the Vatican. Pius IX considered himself a prisoner of atheism and Freemasonry, while French chauvinism came to a boil in the face of its other foe, the one across the Rhine. Loyson and his church came to prominence in the first years of the anticlerical Third Republic. Republicans, like their ancestors in the generation of 1789, identified Christianity with the reaction and privilege of the aristocracy, but Loyson, having cut all ties with Rome, enjoyed a certain esteem for at least promoting a French church. His rise and fall signified that Christianity of any sort could not take a firm and lasting root in an increasingly secular terrain.

Loyson founded his new community on four tenets: the rejection of infallibility; the election of bishops by congregations and clergy; the celebration of offices in the national language; and the marriage of priests. The larger, blurry intent was to promote monotheism without dogmas, a kind of proto-ecumenism, as well as an *entente* with the secular world of democracy and scientific progress. That last tenet was fatal because it amounted to a forfeit of any final hegemonic voice; it was a piteous concession to the overwhelming power of the modern, especially to the prestige of science. It was the weakness that Dostoevsky identified as endemic to Protestantism, a running after every fashion so as to win acceptance or, at the craven least, toleration.

Initially, however, Loyson reaped the benefit of publicity and scandal. As a personality cult, which to some extent it was, his breakaway church had the sensational appeal of a married priest. Its founder insisted from the first that he had not broken with Rome in order to marry—three years fell between apostasy and matrimony—but the charge was always there to be made. Loyson went so far as to insist that not only was celibacy not an article of faith but that there was no incompatibility between ordination and marriage. He could point to Rome itself in its policy of tolerating the marriage, preceding ordination, of priests in its Eastern dioceses. Alluding to sexual misconduct he asserted that many priests "need to be reconciled with the interests, the affections, and the duties of human nature."[6]

In a testamentary letter published on Whitsunday of 1893, when his Gallican experiment was fading beyond resuscitation, he claimed he had never abjured Catholicism, but he sharply criticized as pagan and puerile the cultism of movements such as the Sacred Heart, which served, in his estimate, as fanatic guises for what he saw as Rome's quest of temporal power. He also dismissed popular accounts of the Virgin's apparitions. Such postures documented the Anglican bias with which Loyson had been tinged during his years in England (he was married in London) and his tour of America, where he is alleged to have received an enthusiastic welcome. Such celebrity proved a foil to the execration he had to endure, with charges of criminality and heresy. No one could deny, however, the fortitude he showed in going his own way. His ecclesiastical critics, however, noted that going his own way was what put him in the dubious company of Luther and to go one's own way defined apostasy.

Although France sustained a Reformed Church, that body never attained the vigor of the Old Catholics of Germany. Loyson's legacy, however, does not lie in his movement but in his prophetic remarks, pseudo or not, on issues that have dogged Catholicism to the present day. To consider him in a positive way, he was an earnest would-be reformer of what he saw as backwardness in the Church, especially its failure to accept modern science. With an overtly sanguine view of where the Church would go once wedded to the age, he predicted that "It will not close the door with fear against the grand hypotheses of Darwin, hypotheses which science has not confirmed, but which it certainly has not disproved."[7] For all of his rationalism, Loyson could not see that his apostasy, the force of a vivid personal example which by his marriage became a defiant one, went far to discredit the very initiatives he was urging. He was in effect calling upon the Church to submit to the world Christ had overcome.

George Sand, who recognized Père Hyacinthe as naive, courageous, and Protestant, and who yet recognized no mediator between herself and God, hailed him for facing squarely what she called "the baneful and infamous consequences of priestly celibacy"[8] but even she was puzzled by the anomaly of a married prelate. The history of controversies on the issue dated back as far as the pontificate of Nicholas I, in the ninth century, but they were of no concern to her. For this woman, whose fictions had been placed on the papal index, the question was how Loyson could reconcile his cozy view of conjugal love with the confessional. And didn't his special pleading savor, she asked ironically, of the casuistry of a priest? Even so, she took delight in what she called Loyson's heresy and congratulated him on it, alleging that heresies are a kind of vital nutriment for Christianity.

Perhaps nothing was so forward as Loyson's preaching that an everlasting Hell simply did not exist. God's wisdom and goodness meant that evil could in no way triumph forever: "if divine justice chastises sin severely on both sides of the tomb, it is always for the final good of the sinner."[9] This excessively charitable view on divine intent and human foibles, known as apocatastasis, had some pedigree in Church history. Saint John Chrysostom, for one, preached that Christ had not only visited Hell but shattered forever its gates. Loyson had extended his own universal charity toward Jews and Protestants, toward positivists and even Jansenists. For him, the only real blasphemy was despair.

It remains to his credit that unlike Lamennais, another discredited prophet, Loyson did not forsake Christianity. Although likened to Luther, he did not break with Catholicism itself. Unlike Renan, his rationalism never went so far as to abandon, let alone explain away the gospels. Despite excommunication, he believed to the end that he was both in and of the Church but he was rapt into a too rosy vision of its future, on his terms.

How did Thérèse respond to this singular priest? At the beginning of her mission and even before she entered the Carmel Thérèse prayed to secure the salvation of the tabloids' killer, Henri Pranzini, and she rejoiced that that prayer had been answered when newspapers reported that, in the face of the guillotine, Pranzini kissed the crucifix of the attendant priest. She referred to Pranzini thereafter as her first child. Toward the end of her mission Thérèse turned to Père Hyacinthe in the hope that he would become another of her children, perhaps the very last.

But unlike Pranzini, a young and sinisterly charming vagabond thief, Loyson was all too well known to the Carmel for the disgrace his apostasy had brought. Perhaps worse yet were his pronouncements on marriage, a peculiar defiance, in its fashion, of the Order whose sisters he had overseen in Paris. In the way of Peter and the other disciples, those sisters had left everything of their lives, including families, behind them; they had given themselves to God as perpetual brides of Christ. For over a generation, Loyson in effect flaunted earthly marriage as no less sacred a bond than theirs. To the Carmelites, perhaps the most painful, if not the most ghastly anomaly, was that he continued to regard himself as a priest after his excommunication. He remained Père Hyacinthe, as indeed even canon law would have acknowledged.

The first occasion for Thérèse's taking notice of Loyson was his tour of Normandy during the summer of 1891. By July 8, she had heard of his *conferences*, a series of public talks he held in Caen and Coutances, the latter the site of a daughter Carmel, founded by Lisieux's in 1866. Her informant was her sister, Céline, still in the world. Thérèse wrote to her of the Carmel's singular desire to save "a soul who seems forever lost.... The particulars have very much interested me, causing my heart to beat very hard."[10] What prompted such palpitations was the curious but dramatic fact that she knew Loyson was four years younger than her father and four older than her mother, so that he could have seemed a nightmare parent. He was a priest who had beguiled women, married one, and became a father.

She had entered the Carmel, as she stated immediately before her profession, "to save souls and especially to pray for priests."[11] Now she was called to pray for a most unusual soul, a lost sheep who persisted in believing that he was a shepherd. Loyson was by then sixty-four, aging as well as errant. It was her father's precipitous confinement to Bon Sauveur, the sanatorium at Caen, which had brought the cruel spite of gossip into the Carmel itself, in February 1889. A particularly harsh blow to the infirm and confined M. Martin fell four months later when, on a lawyer's urging to Uncle Isidore, he was dispossessed of his property. Loyson,

I would submit, became for Thérèse a kind of anti-Louis, a counter version of isolation and notoriety. Both had led ascetic lives that turned to matrimony. Louis in his twenties had longed to become a priest but had been denied the possibility because he did not know and could not learn, though he tried, the requisite Latin. He had settled into a quiet celibacy until his mother prompted him into a marriage as he reached the biblical midway point of his life. Loyson had gone in the same direction, a priest who might have remained such had he not been allured by the adoring audiences of women—in that company he is strangely akin to the charming Pranzini[12]—into an exalted view of marital bonds. Louis, for his part, always showed a reverent, almost awed deference to priests.

That such parallels as I have drawn were apparent to Thérèse may be contested, but her July 1891 letter shows she was aware of the indispensable nexus in Christianity that conjoins suffering and love. She begins by mentioning an illness afflicting Mère Gonzague: "it is sad to see those one loves suffering like that," a remark that must have left a bitter resonance with Céline. She, not Thérèse, had watched helplessly over Louis's decline and had visited him for the one hour allowed her weekly during his first three months at Bon Sauveur. This remark's pertinence to Loyson is that Thérèse was convinced of something that does not surface in any of his writings, that he was "the wretched prodigal," a lost and therefore necessarily unhappy soul. She even construed his tour as evidence of his anguish: "...it's easy to see that remorse is gnawing at him; he traverses the churches with a large crucifix and seems to be showing great reverence."[13]

These remarks indicate that Thérèse was seeing Loyson as a sinner akin to Pranzini, brought to the cross in penitence at last. Yet his turning to Christ was the more urgent, for if Pranzini had been the worst sort of criminal, Loyson was "more culpable perhaps than any converted sinner ever was." Indeed, as with Pranzini, she felt the profound assurance that had guided her in the summer of 1887 and all her conscious life, that God instills in the soul only desires that are meant to be fulfilled. With Pranzini she had stood alone, confiding only in her sister. Now, however, within Carmel, she was but one of Jesus's "poor little spouses" assigned "to bring back to the fold this poor lost sheep."[14]

If it is fair to fault Thérèse for naïveté about sin, if not blindness to it, it can also be argued that she was subject to a kind of charity by prolepsis: she had almost desperately anticipated a salvific sign from Pranzini. The drama of that wretched man's final penance had been assured by the certainty that she had desired it, and God would not cheat that desire. So, too, with Loyson. She even had a kind of scenario prepared for him, this time adducing one of Jesus' healing miracles[15]: "...a day will come when [Jesus] shall open his eyes and then who knows if he'll not pass through France in a mission wholly different from the one he's on now."[16]

Through the rest of July, 1891 she gathered up accounts of Loyson's tour from the local paper, *La Croix du Calvados,* a supplement to the main issue, which came from Paris. The July 9–16 issue addressed him as "a defrocked priest and a married one, protégé of Free Masons and of the impious everywhere you go."[17] In the third of the clippings, the issue of July 23–30, the following passage bears what is most likely Thérèse's underlining (not Céline's): Loyson was quoted that "... if the Church proves to him that he's at fault, *he's quite willing to acknowledge his error and to resume humbly his place in Christian unity.*"[18] It might have seemed to Thérèse that, twenty years on, Loyson was growing tired of his own apostasy, even though, as the Catholic journal noted, he was being applauded all over by Jews.

She probably did not know that the membership of his Gallican venture was declining and that, with an unruly adolescent son who, turning the trick, rejected all religion, Loyson had possibly learned to perceive himself as a prodigal, if not a lost sheep. But no. He made that tour in Normandy in his sixty-fifth year, when he was well on the way of iterated justifications for his life's turns. His apologia had too long become a private dogma, accruing many times, like a succession of tree rings, ever circular and sealed with a sturdy bark. After the summer of 1891, he was again hidden within the inviolable recesses of Thérèse's prayers for him.

Twenty years later, in January, 1911, when Pères Roulland and Pichon were testifying at the first hearings for Thérèse's beatification, the Carmel of Lisieux sent to Père Hyacinthe (not so addressed) the latest edition of *Histoire d'une Âme,* including a written note that Thérèse had prayed for him.[19] In acknowledgment, on February 5, Loyson lost no time defending himself to her sister, Pauline: "... this beautiful soul had offered to God her prayers and sufferings for what she called my 'conversion,' meaning to say my submission to the precepts imposed by the Pope on consciences which abdicate between his hands."[20] He added that while genuinely moved by what he had read in Thérèse's writings, he remained unconvinced and quoted St. Paul (Romans 10.2) on the Jews who have a zeal for God but without knowledge of God.[21]

Loyson was arguing not only against Thérèse but against Rome, then in the papacy of Pius X, that the Church via the dogma of infallibility had, in his estimate, chosen to stand in its own righteousness rather than in Christ, who had displaced all the Judaic claims of righteousness. As Karl Barth later wrote, "To know God means a relentless honouring of Him in His pre-eminence over all human eminence, even over the eminence of our noteworthy thoughts about Him."[22] No less important in this matter is how Thérèse saw Loyson, *coupable* and in need of *conversion.* These words in her terms merit scrutiny.

Although the Carmelites' *Constitution* dwells in detailed length (Chapters XV–XX) upon *coulpes* or faults, Thérèse nowhere speaks of them in her writings, and she uses *coupable* only a spare eight times: once for Pranzini (A 46r), twice for Loyson; also, in explaining her *offrande* or sacrifice of self to divine Love, divine Justice having prompted a sister elsewhere to take punishments meant for the culpable (A 84r). In LT 226, to Adolphe Roulland, May 9, 1897, she says that being just means not only severely punishing the culpable; it also means recognizing good intentions. She may have seen such intentions in Loyson. She may even have recognized, as George Sand did, a courage in his standing alone against the Church establishment. She had written two plays about acute spiritual isolation, and in them she knew that her special heroine-saint, Jeanne d'Arc, had confronted the grim lot of any heretic or apostate.

Loyson told Pauline: "I may be deceived, my Reverend Mother, I have been so more than once in my life, but I am persuaded that what God condemns in a person is not error, when it is sincere, but egotism, pride and hatefulness. I believe I can say before death and God that such have never been the motives of my thought and my life."[23] It is surprising to read such words from a veteran priest. Not that Loyson was in fact subject to pride and egotism—as who is not?—but that he did not express an awareness of the safeguards any Christian would have to hold against them. As the gospels indicate, the peculiar fact about righteousness is that the truly righteous person does not know he is righteous. Loyson's disclaimer has a tragic ring to it.

Thérèse, however, had learned in her twenty-four years to attain skepticism about human judgment far greater than Loyson had reached in his eighty-four. As she observed to Céline in the last weeks, "It's amazing how, finally, everything anyone can say to me touches me not in the slightest, because I've learned how little substance human judgments have."[24] Eschewing egotism and pride, Loyson did not perceive how they had subtly corrupted his Gallican church; that apostasy and heresy are species of pride by their very resistance, even to what might well be corrupt.

Thérèse realized that pride is inescapable, but she took drastic measures to confront it in herself as best she could: she came to savor, to welcome occasions when other sisters put her down. At the 1910 hearings, Pauline recalled an incident when one of the novices under her sister's training had made some very humiliating remarks to Thérèse (novices were permitted to speak freely and Thérèse encouraged them even to criticism of her). Asked what the matter was, Thérèse answered that she was happy that God gave occasion to remind her that she was "absolutely little and without merit."[25] Had Père Hyacinthe been able to maintain that sort of lowliness, he would not have founded the Gallican Church.

In the end Thérèse saw her Carmelite sisters as indispensable agents in the process of breaking her pride. So as not to allow that pride a furtive re-entry, she made the breaking a condition for her mission: "I can be broken, tested, only by the just since all my sisters are pleasing to God. It is less bitter to be broken by a sinner than by a just person, but out of compassion for sinners and to obtain their conversion I ask you, oh my God, that I be broken for them by the souls who surround me."[26] By the time of this statement, she was very close to death, and there was no evidence that she or anyone else had, through prayer, brought Loyson to conversion. Yet this statement is unusually forceful in indicating that she found herself implicitly proximate to his company: she wanted to be broken by the community in order that she might serve as an example for him.

According to this singular drama, Thérèse knew that she could and should never be one of the just and righteous, those other Carmelites. But she had a sufficient inadequacy, a capacity to be reduced from pride to humiliation, the reminder that she was a nobody, and that reduction would serve vicariously to convert sinners. It is legitimate to infer, then, that for her, sinners were those whose pride goes unacknowledged by themselves. It is a blind obstinacy. Conversion meant a kind of awakening or inner lighting (to use her image for Loyson), such as she had undergone at Christmas 1886, when she learned to stop dwelling blindly and morbidly upon her self. That Christmas "conversion," as she styled it, was the necessary first step toward the Easter conversion of the spring of 1896, when she learned to dwell lovingly on others, both the near and the very distant, those turned to God and those turned away.

Having been confined within that peculiar cage of the childish self, she knew that others similarly imprisoned had need of her prayerful solicitude. Her pity for Loyson was not centered upon his apostasy nor even upon his marriage. She paid no attention to his blasphemous dismissal of relics and cults. What mattered was the self-detention of pride. Loyson admitted to Pauline that he might well be deceived, an extraordinary admission from a priest to a sister. It seems a pity that Thérèse herself never learned of it.

Thérèse, it seems to me, was trying experimentally to resolve for herself the challenge Jesus poses in the Sermon on the Mount, Matthew 7:3. She could see the mote in her brother's eye only if the beam in her own was being forcibly removed. It was a subtle ruse, that only by a steadily held awareness of her own inconsequence could she help those who were astray. She once admitted to Céline that she could not be one to attain heaven by works; she would have to steal her way into it. Something of this stratagem she effected in her relation to sinners, those who, all unawares, were in need of compassion.

If it is to be wondered what within Thérèse's writing prompted Loyson's criticism of her "zeal,"[27] it is almost certainly a passage in C where Thérèse pays loving and grateful tribute to Gonzague for the severities by which this mother had shaped her. She writes of those whom Teresa of Ávila had called saintly simple souls, the blessèd sisters who unquestioningly obeyed their superiors and were thus happily assured of being on the right path: "they don't have to worry about deceiving themselves, even if it seems to them that their superiors are deceived." Obedience, in sum, is "their sole compass." "But when one stops looking at this infallible compass, when one strays from the way it says to follow on the pretext of doing God's will, which does not enlighten well those who yet remain in place, immediately the soul has wandered onto dry paths where the water of grace is soon lacking."[28]

Thérèse was at last speaking of and to Loyson directly, but she was telling him about much more than the inestimable value of obedience, given, as she notes, even to those who might seem errant. What weighed no less vitally for her was the perception that Gonzague was the compass given to her and the Carmel by Jesus himself, "living in your soul and communicating to me his will through you."[29] In his apostasy Loyson had tragically forfeited the charity of reading the will of Jesus in another Christian soul.[30] Central though obedience was to Thérèse, as to any Carmelite, love was always the final measure, the needle, as it were, of that compass.[31]

She was just strong enough to take communion on August 19, 1897. It was the feast of Saint Hyacinth, a Polish Dominican of the thirteenth century, famous for converting sinners by his sermons. The breviary told the Carmelites that day of how St Hyacinth had practiced a perpetual chastity: "He didn't pass a day without giving some luminous proof of his faith, his piety and his sanctity."[32] It was Thérèse's last communion. She dedicated it to Hyacinthe Loyson.[33]

II. Broken by a Sinner: The Too Credible Antics of Léo Taxil

"Je m'étais accusé d'un assassinat imaginaire, dans ma confession générale au père jésuite de Clamart. Eh bien, à vous, je fais l'aveu d'un autre crime. J'ai commis une infanticide. Le Palladisme, maintenant, est mort et bien mort. Son père vient de l'assassiner."
["I accused myself of an imaginary murder in my general confession to the Jesuit father at Clamart. Well, I'll admit to you another crime. I've committed infanticide. Palladism is now good and dead. Its father has just killed it."] The Confession of LÉO TAXIL, *April 19, 1897*

For several weeks the beaches of Marseille were deserted. Disturbing letters had come to the city's newspapers from fishermen telling how they had barely escaped the danger. A municipal commission was set up and it was determined that sharks had indeed arrived, probably from Corsica, lured by the meaty refuse dumped from some ship. The city entrusted to a general and a hundred men armed with rifles and lots of cartridges the task of clearing the seas of this menace. They swept the coastal waters and then returned to the harbor, with nothing to report. A subsequent inquest revealed that the published letters were all fantastic. Not only were there no such fishermen in the villages from which the letters had been posted; the letters had all been written in the same hand.

That hand belonged to a nineteen-year-old named Gabriel-Antoine Jogand-Pages. To Free Masons and the world of occultism he is known as Léo Taxil. This name he assumed when he had to flee to Switzerland in order to avoid a stiff fine and eight years of imprisonment for defaming religion. That was in 1876, when he was only 23, but his career in villainy had begun well before then.

He had been educated by Jesuits and was even pious enough to be appointed an instructor at the newly founded College de Saint-Louis in Marseille, but in his rebellious adolescence he had become acquainted with Masonic literature. When he ran away from school, he was tracked down en route to a journalist's career in Belgium. On his father's orders, he was sent to a reform school. A priest once refused him communion after a confession that had sounded more like boasting than contrition. The next day Gabriel-Antoine took communion, anyway. Was that sacrilege responsible for the confessor's heart attack immediately afterward at the back of the chapel?

In Switzerland Taxil had a hard time making a living with anti-Catholic satires and he returned to France under a general post-Commune amnesty in 1878. After marketing pornography, he founded a press for his salvos against Rome, the Librairie Anticlericale. In 1881 he established an anticlerical league and joined a Masonic lodge, Le Temple de l'Honneur Français, but he was permanently expelled from the order when he was found guilty of lies, having falsely claimed the patronage of such eminences as Louis Blanc and Victor Hugo. He had also been sued for plagiarism. His publications, including *Les Amours Secrètes de Pie IX* (1881) and *La Bible Amusante* (1882), had earned him the contempt of all good Catholics, but after he was expelled from masonry, he discovered a new career by shifting into reverse, writing books purporting a Masonic conspiracy against Christian Europe. He had learned well what his imaginary sharks had told him, that fearsome rumor is mighty over many, and far more effective than mere ridicule or calumny.

In 1885 he made a general confession to a Jesuit priest in Paris, who put him through the Spiritual Exercises of St. Ignatius. He astounded his confessor by pretending to have committed a premeditated murder. Directly, the anticlerical league he himself had created voted his expulsion as a traitor, a peculiar sort of relegation, but he met the charge with equanimity, telling his indignant fellows that someday they would understand what he intended. They did not know they would have to wait twelve years for the revelation.

Taxil's anti-Masonic exposés became international occasions. His books, some running up to a thousand pages, sold in German, English, Spanish, and Italian translations. His accounts of murderous initiations into lodges drew vigorous denials from such Masons as Edward, Prince of Wales, Bismarck, and Kaiser Wilhelm I, thereby securing even more sales. His new notoriety also brought a journalist from the *Catholic Times* of London, who offered to introduce him to the papal nuncio in Paris. Taxil surprised the nuncio by expressing hope that he could enter the Carthusian Order so as to escape his wife's nagging. In 1887 he had an audience with Pope Leo XIII, whose encyclical, *Humanum Genus* (issued April 20, 1884), had possibly inspired Taxil's writing against Masonry. Pope Leo had called for an unveiling of Freemasonry's intent, fearful as he was that it had fueled republican appropriation of the papacy's Italian territories in 1870. Hence, the pope was indebted to Taxil for his efforts and proved staunchly gullible about their substance. It is hard to believe that no one in the Vatican knew enough about historical and contemporary Freemasonry to see through the sensationalism Taxil was churning out. Later, the pope did learn that the published account of Luciferian orgies of the Masons' Scottish Rite in America (Taxil made the mistake of locating them in Charleston, South Carolina) were completely bogus, but he kept a discreet silence. Besides, how was the pope to know fact from fancy regarding such an underground?

Taxil wrote of Masonic seances in which the spirits of Luther and Voltaire were invoked, but sales probably depended far more upon his account of black masses and obscene sexual practices. He invented an Order of the Palladium which took its instructions directly from Lucifer. He identified its earthly leader as Albert Pike, who was in fact the head of the Scottish Rite in Britain, but his master stroke came with the invention of a priestess. Such royalty was an office foreign to Masons but indispensable in tainting Freemasonry with the paganism that unwary readers would impute to a secret organization inimical to Catholicism.

The priestess's name was Diana Vaughan, who was in fact Taxil's secretary, a young woman from the United States (but of a French family) whom he met in 1893 while she was working as a representative for an American manufacturer of typewriters. Clever, amused, and, as Taxil was careful to determine, a free-thinker, she sportingly joined the grand ludification into which her new employer enlisted her: she would pose as an escapee from the Masons' satanic cult, have confessions published in her name about the harrowing ordeals to which she had been subjected, stay in hiding for her life's sake, and answer the solicitous correspondents who were sure to contact her through a private postal agency. Taxil later boasted that Vaughan received and answered letters from bishops, cardinals, and even from Pope Leo's secretary. "This vessel of Palladism has been a real battleship compared to the tugboat which, for my debut, I had sent out on the shark chase in Marseille's harbor."[34]

Catholics had already been praying for Vaughan's conversion to Catholicism when on May 8, 1895, *La Croix* asked its readership to entreat Jeanne d'Arc to secure it. (Pope Leo had declared Jeanne's veneration in January of 1894.) With yet another master stroke of mass psychology, Taxil, who in 1890 had published a book on the martyrdom of Jeanne, now had Vaughan claim that the Maid of Orleans herself had rescued her from satanism and on June 6, 1895, had converted her to Catholicism. In her serialized *Mémoirs d'une ex-Palladiste* Vaughan now offered to become a new Jeanne for a Catholicism beset with an international conspiracy far more sinister than British occupation of French soil could have been in Jeanne's time. Conservative Catholic journals, having swallowed the hoax whole, endorsed what seemed to be a divinely appointed crusade.

The fact that so many people were taken in by Taxil and his minion can be in part glossed by the contentiousness of the age. The Third Republic's anticlerical campaign, which closed Catholic schools and dispossessed orders, had engendered a siege mentality in French Catholicism. There were even fears of reversion to the Terror. (The martyred Carmelites of Compiègne, who had been guillotined in the last days of Robespierre's murderous regime, had been introduced for beatification on the centenary of their deaths, in 1894.) But hostility to Christianity was not merely governmental. Pope Leo's *Humanum Genus* had pointed to the dark populism of Masonic secrecy, an international movement he believed demonic in its designs against the Church. If the Church could mount only a vigorous but rather baffled opposition to ascendant secular ideologies such as socialism and Darwinism, it had no difficulty recognizing the spiritual adversary who had destroyed Eden. In Diana Vaughan, the arrival of a Jeanne-like figure out of nowhere was enormously appealing, a populist liberator who had already been martyred, in her way, by the subterranean foe of the Faith.

Another gloss on the Taxil-Vaughan hoax comes from a now hoary tract in social psychology published in France in the very year of Vaughan's "conversion" and initial "memoirs." Gustave Le Bon's *Psychologie des foules* argued that collectivities tend to be suggestible, reactionary, fanatical, yet deferential to authority. Le Bon was not speaking of the readership of conservative Catholic journals, but his remarks on *le sentiment religieux* have bearing on Taxil's extraordinary success in duping millions. Whereas individuals pursue in the main their private interests, in collectivities, says Le Bon, they can turn to an exalting morality of sacrifice, adoration, and cultic veneration. A hero once proclaimed becomes almost divine. Secular cultures have purveyed savior figures as imposing, if not so lasting, as religious ones: from Caesar to Napoléon, not to mention the twentieth century's State idols. But sectarian crowds, by which Le Bon meant religious collectivities, are distinctive in their homogeneity, in their need of an appeal to tradition, and in the role of illusion or myth within that tradition.

Taxil's initial anti-Masonic propaganda had played to Catholic dread, but his invention of a pagan priestess turned martyr provided an irresistible antidote to that dread. Even though no one had actually seen Vaughan or so much as a photograph of her, how could sane, skeptical voices (and there were some) be heard when Vaughan's revelations were credited chiefly because people wanted to believe in them? Her written words were mighty enough, not least because they were confessional in tone. Besides, she had intimated that she might soon be withdrawing into a convent. This was all too good to be false. (Figure 4.2.)

FIGURE 4.2 Léo Taxil in 1890, a sensationalist and buffoon, who duped millions of Christians, and taught Thérèse much about spiritual darkness. Copyright The Image Works'

The controversy over Vaughan's credibility, even her existence, was fed by the assumption that to deny either was to participate in the Masonic conspiracy itself, to abet its secrecy. Besides, reputable Catholic journals were supporting Vaughan. The Jesuit *Civiltà Cattolica*, on September 19, 1896, celebrated her in these grandiloquent phrases: "...summoned from dark shadows to the light of God, prepared by divine providence, and armed with knowledge and personal experience, she is turning to the service of the Church; she's inexhaustible in valuable publications that have no equal in precision and usefulness. Masonry has been consternated by them and to get back at this fiercely brave woman it spreads word that she doesn't exist, and it's a complete myth."[35] Given such an official endorsement of the Vaughan story, it would have required of ordinary, pious believers a stupendous skepticism to have doubted her.

In another Catholic journal, *Rosier de Marie*, the following month, Pierre Lautier, presiding general of the Ordre des Avocats de Saint-Pierre, announced that Vaughan existed because nearly three years before, in 1893, well before her conversion, he had spent two hours interviewing her and Taxil in the presence of an artist who was painting her portrait. He recalled that she served him chartreuse after coffee but took cognac for herself. "Hostility to the Church, going as far as abstention from Carthusian liqueur, well, that's typical." But Lautier had all the more reason now to rejoice: "Today, Miss Vaughan is a fervent Catholic, fighting the good fight as a true champion of the faith."[36] One of Vaughan's most ardent supporters, the bishop of Grenoble, Monseigneur Fava, who had received letters from her, urged an inquest before she could be condemned to death by Masonic satanists, as though she were another Jeanne, indeed.

Thérèse was only one of millions caught in the web of fantasy that Taxil had spun, but she had her own special reasons for being attracted to Vaughan and her story. From childhood, Thérèse had nourished a lively identification of herself with Jeanne, feeling that she, too, had been born for glory and "the same heavenly inspiration."[37] But she noted in her reminiscing that her own glory would not be conspicuous before others as Jeanne's had been. Instead, hers would be the true glory of Carmel, the willingness to be unknown and reckoned for naught (Ms A 71r). Now, Vaughan, in the *Mémoirs*, had claimed the salvific intercession of Jeanne, a saintly power that no Catholic would likely ever have the temerity to contest as fake. Not the least weighty factor in the enthrallment was Vaughan's choosing to retire into monastic life, that glorious obscurity, thus ratifying Thérèse's own choice and destiny. Uncannily, on June 13, 1895, Vaughan was reported to have offered herself as a victim to divine justice, only four days after Thérèse, in a burst of inspirational fervor, had written her own *offrande*, proclaiming herself a victim to be given to God's love. That fortuitous proximity of dates must have impressed Thérèse deeply. She even paid Vaughan the particular homage she had given to San Juan de la Cruz, transcribing: she copied passages from Vaughan's *Neuvaine Eucharistie pour réparer*, A Eucharistic Novena of Atonement.

Thérèse was duped, not because she was gullible or credulous—she was neither—but because in the instance of Vaughan she could not bring to bear the full acuity by which she had learned to penetrate hearts. She had learned to read them by reading faces and gauging tones and gestures, and it was her service as novice mistress that ripened her in such skills. In the mostly silent Carmelite world, what a sister said carried a gravity unknown to the loquacious outer world, and much of what was said was confessional or supplicatory in nature, whether collective, in the offices, or individual, in the meetings Thérèse held daily with the novices. When Vaughan proclaimed her intent to enter a cloistered order, the Catholic faithful might well have sighed with delighted piety, but to Thérèse Vaughan was saying, I wish to become a novice. It was as though Vaughan was speaking not to the Carmelite community but from within it, as a postulant. How could Thérèse not have responded to that? When there was an occasion for charity, she could not refuse it, but this occasion was golden with promise and high in drama. She had never known of a soul struggling—a young woman like herself—to escape from a cruel, demonic world into the welcoming Church.

There is more. Vaughan, though merely a salaried amanuensis of the cynical Taxil, seemingly shared with Thérèse the particular bond of writers. She had composed an autobiography, which in some ways complemented the first manuscript Thérèse was composing at the very time the *Mémoirs d'une ex-Palladiste* appeared. Manuscript A, while diametric to a sensational exposé, was following the same trajectory as Vaughan's, a story of a young woman's soul moving from darkness and the demonic toward redemptive light. Thérèse had interpreted a decade of her childhood, from the death of her mother till her Christmas "conversion" of 1886, when she was just short of 14, as a prolonged moody selfishness, the acme of which was a hallucinatory illness. It was, she writes, Satan's own work: "The sickness with which I was attacked certainly came from the Devil.... I believe that the *Devil* had been given an external sway over me."[38] However surcharged with melodrama, Vaughan's appeal for rescue from a cult of Satan-worshippers spoke to Thérèse's own experience of evil.

When the Christmas "conversion" of 1886 had at last set Thérèse on the way of self-humbling, thus preparing her implicitly for Carmel, she still faced demonic obstruction, in the very desire to enter the order. She recalls that on the evening of September 8, 1890, when, following her retreat she had professed her vows and her life's dream had been at last realized, she was suddenly beset with an acute sense of unworthiness which made her feel that to go on into Carmelite life would be tantamount to fraud: "I found Carmel's life quite beautiful, but the Devil prompted in me the *certainty* that it had not been made for me, that I'd be deceiving the superiors in proceeding on a path where I had not been called. My shadows were so great that I saw and understood only one thing: I had no *vocation!*"[39] Here was yet an ironic turn, that Thérèse, who had once been tempted by Satan to abandon the route into the Carmel which she had been taking for years, could understand how dreadful it must have been for Diana Vaughan to feel the scorn of anyone who charged her with fraud.

Thérèse was able to get past the temptation against her devotion to the Carmel only by the very means that showed she did have the vocation, by confessing her unworthiness to her novice mistress. The gentle and shrewd Sr. Marie des Anges, who had known such darkness in her own early Carmelite life, assured her that her sense of unworthiness signaled the humility requisite to going on. When Thérèse further shared her scruples with the prioress, Mère Gonzague had the rugged good sense to laugh at her.

This small but revelatory incident might well have been called the triumph of humility, which became in fact the title of Thérèse's drama centering upon Diana Vaughan's memoir. Taxil had written that Vaughan had become the betrothed of Asmodeus, a companion of Lucifer and Beel-Zebub, at the time she had been freed of Masonic diabolism via Jeanne d'Arc. In Thérèse's drama, these devils immediately upon entry[40] fall into comically bitter reproaches of one another for having lost so many initiates to the saints. When Lucifer upbraids Beel-Zebub for losing adepts to Saint Michael, Beel-Zebub passes blame on to Asmodeus for having forfeited his fiancée "in a fashion grievous for our cause."[41] Although, after the exposure of the hoax, some of Asmodeus's response, including references to Diana, was deleted from the manuscript, the purport was that he intended to find out where she had hidden herself so that he could avenge himself with new torments for her. These remarks, not to mention the catalogue of demons Asmodeus later provides, suffice to indicate that Thérèse had read the serialized *Mémoirs*, most likely supplied to the Carmel by Uncle Isidore.[42]

However ludicrous it might seem, that demonic melodrama which Vaughan's story had provided, her miraculously thwarted engagement to Asmodeus was, for Thérèse, integral to the rescue from Freemasonry which Jeanne the virgin martyr had effected. Thérèse's own sister, Céline, had been delivered to Carmel only after Thérèse had made intercessory prayers that a budding courtship with their distant cousin, Henry Maudelonde, be foiled. Only a marriage strictly kept within the bounds of Christian piety could be secure from worldly contamination, and even some within those bounds, as Céline's with Maudelonde presumably would have been, were insupportable to a virgin's imagination.

No less so was another male ensnarement. Céline's delivery to Carmel had been achieved only when her sisters had mounted a fierce opposition to the man who had exerted a hegemony over her life that was close to exploitative. That man was Almire Pichon, S.J. He had been a friend of the Martin family since Thérèse's childhood. He had helped Pauline to get the dithering, hapless Marie, her older sister, settled into the Carmel. But he also conspired to take Céline with him to Canada for the founding of a mission, and the secrecy he imposed on her to that end was cruel and duplicitous. He was hardly in Taxil's league, but as a popular preacher with a gift for fascinating people in large numbers, especially young women, his influence remains strangely suspect in the chronicle of the Martin family. If Loyson was a counter to Louis, Taxil was a counter to Pichon, but if Thérèse showed no informed wariness of Taxil, it was because Vaughan alone held her interest.

The worm in the bud briefly but tellingly turned toward Thérèse when Taxil-Vaughan forgot for a moment the role of victim-martyr in hiding. When the Vatican set up a board of inquest, headed by Monseigneur Luigi Lazzareschi, Taxil, with Vaughan's name affixed, published an attack upon the board for questioning the veracity of what had been published under her name. The commission was able to arrive at no conclusion, neither for nor against Vaughan. Thérèse, taken aback by Vaughan's effrontery and impudence, remarked merely, "It's impossible that that came from God."[43] It may be that at that moment the whole hollow edifice of the hoax, which her trust in Vaughan and her hope for Vaughan's coming into Carmel had sustained, began to collapse. She makes no subsequent reference to Diana Vaughan but there is one reference, obliquely put, to Taxil.

Taxil's massive deception came to light by his own boastful and protracted admission at the Société de Géographie in Paris, on Monday, April 19, 1897. There and then, Thérèse's photo of herself dressed as Jeanne d'Arc for one of her *récreations,* together with Céline as Saint Catherine, was projected by an oxhydric lamp on a screen overhead for all the invited (clerics, reporters, even some Masons) to see.[44] The press had been promised instead a screen-size view of the original compact between Vaughan and Lucifer, as well as an address by Vaughan herself after Taxil had given his presentation entitled "Douze ans sous la bannière de l'Eglise," "A Dozen Years under the Church's Banner." Thérèse was not identified nor was anything made of the photo in Parisian accounts but the local paper in Lisieux, *Le Normand,* observed that perhaps the photo, like everything else about Taxil, was bogus. Taxil made no reference to Thérèse nor to the photo, which she had admiringly sent to Vaughan. Neither did he say anything about the Carmel.

His target was much larger. For twelve years he had hoodwinked Rome and millions of Catholics. The tone of his endless remarks that April day is consistently one of self-amusement and self-congratulation, spurred on by secular laughter at his witticisms and shouts of outrage from the betrayed. It is difficult to imagine how someone could be sustained for so many years by what amounted to a grotesque prank. This was no requital for injustices suffered in a Church-schooled childhood, nor was it even a plea for toleration on behalf of Freemasonry, some of whose members were as appalled and incensed as were Catholics by what Taxil had perpetrated. Although he had made a hefty fortune from his sales and was able to retire to a country estate thereafter, Taxil does not seem to have been prompted even by avarice. His sole aim was to savor his own well-honed skill in deceit.

As no one had lost palpably anything—this was no Panama scandal—nor suffered damages beyond the immeasurable humiliation of credulity, Taxil went away free from prosecution. He attempted no more hoaxes. (He could not have mounted anything to surpass Diana Vaughan and *palladisme.*) Even though sensationalism such as this incident affords usually insures that its agents vanish into obscurity, Taxil remains an ominous figure. His shallow merriment apart, he left an example of how immense numbers of people could be enticed by the bait of a well-calculated lie. As a genius of publicity, Taxil might be called the godfather of modern conspiracy theorists, albeit one with a sense of humor, and his work stands in tandem with the most infamous of subsequent documents in this genre, the anti-Semitic *Protocols of the Learnèd Elders of Zion,* which calumniated Jews as he had calumniated Freemasons.[45] The denominators are similar: an impenetrable, nations-wide conspiracy against Christianity, diabolical rites, the naming of prominent figures, the appeal to dread with an undertow of menace to justify it.

Taxil's was an extraordinary achievement. He promoted a baroque image of evil and then exploded it as a sham, a gesture that seemed to explode the very notion of evil itself. A gigantic stunt had deluded masses of people by playing on their own quaint, not to say mediaeval, fears of devils and devil worship. It was one thing to mock what is sacred and sanctified; Taxil's initial outings against Catholicism had been tasteless, pointless, even threadbare, given that the Church had suffered secular ridicule for generations and from wits far greater than his. It was another and much shrewder thing to mock what Christians took no less seriously than sanctity, which was its antonym. Playing upon the gospels' own word that Satan is the prince of this world, Taxil brought him home and then made him a phantom. The commonplace that the devil's final trick is to convince people that he does not exist finds its playing out in this escapade.

In Taxil's surcharged landscape toward apocalypticism, what he did to Thérèse might seem incidental. Her sister Pauline said that when the news of Taxil's public appearance reached the Carmel, Thérèse without comment tore up the letter acknowledging the photo she had sent to Vaughan and tossed it onto the garden's trashheap (*fumier*). "She had a genuine horror of the smallest lies, even light-hearted ones. She was honesty personified."[46] But this statement deserves some semantic latitude even beyond Pauline's awareness. It was not only lying that unsettled Thérèse. It was also illusion, a connotative sense of *mensonge*. Taxil had deceived her and other Catholics beyond number, yes; but the strict honesty to which Pauline alludes suggests that Thérèse was alert to self-deception. To some extent she had unwittingly colluded with this strange and repellant man.

Her first autobiographical manuscript relates the story from which Thérèse's will to truth was begotten. When, at the age of ten, she had survived a months-long bout with fever and hallucinations and was delivered from the malady, as she saw it, by a statue of the Virgin Mary suddenly smiling upon her in her sickbed, she had related this miracle to Pauline, who was by then a novice at the Carmel. Other Carmelite sisters wanted particulars about the vision, and Thérèse recoiled in intimidation. She was not used to being challenged, however benevolently, by interrogative curiosity: "Alas, as I had sensed, my happiness vanished and was transformed into bitterness.... All these questions disturbed and hurt me.... I figured that I *had lied*...."[47]

Thérèse does *not* say, nor would she ever have implied, that the Carmel's sisters, Pauline and Marie among them, had even hinted that she was lying about the Virgin's smile. Their curiosity simply proved so great that she could not satisfy it with words, and, overly sensitive as she was at that age, she could only become dubious about her own perceptiveness. Had she deceived herself? If so, then, of course, whatever she was telling them amounted to a species of lie. It is important to note in this episode that she did not palliate or extenuate by suggesting through her pen that she might have been mistaken, merely. No; to be deluded was to be collusive with a lie. Such was her rigorous orientation to truthfulness.

She had to suffer another abrupt change from joy to grief in the Vaughan hoax, but at twenty-four, she did not have the protective cover of childhood for any explanation of why she had been taken in. She had learned to be wary of illusions. She believed she had entered Carmel wholly free of any concerns about the rigors of its sacrificial life. She had not, however, been prepared for the possibility that someone might instill illusions into her, mischievous, harmful ones. Taxil taught her the gratuitous nature of such deceit and, no less, her susceptibility to it. Mewed up in Carmel, she had left herself unguarded. Having presumed to flee the world, she learned from Taxil that she had to confront it. It may well be that the impetus to gather her writings and present them to the world posthumously was implicitly driven as a counter to the harsh lesson she had learned from this agile buffoon. The fakery of the Vaughan world would be met and confounded by revealed writings of an entirely different sort, and in a voice from that cloistered world to which Vaughan was purported to be going.

No matter how bounteous and sustaining the mystical literature of Carmel and foremost the works of San Juan de la Cruz in her formation, I would maintain that Taxil emerges as her most important guide, a man who never met her nor would likely have cared a smidgeon about her. He was not one to inspire. All he could do was to fabricate in order to laugh with scorn at anyone who took his bait. Yet it was he who opened to her, howsoever obliquely, the dark world that she, in her adolescent urge to mission, had always sought. It had been, however, a world she saw on her terms, those of a dreamy, wholly uninformed naïveté, a rescue mission that enticed with the prospect of martyrdom among benighted, exotic peoples in vastly distant lands. The wilderness into which Taxil hurled her was immediate. Indeed, it was a desert with which she was already familiar on the terms of her own sensibility but which she characterized as a misty land where light penetrated only at irregular and unsparingly brief intervals. Thanks to him, that terrain became dark, sinister, and populous.

Although Thérèse had nothing to say or to write expressly about Taxil or Vaughan after the revelation, she wrote a poem to Jeanne d'Arc a short time later. There, Jeanne's greatness is proclaimed not from the battlefield nor even from the stake but in her bitter cup, that she was rejected by all. Sequestered to a dungeon hole (*cachot*), she lay chained as "The cruel stranger [or foreigner] overwhelmed you with sorrows,"[48] a curious line, which suggests Taxil more than Jeanne's real tormentor, Pierre Cauchon. It is as though Thérèse is writing to atone for her part in besmirching Jeanne by setting up in her mind a series of correspondences between her own final life and Jeanne's. Thérèse had been confined to the *cachot* of spiritual darkness, where she had to resist the torments of demonic voices tempting her to despair. In Taxil and Vaughan, she had been betrayed as well. The poem's fifth and final quatrain says that as Christ came seeking his own betrayal and death, so suffering is one's treasure, (mine, Jeanne's, and yours), too. Taxil's deriding and venomous sport became a necessary avenue to the Cross. She could never have guessed, upon entering Carmel eight years previous, that she would have to go down that path.

Had Thérèse gone only that far, had she been content with this imitation of Christ, she would be commendable to one's contemplation, noble and yet not entirely Christian. Taking abuse and torment with dignity and without the very human urge to strike back—that is altogether admirable and stoic, but it is not enough. Thérèse had to go further. She had to reach behind and beyond the enmity Taxil himself had implicitly demonstrated, even though in Voltairean fashion he seemed to take nothing seriously. Loving one's enemies, forgiving them from one's cross is so tall an order as to seem impossible. It *is* impossible, short of grace, as Thérèse herself acknowledged.

She claimed that it was more bitter for her to be broken and humbled by the just and righteous, by her sisters in the Carmel, than by the unjust and unrighteous; by sinners, that is. This statement seems to point to Taxil, as no one else in her life's closing months could have competed with him in the profound injustice of deceit. That his trickery proved less bitter for her seems hard to construe, unless Vaughan's collapse of the "celestial inspiration" and all the fraudulent piety actually savored of the darkness that Thérèse believed she had been entrusted to by Jesus. Taxil's whole performance formed a drama worthy of the table of sorrow; it furnished the bitter bread, and he was as worthy to sit at that table as anyone else. Her way of forgiving him is unique for being wordless.

5

Final Charity: The Last Autobiography

If the righteous scarcely be saved, where shall the ungodly and the sinner appear?

I. Peter, 4:18

You blockhead, cried Don Quixote incensed, it neither concerns, nor belongs to knights-errant, to examine whether the afflicted, the enslaved and oppressed, whom they meet on the highway, are reduced to these wretched circumstances by their crimes, or their misfortunes; our business is only to assist them in their distress, having an eye to their sufferings, and not to their demerits.

Volume I, Book IV.3 (Tobias Smollett translation, 1755)

Je voudrais pouvoir exprimer ce que je sens, mais hélas je crois que c'est impossible. Il faut avoir voyagé sous ce sombre tunnel pour en comprendre l'obscurité.
[I'd like to be able to express what I'm realizing, but alas, I believe it's impossible. It's necessary to have traveled beneath this somber tunnel to understand its darkness.]

Manuscript C, 5v

Elle était comme envelopée d'innocence, mais d'une innocence éclairée, qui a deviné la boue de ce monde et a résolu, avec le secours de la grâce, de ne pas en souiller son âme.
[She was as though wrapped in innocence but it was an enlightened innocence, which sensed the mire of this world and resolved, by the help of grace, not to soil her soul with it.]

Mère Agnes de Jésus on Thérèse, NPPA
I was in prison and you visited me.

MATTHEW 25:36

I. Thérèse as a Mythic Figure

In the south of Switzerland a mountain range named for Saint Gothard reaches nearly 10,500 feet. The pass through that range lies at 6,935 feet. Lucerne lies far below to the north at some fifty miles distance, and Milan waits over a hundred to the south. On the morning of November 8, 1887, Thérèse, Céline, their father and more than one hundred other jubilee pilgrims of four French dioceses were en route by train to Rome as they entered the tunnel of the St. Gothard pass, completed only a few years before. Those among the passengers who were playing cards had to suspend their hands. It was perhaps at that time that Louis Martin suggested that everyone pray, only to hear from one of the players that, thanks be to God, there weren't many pharisees these days. The 5.4 miles in total darkness required nearly forty-five minutes to traverse. For a fourteen-year-old girl who had spent her childhood in fear of dark places, that eerie protraction might have been a terror made vivid. (Figure 5.1.)

She didn't say. But it was almost certainly in her mind when, three years later, Thérèse was writing to Pauline about Jesus. He had asked her, she writes, what path she wished to take in following him, and she had answered by asking him in turn to take her on the path he himself preferred.[1] Pauline, who had undergone a private retreat that was hooded by a cloudy, starless sky, was probably not surprised by what that chosen path would be for her sister: "Then Jesus took me by the hand and made me enter an underground where there is neither cold nor heat, where the sun does not shine and where neither rain nor wind make a visit, an

FIGURE 5.1 Construction workers at the mouth of St. Gothard Pass, Switzerland, 1881. Forty-five minutes of total darkness within it gave Therese her image of the spiritual tunnel where she sought to follow Jesus.

underground where I see nothing but a half-veiled brightness, the splendor which the lowered eyes of my Fiancé diffuse around them....[2]

Some of Thérèse's best writing comes in the inviting way of a fairy story, and this letter exemplifies such an invitation. It is not hard to imagine the Jesus of this account as a princely lover who is forced to put his young belovèd (and himself?) through a test. He is like Mozart's Tamino leading Pamina through fire and then through water, each time to the sound, a gentle sustentation, of his magic flute. Or possibly a better fit would be the story of Psyche, who could come to her adoring and adored Cupid only by night, as he obliged her to do, without a lamp. Thérèse writes: "I don't see that we are proceeding toward the mountain's end since our journey is being made under the earth, and yet it seems to me that we're getting there without knowing how. The route that I'm following is no consolation for me but it brings me every consolation as it's Jesus who's chosen it and as I want to console him all alone, all alone!"[3]

This primary document from August 1890 foreshadows the onset of the other, deeper and darker passageway through which Thérèse passed in the last eighteen months of her life. It is of more than ancillary importance, however, because in it Thérèse provides explicit focus upon what she would later lose in a subsequent passageway: the company of Jesus, the sense that the darkness was coming to an end, and the treasured mission of consoling Jesus who, as she rather strangely remarks, is all alone. It seems that her presence does not count. As his eyes are lowered and she can see only the diffusion of light they afford, she is evidently following him, perhaps from some distance, for she has yet to console him. In the narrative, she says only that she wants to. Even so, the tone is positive with resolution and expectation, as though this Psyche, like her mythic namesake, did not know that she would be parted from her Cupid and made to suffer sorest trials for her love of him.

Much of the appeal that Thérèse has won over several generations lies at this subterranean level of the mythic, even though it is not centrally a part of Christian tradition; she is the maiden tested for her belovèd and bereft of him. The sister, Thérèse de l'Enfant Jésus, had tended the sometimes distant and almost always somnolent saviour—Jesus was asleep in her little boat, she used to say—but in her ripening adolescent years Jesus remained the doll-like child. Céline had given Thérèse a toy boat, labeled it the *Abandon*, and placed in it a figurine baby Jesus.[4] Thérèse never fancied herself the helmsman of this boat—how could she have dared to presume such a mannish business was suitable for her?—and she remained in her imagination and her complicit sisters' only a plaything for whenever Jesus was awake.

The overly cherished image of the divine infant in the boat was a deft conflation of two gospel narratives, the nativity that placed the newborn Jesus in a feeding station (Luke 2:1–14) and the mature Jesus's crossing of Gennesaret (the Sea of Galilee) during a violent storm (Mark: 4: 35–41). In the little, private storm of Thérèse's coming of age Jesus was to arrive as a spouse, but this bride was left ever waiting, exquisite and exuberant though the waiting often was.[5] As a novice, she secured him anew when she became Thérèse de la Sainte-Face. It is in that penultimate role, Jesus staggering on the Via Dolorosa toward crucifixion, that he takes her through the mountain's subterranean path.[6] Following him in ardent anticipation, she calls to mind yet another mighty mythic passage, that of Eurydice guided through the underworld by her Orpheus. The force of this analogue comes from its being a rescue, and one that finally fails and leaves the young woman in her darkness, perhaps forever.

For any Carmelite sister the only admissible tale of a bonding with her divine spouse was Solomon's mystifying *Canticum Canticorum*, but the surcharged eroticism of its eight chapters remained impenetrable, and finally it does not comport with Thérèse's experience. She never claimed to have had a *unio mystica* with Jesus that could be conformed to the spouse's impassioned meeting with his young woman.[7] Thérèse lived out her life in Jesus as both the Psyche and the Eurydice of the Christian journey, loving intimately and faithfully, yet being left behind. She is venerated for having given to these two young, vulnerable and tormented selves a role that could never have been imagined among the pagan and uncharitable Greeks. The role had been given to her by Jesus.

II. *From Professed Vows to the Easter Conversion*

How long she passed through the darkness she had announced to Pauline in that summer of 1890 remains unknown; a kind of darkness clouds the time that the Carmelites call Thérèse's *années obscures*,[8] running from the autumn of 1890 into February, 1893, when Pauline assumed the priorate. Of the extant 266 letters from Thérèse only a piteous nineteen unfold themselves from these thirty formative months. What she wrote and received from Céline and what Céline destroyed begs a helpless guessing; likewise, what Thérèse wrote to Pichon. As for her first manuscript, she gives those thirty months only five pages, 76r-80v.

Nonetheless, there are a few glimpses of that vanished time. Pichon upbraided her in his characteristically imperative, then hortatory manner when she admitted to him that she doubted Jesus's love for her. Sometime within the next year Mère Gonzague was attempting to console her, *mon cher agnelet* ["my dear little lamb"] over the tribulations of a life which, for Christ's own, could only be a desert not intended to hearten the soul. Gonzague refers to Thérèse in the third person: "she is seeking only the cross of her belovèd, who has been abandoned by everyone...."[9] But was that truly so? Thérèse was *not* seeking the cross of Jesus but Jesus himself. Her iterated injunctions to her natural sisters—let us be this for Jesus and let us do that for Jesus—proclaim the urgency of girls preparing for a party to which a very special guest has been invited, and only he. But Jesus continued not to appear at their garden party. Why had he declined to come? Without receiving an answer to that question, Thérèse could not help but wonder whether Jesus loved her.

Gonzague went on: "Soon he's leading us to Mount Tabor or more often to Calvary, as it's there that he's given to us in the way of a child for his Mother."[10] These are sage words, but that does not mean that Thérèse was able to assimilate them to her own keen longing for the person of Jesus, the divine presence of him. She needed him so that she could give him all her solicitous love. In effect, she was being a true Carmelite, fired by zeal. *"Zelo zelatus sum pro Domino Deo"* ["I am zealous with zeal for the Lord God"] rang the motto of the Carmel, taken from the story of Elijah on its mountain after he had slaughtered the priests of Baal.[11] But Thérèse was zealous with zeal in her own, singular way, as the closing pages of Manuscript A reveal. There she admits to Pauline that she had experienced "the most absolute dryness" in her soul during her retreat, beginning August 28, 1890, before taking her vows. She goes on to make an astoundingly presumptuous remark: Jesus, asleep as usual in his little boat, would undoubtedly not awaken until she made "[her] great retreat in eternity."[12] She does not say how she could be so sure of this peculiar sequence, but she makes clear that she prefers it so. She would not trouble him as others do but leave him to sleep. She herself, as she notes, has spent her seven years in Carmel dozing off during prayers, but that has not perturbed her.

Here at the end of her first manuscript and within two years of her death appears one of the central elements of Theresian spirituality, the calm admission and embrace of personal limits; of failings, even. At twenty-two, when most young women might feel a bristling need to define and assert their independence, Thérèse had already attained an acceptance of internal weaknesses usually found only in a well-seasoned maturity. A retrospection from Manuscript A, completed in January 1896, to September 1890, when Thérèse wrote a prayer upon taking vows, serves to show how far she had come—and not come.

Her explicit desire for martyrdom of heart and body, her request that all her vows realize their completion in her love of Jesus, that Jesus bring her to understand what his bride must be for him—all of this comports fully with the Carmelite ethos of spiritual perfection. Altogether singularly Thérèse, however, in her missionary urge, extended well beyond the Carmelite sense of mission, to make hell and purgatory itself void of souls. It is a strange profession of vows that ends with a special pardon being asked "if I'm saying things that mustn't be said," but this writing makes apparent the peculiar amalgam of eager submission and no less eager, in fact exhilarated expectation so often characteristic of the writer in her relationship to her spouse. What proves salient in this profession is her request to become no burden to the community of her sisters but rather to be "forgotten like a little grain of sand for you, Jesus."[13] This image of herself occurs frequently in her early letters and as late as September 3, 1890 (LT 114), when she signed herself "the little grain of sand" but then it disappears, only to recur a good seven years later, at the beginning of C. There, she finds the saints as distant in their perfection from her as a mountain with an invisible summit is distant from "the little grain of dark sand trodden under the feet of passersby."[14]

In short, a clear trajectory conjoins Thérèse's profession of vows in the autumn of 1890 and the ripest writing of her spirituality, in the summer of 1897. Of obvious note is the change in perspective regarding the grain of sand, herself. From an initially out-of-the-way, unobtrusive granule within the Carmel she becomes a granule much trodden upon by passersby and sullied: now, a *dark* grain of sand. Trivial as these two passages might seem, they speak amply, and the alteration of the sand of grain by one attribute shows how careful and suggestive in her diction Thérèse was. A shrewd writer, she leaves many signposts, however small. She enjoyed one of the hidden perquisites of Carmelite life: that in a community sustained mostly by silence, when someone expressed herself, it was to say something.

One of the best known passages of Manuscript A is Thérèse's account of how she quite suddenly came to an awareness of her pathetic and selfish occupation with herself and learned to think of others. This story, known as her "Christmas conversion" of 1886, served to authenticate her claim that, although only fourteen in the following year, when she undertook to plead with the ecclesiastical authorities for her admission into Carmel, she had become older and far more ripened than her biological years indicated. Such, although illustrated in a minor domestic incident, was her Damascene moment, an abrupt and decisive turning point in her life.

There seems to be little point in wondering whether it is truly possible for someone to grow up within half an hour. What matters is that Thérèse wrote that it happened, believed that it happened, and furnished for herself the singularity of a drama, an event, rather than a perhaps more credible record, which would have tracked the glacial pace of an ordinary, adolescent peevishness into something quite different. A grace for her was a theatrical occasion, not a process. For example, she designated the direst grace among those in her life as "Our great treasure, February 12, 1889," the day her father was admitted to the sanatorium at Caen.[15] That this affliction went on for over three years mattered less than the sign of its sudden onset. The metonymous manipulation of time here, as though one horrible day could stand in for the hundreds that ensued, is not so callous as it might seem. Thérèse staunchly adheres to the calendric consciousness of Catholicism; precise and economical, one day may entail much more than its twenty-four hours. The sum of many years was compacted into the day of her *offrande*, June 9, 1895.

In Manuscript C she underwent what I shall call her Easter conversion of 1896. She does not name it so, but much speaks for this denomination from within her writing. If the Christmas "conversion" marked her birth into Christian life, the Easter conversion marked a kind of death. What remains to be determined is the nature of that death. To put it in gospel terms, how did this seed of grain fall into the ground to be reborn?

III. Notes on the Fretful Manuscript B

The seed that fell into the ground is depicted in Manuscript B, eight densely-written pages Thérèse composed in September 1896, during what she knew was to be her last private retreat.

As two of her natural sisters attested after her death, retreats were exceedingly trying times for her. Céline, not one to put a fine point on anything, characterized them as "a torment" for Thérèse. Pauline noted the preached retreat's standard admonitions about the hazards of mortal sin into which a retreating soul could so easily fall, even by a simple thought. Since her childhood years, Thérèse had been used to porting such morbid baggage, but it never became lighter for her to bear: "To her it seemed so difficult to offend God when you loved him! During all the time of these exercises, I saw her pale and wasted. She couldn't eat or sleep and would have fallen sick if it had gone on."[16]

Her sisters' testimonies indicate only one of the reasons, but a very weighty one, why B has particular importance: it was her last opportunity, as it then seemed, to affirm her unequivocal and unyielding trust in love as the essential integument between God and the human soul. Tacitly it rejects—if it does not altogether confound—the grim and hoary preoccupation with sin, as though such a focus was itself a sin, an implicit slighting, even a denial of God's compassionate love. This private retreat answered many torturous years of preached ones. Brief though it is, B deserves to be counted as a deeply moving literary self-portrait. I shall establish here its significance as a prolegomenon to Manuscript C.

First, a broad context in gender for both writings. In her sociology of women's writing in France, Beatrice Didier remarks how autobiography affords a plasticity for self-expression that has freed women from the limiting, male-dominated conventions imposed upon their sex: "the revenge of the imagination authorized their 'me' to forge a universe which escaped all constraint." She then remarks the aesthetic preference that women writers tend to evince for "the wondrous, where the tying between the real and the supernatural is effected without a jostle, where the wondrous is commingled in the most daily living."[17]

If all that is so, Thérèse's should be counted as the supreme exemplar of the feminine script. Her "me" was daily implicated in the exalted rapport of the Carmel, where one's life was (and is) turned to God. From there extends the one crucial difference setting her apart from other French autobiographers—George Sand, Simone de Beauvoir, Natalie Sarraute occupying first chairs—that her "me" remains, first and last, as intimate and as private as a confessional. Her recounting of her life, meaning her spiritual life (she had no other), amounts to a prayer to her belovèd spouse, Jesus. It might be called a love letter carried to the most exalted degree possible and the more remarkable for its writer's urging the feebleness of her shortcomings, her ontic inadequacy, as the very grounds for Christ's acceptance of her. Her writing empowers her to say how weak she is—weak in a fantastic way.

While Didier's female heroes of the pen "forged" their own universe and furnished it with marvels for daily use, Thérèse was born into a universe of marvels, one that Christian spirituality afforded her. It was the chief of those marvels that she had become the chosen bride of her deity. It is apt, then, but also surprising that her prayer in Manuscript B to Jesus begins with the formal *vous* as though she were meeting him for the first time, at the altar. She thanks him for guiding her little soul gently during a storm that had been building within her for many years and was loosed five months before, the time of her Easter conversion. She is writing in the midst of this storm.

She then relates to Jesus a dream she had on the night of May 10th.[18] Three Spanish Carmelite sisters from the time of the Carmel's foundations in France, which began in 1604, came to her while she was in the presence of Mère Gonzague. She recognized Madre Aña de Jesús, whose face glowed with a celestial beauty and who overwhelmed her with maternal caresses, assuring her, upon being asked, that Thérèse would die soon and that, yes, God was pleased with her. Thérèse tells Jesus what he already knew, of course, but which it was important for her to proclaim: this oneiric event restored her vision of heaven, "I *believed*, I *realized* that there is a Heaven and that this Heaven is filled with souls who cherish me, who regard me as their child."[19] What gave the dream its convincing gravity was that Thérèse had never been attentive to Madre Aña beyond what little she had heard of her. The visitation was sublimely gratuitous, and Thérèse felt boundless gratitude to Madre Aña and to the celestial company, which seemed to have deputized this Spanish mother.

Thérèse claims that this dream informed her of God's contentment with her as she was, but it seems also to have begotten what she saw as the innumerable other graces of wanting "to accomplish for you, Jesus, all the most heroic works."[20] It was not enough for her to die (soon) a Carmelite spouse and mother of souls. No; her wishes subsumed priesthood, apostleship, and martyrdom, the last being most important as the sacrificial love that would put her in the company of Jeanne d'Arc and the early Christian martyrs, Saints Agnes and Cecilia, women whom she had grown up longing to emulate. Coming down from this giddy rhetorical flight, she admits to the absurdity of her foolishness, since her soul is the smallest and weakest of all. Such is the range of her hyperbole, from the alpha of "all the most heroic acts" she wishes to accomplish, to the omega of her soul's uttermost incapacity to accomplish anything. She notes with irony that her real martyrdom has not been some outpouring of her blood on a battlefield but precisely this torment of carrying immeasurable desires in the pettiest of mortal frames.

Thérèse had long been buoyed by her extravagant ambitions, and only now was she reconciled to fully facing their almost comic sterility. It is a measure of her incongruous audacity at work even in childhood that she had allowed herself to get started toward these trouser heroisms, she, a timid little bourgeoise in a pedestrian age. Help came finally in her humbling herself to scale, and with that scaling down to reality came the invaluable corollary to humility, the capacity to see through the deceits of wishfulness and to cherish truthfulness to a ruthless degree, especially toward oneself. In B, though, she had not made that transition complete.

Instead, as in a fairy tale, just when the heroine has reached her lowest point (Snow White put to deadly sleep by the witch), Jesus fulfills "my *little childish desires*" as well as "other *desires greater* than the universe." She refers to a reading of St. Paul's first letter to the Christians of Corinth. There (chapter 12) he reviews the Pentecostal gifts, one given sufficient to each soul under the divine afflatus. Desiring *all* the gifts, Thérèse read on and discovered that none of these counted for anything without love. At once she was ravished by the realization of her desires: in becoming love, she would become everything, thus fulfilling her dream of many vocations. In her poetic turn, she speaks of descrying finally the lighthouse that shall guide her safely into port, of having found the secret of the lighthouse's flame. And yet she says it is God that has given her "my place in the Church."[21]

Although she writes of St. Paul's hymn to love as a revelation, her voluntarism wins out when she says that, like Mary Magdalene, she lowered herself into the depths of her nothingness and thus rose and attained her end. It is not clear whether she perceived that humbling as sufficient unto itself or as strategic, that is, as the condition to which God would respond by lifting her up.[22] It seems likely that just as she found God had given to her this special place in the Church (that is her sequence of verbs), so she rose and was raised from nothingness to Love.

Halfway through Manuscript B Thérèse reveals what it is finally all about: the search for parity with Christ himself. She does not refer to Philippians 2 where St. Paul speaks of Christ lowering himself from heaven into the near nothingness of human slavery, but she knew that he did so from love of fallen humanity. Her own lowering of herself *within* her particular nothingness was her gesture as Love transforming that nothingness into fire. That she could be a fitting sacrifice came from her assumption that, as in the Old Testament the sacrifices to the mighty god of justice had to be pure and perfect, so the sacrifices made to divine love could be imperfect and—not impure—but weak.[23]

Her finding appointment for herself as Love in the Church allowed her to realize, as she understood it, the dynamics of love that she had found in the *Cantico* of San Juan de la Cruz: "love is not paid for except by itself."[24] So weighty were these words for her that she had inscribed them onto the *armoiries,* her fancied coat of arms at the end of Manuscript A. San Juan contends that the human soul seeks a love for God that will be equal to God's love for the soul, an equality which, to Thérèse, followed as naturally as the parity of the lover and the belovèd in Solomon's canticle.[25] But as her Solomonic spouse was Jesus, she yearned for the validation of her love, a sign that would establish her claim to parity. Shrewdly, she finds it in her child-like weakness, the very thing which had made her incapable of carrying off those most heroic works of her childhood's fantasies.

With all the coyness of a wheedling child, Thérèse contends that parents do not hesitate to grant the desires of their little ones. The blessed souls she alluded to in her narrative about dreaming of Madre Aña included her own parents, so that when now she calls upon those souls, "O blessed inhabitants of Heaven, I beg you to *adopt me as your infant,*" Thérèse surely has Louis and Zélie in mind.[26] It was Louis who had taught her how adroitly extortionist a child could be with an indulgent father, so it is odd that she never addresses either of her parents in her prayers. She was too aware of their weaknesses, their endearing littleness and helplessness, and parents usually do not adopt their own children.

Well and good, the celestial adoption, but what has happened to the longed-for parity of love? It has fallen away completely as Thérèse resigns herself once more to her own feebleness, as though the consequences of being a child before a loving parent (all taken and what given in return?) had come home to her. The proven works of love that come from such a weak little person can only be little themselves. It is here that she interposes the minor chore for which she became world famous and iconically defined, the strewing of flower petals. This gesture she identifies as a metonym for performing any little sacrifice, giving any little glance, saying any little word, all done in proof of a love for Jesus.

Then, having reached this lowliest point, Thérèse bounds once again to the highest. She imagines Christ taking up the petals of her littleness—"these nothings will give you pleasure"[27]—and, with his divine touch, giving them to the Church Triumphant, the heavenly mother, who shall pass them to the earth-bound Church Militant, bringing victory. The flowers of Thérèse's tortured inconsequence shall be given a celestial manumission and thus empower the Church of missionaries and martyrs. It is an astonishing sequence in its reaches, from earth to heaven and back. It might be called the triumphalism of humility.

As though seeking to validate her petal strewing, she turns again to San Juan de la Cruz and a favored saying about Mary, the sister of Lazarus. This Mary is sitting lovingly attentive before Jesus as Martha works apart. Juan writes: "more precious before God and the soul is a little of such pure love and more beneficial to the Church, though it seems that [the soul] is doing nothing, than all those other works combined."[28] But, that affirmed, Thérèse torments herself yet again, wondering if her love is truly pure.[29] She has already admitted herself imperfect, but she has yoked perfection with purity. Implicitly, because she is imperfect, she is impure. How, then, can her love for Jesus be pure?

Thérèse at this point has to consider whether *all* of her desires, both the careerist sort and the flowery, the grand and the minuscule, are only foolishness within her. She asks that if she is being rash, Jesus should remove these desires, as they, unavailing, are her greatest martyrdom. Yet the true rashness, a most poignant one, comes when she adds that "after having aspired to the highest regions of Love, if I must not attain them one day, I shall have tasted more *sweetness in my martyrdom, in my lunacy,* than I would taste in the bosom of *celestial joys.*"[30] Here she carries her audacity to the outermost limit, telling Jesus that if there is no heaven, then he should let her go on savoring the sweet bitterness of her unrealizable desires. It would be difficult to imagine a more grievous and wrenching plea, as from an addict hugging her narcosis.

Once more, however, Thérèse recovers herself—likely beginning the next morning's writing—with a rescuing image: she cannot understand why God would permit impossible desires in so poor a frame as hers. She says they belong to the high-flying, the other and worthy Carmelites and the saints, all eagles. She remains earthbound, a piteous sparrow helplessly flapping its wings in the storm. Even so, she writes, this little bird has fixed its eye, eagle-like, upon a sunlight that is not there, a light obscured by the storm's clouds. (Implicitly, her sparrowy vision is superior to any eagle's.) What makes this passage both so forlorn and so unusual is that Thérèse speaks of herself as fallen and sinful. She is occupied with earthly trifles (*bagatelles*), but not disposed to lament her own misery for "all her misdeeds" or to hide (like Adam in the Garden?) or to die of penance. She says she is ready to confess in detail her infidelities, singing their sweet song with a bold abandon. Did not Christ come for the sinners rather than the just? And should he not come, this bird shall rejoice in "this deserved suffering."[31]

Here, tucked away in a fretful, meandering minor key lies arguably the real magnificence of B, so far as a radical humbling can be called magnificent. It comes as an antipodes to what is usually culled from B for triumphalist, consolatory, and therefore spurious ends, Thérèse as Love at the Church's Heart, as she had proclaimed herself only a few days before. Now, Thérèse admits to herself that she is a wretched, broken vessel of faith and hope. She is a sinner, consciously embracing her cherished lies and yet—here sounds that ruthless truthfulness—ready to admit everything about her imperfection *and* impurity. She has discovered that the recompense for unsparing candor about the inner life is a priceless equanimity, as though in stripping oneself down and down, one becomes ready for the peace that Christ had promised. The candor and the peace are alike sublimely incomprehensible. Best of all, the koan of a rejoiced suffering.

In this nadir of her darkness inscribed in words far more bitter than anything to be found ten months later in C, Thérèse affords no gloss on what she means by her deserving that suffering. Although she claims that the celestial eagles, that blessed company from which Madre Aña had come, would protect her from the vultures of despair seeking to devour her, her pathetic avian self hides its head alone under its own wing. Even the consolatory Virgin, under whose robe the Carmelites often sought refuge in their private tribulations, is absent from this stormy scene. Thérèse had not thought to turn to her, because the real drama is with Jesus and the storm between them.

Within such unmitigated bleakness and as though braced by it, Thérèse creates an almost theatrical contrast to the stormy setting. The little bird becomes "happy to be *weak* and *little*," at peace in her heart, and confident that she will be the prey not of the vultures but of *the Eagle* (the italics and capital signifying Jesus) who comes from the solar center of love.[32] She is buoyed by a proleptic gratitude for this deliverance. Such is the outermost degree of her *confiance*. It is so absolute that it goes beyond hope itself, so far as hope is always girded or countered by fear. Thérèse's *confiance* has as its chief predicate a rugged fearlessness as it rests upon the fact that, however distant he may be from the soul seeking him, Jesus is always present at the same time in the valley of tears, "hidden under the appearance of a white wafer."[33]

It then occurs to Thérèse that even as her desires were madness (*folie*), Christ's descent to sinners and his dying on their behalf were also madness, and such madness was drawing her toward him. This divine centripety, the love from Jesus drawing the soul to him, is one of her most iterated images. The key verb *attirer* occurs sixty-five times in her writing. But imperturbable though her helplessness might be, she does not feel Jesus himself exerting that pull. She says she must call upon her siblings in heaven to intercede and secure for her the eagle wings that shall enable her to fly upward. That, she claims, is yet more of her madness.

Not quite crediting her siblings' intercession, Thérèse closes with the prayer that sometime Jesus will descend like an eagle, bear her up to the foyer of love, and plunge her into the fire of divine love's abyss, there to complete her pledge in the *offrande* of June 1895. Here, though, she closes with the crucial petition, one that transcends the unhappy vagaries of her anxious self in this document and that serves as an entry into C. She asks that Jesus descend to *other* souls, little as her own, a great number of them, and recruit them into a legion worthy of divine love. She has at last ceased to think of herself, and in that cessation she picks up for the first time the light that she carries through the darkness of her last summer.

The retreat of September 1896 affords a kind of relief map of Thérèse's spiritual itinerary. It has peaks, valleys, and very little level plain. Thus it reflects well the extreme contraries of Thérèse's temperament, her infinite longings and her profound inadequacy to bring them to fruition. In her inflated mesmeric moments, she calls herself Love (and how many readers applaud!), but when she humbles herself, she is with Luke's publican and closer to Gethsemani. As a series of explorations into her self, Manuscript B affords false starts and false endings, false in that she herself cannot rest contentedly in them but cancels them all, excepting one. She is trying to find her way in a darkness that has encircled her for more than four months. Having lived in and for the love of Jesus, she must now face the challenge of feeling cut off from him, from heaven itself. B is about her search for a final reckoning of herself before the mystery of God and the mystery of her spiritual affliction: she wondered why God instilled in her such boundless desires if they were all inopportune and pointless. Why, after a lifetime of seeking to love God, was she now denied the grace of faith and hope? These nail-driving interrogatives produce no answers for her. Such are the torments running as an undertow beneath the frothy waves of B's often billowy rhetoric. It is easy to confuse the foam with the current.

For B affords perhaps the most celebrated of her self-depictions: not the little bird in the storm, the weakling she knew herself to be, the unabashed sinner sitting in song about her sins, but "Love at the Heart of the Church." Devout Christians understandably want their saints to be unequivocal, requiring no engagement with contradiction or ambiguity, even though this document is primarily about the physics of contradiction in the writing self and about the ambiguity by which to acknowledge finitude and helplessness. The almost strident major-keyed note of Love at the Heart that Thérèse sounds and rejoices in so very briefly has echoed over several generations, but for her own searching self it proves temporary. She moves on. Far less conspicuous has been the very propulsion that informs all of B no less than of C. It comes simply: "I'm seeking the truth."[34] The proof that she is doing so lies in the urgent forthrightness of her momentum; she no sooner arrives in one station of rest than she sets off toward another to test it in turn, as though nothing could be more deadly to her than fakery and pretense, the false arrival. Consolations she believes she has reached suddenly become unsavory to her. Repeatedly, she flies high but remembers to bring herself low. She is indeed a queer little bird, knowing only summits and chasms.

The definitive value of B lies not in the nominal badges Thérèse awarded herself so restively but in the tense compaction of opposites that make her so engaging. Hers is an exuberant longing that can convince itself by its own need and take flight only to be countered and confounded by a gravitational pull toward the self-humbling, which as a Carmelite she daily, dutifully felt. She could not proclaim herself Love at the Heart when she unhesitatingly ended this missive to Jesus as she regularly ended her letters, *rel. carm. ind.*, "unworthy Carmelite sister." The September retreat became the optimal and ultimate occasion during which to submit herself to the extremes of her own temperament.

She knew she was being tested, and left a record of her bouts within that testing. Nothing would have been more satanic than for her to convince herself that she was not in darkness or that she was sure to find a way out of it. That would not have been Thérèse, especially not now, when she was under the exigencies of death and pushing herself on toward truth-telling at its most merciless. The result is a series of the fond presumptions she wanted to embrace but discarded. The novices she worked with testified that she was a stringent and exacting *compagne*. In B she is that way with herself.

In the dynamism of her mere eight pages of retreat, the first peak, as it were, comes in that vision of Madre Aña de Jesús. So lovingly within it is Thérèse sustained and so mighty is the assurance that it gave, and that she needed, of God's calling her contentedly, that it is strange she was not contented with this dream portent. She remembered its sweetness but she was unable to let it suffice, as though this grace would somehow not avail. She may have feared it was a delusion. She leaves it as merely "the prelude to much greater graces with which You wished to overwhelm me."[35]

My sense is that as the dream was speaking to her inadequacy, God's proclaimed contentedness could not give her the assurance she needed within herself. That is human. A woman self-convinced that she is plain will never be dissuaded from that certainty by anyone's protests that she is beautiful. Thérèse needed a grace that gave her an activist's momentum, and that is what "all the works" come to, a large-scale project to vanquish her smallness and inadequacy by making her too busy to notice them. To put it in gospel contexts, this was a Mary who found herself wanting to become a Martha. But her sense of inadequacy proved too deep, and the very projects she wished to undertake tormented her because she knew she was an impossible agent. Inadequacy and littleness return with renewed force and form a coda, sounding the theme from which the oneiric Madre Aña had taken her cue.

Inadequate, weak, little—her essential falling short became a springboard propelling her to seek a self beyond herself, one she knew was fantastic but that filled the void created by her yearning for consequence. As only God could have instilled that yearning in her, surely it *had* to be realized. Only heroic deeds would do because they were exemplary and would allow her to become exemplary. A Christian heroism, especially in martyrdom, would not only enlist her with those saintly women she had treasured throughout her childhood: Agnes, Cecilia, Jeanne d'Arc; it would identify her as a saver of souls in the Church's posterity. (Figure 5.2.)

A saintliness of the heroic sort was not, however, part of Carmelite spirituality. No Carmel was ever a training ground for a combat mission; every Carmel has always been a house of prayer (for embattled priests), and pretends to nothing else. A contemplative life passed in obscurity would necessarily have nothing to do with "all the works." Nothing; but neither of the magisterial first voices of Carmel, not Teresa nor Juan, brings Thérèse back down to the firmness of earth. It is Francis of Assisi who refused, as she oddly puts it, "the lofty worthiness of a priesthood." So

FIGURE 5.2 Prayer card depicting Jeanne d'Arc, which Thérèse held on her deathbed. Copyright Archives du Carmel de Lisieux.

it is he whom she says she must imitate. It is touchingly characteristic of Thérèse in the restiveness of this retreat that even Francis's model of earthbound humility, the lowest point coming in his living with lepers, she responds to with emulous tones: "I admire and envy Saint Francis's humility."[36] It is as though she would have liked to contest with him for the title of most humble.

Thérèse was showing herself altogether conventional in wishing she could become a saint. Every Christian would wish to be both called and chosen. The Carmel itself, in affording a disciplinary way to perfection, was implicitly making saints, and yet, as every Carmelite and every Christian knows, the true saints are known only to God. Those proclaimed as saints by the Church serve as models of Christian life, as intercessors, as teachers, and there is a fixed aura that keeps them elevated in the performance of those roles. Their greatness inspires, sustains, and teases. Most Christians move on with a humble acceptance of their mediocrity, but there are always those who, with Léon Bloy, feel that the only sadness in life is not to be one of the saints. For Thérèse, it was at times an unbearable sadness.

Thérèse seems to have forgotten or to have laid aside an injunction from the first formative text of her spirituality, the one committed to memory, the *Imitatio Christi*, that a Christian must not seek to become a great name, that is, a saint.[37] Every true saint is inwardly condemned to the awareness that she or he is not one. With that humbling fact goes the far weightier caution Jesus himself provided (Luke 6:26) against the sociology of awe: "Woe unto you, when all men shall speak well of you! For so did their fathers to the false prophets."

Too keenly aware of her unworthiness, as though she were fenced in or walled off by her insuperable inadequacy, Thérèse trumped her weakness by claiming that exactly because of it, Jesus was pleased to fulfill those desires greater than the universe by giving her the vocation of becoming Love at the Heart of the Church, a role subsuming all missions, martyrdoms, priesthoods: "in that way I shall become all... in that way my dream will be realized!!!" The fervid, child-like egotism of this exclamation, transparently reminiscent of her famous infantilism at the age of three, "I'm choosing everything," shows Thérèse at her most lovable, *not* because that title of Love has been substantially conferred upon her by adulating posterity, as though it were of prophetic moment, but because it exposes her need, the desperation of a convinced nobody seeking to become a supreme somebody.[38]

Thérèse is telling on herself (indeed, the whole of B is such a record), and having tasted the joy of becoming Love, she subtracts it at once and reverts to her real business, facing weakness and powerlessness. She has to do so, because that is where truth-seeking inevitably leads, back and back again. Turning from scripture to her life's own witnessing, she calls up her *offrande* of fifteen months before. As sacrifices to the Hebrew God of justice had to be stainlessly perfect, so her sacrifice of herself to the Christian God of love was (had to be?) weak and imperfect. She says divine love had so willed it because such love descends in compassion and lowers itself to the nothingness (herself) which it is to transform into holocaustic fire. She has come full circle within a single page, from being the all of Love to being a nothingness to which divine love descends.

Although San Juan de la Cruz seems to have inspired Thérèse to make something of her nothingness, whether as pure love or as reciprocal love, in both instances she asks herself whether such love is genuinely hers to offer. How could she love reciprocally, love Jesus as he loves her? How could there be pure love in her, given her wretchedly ineffectual self? Her stopping short on these crucial matters affords a key to the peculiar nature of B, that the most exalted moments, the widening gyres, become suspect, as the truth-seeking that has impelled her threatens to disappear into fantasy. Conversely, the abysmally confessional passages of defeat are the genuine. Suffering does not lie. The exclamatory arrivals that pass so quickly point to their phantom-like nature. They glow and then fade, a will-o'th'-wisp. It is in the lower depths of herself, when she is helpless, that everything rings true, as when she admits, "I'm afraid of finding myself overwhelmed under the weight of my audacious desires."[39] Her expansive desires, in sum, are oppressions. At times, she seems to be very close to the breakthrough that will tell her *why* those desires are oppressive.

Thérèse's crying out for adoption into heaven suggests she had rejected even the dream vision of Madre Aña. She simply could not get enough assurance and re-assurance about herself, especially in regard to Jesus. (The many lost letters to Almire Pichon were probably centered upon that insatiability.) Wondering if she could be up to loving him, she all but gives it out that perhaps Jesus is not so loving of her. There is the faintest hint of reproach. If that doubting, left inexplicit, seems an absurdity, there is evidence that she felt qualms of this sort even about the most solicitous and loving presence in the Christian heaven: "I would like to be certain that she *loves* me, the Blessèd Virgin."[40] There is probably no greater measure of the depth of her suffering than those few, unadorned words.

As though seeking out the cause for her unease about her love-worthiness, Thérèse resorts with surprising artifice to the language of sin and applies it to herself, but that, too, she lets go, as though she could not even convince herself of being a sinner. If she could, she would then be in the attention-getting posture of Mary Magdalene. Jesus came for sinners, but poor Thérèse cannot assure herself that she is one. These are spiked ironies: just as the Juanist injunctions to the extreme exigency of love match her temperament but not her stamina or her sense of self-worth, so the notion of sinfulness is another shoe that resists fitting, and she denies herself even the consolation of needing Jesus.

Manuscript B is the witness to a tortuous inefficacy, a *huis clos* of frustration and irresolution. Beginning with a storm, it ends with clouds still looming thick. Its pricelessness lies in its sustained combat between truth-seeking and phantasy, the candor of spiritual lowliness and an obfuscating release into the highfallutin. Two images mark these polarities: the small, insignificant bird, huddled under cloud and wind, and the strewn rose-petals, the merest small actions empowering the Church through Christ's own hands. In my estimate, the first speaks far better than the second of Theresian spirituality, as it concerns humble, unperturbed acceptance of suffering, the acquiescence known as *abandon*. The second, enticing though it may be as a gesture of littleness, turns triumphalist, arrogating a spiritual power that God has not granted. (The Holy Spirit cannot be maneuvered nor cantilevered.) After Thérèse's death the strewing of rose petals assumed the unsettling aroma of consolation, and not far behind consolation invariably comes the vulgarity of the carefully staged, the fake, an emblem made into a commodity of folkish consumerism.

These last remarks seem to mount an attack upon Thérèse, but in fact, so far as they may seem an assault, it is the iconic Thérèse that is at issue here, not the dying woman: *pluie de roses*, the shower of testimonies that rained down as though on cue from the stormy Manuscript B, in volume after volume prior to her canonization (what Paul Claudel might have meant in lamenting "the Thérèse industry"), mark only what the populist enthusiasm for this young sister of Carmel came to: she was obscure—all the better—but solicitous of the little souls of the Church as no one else had been before. As a self-proclaimed nobody and yet a religious, she was their apparent champion and their long-needed voice. More than that, the *pluie* democratized the notion of sainthood for Catholicism, and the swell of popular enthusiasm for making this sister a saint amounted to a covert revenge against ecclesiastic hierarchism. It was, in its way, a revolution within the Church, one that the Church's hierarchs met just in time and handled shrewdly.

The iconic Thérèse, the plaster Thérèse of chapels, the Thérèse seized upon at B 5r-v (but never at B 6r-v, with its little bird) has nothing to do with what makes her so amazing, that she fared through the darkness of storms in B and the darkness of the tunnel and the vault in C with an uncanny ease, clinging to her own love for God and discovering its farthest reaches, well beyond those souls clutching the rose petals. If she discovered anything of lasting import through her eight days of B, it was that the real shower is the suffering that Jesus sends down upon meager, redeemable selves. The storm Thérèse had to endure is inextricably bound to the cross she finally picked up.

A remembrance of Thérèse's darkness written by Céline in 1908 seems as dark as those Thérèse herself penned, and it jibes convincingly with C. When Céline ventured to ask her about it, Thérèse exclaimed, "Oh, if you were to spend just five minutes in the testing I am going through!" Sometimes, when talking about something entirely different, Thérèse would break off in an anguished tone with "Is there a heaven? Tell me about it." But Céline's resort to sweet soothing platitudes about the celestial realm were to no avail: "Most often, it was necessary to change the subject, as my words seemed to increase her torments.... I understood then the horrible state of the damned who live without faith and without hope."[41] When Céline edited those remarks for her *Conseils et Souvenirs*, she omitted the last sentence. Preferring charity to judgment, Thérèse herself never refers to damned souls.

IV. An Initial Misplacement: The Disaster of Histoire d'une âme, *1898*.

Thérèse's story of her self has been known to the world for over one hundred years. For more than half of those years the story was edited, issued, and re-issued in a way that distorted the trajectory of her life and her dying. Those responsible—Père Godefroy Madelaine, Gonzague, and Pauline—chose to place the final manuscript, C, in immediate succession to A. That made sense only in terms of the two works, the second being a resumption or completion of the first. Thérèse had been instructed by the prioress to resume the account of her life in Carmel, an account that she had only begun to develop when she concluded A.

The *Story of a Soul*, however, came to much more than A and C. It was distended by an appendix that included all of Thérèse's poems, a few of her letters and prayers, her *conseils* recalled by Céline, and in the course of new editions an ever-growing heap of populist testimony to her miracle working, denominated *Pluie de roses*, the shower of roses. There were over one hundred pages of these entries by the time of the 1911 edition. Within this oversized *circulaire*, twelve chapters subsumed her autobiography. Ms C, however, began as the ninth chapter and ended in the eleventh; it was edited in such a way as to obscure the fact that Gonzague was a new addressee. Gonzague wanted all of the autobiography to seem to have been addressed to her alone. That meant that B, which was addressed to Marie, had to be recast at the start, "my dear sister" becoming "my dear Mother." B unfolded within the eleventh chapter immediately after C was abruptly dissolved into the story that Thérèse asked Pauline to append, *Histoire de la pécheresse convertie et morte d'Amour* ["Story of a Sinful Woman Converted and Dead from Love"].

In that way chronology was ruinously ignored. The impression that the printed sequence gave was that the fretful exuberance of Ms B came *subsequent* to the illuminations of C. September 7–18 1896 came after June 1897. It is as though the testing in the tunnel, under the vault, at the table of suffering—all of that had been cleared away or overcome and now the young Carmelite was seeking a way, an outlet for a dynamic careerism. The *Story* ends with a wholly spurious upbeat that does plain violence to documentary facts.

There is no point in inveighing against the editors. They had assumed a task that was extraordinary for each of them and for which none of them had professional training. They can hardly be faulted for not having the objective criteria such as a historiographer or biographer would need to follow, the rigor of a consistent chronology to indicate how Thérèse had made her Christian way as a writer. In their time and by the very nature of hagiography itself, which is what *Histoire d'une âme* came to (Thérèse's audacity at last becoming infectious), there would have been no need nor expectation of explanatory notes such as abound in the indispensable centenary editions from CERF.

Neither is there any purpose in criticizing Pauline for her changes in Thérèse's diction and even her phrasing. Thérèse always looked to Pauline, far better educated than she and her adoptive mother to boot, as her instructor. It is wholly credible that she authorized Pauline to make whatever emendations she thought fit. There are some seven thousand of them, but the great majority is slight. A look at the substantial changes would be revelatory, but such an effort belongs to someone's study of Pauline and her spirituality. Her many changes are helpful in signifying what was *not* Thérèse, but they raise a key point in the reception history that made her a folkish saint: Pauline's presentation (not to say recasting) of

Thérèse, especially in the memorializing final chapter of the *Histoire d'une âme*, determined the image that generations of cultists would carry.

That is not all Thérèse has been edited decisively, if not incontrovertibly, as an image attended by one-line statements or even mere phrases (such as *spiritual childhood*, now deemed inappropriate) iterated into cliché. This editorial imbalance, reinforced by the staggering simplicity of the iconic, means that one's response to Thérèse is preconditioned to become more reflexive than reflective. If, as Jesus tells us, a prophet is dishonored within his own house and family, is it not enough that a saintly figure such as Thérèse should suffer for the Church? Must a saint also suffer at the hands of the Church?

Two of the most important people in Thérèse's heart suffered in that way. Through exhaustive documentary details available to her she knew about Jeanne d'Arc, about the sinister pharisaism of her ecclesiastical interrogators, and about the ghastly death to which she was condemned. Thérèse did not know about the sufferings of her beloved Juan de la Cruz, about his sequestration by and from his brothers, about the ignominy he endured to the end of his life. Her own suffering is of an order quite different from Jeanne's or Juan's. It comes from manipulations and distortions, however benignly meant, of who she was and what she has written. A part of that effort has involved the comparative negligence of Manuscript C and especially of the darkness attested there.

The following discussion is meant to overcome that seemingly willful ignorance. Denial, evasion, and the adroit cosmetics of triumphalism have had their day. Thérèse is now a doctor of the Church. How is it possible to learn from her, genuinely learn, if the dark mysteries she recorded continue to be dodged?

V. Thérèse and Mère Gonzague

The first fact that launches the reader into C, and one worth remembering along the way, is that Thérèse was addressing her writing to the only sister who could follow her critically into its byways and its depths, Mère Marie de Gonzague. By a great mercy Gonzague resumed the priorate upon election, March 21, 1896, less than a month before Thérèse's entry into what she called the densest of shadows. Thérèse speaks of "your blessèd priorate" as though only Gonzague, not Pauline, could be a fit accomplice of God when Thérèse was undergoing her temptations.[42]

It is idle to speculate upon what Thérèse would have written to Pauline, had her sister been re-elected to a second term. The manuscript addressed to Pauline, A, for all its wealth of reminiscence, says very little about Thérèser's spiritual development. Pauline herself pointed out this deficiency during the beatification hearings.[43] How different, how much spiritually richer, might A have been, had Gonzague been the addressee, someone impatient of familial anecdotes, unimpressed by sentimentalities and adolescent hyperboles shared among natural sisters, exigent of an unsparing reflection upon a wee self summoned by Christ to Carmel. Yet it is well to have A just as it is, so that it is possible to chart the almost miraculous progressions marked variously by B and C.

A second fact about C is that both Gonzague and Thérèse knew it would be of a most unusual genre, an autobiographical obituary. Pauline had told Gonzague that Thérèse could be assigned to write her own death notice. In the Carmel's tradition of *circulaires*, the necrologies posted to all francophone Carmels around the globe, the prioress gathered as much information as she could from the community in order to write of the dead sister's early formation and vocation, her life and work in the Carmel, including all the administrative and service positions she had held, and her exit into eternal life usually inwoven with an account of her final illness. The standard length of such a narrative was four printed pages, but some *circulaires*, particularly those for prioresses and co-founders of what were called daughter Carmels, ran to many more. In 1891 Pauline had written by Gonzague's assignment a 21-page *circulaire* on the Lisieux Carmel's co-founder, Mère Geneviève. The longest in Thérèse's time came just short of a hundred pages, with one prioress writing over eighteen months about her venerable predecessor, Mère Agathe of Nantes. The inordinate length was justified by the prioress's having turned the *circulaire* into more than a biography; it was a manual, with generously lengthy quotes from Mère Agathe's reflections on the daily practices and exactions of Carmelite spirituality and how a community might best be run. Apparently, the need for a kind of updating was felt, and in 1904 a prioress's handbook was issued anonymously to all the French Carmels.

It seems plausible that the Lisieux Carmel, or at least Pauline, Thérèse, and Gonzague, took inspiration from the distention of Mère Agathe's *circulaire*. But that a young novice should be permitted to write at an indeterminate length about her own journey, an account meant for printing—what presumption! Céline, who had entered the Carmel in September, 1894, just three months before Pauline had ordered Thérèse to commence her autobiography, was the first reader of A. Thérèse shared with her each of the six *cahiers* (notebooks) as it was completed, and Céline was so delighted with them that she urged their publication. Thérèse laughed off the suggestion at the time, but Céline may have urged it further with Pauline. Céline was the first to realize that her little sister was a print-worthy writer.

Pauline informed Gonzague for the first time about Ms A on June 3, 1897, only days after Gonzague replaced Thérèse with Sr. Marie des Anges as the trainer of novices, with the full and proper title, *maîtresse*. Gonzague accepted Pauline's suggestion—it must have been very tactfully put—that Thérèse be ordered to resume her narrative. Not exclusively autobiographical, Ms A had closed with reflections on Carmelite life. A resumption of the writing could only, then, be further reflections. Not initially certain what she would write about, Thérèse took topical suggestions from Pauline. But she was not addressing Pauline now. She was addressing Gonzague, and that difference determined what she would say and how.

This matter deserves emphasis. Through the poems she was asked by individual sisters to write on their behalf; through her correspondence, and especially through her work with four singular novices, Thérèse had learned the importance of heeding each personality with which she was dealing. She cast her words accordingly. Two of the best texts in evidence of this attentiveness are the letters she wrote to the young priests Bellière and Roulland. It is not that she had to invent a self within her each time she turned from one person to another, but if she had been asked for a few dozen versions of her autobiography, she would have been able to produce as many variations, like a composer rearranging a score with varying instrumentations. Had Thérèse written for her needy and sometimes anxious sister, Marie, she might well have scored heavily for strings; for the lively, chipper Marie de la Trinité, she would have used impish woodwinds; for the bossy, booming St. Vincent de Paul, a lot of brass. With Gonzague she was not averse to a sophisticated percussion but with a full orchestra. Some staccati and sforzandi, too.

Before a look at the crepuscular life of C, its addressee merits more notice. (Like Pauline, Gonzague deserves a biography.) In the second series of hearings toward Thérèse's beatification, the *procès apostolique*, some witnesses, notably Pauline and Marie de la Trinité, spoke critically of Gonzague, thus providing a basis for melodramatic portraiture of her in subsequent texts. But this image of Gonzague—imperious, capricious, arbitrary, mercurial—has a positive underside that has not been appreciated. The Carmelites were unhappily remembering someone whom Thérèse had learned, not without cost, to cherish. Thérèse was alive to and responded to what was the hidden source of the others' complaints, Gonzague's acute insecurities. The office of priorate, the seat of unquestionable authority, perhaps blinded even Pauline to the weaknesses of Gonzague as its tenant, even though by the time of that second hearing, she herself had served some terms as prioress and knew her own weaknesses.

Pauline's assumption of the priorate could have taught her much about Gonzague, but overwhelmed as she was in taking on the post, she had her hands full. A detailed record of the transition remains, however. On February 20, 1893, the day of Pauline's election, Uncle Isidore went to the Carmel, with his daughter Marie. Léonie and Céline came close behind. They found Pauline speechless and sobbing softly. Isidore tried to cheer her, but, a veteran visitor, he sensed the awkwardness immediately as Gonzague was stationed by the parloir grille the entire while. As Mme Guérin observed to her other daughter, Jeanne, "Happily, Pauline will have Mother M. de G. to guide her."[44]

Happily for the Carmel, but not altogether happily for Pauline. Within a few weeks, Gonzague suffered acute bouts of asthma, became feverish, and was convinced she would soon be dying. Pauline was anguished to see her so ill. Alexandre de Cornière, Carmel's physician, warned her that if Gonzague's fever continued (ague, as it used to be known), it would be very dangerous. "She spoke to me last evening like a dying person. I was shattered and wept! She told me the good Lord would help me, that I didn't need her any more, that Mère Geneviève would be with me, etc.... and she gave me her last urgings... imagine my pain!"[45]

It is not hard to discern the melodrama and hysterics of this scene and both of its participants' roles. Gonzague's vanity was deeply wounded when she was replaced in the priorate she had long managed by the young woman for whose novitiate she herself had served as *maîtresse*. Gonzague, nearly 60, and Pauline, only 32, had reversed roles and had to adjust to each other on those difficult terms. As the elder, Gonzague might have comported herself better, for she had once been in Pauline's position before the imposing Mère Geneviève, the now eighty-eight-year-old to whom she was grandly consigning the distraught young prioress. Gonzague's recovery, much prayed for, was deemed miraculous. In the February election she had been appointed, as expected, *maîtresse de novices* and *dépositaire*, or records keeper, a post that allowed her to keep a close watch on how Pauline economized.[46]

Gonzague's return to the priorate upon election, March 21, 1896, began a new life for Thérèse. Under Pauline's priorate, Thérèse wrote forty-six letters, all of them addressed to people within the closed family circle. Under Gonzague, she wrote eighty-one, only half of which went to family members. Among them are some of her most substantial articulations of her spirituality. Now, her world was opening up to the transcendental family of her new brothers, Bellière and Roulland, and her new charges, the novices she was training. (Céline as novice is the obvious anomaly in this new family configuration.) It is as though Gonzague had liberated her from the stifling solicitudes of her natural family and foremost among them Pauline. Pauline's subtle alienation from the Gonzague-Thérèse nexus was registered in her turbulent dismay over the very tardy revelation of her little sister's hemoptysis.[47] Gonzague as prioress was rightly privy to matters that Thérèse, for better or worse, chose not to share with Pauline.

Altogether exceptionally, Gonzague, seasoned by her more than thirty-five years in the Carmel, confided in Thérèse. That much is known from one of those meaty letters, written on June 29, 1896, three months after the tumultuous election of Gonzague. It is cast not as a letter, however, but as a kind of parable or, perhaps better, a *récreation pieuse* with the title, "Légende d'un tout petit Agneau," the story of a very little lamb. Transparently, Gonzague is depicted in the shepherdess of the story, melancholy, taking no joy in tending her sheep but still loving a little lamb: "and as if the lamb had been her equal, the Shepherdess confided to her her hurts and sometimes wept with her...."[48]

In a dream vision, the lamb is delivered to a heavenly countryside where the divine Pastor inquires about her tears and those of the Shepherdess. Told that it had taken seven ballots for the sheep to choose the Shepherdess anew, the Pastor explains that he had willed her suffering and that the flock was his cherished instrument for sanctifying her soul. When the lamb asks the Pastor why he has not shared his intent with the Shepherdess, he says that he has willed her to carry her heavenly cross. Besides, she should rejoice to have a share in *his* sort of sufferings: to be misunderstood, rejected, alienated. But he entrusts this message to the lamb so as to mitigate the bitterness of the beloved woman.

The vision ends prophetically. The lamb asks the Pastor not to leave the flock languishing long in earthly exile. The Pastor, anticipating Madre Aña in the dream recounted in Ms B (2r), promises that soon both the Shepherdess and the lamb will be joining him and blessing for eternity the happy suffering that has earned them so much heavenly joy. Thérèse had fifteen months to live; Gonzague, eight years.

This "legend" goes well beyond the incidentals it records: the grief of Gonzague and the celestial carrot of everlasting bliss at the terminus of that grief. More helpful, I believe, to any reader of this message is Thérèse's bold prescription to her prioress on how to live in and deal with a community. (A twenty-three-year-old is telling a sixty-five-year-old how to manage.) In the parable, Jesus the Pastor speaks of the degrees by which the soul can be raised to heaven: not by withdrawing oneself from others completely, which meant that Gonzague should drop a moody hope for posting to Saigon, nor by despising the love and attention others might give her (but whose love and attention did Thérèse mean?), but to accept those others in order to please Jesus and to serve them by *degrees*, a polyvalent word in French that is most adroit here: degree by rank, by stages of time, and by the steps of a staircase such as the sisters took to re-enter their cells. Here, Thérèse prescribes the very steep and arduous way she famously dismisses a year later for the quick lift of Jesus's elevator arms. "To raise yourself you need to *put* your *foot* in (on) the *steps* of others and attach yourself to me alone...."[49] That is, one ascends by lowering oneself humbly to the stations of others; in the American idiom, putting oneself in their shoes. Tactfully, Thérèse is identifying to Gonzague the vanity of her wounded pride.

The most intriguing and richly ambiguous passage within this prescriptive paragraph is the gloss upon serving by degrees: "for distancing oneself from others will serve only one thing, *to walk* and to rove in the paths of the earth...."[50] The first of the operative verbs, *marcher*, has in the main a positive denotation for Thérèse, even in adverse contexts: one walks in the way Jesus has given, even or especially the route of humiliation but also sometimes by the perilous path of popular esteem. Jesus veiled her faults, she says, so that she could help Gonzague in training the novices. But the other word, *s'égarer*, invariably denotes for Thérèse a straying or wandering off. Her common point of reference is the parable of the sole lost lamb, which the Good Shepherd goes off to recover, leaving the complacent ninety-nine back at their grazing. In short, she is posing as such a lamb herself, isolated as she is by her dream. Jesus, too, wanders in order to find the lost soul. Who would not *want* to stray if it meant that divinity itself would come to the rescue? By the time of this letter, late June of 1896, Thérèse had been in her darkness for over two months, time enough to regard herself as the Carmel's lost sheep. Time enough, too, to realize that wandering in the world might not be such a bad thing: her father had wanted to do it, poor Louis, and Jesus describes himself at times in vagrancy. Thérèse's desire to go to Saigon, like Gonzague's a generation before, was a yearning for the adventure of spiritual displacement and a healing apartness from the community where love could itself go astray amid stumbling, unhappy souls.

After Gonzague ordered her to resume her writing, Thérèse told Pauline that she intended to dwell upon fraternal charity. Pauline may have been startled by the sweep of grandiloquence in Thérèse's explanation of this choice. "In fact I've received too many great insights on this subject and don't want to keep them all to myself. I assure you that charity is not understood on earth and yet it is the first of virtues."[51] How could the Church, how could its Tradition have failed to teach what charity is?

Were she pressed with this question as a response to her proclamation about charity, Thérèse might answer from early remarks within C that by the Holy Spirit Teresa of Ávila had enriched the Church with revelations of what, in an almost gnostic-sounding way, Thérèse calls Christ's secrets, so that he might be better known and more loved of souls. Of course, the gospels and the patristic corpus and all the liturgical and ritual performance of the Church sufficed, and yet the Spiritus Sanctus continues to move about, finding fresh voices for each generation. Citing the abundance of *chercher* and *trouver*, *seeking* and *finding* in her writings, a reader would be justified to assume that Thérèse was now consciously seeing herself in succession, however obscurely, to Teresa. She, too, had revelations to share, even as she observed to Pauline. She was even considering writing on Scripture, an unheard of undertaking for a mere novice.

Her intent at this time (June 1897) to write a commentary on the *Song of Songs* went unrealized, likely quashed by the prioress. If so, Gonzague acted with good reason. For C marks a departure that such a commentary might have arrested, a departure from self-absorption, from Thérèse's anxiety over being and not being with Jesus, which, for her, was what Solomon was singing about. (Figure 5.3.)

The first manuscript was written as a series of acknowledged graces, a prolonged prayer of thanksgiving for those graces, a vernal stretch of remembrance and recordation but with a certain self-congratulation latent in the thanks. Yet gratitude is one of the most attractive of human comportments and Thérèse included among her graces the sequestering of her father in a sanatorium, a not ordinary occasion

DILECTUS MEUS MIHI
ET EGO ILLI.

FIGURE 5.3 Therese's prayer card, known as Our Lady of Mount Carmel, illustrating the *Song of Songs*, "My Beloved is Mine and I am His." Copyright Archives du Carmel de Lisieux.

for thankfulness. It seems hardly possible to be complacent about one's own deeply shared hurt, but even there the thanks seems quietly to say that the Martins were specially chosen by God to be tested, and they had weathered their way through the test, not to forget Louis.

The subtle jeopardy of thanksgiving is that it might sustain preoccupation with oneself. Jesus himself cites the one bad penny among biblical prayers: "I thank you, God, that I am not like other men." Thérèse recognized the stealth of pride at work in her (Gonzague, a sure help in identifying such a lapse), and she would without question have admitted it, had she been in the company of Madeleine de Saint-Joseph, one of the first French Mothers of Carmel, who preferred to think and speak of adoration, rather than thanksgiving, so as to evade the trap of first-person satisfactions.[52]

To be free of self-absorption means opening oneself up to the much wider world. That aperture appears in C. There is a lexical register of the shift in Thérèse's consciousness in this regard, an attenuation of self-consciousness, just as the darkness would seem to have enforced that self upon itself more vigorously than at any time before. In French, *reconnaître* and its substantive, *reconnaissance*, denote not only recognition but gratitude; whereas in English, the sense is restricted to the epistemological.[53] To be aware in the French manner involves, at least connotatively, being grateful. *Reconnaître* enjoys a high frequency in Thérèse's writings as a whole: eighty-three occasions, with sixteen of them in A, three in B, two in C. *Reconnaissance* occurs sixty-three times, with twelve in A, five in B (among which, her claim that Jesus does not ask for great deeds but only *abandon* and gratitude), four in C. But four of these six instances in C are not about Thérèse's thankful acknowledgments; rather about those of other souls.

That does not mean Thérèse had learned to stint on her gratitude. Quite the reverse; she was earnestly grateful to Gonzague for the substance of her formation as a Carmelite, and C is a partial payment of thanks due. She was aware that in her writing she was addressing a sister who had expended most of her many years in Carmel (by 1897, nearly thirty-seven) living on behalf of others, her community of sisters. Thérèse, charged with the welfare of four among those sisters, was following directly in Gonzague's path, as the simile of the painting brushes shows. The novices for whom she was *compagne* had given Thérèse the occasion for benevolences and beneficences that continually drew her away from herself.

To speak of such self-subtraction, however, would seem to controvert her own intent to make herself a model for her sororal charges as she tried to make herself the exemplar of littleness, of helplessness even. In C 4r she tells the prioress that God's greatest of all graces to her was the revelation of her limits, as though a divine warrant were showing to her the impossibility of her treading Teresa's way of perfection. The way of imperfection, in which she had become expert, was leading her to a precipice. If pride goes before destruction and a haughty spirit before the fall, lowliness is at risk as well. Littleness and impotence are no covert safeguards, and humility, too, has its snares. To be self-convicted of littleness and weakness borders on the pride of inconsequence, as though the Holy Spirit could not possibly make an entry nor a use of such radical economy. In the end, a large, dark, faceless community had to take Thérèse farther on the Via Dolorosa than even her four needy novices could have required of her.

VI. *The Structures and Topics of C*

A small number of important, though not collectively coherent facts about the composition of C needs remarking. First, Thérèse was writing an open-ended series of daily letters. She signals each of the days by commencing with *Mère bien-aimée, Well-beloved Mother*, a salutation that gradually gives way to the warmer *Mère chérie*. C as a concatenation of letters recalls the melancholy fact that Thérèse had written at least fifteen letters to Gonzague over the years before C, all of which have disappeared.[54] Like her lost letters to Almire Pichon and like Céline's lost (destroyed) correspondence in the early 1890s, the contents prompt futile guessing. In C, however, there is a sufficient bounty.

As the number of the "letters" addressed in C come to twenty-seven and Thérèse commenced her writing only upon the prioress's order on Thursday, June 3, it is safe to locate in their midst three of her best-known late photos, those in which she kneels while holding in either hand pictures of the Infant Jesus and the Holy Face. (The third of these is on the front cover of this book.)

Those photos were taken on Monday, June 7, in the very middle of her writing to Gonzague about her spiritual darkness and her temptation against love. It is striking that her account of the darkness culminates with her prayer for illumination that God send the light of trust into lost souls' obdurate hearts, on the one day that she expressly dates at the close: June 9, the second anniversary of her *offrande*. She closes that day's entry by telling Gonzague that the trial she is undergoing is removing all "natural satisfaction in the desire I had of heaven ....[I]n fact I no longer have any great desires except to love to the point of dying from love...."[55] It is fair, then, to consider the five-days account of her darkness as a completion of her *offrande*.

Dying from love had initially meant a dramatic immolation, a petition to God that all of her self be consumed by and for divine love. The fire she yearned to elicit on June 9, 1895, did not come as she might have wished. Instead, she had been consumed by a "darkness visible," one in which she would realize divine love by the fact of her being sent into that dark. As she does not give much heed to the Holy Spirit—long-standing qualms about Illuminism were commonplace in the Carmel—it is no surprise that she does not suggest to Gonzague nor to herself that the Holy Spirit was having a singular way with her. Only Jesus is acknowledged, and he is only obliquely responsible, letting the darkness happen. That way she observes with necessary deference and humility the arcane nature of what has come over her, and she can claim that as a testing this dwelling in darkness among unhappy, godless souls amounts to a grace, for within that darkness she finds the necessary occasion to pray on behalf of them all. The self-ratification through prayer, her request that God send the illumination of faith, tactfully succeeds her admission that she no longer believes but simply *wants* to believe.

That same day she wrote to Bellière as though it were to be her last: "O, my dear little brother, how happy I am to die!...because I truly believe it's the Good Lord's will....but I'm not dying, I'm entering into life and what I can't say to you here below I'll make you understand from heaven's heights...."[56] In charitable dissembling to this impressionable young man, Thérèse proclaimed a faith she had just told Gonzague she did not possess.

Beyond that fateful June 9, she was looking to another date, June 21, the feast day of Mère Gonzague. Like the needle to the pole, that date gives Thérèse a thematic direction derived from the five days of discussing her temptation against love. From them she turns to her longing for a foreign mission as a covert means of release from her natural sisters. The foreign mission amounts to a phantom sketch of another table of sorrows, one she was consciously seeking in order to fulfill the itinerary of Juan de la Cruz, to disappear into the world's contempt and to find the oblivion of anonymity. This urging in her brings her closer to Gonzague, who had felt herself pulled in that same direction during her own green years.

After three letters and as many days on that story, she turns to the motif of charity, six days—Sunday, June 13 through Friday, June 18—which form literally the centerpiece of C. By the time of Gonzague's feast day, Thérèse has situated herself within the fourth thematic frame and her training of the novices, a report on how she has fared in Gonzague's place. Those six days—Saturday, June 19 through Friday, June 25—are succeeded by the final six, the summing up of God's mercies to her—Saturday, June 26 through Thursday, July 1—thus bringing full circle the celebration with which she had begun her first manuscript two and a half years before.[57]

VII. Her Christology

C affords a remarkable Christology. First, Thérèse had written of Jesus making use of Gonzague, who had returned to the priorate and was then implicitly renewing what Thérèse calls *"powerful* and maternal education." Drawing upon the gospel message that God causes the rain to fall and the sun to shine upon the just and the unjust alike, Thérèse contracts the divine meteorology into a garden-like frame, one suggestive of Teresa's guiding metaphor in her *Vida*. Jesus himself had caused *His* little flower to imbibe through Gonzague "the life-giving waters of humiliation."[58] Then, again through the prioress, he had caused a gentle sun to shine down upon this flower so that it might grow. The Carmel sisters who were later outspokenly critical of Gonzague perhaps had forgotten that she was, in Thérèse's clearly written testimony, the immediate instrument of Jesus, so closely identified with him that in one exceptional passage Thérèse inverts her usual predications and speaks of obeying Jesus in order to please Gonzague.[59] As Thérèse explicitly preferred Gonzague's bitter watering to "the mawkish water of compliments," it is not difficult to imagine how she might have responded to the panegyrical talk of herself that her sisters gave in reminiscence before the officers of the hearings.[60]

If her would-be sympathizers were averse to Gonzague, they must have been nonplused by Jesus when they learned of how he had called to Thérèse from the morbid gurgling of her own throat. That is what she says about the nocturnal occasion of her initial hemoptysis. She interprets an outward event for its anagogical worth: she writes that she *felt* (*je sentis*) a gush rising to her lips that night, but after confirming the bleeding when she got up the following morning, "I was inwardly persuaded that on the anniversary of his death Jesus wanted me *to hear a first summons.*"[61]

Having established the primacy of Jesus as the agent of all that was transpiring both outwardly, via Gonzague's discipline, and inwardly, Thérèse presents the chief disclosure of C, that "Jesus made me realize that there truly are souls without faith, who by the abuse of grace have lost this precious treasure, the source of the only pure and genuine joys."[62] He brought this realization by permitting (again, her word) her own soul to be invaded by the thickest shadows, obscuring heaven so that the very thought of it became a struggle and a torment. She means that she had become an initiate into the society of souls astray, sinners by their abuse of the divine favor of reason and speech.

Perhaps it is because she has acknowledged the determinant role of Jesus in her last months of life that C, as well as the late letters, abounds in the literally governing verb *sentir*. [63] Beyond the pallid sensuous denotations of "sense" or "feel," as when she felt the rising blood in her throat, the word's heavier valence is "realize." It makes a strong and vivid epistemological claim, signifying that she has arrived at one of the road markers on her truth-seeking way. The signpost does not supply a demonstrable, experimental truth, but rather an intuitive certainty; a private enlightenment, given that the higher awareness she has gained comes within a sheer and unsettling darkness. But the source is unimpeachable: "Jesus made me realize" covers most of C's terrain.

Thérèse had been scouting towards its darkness for a good while. Six months before, in January, she had composed upon request a poem for the sister who occupied the cell next to her own. Sr. Marie-Philomène de Jésus was thirty-four years her senior, but had shared some of her novitiate time with Thérèse.[64] She requested some verses to address her guardian angel. Thérèse herself showed at best a nominal interest in guardian angels,[65] but she gives herself away in this poem when she writes "During my short life I wish to save my brothers, the sinners."[66] As Sr. Philomène was in her fifty-eighth year, her life was not likely the only one she meant.

In May Thérèse composed for herself the poem that stands as a kind of summa in verse for her ripening spirituality, the celebration explaining "Pourquoi je t'aime, ô Marie!" ["Why I love you, o Mary!]. There, she startles the reader (not to mention Mary) with a glance at Jesus's innumerable "brother sinners." Thus, she makes intricate use of St. Paul's gloss on Jesus, "the firstborn of many brethren."[67] Those "brethren," says Paul, God had predestined, called, justified, and glorified. Paul identifies them as those who love God, as Thérèse knew she did. Had she, too, not been called? She had, of course, but having received the grace of convicting herself as a sinner, she knew that one could be akin to Jesus and yet a sinner. Otherwise put, she had lots of brothers.

It is but a short yet telling step from here to the prayer she records with third-person obliquity in C: "...can she not say in her own name, in the name of her brothers, Have pity upon us, Lord, for we are poor sinners!"[68] Now, she is no longer concerned to save her brothers as sinners, as though she were not one with them, but to petition for them and for herself. It is divine compassion she seeks, not salvation. She might have claimed, but she does not, that Jesus had prompted this prayer, for it echoes the plea of the publican, tearless though hers apparently is.[69]

Allusion to Saint Luke's publican and his prayer is apt because Thérèse seems to presume contrition of heart in those at the table, a grief that might not be there at all. It is *her* sorrow at the table that the anticommunity assembled there sits resolutely apart from God, as her prayer tells us she does not. In the Johannine narrative Jesus enjoins his disciples, those who knew themselves to be sinners, to love each other as he has loved them. Thérèse elsewhere makes much of the distinction that these words enforce: as *Jesus* has loved, not as they have. But at the table of sorrow, the assembled cannot love each other on any terms—or themselves, either. Under the vast pall of their spiritual desolation, they would not even understand the injunction suitable to a godless life, "Be indifferent to one another," because the very thought of another person would be alien to them. Thérèse knew that the embrace of meaninglessness had to be loveless. It is the ice of the willfully solitary self in which Dante's Satan is frozen at Hell's bottom.

This young woman, whose whole life had been centered upon the love of God in and through her spouse, Jesus, identifies herself with the barren souls of those who have frozen themselves in the Satanic way, rejecting all obligation to others and even to self. She was not concerned to look or to probe into these wretches; she merely felt their desolation in being apart from God, even though it was by their willing to be so. She does not weigh their motives or the routes such motives took, because she is ignorant of them, lacking the experiential signposts that she always needed and could find only in herself. Taxil's devastating, imponderable cruelty had given her a sense of how she could be an accomplice to the malice of deceit in this world, and that sense sufficed her. She was initiated in spite of herself into the worldliness she had always rejected. Jesus, she believed, had sent her to the table. Taxil had shown her the way.

In this peculiar solidarity, she tells God that she is waiting for the Lord's day before she may rise. That means she is awaiting permission to be released as though from the commission of what the Carmelites called a fault, perhaps such as would have required a penitential prostration, an action of self-humbling, ended only by a sign from the prioress. The darkness, the tunnel, the vault had all come into Thérèse without her volition, but she takes them on as though they were transgressive, the effects of her volition, the props of a sinfulness of which she was not evidently guilty yet in which she was somehow complicit. This is Taxil's lesson to her, a matter that might also be construed as a grace because it was likely the only way she could establish an affinity with the others at the table. She felt accountable not for sin as such but for *their* sin. She who had refused, had wanted to refuse God nothing of her love, stations herself among the supreme and outermost of recusants.[70]

This passage, the early but true climax in C, forms a luminous parallel with a climactic moment in A. When she described there her Christmas "conversion" of 1886, the point where she had passed out of childish self-absorption to an adult's awareness of suffering in others, she stationed herself retrospectively in a Marian position: "I resolved to keep myself in spirit at the foot of the Cross in order to receive the Divine dew which ran down from it, understanding that I had to sprinkle it at once over souls...."[71] (Fig. 5.4.) Now, in C, she speaks in another tone of resolution but this time (again) in the third person: "...she agrees to eat for as long as you wish the bread of suffering and she does not wish to rise from this table filled with bitterness where poor sinners eat before the day you have set."[72] These texts stand two years apart from each other, and they describe experiences separated by more than ten years' distance, but their common denominator is Thérèse's desire to save souls.

In 1886 she concentrated her efforts upon the saving of "des grands pécheurs," grand-scale offenders such as the tabloid villain Pranzini and later Hyacinth Loyson. Having come well down from her adolescent attention to dark celebrities, she learned to read souls anonymously, those, that is, whom she calls "unbelieving wretches." Feeble though that tag might suggest they were, these unhappy souls exerted a mighty sway upon her and finally became those she called "the worst materialists."[73]

What I call Thérèse's *épreuve de l'amour de la confiance*, the testing of her loving trust, came from these unfortunates; those for whom she found the grace to pray were those whose voices she heard in keen, eloquent mockery of her longing for heaven. The most vigorous and sharp-edged utterance in all of Thérèse's writings is like some furtive and agilely metamorphous virus placed in a pure field; it threatens to confound everything else that she wrote. She quotes the demons speaking to her: "'You're dreaming of light, of a home country balmy with sweetest fragrances, you're dreaming of the *everlasting* possession of the Creator of all these wonders, you believe that one day you'll get out of the mists that surround you. Go on, go on, rejoice at the death which will give you not what you're hoping but a night yet more profound, the night of nothingness.'"[74] That is what she heard inside herself.

The bite in these cunning words comes from the aggressive cooption of what was most precious to Thérèse: the light (of faith), the kingdom, being forever with God, as though the voices by knowing of these desiderata somehow took them over, played with their allure, and then despoiled them. Her susceptibilities are laid bare within her own testimony. Worst of all, the darkness she came to know threatened to be only preliminary to one in which she would find not even the malicious tones of those tormenting voices—a total void.

FIGURE 5.4 Four months before her death, Therese strews rose petals at the cross. Sisters Marie of the Eucharist and Madeleine are behind her. Copyright Office Central de Lisieux.

It may be difficult, if not impossible, to believe that a pious young woman could carry such devilish venom within her. Even so, with an incisive, yet unsparing economy she gave it bitter articulation. Because she was truth-seeking, Thérèse was also truth-telling, and in this instance she became a candid amanuensis for the despotism of evil within. Perhaps this was the coy, seductive lilt in "You're dreaming" she had learned from Diana Vaughan and Léo Taxil. As the gospel says, let the reader take note.

At the same time the text moves on. The not-to-be found "torch of Faith" is succeeded by "the torch of love."[75] The stark absence of faith and hope did not prevent her from realizing and expressing the selfless love that overcomes those demonic voices. It comes by her prayer on behalf of those who, in their insistent way, have embraced nothingness within this life. As love, it does not remonstrate nor reproach. Thérèse is no pathologist of evil. It may even be charged that she does not understand it and that nothing in her life and her spiritual formation turned her to dwell upon its mesmeric draw. She knew evil was not her business.

That is why she writes of how she responded to the voices within her by shunning them. Having lost what she calls "the enjoyment of Faith," she tells Gonzague: "At every new occasion of combat, when my enemies come to provoke me, I comport myself bravely, knowing it's cowardice to fight a duel, I turn my back to my adversaries without deigning to look them in the face, but I run to my Jesus and tell him I'm ready to spill the last drop of my blood to confess that there's a Heaven."[76] This is a richly problematic passage.

First, the disconcerting "cowardice" (*lâcheté*). How could it possibly be cowardly to confront evil? Rashness, yes; presumption, probably; foolishness, likely, but taking on a fearsome enemy cannot be judged a coward's work. (Was Luther, proud of his vociferous contests in pride with Satan, a weakling?) Thérèse's usually neat, well-measured diction seems for once to falter. The word she should have used she consciously chose not to use: *imprudence*. Why she evaded the obvious fit becomes clear in her running to Jesus. That was the prudent thing to do, and yet her delight in the spontaneity of *audace*, the boldness that carried her beyond toilsome, tedious proprieties on several counts, was too forward to admit prudence as a desired course. To her, prudence suggested timidity, an excess of caution. In A she cites her Uncle Isidore's refusal to approve of her early entry into Carmel on the ground that such approval would be "contrary to kindly prudence."[77] Citing her beloved *Imitatio Christi*, she contrasts the course of prudence to the Christian message of love's unbounded possibilities: "Kindly prudence on the other hand shudders at every step and doesn't dare put its foot forward..."[78] How could love be among the rewards of caution? Prudence seems all but an antonym to the real companion of love, which for her is trust, *confiance*.

Weighty though these semantic issues may be, the flight to Jesus poses a much greater challenge. When she tells Gonzague of how she addresses Jesus, proclaiming her readiness to shed all her blood in order to confess that heaven exists, Thérèse refers to the many *actes de foi* she says she had performed through the past year.[79] They seem to have been paraphrases of what she has just written: she is prepared to shed all her blood for an affirmation she knows she cannot sustain beyond its utterance, as though the iteration of the act attests at once her willingness and her abysmal helplessness. The tension between her void and her readiness to fill it with heaven marks her version of St. Paul's "hope against hope," where Abraham accepted God's promise of future generations for him despite his and his wife's superannuation.[80] The "despite" for Thérèse was the tunnel and fog created by the inner persuasions of "the worst materialists" who rejected all possibility of heaven. She had accepted their persuasion but not their rejection of God and the divine realm.

Most troublesome about Thérèse's words to Jesus is that her *actes de foi* became a mantric guard against despair; that to keep herself going in prayer she had to resort to a kind of formulaic insistence. What she missed was what she had always cherished in prayer, the immediate and spontaneous expression of what was in her heart and in her own words, not routinized and lifeless by diurnal repetition. Now, in her year of shadows, she had to forge against adversity a shield of recapitulated self-assurances: yes, she was ready to shed her blood, and with each assurance she remained only ready. There is the faintest tone of reproach against God: why has she not been summoned to fulfill that readiness?

So very different is the preceding prayer, which does savor of that indispensable spontaneity of the heart Thérèse had counted upon: the prayer at the table of sinners came at the moment of its composition. One off, it serves almost as a foil to the innumerable *actes de foi* by its succinct grip and gentle vim. My point is not to set off one prayer against another as if to rate them, one as an I-prayer and the other a we-prayer, but to observe that the supplication at the table has an abiding significance; this is the lowly beseeching of an all-encompassing love, and yet the word "love" does not appear within it. It is where Thérèse's littleness and weakness reach their nadir that she reaches love's acme, and all the more effectively because she is not trying to. The absence of all rhetoric about love or "Love" affords love some real space. It is the ripest formulation of her Easter conversion, not a protest against it, as the *actes de foi* might be construed.

Thérèse's love in this prayer, extended to a vast and sorry humanity, is attended by the cross she is carrying for her beloved. It is as though she were sitting at this somber Eucharist in the place that Jesus, notorious as a banqueter in the gospels, would have occupied, but nothing in or beyond the text tells us that she thought she was there in his stead. All the better that she says nothing of what she knew through Saint Paul, that the absent Jesus was also within her.[81] For her, Christianity establishes a juncture between human suffering and divine sacrifice. Here that suffering and that sacrifice are conjoined in and through a young daughter of Carmel.

I have called attention a few times to what Thérèse might have said but did not. No matter how buoyant, warm, and uplifting her writings—and C affords many instances for these terms—very often it is what she does *not* say that says more. In the not saying, she is observing in strict Carmelite fashion the blessedness of silence, the language of angels, as Pauline had written in paint over the convent's *dortoir*. The autobiographical manuscripts are rife with unrecorded, prayerful pauses, signified by more than the succession of dots at the end of an entry. These silences are like rest notes in a musical score, aiding the theme by the simple might of an absence, an eloquent quiet strategically placed on behalf of a phrase. In a most dramatic instance, Thérèse calls attention to the hidden value of silence, that in her account of the darkness, she knows she is risking blasphemy. She has to put her pen down.

Blasphemy had a particular history within Thérèse's life. When a child of eight, she was often accompanied to school by a maidservant of her Uncle Isidore's house, Marcelline Huse, then fifteen years old. (This girl became a Benedictine nun.) At the first beatification hearing, Huse recalled how she and Thérèse heard blasphemous talk from workmen, and her young charge, with her father's gift for charitable extenuations, remarked: "We must not condemn souls, as those people received far fewer blessings than we, and they were more unhappy than guilty."[82] It could have been Louis talking, someone who deserves to be reckoned as one of Thérèse's spiritual guides; unquestionably, he was her first and maybe finally the most important. And it was he who would have taught her the peril of words approaching blasphemy.

Perhaps it was such unfortunates as those workmen that she remembered when composing a prayer for herself and for Marthe de Jésus, which opens: "Sinners' blasphemies have painfully reached our ears."[83] But the ready text for this situation of hapless profanity is not that prayer. Rather, it is Thérèse's most celebrated poem, "Living by Love." There, apostrophizing Jesus, she defines this living from love, by and for love in regard to those who have no such boon: "It means wiping your face / It means winning pardon from sin for sinners / O God of Love! That they may enter anew into your grace and forever bless your name.... Blasphemy reaches to my heart and to blot it out I want to sing ever 'Your Sacred Name I adore.'..."[84] In this poem, vibrant with warmth, as though to stave off the harsh cold of that February 1895, the blasphemy has passed beyond workmen in the streets and has penetrated Thérèse, so that only by her singing can she drown out its baleful noise within her.

Wiping Christ's face was her chief consolatory gesture. She uses the verb, *essuyer*, thirty-seven times in her writing, and in virtually all the contexts it is Christ's tears that are being wiped away. In this poem, however, it is the spittle of the sinners that Love's transcendent liveliness removes. Spitting is the first blaspheming. The second is vocal, a malediction that only benediction can overcome. Thus, Love would effect the conversion of their blaspheming into an everlasting blessing.

The convergence of this poem with Thérèse's prayer at the table of sorrow is apparent, as though the prayer could be appended as another stanza or, conversely, as though the poem reaches its resolution into praxis at the table of sinners. It is significant that Thérèse affords the sinners no voice at the table, no occasion for blaspheming. Like the lions before Daniel, they have their mouths stopped. This silence proves to be one of Thérèse's little mercies, as though she had bidden her company to listen to her intercession, and they finally had the humanity to do so.

VIII. In the Absence of Jesus

In speaking of one of her *fundaciones*, Teresa of Avila characterizes herself among the young women there as "this wretch amid these angelic souls,"[85] but Thérèse at the table of sorrow might be called "this angel amid those wretches." That temptation aside, she might be situated once more within the gospel contexts where she seems so naturally at home. The context this time is the banquet laid for reluctant guests.[86] After the host has received all of the begging off excuses of those he has invited, he bids his servants to call in a miscellany of people off the street and sit them at the banquet table.

At the dark banquet of bitter bread, however, it is the table's Lord who is not present, and Thérèse, as the only speaker, is left, it seems, in minor substitution for him. It is not certain when or if he will come. It is even more awkward that this table's bitter fare is furnished to those who, like the gospel's guests on the list, would have made any excuse not to be there. They are the truly poor and lame by their desolate selfness, their insistent lovelessness. The scene cries out for the eloquent scorn of the immortal Bernanos, but, if it be called existential, Thérèse herself rescues it from gloom by a solicitude wholly beyond the deserving of those around her. If there is one text from Christianity that fitly and succinctly addresses the bleak narcissism of an unhappy age, it could be Manuscript C, its sixth folio.

The table of sorrow realized Thérèse's desire to escape the claustral sustenance of the Lisieux Carmel, specifically the too comforting and therefore spiritually hazardous presence of her natural family in its four warm partisans, her cousin Marie included. The table became the unsought, grace-given goal of her once-cherished knight errancy, her adolescent desire to be a warrior or a missionary or a martyr for Jesus now made idle by an inexplicable forging that shaped all those roles into one. Her long longing for the Carmel in Saigon, where she could live out the imperative of Juan de la Cruz, to be despised, hidden, and forgotten in imitation of Christ, had been denied her by the debilities of her unremitting sickness. As early as the spring of 1896, presentiment of her death denied her the safe harbor of at last finding Jesus, a harbor that she had envisioned from childhood and thought she could find in Asia. In the end, the table was her *Indochine*, her Vietnam, her mission. What better than to be a hidden warrior, a despised missionary, an unacknowledged priest, and a forgotten martyr!

From the table's episode early in C, twenty-five folio pages remain in anticlimax, a descent into a Canaan land where in various patches Thérèse wanders anecdotally among the people she found in her other mission, the one for her spiritual sisters within the Carmel's walls. It is as though, having recounted to Gonzague the fairyland turned nightmare within her soul, she could now address the quotidien life that she and the prioress knew well. But that coming down is no concession to ordinariness. Thérèse, wittingly or not, takes on the steep task usually associated with poets and novelists, to transform the common by the revelation of what lives mysteriously within it. In Christian fashion, she follows the path of inconspicuous sufferings, teasing out the mortality of weakness and littleness in herself and in others and binding them in singular fusions. After offering a jolt from deep darkness, C affords wondrously tiny lights on a level plain. In its way, it can prove a snare for the unwary, who presume that little stories can only be trivial. Without such saint-life grandeurs as levitations, miracles, and the sublime heraldry of visions, crumbs of circumstance are brushed off as from a table, another sort of table, occasions of apparent inconsequence that seem not much different from gossip. Initially, even the most patient reader might be inclined to protest that these tales are so random and petty as to seem pointless. But Thérèse is no postmodernist, eagerly embracing meaninglessness as some precious nourishment for a barren, loveless life. To the contrary, the minor incidents she relates take on a magnitude for her reflection.

Thérèse establishes their connection with the table of sorrow by this audacious interrogative for Jesus: "Is there a greater *joy* than to suffer for your love?" At the table, her suffering, the eclipse of heavenly light, meant for her that Jesus was opening up that very heaven and its light "to poor infidels, forever."[87] This extremity in expiatory suffering, one soul's privation for a multitude's gain, stands, I believe, unique in Carmel spirituality. By fixing her attention upon the spiritually desolate with whom she is seated, Thérèse sees beyond Teresa and even Juan to what I call "the dark night of the us." For her own part, she remarks that her acceptance of the darkness has sufficed Jesus, so that she is not obliged, as she puts it, to drink of this chalice down to the lees, that is, to stoop to the atheism of those who have abused their graces. Although she ceases to feel heaven, she does not concede to the irremediable bitterness of despair by rejecting God. Quite the reverse; in her darkness, she recognizes that Jesus is free to do with her as he wishes.

This willing passivity marks a decisive shift in momentum from the activism of Thérèse's grand-scale desires in B. Those desires culminate there in her self-appointment as Love, a role that she no sooner announces than she loses sight of. In C, however, she makes no role-playing claims but rather is assigned her stations, first as a banqueter over the bitter bread, and then as a student of a few

Carmel sisters putting her to tests very much of their own. From this vantage, the transition from B to C does not mark some kind of recumbence or inertia. In C Thérèse learns the meaning of her own *confiance* in full, that a genuine trust in God cannot be programmatic or on terms of one's own choosing but must leave one a ready, willing cipher for divinity to use.

In that second mission, at the Carmel itself, Thérèse suffers quite differently. There, she is at the hands of those who bear her certainly no malice nor the indifference of the table's sinners, but nonetheless they give her occasion for a disconcerting awkwardness, an embarrassment, or a vexation that challenges her capacity for charity. She reads each incident as one that brings an unexpected grace, a revelation of how charity works as subtly as whatever threatens to defeat it. Best of all, and this is a concession to anyone who finds her an insufferable Uriah Heep, she exposes herself to the pride that lurks within virtually every conclusion she draws, as though it were a breakthrough or a victory, on behalf of charity. The at times overbearingly didactic or even frankly tedious passages of C,[88] her writings from June 13 through June 18, are the ideal challenge to those who presume that she had somehow become "a wise old crone."[89]

In dwelling upon what seem minutiae, Thérèse is following a long-established practice of monastic life, in which the slightest falling off or down in one's spiritual life must be seen as perilous, the portent of a harm that might prove much greater than what has initiated it.[90] Habits, bad or otherwise, begin in unnoticeable increments until they are suddenly one's second or elected nature, like a garden's weeds that seem to grow exponentially overnight. Hence the necessity of ever-vigilant attention to one's failings and the candor of confessing them openly to the community. Thérèse makes clear that each of her sisters has been effectively the instrument for her good by challenging her. They have in their way taught her all the more effectively by the complete absence of didactic or preachy ripostes. As a *compagne* to other novices, she came to realize that a guide is often shown the way by the guided.

Thérèse's own metaphor framing her brief stories involves painting, that pursuit in which she had seen Gonzague and herself as larger and smaller brushes at work on the four novices. Any sister's outer self, daily met and transparent, is the one that Thérèse must deal with, but she can do so only by remembering the interior self where Jesus indwells. Only then can she make a charitable response, applying her minuscule brush. Her brief episodes in C emerge as a series of minor brushstrokes. In gospel language, she has based this spiritual portraiture upon Jesus's words to those who unreflectingly served him in tending others: the hungry, the naked, the imprisoned.[91] Jesus tells the faithful that he was there in those unfortunates whom they had served. Yet Thérèse hazards a terrible pharisaism in portraying her Carmel sisters, most of them older than she, as unfortunates, victims of their own foibles and unaware of the fact.

Probably best known of the episodes (caricatured in a film on Thérèse) involves one of the most challenging of the older Carmelites, Sr. Saint-Pierre de Sainte-Thérèse. She was a lay sister or *converse* who had entered the Carmel in 1866 at age thirty-six. Rheumatoid arthritis crippled her in her later years, so that she was unable to sustain the normal work load of her responsibilities. For a while she could move on her own by crutches but eventually had to be helped on the way to the refectory and to the choir. The pain she continually suffered, keenly aggravated by a pluvious climate and the unheated rooms of winter, made her irascible and testy. Her dependence upon assistance did not help, prompting her to become more anxious that she would fall and break a bone, a constant dread for an arthritic.[92]

As sisters at work in the infirmary were too occupied with their charges, Thérèse volunteered herself to Sr. Saint-Pierre, who reluctantly accepted, wary of this novice's youth and inexperience in so delicate, demanding, and awkward a task. Thérèse tells Gonzague that it cost her a lot to offer help as she knew Sr. Saint-Pierre could be difficult, but, as she reports rather immodestly, "I set to work and had so much good intent that I brought it off perfectly."[93] In the broader context, the story of someone self-confessed to be weak and inadequate, this claim to perfect success sounds jarringly novel.

This remark carries revelatory import. It suggests that as Thérèse took inspiration from Christ's teaching that God weighs intentions more than the extent of their action,[94] she had concluded that an intention has its own efficacy, at least in occasions such as her service to Sr. Saint-Pierre. If the scale of the action is limited, its experimental value is the more easily determined. That is why Thérèse gives an almost clinical thoroughness to her narrative of a brief undertaking.

Small though it was, walking a crippled old woman for all of ten minutes, she makes much of it by recounting it at length as what she calls a ceremony that included a promenade. What she intends to convey as a comic routine, including Saint-Pierre's exclamatory alarms about Thérèse's pace with her, might seem disconcertingly insensitive, but that may be too solemn a response and may undervalue the hardiness that Carmel life had conferred upon its daughters, even the infirm. Sr. Saint-Pierre was expecting only to be helped to the refectory and seated there, but Thérèse went to extra, little lengths, breaking the bread to spare her sister's gnarled, claw-like hands and smiling at her broadly, thus mollifying the poor woman, as Thérèse learned later from Céline.

Thérèse appends to this story another incident that occurred one wintry evening when she was escorting Sr. Saint-Pierre in cold and dark. She heard party music coming from just beyond the walls, and like a Cinderella she imagined the glow and splendor of the proceedings, "a very bright salon, elegantly dressed young girls exchanging compliments," but the fairytale wonder dissolves in an instant as to their festive music she offers the counterpoint of arthritic groans and to their lights she contrasts the pallor of a brick wall along the cloister walk. She says she *knows* that "the Lord made shine the rays of the truth which surpassed the shadowy brightness of the festivities in such a way that I couldn't believe my happiness."[95] By that truth she meant those moments when Jesus is present in the naked, the ill, and the imprisoned (Sr. Saint-Pierre being a prisoner of her disease), testing one's charity.

In another key, Thérèse relates a contention she had with Marthe de Jésus. Their squabbling outside the door of the prioress occured when Thérèse as *sacristine* was fulfilling her duties by returning keys from the communion grill to Gonzague, who as prioress was in charge of all the keys. At this time Gonzague was ill with bronchitis, and Thérèse was eager to see how she was faring. But Marthe de Jésus,"enlivened by a holy zeal," thought that Thérèse was intending to wake Gonzague and blocked her way to the prioress's room.[96] Their exchanges at that point reached a volume sufficiently high to wake the convalescent. When Marthe de Jésus began accusing her of causing the disturbance, Thérèse decided on the spot to leave without remonstrating.

Thérèse says she realized that had she chosen to justify herself, she would have forfeited peace in her soul. Moreover, she saw that she did not have enough virtue in her soul to allow herself to be accused without rejoinder, and so she fled the scene. In so doing, however, she was merely upholding the letter and spirit in the Carmel's *Rule*, which forbade a sister who was accused of any fault from a self-defense that amounted to a counter-attack upon the accuser.[97] This trivial episode illustrates how from something petty a grievous harm could grow.

Like the awkward escorting of Saint-Pierre, this unhappy exchange with Marthe de Jésus furnished Thérèse with an insight far greater than the event itself warranted. Looking back she realizes she had fussed so much over so little. This is the remark of a dying person who had attained the peaceful equipoise that sees how much of a life has been passed in foolishness and vanity, but here that final peace comes with a difference. Thérèse not only rejoices in what the incidentals have revealed about herself, a self so imperfect; she is even happier that she has remained "*weakness* itself... in that that I boast, and I'm waiting every day to discover in myself new imperfections."[98]

Cultists naturally want their saints to be better than human, but saints know themselves far better. Thérèse offers a transparent example of an insistent regard for repeated failures. Her straightforward telling on herself is not some kind of phony humility. What gives glory, if that word is admissible, to C is that the writing itself exposes some imperfections that would have made her happy, had she caught them. She had failed in charity to the miserable party-goers, vaunting her own life over theirs. And in recounting the hot little contretemps with Marthe de Jésus she writes that she went off to savor "the fruits of my victory" meanwhile "leaving the sister to go on with her discourse, which was like Camilla's curses upon Rome."⁹⁹ Beneath an amused exaggeration there lay at least a trace of ridicule, even though she knew (and says so) that Marthe loved her. Gonzague was alert to these shows of pride in Thérèse.

It does not seem to me picayune to notice such failings in Thérèse, given that she herself was looking to collect them. C validates her self-estimate by documenting it so well, as though by that writing she were helping Pauline and others, reminding them not to exalt her by cheating her of what was hard won, the perception of her abiding lowliness, that in her last months she was as imperfect as when she had first entered Carmel. In that realization she matured and came to savor the joy hiding out within an apparent bitterness. Jesus, she writes, makes the bitter into the sweet. In all but admitting that in her shows of pride and kindred faults she has failed as a Carmelite, she is lying squarely under her cross. The sweetness came in knowing that that was where Jesus was, too. (Figure 5.5.)

FIGURE 5.5 Christ prepared for crucifixion. Therese kept this card in her breviary. Copyright Archives du Carmel de Lisieux

Thérèse's prayer at the table of sorrow is an intuitive reading of anguish in the lost souls around her. It does not matter that they might be spiritually base or even bestial. What matters to her is their bitter fellowship of grief. Thérèse herself develops the notion of reading Christ hidden within the soul. The portraiture she accomplished with the prioress, Gonzague by the larger strokes, Thérèse by much smaller ones, always comes to the same end, Christ's self-portrait in each of the sisters.

Thérèse is not at all dismayed nor even attentive to obstructions of her view. Instead, she occupies herself with the defects of means to finding Jesus within the other soul. She seems to marvel at the paradox of inadequacy, that such inadequacy is exactly what Jesus will choose in order to pursue his artistry. This notion, inspired by the fecklessness and bungling of the disciples, those lovably fallible men whom he enlisted, enjoys several occasions in her earlier writing. In an August, 1893 letter to Céline she claims that Jesus makes use of all means and that every creature (the French *créatures* denotes people, not beasts) is at his service. In her dramatic phrasing, Jesus "despoils utterly the souls dearest to Him. Seeing themselves in such great destitution these wretched little souls are fearful; it seems to them they're worthless since they receive everything from others and can give nothing back, but that's not so. The *essence* of their *being* works secretly. Jesus is shaping within them the seed that shall be grown on high in Heaven's celestial gardens." Having revealed to them their nothingness, Jesus employs them as "the most *meager* instruments so as to show them that it's he alone who is at work."¹⁰⁰

In a homey vein Thérèse likened herself to a bowl containing milk at which kittens (her novice charges) were jostling one another to drink.[101] Jesus, having supplied that milk, was watching from the side. Her only concern, she said, was to make sure the bowl was not turned over. With this simple good humor and wit, she underscores her role of mereness, literally a vessel through which grace works on behalf of others.

Consistently throughout C and throughout her darkness she saw herself in this utilitarian way. Even—rather, especially—at the table of sorrow she was God's lowly tool through which others were being served. That perspective, hers, is finally the best way to construe the meaning of the table: not through the gloom that pervades the sinners themselves, nor even by the bitterness of the bread, which, to her trusting, would finally turn sweet, but in her serving others in suffering, a serving given beyond all measures of time.

IX. *A Partial and Partisan Summing Up*

In porous, protean B, Thérèse subjected herself to the exactions of a personal retreat, her last. Although private retreats had always been trying for her, in this ultimate confrontation with herself she squirmed brilliantly and produced some vigorous, even intoxicant prose, not without dangers. Nine months later she was fearful of writing blasphemies, but a blasphemy exclaims in B and has gone unnoticed as such. For Jesus—Jesus alone—is love at the heart of the Church. However poignant and painful to read, this self-identification with "Love" in an anxious heart cannot be taken with doctrinal assurance. It remains touching but flabbergasting.

At her best in B Thérèse was lowly, sounding her own depths, and the sounding line went to fathoms she had not reached before. Her sinfulness was accepted and at once revealed as the surest predication of *abandon,* a kind of snare Jesus could not avoid, for he came on behalf of the sinners, not the righteous. That is capital wit, a warrant that a gentle dove can perform as a subtle serpent. Yet she was not entirely convinced that she was a sinner, and she moved on. In her closing words, she laid out the seedbed for the next summer's masterwork.

The third manuscript brings to completion Thérèse's life journey as a Christian, her passing into a darkness of particularly little, yet sufficient light. Wholly without intent and contrivance, she descended and took on the semblance of a slave to sin, identifying herself with the most wretched, those who have lost God and those who have rejected God and all sense of God. She participated fully neither in the loss nor in the rejection, but she did feel, I believe, the acute sorrow hidden within these privations. That movement toward what might be called solidarity freed her at long last from the anxious possessiveness she had suffered after Almire Pichon had told her, authoritatively, insistently, incautiously, that she was abiding in a state of prevenient grace, that she had never committed a mortal sin, that she was, in sum, securely en route toward the spiritual perfection that Teresa of Avila had set out for her as for all her spiritual sisters.

The Theresian passage to darkness is noteworthy because it so dramatically and imposingly reverses the progression St. Paul marks in speaking of the soul's redemption. As Pauline spirituality has bedrock status for many Christians, especially the ecclesiastical communities of Protestantism, it is useful to summon his witnessing. For Paul, the "old man" of sin is pronounced dead through Christ so as to become the "new man" of righteousness.[102] The soul proceeds from seemingly irremediable sinfulness under the Hebraic law (more formidably, The Law) into the light of faith through Christ, from all the cunning of evil into holiness. Thérèse, however, began with that light, the radiance of a never questioned, never questionable faith, the certainty of God's love, of Jesus's presence in her life, of sure election and of a heavenly hereafter. Throughout her maturing adolescence, she found herself threatened with the loss of all those sureties. In the end, she had to deal alone with an indefinitely extended loss for which she had never been prepared and in the subtle void of which she could find no succor. There was nothing in the Carmelites' Rule and Constitutions to equip her with spiritual armor for the combat she had to undergo. Such armor could be taken up and worn only by the holy and righteous, the "new" men and women. Such a possession, the ownership of the new person, prompts big-headedness in Paul, a writer at times preoccupied with boasting. It was a necessary defense, possibly, against adversaries he had in Galatia and elsewhere. Thérèse for her part had no ground for boasting.

She did not have even the bracing challenge of real, living opponents. She had only phantom voices she heard within her shadows. Yet she found herself wholly stripped down, helpless, empty-handed. In her spiritual self-portraiture the primary colors are of her weakness and littleness, inadequacies that do not, even so, bring her to dwell upon Paul's onerous *sense* of sin or sinfulness. In B she admitted to being a sinner and audaciously proclaimed she would sing of it—what a lucid tonic against neurotic preoccupations! It would be uncharitable to construe her iterated admission of her deficiencies as self-excusing, but for her the weakness amounted to simple, daily, observable fact. Her implicit failure as a Christian, her inconsequence, made her the more dependent upon Jesus and his love, and that dependence could only be good. She discovered that failure can be fail-safe.

Thérèse was and wanted to be wholly dependent, as might be anyone so aware of helplessness as to become beggarly toward God.[103] Her "little way" proves inextricably bound with the first of the beatitudes: she was blessed in her absolute neediness, her straightforward and unmitigated indigence, which allowed her to look nowhere else but to God. In a sense, her trust, her *confiance,* signifies that she could turn only to God, even God apparently *in absentia.* Such was her poverty of spirit. C remains incisive and invaluable as the record of her reaching the rock bottom of that poverty. Whether she knew that she attained a sacred destitution remains uncertain, but it complements the rejoiced suffering at which she arrived in B.

The fifth beatitude, blessed are the merciful, is also implicated in C. Far more toward those at the table of sorrow than toward the neglected sisters of Carmel Thérèse showed herself merciful, sympathetic in the old, root sense in that word, insightfully capable of feeling as the other person feels. This capacity was far more a solidarity or self-identification with others than a mere pity for them, pity bearing the unhappy residue of "feeling sorry" for another person from one's superior (and enjoyable) station. Her preachy anecdotes on pain-wracked Sr. Febronie, on possessive Sr. Marthe, and on teeth-rattling Sr. Marie de Jésus are unsettling because she gives us the sense that she learned how to put up with them and thus she rewards herself. It is not hard to imagine Gonzague's reproachful eye passing through these stories. Better had Thérèse stayed at the table and written further of how it feels to be bereft of God. There, at least, her mercy is egalitarian, necessarily so, given her absolute poverty in spirit. Not incidentally, the fifth beatitude suggests the incarnation itself, a divine entering into the human condition to share its burdens.

In logical complement to spiritual poverty and to mercifulness, the sixth beatitude, which celebrates purity of heart, also claims its due in the context of C. A true purity of heart is free of self-interest and special pleading; it is without the alloy of reward for the self. Thérèse's fretful preoccupations with herself in Manuscript B suggest that in that autumn of 1896 she was still short of that supreme disinterestedness, which, even so, she had known of and wished to claim: the love of Jesus, a love for his sake, not for hers. She finally reached a purity of heart in C, praying on behalf of others in darkness, mercifully identifying herself with them and acknowledging with them her own helplessness, even though she, unlike them, remained God-centered. It is at the dismal table of sorrow that her love for God shines brightest. Miraculously, in that passage she says not a word about love.

Again, the contrast between the table and the subsequent settings of charity at Carmel is painfully evident. Thérèse's merit badge consciousness within the midst of pitied sisters may well be self-satiric. She may have been congratulating herself on her achievements in charity with an eye to Gonzague's putting down her pride in such declarations. Or she was simply too eager, having been charged in her post-adolescent years with a tremendous responsibility toward others, to claim some achievements for herself, to show that she had lived up to Gonzague's expectations of her. In either case, she has left her readers the record of how she remained subject to pride even in her feverish last months. C is the account of her stumbling and falling and stumbling yet more. In that sequence, C proves invaluable. It teaches that Thérèse should be taken at her word, that she was weak and inadequate to the Carmel's demands of her.

FIGURE 5.6 After Therese's death: Marie de Gonzague (seated left), with Therese's sisters, Marie, Pauline, Celine, and their cousin Marie (seated right) Copyright Archives du Carmel de Lisieux.

That was a sore lesson that her natural sisters could not have understood nor accepted, but it was one that Gonzague perceived from the first (Figure 5.6.)

Love was the immoveable center of Thérèse's life, a singular, fervent, and subtle energy, and the abiding problematic. Her writings show that she was beset with ultimate questions about it. Did God love her? Did Jesus love her? Did she love God even though, in her almost continuous dryness, she did not feel that love? Did she ever ask herself how Teresa had fared when posing that last question to herself near the end of the *Camino de perfeccion*? When Thérèse was asked in turn, as indeed her novice sisters must often have asked her, about what love of God meant, she likely answered that it was nothing other than a total reliance, a trusting first, last and only in Jesus, in God as he is both humanly and divinely needy of us. If she was tried in her insecure, labile disposition, she held firmly to that need, to the fancy that Jesus, despised and rejected of men, betrayed by ingrates, would have at least a few loyal loving souls, and she would always be among them to assuage his grief and his pain.

None so loyal nor so loving souls are situated at the table of sorrow. Here, Thérèse combines her Martha and Mary selves supremely well, doing the fellowship's work of eating in the midst of dismal people while praying on their behalf, her Marian self addressing God in a request for light. In another gospel way, she reverses the story of the lost lamb. Jesus tells of the good shepherd who leaves ninety-nine sheep to find one gone astray. Now, the lost lamb herself has found a whole flock of strays and marginals, and her own nethermost nothingness, cued by Juan de la Cruz, waits to ensnare Jesus. He is bound to come, is he not, to assuage the grief and pain of this forlorn flock?

But who was to assuage her own grief and pain, when she fretted to Pichon in those innumerable letters, most of which he never found strength to answer? When Louis was tormented at Bon Sauveur? When the bottom fell out during the Easter season of 1896? When Taxil humiliated her? The answer had to be, No one, as that was what bearing one's cross meant.

In the *Paradiso* an arresting moment comes when Dante, suddenly made blind amid the heavenly host of saints, must answer questions about love that Saint John is putting to him. Dante has already faced interrogations from Saints Peter and James about faith and hope, but he has fobbed them off with a catechumen's responses, a text-perfect assent. He has arrived in heaven itself, so issues of faith and hope seem curiously, not to say comically, otiose. But Saint John does not let him go so easily. He wants to know how love itself seized and held Dante captive. He asks with unsparing vividness, what about the teeth and the cords of love? How has Dante been bitten and bound by love, made prey and captive? Only from the depths of his hurtful experience of love, its travails, its immitigable losses, can a genuine, nontextual answer come. For Dante it is the warrant of a life borne in ignominy and exile.

Stretched though the comparison may appear, Thérèse seems to me closely akin to Dante on several germinal counts. Like him, she had to face calamitous reversals of fortune and testing, and she had to make her way alone. Like him, she had to write her way through a private and life-menacing darkness. Like him, she arrives at an intimately and arduously won, if heterodox, view of Christian life. Both of them could be charged as heretics. Like him, she comprehends everything within divine love, even as love was for her, as for him, the dynamics governing life itself, a bottomless need for God, a restive longing for completion and peace.

Thérèse, despite her protracted periods of dryness throughout the years at Carmel, never wrote of being tormented by fears of Dantesque damnation, of hellfire, nor even of Purgatory's staple of agonies.[104] The simple reason for her freedom from such anxious and conventional burdens is that she could grasp only the lovingness of God and, accordingly, only an intimate rapport with Jesus, even when he was asleep or otherwise absent from her. Much of her latitudinal, almost instantly realized appeal to so many people in and well beyond France may derive from this almost familial closeness, which any believer would want for her or his own. If it is difficult to realize this fiduciary bond with Jesus and the Father, perhaps it can be found obliquely through Thérèse. She promised to draw all those who love her toward God. Devotion to her seems to be in reach of this divine centripety. What else are saints for but to show their way to God? And hers is supremely simple, human, and welcoming.

To that decisive degree, Thérèse proves herself a kind of anti-Dante, a witness not for the prosecution of human weakness and straying but for its defense. That fact points to a central truth about the table of sorrow and her position at it. There she is, seated and ready in what may be an everlasting expectancy of some indiscernible, God-appointed moment, the divine summons for her to rise up from the table, reborn, reclaimed. This setting appears static, a tableau fixed and immobile like a Renaissance version of the Annunciation or the Stabat Mater, but it is not. Thérèse makes clear that she is "in process," waiting for God's response. She has deftly put the ball into God's court. It cannot be determined whether the bitter bread has no leavening or has just enough to turn that bitterness into the sweet salvific she might have confidently looked for prior to the tunnel, the vault, and her new company, the godless with their anthill convictions about human life and human destiny. While sitting at the table, she is effectively setting off on the long journey of a late, post-literate, pre-God humanity, a journeying that is her distinct and distinguishing contribution to Christian eschatology.

In regard to someone who rejoiced in being little and helpless, it would be incongruous to speak of magnificence. The same holds true for that threadbare tag, genius, which always requires and seldom receives definition, but which is occasionally awarded to her, as though sainthood were not a cutting from suitable cloth. But "genius" does not fit her, and all puffing up of her is sure to bring her smile upon its vanity and folly. A more helpful inquiry might be, is her prayer meant to assist the godless to begin the long road of their own humbling, their own arrival at a redemptive littleness? Has Thérèse herself reached the utmost point of littleness, or is there a smidgeon of self still at impish work within her?

Given her repeated self-identification as a *rien*, a nothing, her assertion that *she*, God's child, "does not want to rise from this table before the day that you have appointed,"[105] seems to empty her prayer of its sublime solidarity with other poor sinners by saying nothing of *their* rising from the table. It may be assumed that they will be raised up when she is, but there are no clear grounds for such an assumption. She concludes her prayer by dwelling upon herself.

Simple as it may seem, ego is always in the way for her. Human life is substantially a prison sentence as far as each is condemned to the first-person, hazardous, and at times baleful in both the singular and the plural. If the Church has necessarily dwelt upon the plural as the Body, it has done so with tremendous cost, yet Thérèse seldom creates the impression (beyond Ms B) of being consciously implicated within this corporate, institutionally propped, mystically furthered magnum. It is ill-advised to celebrate her sainthood as the model of a submissive (and therefore ideal?) femininity before masculine ecclesiastical authority. In her peculiar and definitive *audace,* she was throwing off such fetters while she was alive. Her relationship with the Church is not finally decisive in the way that her relation to Christ and humanity are. This is why Thérèse undertook her itinerary with the ironic resolve "to do good upon earth" as *her* heaven to spend. She discovered that a communicant can live what Augustine thought impossible, a blessèd life in the land of death.

Her pronouncement suggests that she attained the perception that one is with Christ not only on the Cross but in the desert of the first person, too, in the bestial terrain of the self, at best only intermittently relieved by angelic serenity. Yet only within that terrain of selves could she make herself a living emblem of a longing for the divine, for what is sacred within or above the tatters of life. Thérèse's prayer may be her Marian self-portrait but her doing good upon earth would make her Martha-self predominant. She recoiled at the prospect that heaven would mean idleness for her, howsoever blissful. Her prayer's *envoi* to God seems to say, "I want employment until I am no longer 'I'" for God shall raise her up when she truly does become nothing but love of Him, when the transforming fire hymned by Juan de la Cruz unites the loving soul and the beloved. That far-off divine event is the real *kenosis* bruited about by theologians; not the emptying of self but the end of any self to do the emptying.

Her sister, Pauline, was duly concerned that people not make of Thérèse somebody that was not Thérèse, and any reader of her life may be subject to the delusion of some kind of arrival at what may well not have been her station of the Cross. But it is fair to ask whether attempted understandings of Thérèse jibe with all that is known of her. Never does she say she wants her imperfect self to disappear into God, only that it may hide in Jesus. She claims that bearing gently one's imperfections is the true sainthood, thus implicitly giving herself a saintly tag.

She had an abundant supply of what Dostoevsky called accursed questions: Why has heaven been sealed off from me? Why has Jesus departed from his loving spouse? Am I left to live on without God? Have scoffers been right all this while, and have I been unapprised? Is this darkness the truth I have always been seeking? These questions do not require an answer; rather, they provide a relief map or, better, they close up the furnace of doubt in which Thérèse found her love of God refined and her *offrande* of June 1895 definitively answered.

Just as in C when she begs to borrow God's love so as to give it back, her own love is not so paltry as she deems but has reached its acme, so when she is in the bleakest darkness with spiritual derelicts she proves most trusting of God by praying on their behalf. It becomes her particular trust that God might give her the strength through a near eternity to bear the cross that she has been given. She is not carrying it for herself alone.

It is no use pretending that Thérèse all the while had held on to her faith and her hope, and was merely concealing them from herself in her darkness, as though to say, as is said of Dostoevsky's somber hero, Stavrogin, that she believed when she did not believe that she believed. That nonsense monstrously cheats the very nature of her trial and all her years spent at Carmel in profound aridity and anguish. It was not faith (or belief) and hope that were tested. They were gone. It was her absolutely blind love of God that was tested, rather like the memory someone has of a dead and departed beloved. Would that memory last?

Hers did. And the proof of it, mercifully a not proclaimed, not trumpeted proof, lies here and there in the whole length of C and in those talks with her hovering sisters, over the summer of 1897.

Conclusion: A Human Passion

AS A MEMBER of one of the great mystical orders of Catholicism, Thérèse of the Enfant Jesus and the Holy Face occupies a securely central position within the Christian tradition. She is one of its best-loved saints and is officially a doctor of the Church. Her writings, like her relics, enjoy a cosmopolitan reach. Moderately educated, dying young in a convent's obscurity, she has attained without much effort a spectacularly high profile, which, in an age said to be spiritually athirst, shows no sign of diminution.

Yet when considered within the terms of her life and writing, Thérèse remains an anomaly. Sorely tested, she identified herself with atheists in a darkness at the farthest remove from Jesus, the spouse she courted from her adolescent years. She is known for her "little way" of trust in God, but she became a powerless servant, a slave to the very humanity that was ignorant, even contemptuous of her spiritual devotion to God and to itself as well.

The most striking aspect of Thérèse's spirituality is that she ended in a position diametrically opposite to the Carmel of the founder, Teresa of Ávila. Coming from the margins of her background and gender, Teresa urged the perfection Jesus himself called for in the Gospel According to Matthew, 5:48: "Be ye therefore perfect, even as your Father which is in heaven is perfect." Thérèse, remaining within the abiding limits and the helplessness of her disposition, answered with the mercy Jesus called for in the Gospel According to Luke, 6:36: "Be ye therefore merciful, as your Father also is merciful."

Thérèse offers another diametric position. The emblem of the Reformed Carmel comes from the First Book of Kings, where Elijah the prophet says he is zealous for the Lord God of hosts (in the Vulgate, *zelo zelatus sum*). Elijah, dwelling in a cave to escape persecution, is ordered by God to go into the wilderness of Damascus. In starkest contrast, Thérèse arrives at a cavernous darkness where those hostile or indifferent to her Jesus dwell. She does not confront them nor preach to convert them; she sits with them in compassion and solidarity. That is how she brings to life Jesus's injunction to be charitable toward those who revile or detest the life he would have his followers lead.

Thérèse comes to that extraordinary station not by conviction but by the experience of prolonged doubt. By regarding doubt, even despair, in a compliant rather than defiant way, she overcomes herself. Enduring without the consolations of faith and hope, she contents herself with the suffering of love, love cast into a void she does not presume to fill.

This saint is well-known for audacious pronouncements in both her writing and speaking, but her errand into the wilderness, where she sits as one within a fellowship of sin, is remarkably undramatic. It lacks the exclamatory force she often relied upon as a conventional way of imposing emphasis. As Teresa of Ávila ended life declaring herself a daughter of the Church, Thérèse ended hers as a proclaimed sister of blind, stumbling humanity, the humanity that the gospels reveal in Jesus's disciples, in those he heals, and in Caiaphas, Pilate, and foxy Herod Antipas.

There is no negative triumphalism at Thérèse's table of sorrow, no spectacular quake or fire as presented to Elijah when he was standing upon a mountain. Instead, like Elijah, she at that table hears something of a still small voice. She believes that Jesus has allowed the darkness of doubt to descend upon her, and that was her left-handed way of finding strength in his very testing of her.

Thérèse practices mercy within her testing by not dwelling upon the sinfulness of those with her at the table—nor on her own. She is sometimes compared to Luther in looking so resolutely upon human inadequacy, but she responds to that inadequacy without Luther's vehemence. She welcomes it, even rejoicing in what it declares of her imperfection. In addition to her audacity, there is impishness in her that merits attention; she does not tire of finding grounds for marking herself down, and the table of sorrows marks the nethermost point of her estimate.

Thérèse's life before she reached that table might be read as a sequence of unexpected turns. She did not enter the Carmel to become a writer, but by the time of her last autobiographical work, which she knew would also be her obituary, she had filled hundreds of folio pages with poems, prayers, plays, and letters. In the Carmel there were no mirrors—a temptation to vanity—but her writing became her mirror for self-examination and self-discovery. Without ever saying or even knowing it, her life in the Carmel was experimental. Like Teresa before her and Ignatius of Antioch before them both, Thérèse learned that a follower of Jesus is always beginning to be a Christian.

Thérèse entered the Carmel at a hazardously early age. Marie de Gonzague as prioress considered her a spoiled child who needed to be chastened severely, but during her nine years within the walls Thérèse became the spiritual guide not only to other novices; she consoled and counselled the two prioresses and other older sisters who revealed to her their many flaws and frets. From them she gathered the evidence that gave her confidence along the common way of imperfection.

When Teresa of Ávila set a very high bar of perfectibility, which Thérèse knew she could never reach, she in response and after much suffering set a very low bar of imperfectability, one that a soul can pass under only through a steadfast and disciplined humility. Both bars require arduous effort and depend first and last upon divine grace. Teresa and Thérèse, mother and daughter, complement one another in the extremes of love and self-sacrifice that they present to those who give them heed. In both of them one finds a rugged and exacting compassion, a love that is strenuous and unflinching.

Catholicism enjoins upon its faithful the practice of intercessory prayer. That is a Christian's direct access to the saints. Millions of people over the generations since Thérèse's death have prayed to her, a saint they know from hagiographic images; from the photography of her sister, Céline; from her messages on devotional cards; from her autobiographies and other works. To those who, like Teresa's brother, Lorenzo de Cepeda, do not or cannot practice intercessory prayer, all of these resources are available as occasions for reflection and contemplation.

No resource, however, is so rich as the gospels as the avenue to the Carmel. Because Thérèse needed and sought from them direction for her self and for those needy in her community and beyond it, she brought the gospels into her life and theirs. For her, the gospels had no distancing historical value, nor was she interested in exegetical or theological constructs from them; they simply imposed themselves as the sole light upon the shadows and darkness of immediate, daily life.

Like the gospels, Thérèse's story teaches best if it remains experimental, not set in historical recesses but brought into the challenges of any here and now. At its end, her life is stripped of everything save her love of Jesus. In geometric terms she is stationed on the horizontal plane of human failings; the stretch is immeasurable, and her reach through prayer extends immeasurably in a vast first person plural. At the same time, her prayer forms an axis with the vertical plane conjoining humanity with God. A double helix coils along both planes, the complementary gyring of human helplessness and of divine love. In the cruciform axis, human passion becomes one with the divine passion: on the cross, Jesus in total helplessness looked mercifully upon his tormentors; at the dark and obscure table of sorrow Thérèse in her total inadequacy asks for divine light to be given to all who negate the struggle and mission of her life.

Thérèse experienced that negation within her and asked God to loan her the love she knew she did not have for him so that she could give it back. She gives it back at the table of sorrow. In the most exemplary charity imaginable, she draws with her through prayer a lost and suffering humanity.

That is the definitive fact about Therese of the Child Jesus of the Holy Face. Everything else is froth on the surface.

APPENDIX I

The Text of Thérèse Witnessing to Her Doubt: Manuscript C 5v–6v

"In the joyous Easter days, Jesus made me realize that there truly are souls who have no faith, who by the abuse of graces lose this precious treasure, source of the only pure and true joys. He allowed that my soul be invaded by the thickest shadows, and that the thought of heaven, so sweet for me, be only the subject of combat and torment. This testing was supposed not to last a few days or weeks, it was supposed to go on till the hour designated by the Good Lord and . . . this hour has not yet come . . . I'd like to be able to express what I feel, but alas I believe that's impossible. It is necessary to have journeyed under this dark tunnel to grasp its obscurity. I'm going to try nevertheless to explain it by a comparison.

"I fancy that I have been born in a country surrounded by thick fog; I've never contemplated the smiling look of nature, inundated and transfigured by the brilliant sun; it's true that from infancy I've heard of these wondrous things, and I know the country where I am is not mine, that there's another toward which I should unceasingly aspire. It's not a story made up by an inhabitant of the sorrowful country where I am, it's a sure reality that the King of the brilliant sun's country came to live for thirty-three years in the land

of shadows. Alas! The shadows did not comprehend that this Divine King was the light of the world.... But Lord, your child has comprehended your divine light, she's asking your forgiveness for her brothers, she agrees to eat for as long as you wish the bread of sorrow and she does not wish to rise, before the day you have indicated, from this table filled with bitterness where poor sinners are eating.... But can she not also say in her name, in the name of her brothers: Have pity on us, Lord, indeed, we are poor sinners!... O Lord, send us away justified.... May all those who are not enlightened by the luminous torch of Faith see it shine at last.... O Jesus, if it is necessary that the table soiled by them be purified by a soul that loves you, I truly wish to eat alone the bread of testing till it please you to introduce me into your luminous realm. The only grace I am asking of you is never to offend you.
"...*suddenly the fog surrounding me is becoming thicker, penetrating my soul and enveloping it in such a way that it is no longer possible to rediscover in it the sweet image of my Country, all has disappeared. When I want to restore my heart, weary of the surrounding shadows, by the memory of the shining land toward which I aspire, my torment doubles; it seems that the shadows borrow the voice of sinners who speak to me mockingly: 'You're dreaming of the light, of a country made fragrant by the sweetest perfumes, you're dreaming of the everlasting possession of the Creator of all these marvels, you believe that one day you will part from the fog around you, go on, go on, rejoice in the death that will give you not what you're hoping but a night even more profound, the night of nothingness.'*
"*Well-belovèd Mother, the image I've wanted to give you of the shadows darkening my soul is as imperfect as a sketch compared to its model, but I don't want to write about it any longer, I'd be afraid of blaspheming... I'm even afraid of having said too much about it....*"

["Au jours si joyeux du temps pascal, Jésus m'a fait sentir qu'il y a véritablement des âmes qui n'ont pas la foi, qui par l'abus des graces perdent ce précieux trésor,

Appendix 1

source des seules joies pures et véritables. Il permit que mon âme fût envahie des plus épaisses ténèbres et que la pensée du Ciel si douce pour moi ne soit plus qu'un sujet de combat et de tourment.... Cette épreuve ne devait pas durer quelques jours, quelques semaines, elle devait ne s'éteindre qu'à l'heure marquée par le Bon Dieu et... cette heure n'est pas encore venue... Je voudrais pouvoir exprimer ce que je sens, mais hélas je crois que c'est impossible. Il faut avoir voyagé sous ce sombre tunnel pour en comprendre l'obscurité. Je vais cependant essayer de l'expliquer par une comparaison.

Je suppose que [je] suis née dans un pays environné d'un épais brouillard, jamais je n'ai contemplé le riant aspect de la nature, inondée, transfigurée par le brillant soleil; dès mon enfance il est vrai, j'entends parler de ces merveilles, je sais que le pays où je suis n'est pas ma patrie, qu'il en est un autre vers lequel je dois sans cesse aspirer. Ce n'est pas une histoire inventée par un habitant du triste pays où je suis, c'est une réalité certaine car Le Roi de la patrie au brillant soleil est venu vivre 33 ans dans le pays des ténèbres, hélas! les ténèbres n'ont point compris que ce Divin Roi était la lumière du monde.... Mais Seigneur, votre enfant l'a comprise votre divine lumière, elle vous demande pardon pour ses frères, elle accepte de manger aussi longtemps que vous le voudrez le pain de la douleur et ne veut point se lever de cette table remplie d'amertume où mangent les pauvres pécheurs avant le jour que vous avez marquée... Mais aussi ne peut-elle pas dire en son nom, au nom de ses frères: Ayez pitié de nous Seigneur, car nous sommes de pauvres pécheurs!... Oh! Seigneur, renvoyez-nous justifiées.... Que tous ceux qui ne sont point éclairés du lumineux flambeau de la Foi le voient luire enfin....ô Jésus s'il faut que le table souillée par eux soit purifiée par une âme qui vous aime, je veux bien y manger seule le pain de l'épreuve jusqu'à ce qu'il vous plaise de m'introduire dans votre lumineux royaume. La seule grâce que je vous demande c'est de ne jamais vous offenser!...

"...mais tout à coup les brouillards qui m'environnent deviennent plus épais, ils pénètrent dans mon âme et l'enveloppent de telle sorte qu'il ne m'est plus possible de retrouver en elle l'image si douce de ma Patrie, tout a disparu! Lorsque je veux reposer mon cœur fatigué des ténèbres qui l'entourent par le souvenir du pays lumineux vers lequel j'aspire mon tourment redouble, il me semble que les ténèbres empruntant la voix des pécheurs me disent en se moquant de moi: "tu rêves la lumière, une patrie embaumée des plus suaves parfums, tu rêves la possession *eternelle* du Createur de toutes ces merveilles, tu crois sortir un jour des brouillards qui l'environnent, avance, avance, réjouis-toi de la mort qui te donnera non ce que tu espères, mais une nuit plus profonde encore, la nuit du néant.'

"Mère bien-aimèe, l'image que j'ai voulu vous donner des ténèbres qui obscurcissent mon âme est aussi imparfaite qu'une ébauche comparée au modèle, cependant je ne veux en écrire plus long, je craindrais de blasphemer... j'ai peur même d'en avoir trop dit...."]

APPENDIX 2

On Another Darkness: Once More, Teresa of Ávila

This book began with a brief portrait of the founder of the Reformed Carmel, Teresa de Jesús. I noted in passing her spiritual itineraries in the great trilogy of her writings, the autobiography, the *Camino* or *Way of Perfection*, and the culminating work on Carmel's life in prayer, the *Moradas*. I suggested that her history of the founding of Carmels throughout Spain, *Fundaciones*, constitutes a second autobiography. The weighty correspondence or *cartas* she wrote over the last score of her years complement that foundational history and profile her as an indomitably entrepreneurial yet acutely circumspect personality, someone ever in the world, however she sought to turn beyond it.

One of her other writings deserves scrutiny in giving acute insight into Thérèse and the darkness of Manuscript C: Teresa's psalmic mirror in which she saw herself and addressed heaven, a work known as *Exclamaciones del alma a Dios*, [Outcryings of a soul to God]. There are seventeen meditations under this rubric, not one of them dated. Even so, their value proves fourfold: first, they afford the most intensely private portion of her work. She dwells only upon her innermost, yearning self, seeking God. Here, there is an eye neither to sisters nor to confessors nor to any other spiritual overseers. All the politics that inform the other works has receded. Second, Thérèse read these outcries from her spiritual mother. She refers twice to the thirteenth of them, both times to a passage in which Teresa speaks of life as a dream—a cliché but not for Thérèse's purposes. Third, the outcries contain valuable notes on Teresa's own darkness. Fourth, they provide her own notes on the kind of company Thérèse kept at the table of sorrow.

Teresa's exclamations initially appear as a road to nowhere, for unlike Augustine, her confessional model, she admits to no ripening into a sudden conversion. Part of the sequestration that women lived under in her time, as long before and long since, meant substantially narrow latitude and not much access to the sort of recklessness men could live out and recover from via dramatic transformations.[2] Women were at considerable risk in making themselves known at all, let alone as chroniclers of their own pinched lives.

While in her major works Teresa often refers to herself as a lowly, worthless creature, in the *Exclamaciones* she laments her epistemological limits before God. Her understanding remains inadequate, not because of any defect in her education or character but because she is human, which means a kind of imprisonment.[3] Yet she exercises a sophisticated skepticism upon herself. If she is in helpless ignorance, she can at least pose questions—a reminder that she was raised by a Jewish father. If God is within her, as Jesus tells believers He is, then what is the point of prayer? But can she not also be separated from God? Of course, and when that happens, there is no avenue to understanding why that separation should happen at all. The soul knows the chilling apartness of God and sees no remedy. Only God can cure what she calls "the wound You have given." By such a wounding the soul loses hope of salvation and joy, the only solace, a grim one, being that suffering has been "so very well spent."[4]

Teresa admits anxiety lest God terminate all his favors to her, meaning undoubtedly the grace of many visitations.[5] Indeed, in her writings subsequent to the *Vida*, the visions and voices fall away markedly, as though in her undertaking to reform the Carmel she had no time for them. Having lived a Marian life of contemplation, she became a Martha, as did Thérèse in her turn.

Worst of all is Teresa's pondering the Dies Irae, the Day of Judgment, an occasion for which she had many times envisioned God turning from her in anger.[6] This fear of being cut off and damned abided within her to the end of her life. If her hope of contenting God remained uncertain and full of hazards, it was because her self-condemnations were always under the surface of her piety, darkening it toward despair. Never did she entertain the possibility that her morbid trepidations derived from the view of a punitive, vengeful deity. Rather, she was so burdened with the weight of former sins and present worthlessness that she felt she deserved hell and would only be receiving justice in God's dispatching her to its torments. All the more wondrous it was that God had granted her, least worthy of creatures, so many graces. They seem to have convinced her all the more that she was God's traitor.

It may be idle to hypothesize what was at the sinful source of such fear, that, for example, Teresa was all too aware of her Jewish legacy, which made her tacitly one of its *conversos*, or, to draw on a once-fashionable assumption, that she had enjoyed a lesbian sexuality with a cousin during their budding years of youth. My sense is that her burden weighed as much, perhaps even more in the secrecy than in any behaviors or particular acts it covered. She felt a keen compunction in never having admitted to herself through her writing what her sin or sins or adolescent straying had been. Her friendly Dominican confessor Domingo Báñez forbade her to write anything of them. What the effect of that obligatory omission was upon her could not have been salutary. The enforced secrecy may have made her feel fraudulent or hypocritical. That it was among the most onerous of her crosses seems plausible. It remains an ironic pity that this woman of unsparing candor was prohibited from directing such candor toward and even against herself where it was apparently most important and in the way that was most important to her, her writing.

Teresa even torments herself when celebrating the Trinity. Since the Holy Spirit unites Father and Son in mutual love, there is no need of her love.[7] The paltry human soul, so she concludes, is left to rejoice that God the Father is loved as He deserves, if only by Jesus. It would seem a sufficiently dismal fact that any mortal's love for God must be inadequate; that it should be superfluous as well amounts to a decisive brief against any attempt at loving God. That is not to mention that any genuine love of God is a grace bestowed, not some herculean achievement of an aching, puny self. But Teresa goes on, fully aware that as a Christian, she knows the cards are stacked against her by God: all good the soul achieves is the effect of grace, not voluntarism; all that is evil in oneself one can safely claim as one's own. In a keenly painful moment, she defines death as not loving God. But then, apostrophizing death, she wonders why people are so afraid of it. After all, she adds, there is so much life in death.

Innumerable times Teresa shifts from the confessional clamors of self to the generic, implicitly more sedate plaints of the first person plural. The central problem of helpless ignorance remains, however, no less for the collective than for the individual. If she complains of perpetual blindness, so might any Christian. She is asking divine pity for all souls when she says we do not understand or even know what we desire, nor do we attain what we ask for. These are remarkable assertions, given that the imperatives of Christian life clearly map out the way and leave few choices for one's desiring and asking: the love of God, the love for God, renunciation of worldly pursuits and interests, love of others as shown in charitable works. But Teresa's shift from "I" to "we," which then moves to "they," imports a great deal, as she is leaving self-commiseration and moving on to the wider reaches of concern for others, the nearly damned. That concern predominates in several of Teresa's outcries.

She asks God's pity for those who do not turn to him. She pleads for those who neither wish to plead for themselves nor know how to do so. How forgetful are mortals when they offend God, she exclaims, how forgetful even of themselves![8] May God cure them of their ingratitude toward his mercies! In fine, she covers the range of dissidents: the oblivious, indifferent, ungrateful. (The only ones missing are the indignant, the active scorners of God.[9]) As she is never one to undervalue the power of sinfulness, her solicitude for nonbelievers and antibelievers is neither soft nor sentimental: "O, hardness of human hearts!"[10] It is such a flinty insistence upon always getting their own worldly way, as she sees it, that will lead them to eternal torment. Hell, their receptacle, she sees clearly, having had visions of herself there; it is a stenchy lake full of serpents. With her penchant for drama at full tilt, she asks that God vouchsafe to just one soul (she means but does not name herself) to reach for the divine light, so that that soul may be a light for the many who have none. This *exclamación* may have inspired Thérèse's prayer for divine light on behalf of those lost at the table of sorrow. The cardinal difference between Teresa's prayer and her daughter's is that Thérèse in hers received the supreme grace of praying not merely for but among the lost.

Teresa, even so, had turned to them. Her prompting to do so provides the closest nexus between her and Thérèse. She claims that those who love God find that their delights in divinity are tempered when they realize that others are not enjoying God's good. The soul loving God wishes to impart its joy to those others; in effect, it sacrifices something of that joy so that others may have a share in it. Charity toward nonbelievers means turning away from God for their sakes. She is explicit: "O, my Jesus! How great is the love you bear to the sons of men, that the greatest service one can do is to leave you for the love and gain of others."[11]

These are astounding words. Had not Jesus enjoined his followers to forsake all human bonds—of family, friends, everyone—in order to join him? But love of others he himself had also identified as the second of God's two commands. Love of God and love of neighbor make up the summa of Christian ethics. Jesus's parable of the beneficent Samaritan answered the discipular question, who is my neighbor? For Teresa, that neighbor, that "Other" was everyone without God: all those countless pagans of America against whom her brothers and other conquistadores had been fighting. Her impetus to extend love abroad is not so colonial nor imperial as to make such faceless hordes explicit in her writing, but they were there for the missionaries to convert. The sword was followed closely by the cross, effecting that grotesque fusion by which Caesar and Christ became as one and rendering unto Caesar was tantamount to rendering unto his victim. The sword's dispensation was, of course, allotted to Muslims and Jews within Christian Europe and beyond. Teresa knew more about what evangelists call "decisions for Christ" than she admitted on paper. Whether she knew of rank atheists within Spanish and Catholic culture itself is not known: she might well have known of some within the orders who had privately descended into the lowest depths of darkness.

What matters far more for now than the recipients of Teresa's charity is the impression the *Exclamaciones* give, that in turning to them and leaving Jesus behind, she was escaping for the while the burden of her unworthiness before God. Implicitly, she was escaping from God as well. She discovered in the itinerary of the *fundaciones* that it suited her better to perform as a Martha than as a Mary, not least because Martha must have been inferior to her sister, having not chosen what Jesus told these sisters was "the better part."[12] Teresa's brief, as it seems to be, for Martha is that perhaps Jesus had no compassion for her in the work she was doing nor even cared whether she was in his presence or was not. Maybe she thought that Jesus had a greater love for Mary. Yet according to Teresa, it was Martha's own love for Jesus that emboldened her to ask why he did not care for her.

Her founding of the Reform's houses was a supremely Marthan enterprise.[13] Her Marian, visionary years in the Carmel of the Incarnation taught her a tormenting awareness of her unworthiness before the divine favors. In a way, she seems to have undertaken the Reform with herself as much the intended object as the lax house. At great physical and psychological cost to herself, as she importuned ecclesiastical councils for permits to buy houses for the convents, wheedled consent from local clergy, and risked offense to other orders (such as the Jesuits in Sevilla), she immersed herself in the worldly ways of politics. When she says she despised the things of this world, she is credible because she puts them to the fore in the *Fundaciones*.

This careerism in Teresa accounts in part for the substance of interest in her among feminist scholars and journalists. The Marian paraphenomena, the prayerful centering upon God, the talks from God—for a time dipped in Freudian bunkum—have been dried and set, more or less permanently, aside.[14] Yet the Marian session, the ever-yearning reach of contemplation toward God is, as Teresa herself would unquestionably insist, the centerpiece of her life's drama. As she put it, she was dying from not dying, so great was her desire to get past the burden of both her loving in a void and the ever-refined sense of her unworthiness. Life itself, in her apt and oft-quoted phrase, was a night for her spent in an obscure inn. Such was her darkness.

Notes

PREFACE

1. "A cette heure matinale les habitants de la Galerie de Navarin faisaient leur toilette et nous nous amusions à les regarder en passant. Un jour, mon père nous dit: 'Faites attention, mes enfants, à tout ce qui pourrait ternir la pureté de votre coeur, ne jetez pas à droite et à gauche des regards indiscrets.'" NPPA, p. 5 of Sr Marie du Sacré-Coeur. La Société Historique de Lisieux has, through the courtesy of the Carmel archivists, afforded the following information on the Galerie de Navarin: across the Boulevard Carnot from the public garden (next to the cathedral), one can still see the arcaded Galerie de Navarin. It was built around 1830 and named for the victory of the British, French, and Russian navies against the Turks and Egyptians in 1827. In the 1990s the building was bought, destroyed and rebuilt identically but with an expanded garden in the center. It is still known as the Galerie de Navarin.
2. "Tout près de la maison aux Buissonnets habitait un officier; sa femme, un peu légère, riait et courait dans le jardin avec l'ordonnance et cela ne nous échappait pas. Nous la guettions quelquefois à travers les arbres; mon père le vit et nous racommanda de ne plus la faire parce que c'était un danger." NPPA, p. 5 of Sr. Marie du Sacré-Coeur.
3. "Il avait un soin extrême d'eloigner de nous tout ce qui lui semblait une occasion de tentation." PO, 239, col. 1.
4. "Je vais entrer au Carmel, je veux vous laisser un souvenir, promettez-moi que vous le garderez toujours" and "Je lui tiens parole et je mourrai avec." "Préparation de Déposition," Sr. Geneviève de Ste. Thérèse, 1908.

INTRODUCTION

1. See Kathleen Norris's *Acedia and Me* (New York: Riverhead Books, 2008), especially her "Commonplace Book" of widely chosen sources, mediaeval and modern, theological, psychoanalytic and literary, pp. 287–329.
2. Émile Littré, *Dictionnaire de la langue française* (Paris: Hachette, 1881), IV: 1866, col. 2. The divines are Jacques Bossuet and Jean-Baptiste Massillon.
3. Rowan Williams, *Teresa of Avila* (Harrisburg, PA, Morehouse Publishing Co., 1991), 158.

CHAPTER 1

1. "[F]es versificadora, no poeta," says Maximiliano Herráiz in his magnificent edition of her *Obras Completas* (Salamanca: Sigueme, 1997), 1103. He notes, however, that her doggerel was part of the wide and abundant circulation of verses among the Carmel sisters, the genres being known as "coplas" or popular songs, "villancicos" which became what we call carols, and "cantarcillos" or little tunes. The songs were characteristically octosyllabic, framed in short stanzas, and with cued refrains so that a soloist could be joined by the other sisters. Most of Madre Teresa's thirty-three extant poem-songs follow such patterns. Probably the best introduction to this subject is a recording by the Spanish ensemble Ars Musicae with the immortal soprano Victoria de los Angeles for Angel Records, Angel 35888, in 1961, which includes valuable notes on instruments: *Spanish Songs of the Renaissance*.
2. 5:8: "entre los pucheros anda el Señor ayudándoos en lo interior y esterior." I have used the edition of Victor García de la Concha, *Libro de las fundaciones* (Madrid: Austral, 1991), 79.
3. *"Pobreza y alegría."* This coupling occurs in one of the *avisos*, the nineteenth, in the 1662 edition of the correspondence, *Cartas de la Santa Madre Teresa de Jesus*, edited by Don Juan de Palafox y Mendoza, published in Madrid by María de Quínones.
4. For the reader of Spanish, a detailed discussion of Teresa's style can be found in María Jesús Mancho Duque's edition of the *Camino de Perfección* (Madrid: Espaca, 1997), 22–51.
5. His writings, translated into Castilian, were sent into Spain as early as 1521 and swiftly proscribed by the inquisitor general, Cardinal Adrian of Utrecht. The order that all copies be confiscated was, of course, wonderfully pointless.
6. The most frequently cited phrase in Plotinus, on the flight of the one to the One, is the most economical way of putting the third or unitive stage of mental prayer.
7. For a well-documented discussion of "The Myth of the Inquisition" see Henry Kamen, *Imagining Spain: Historical Myth and National Identity* (New Haven: Yale University Press, 2008), 126–149. He notes that the superstitious horror built

up about and against the Inquisition is largely the propaganda of nineteenth-century Liberal exiles, Antonio Puigblanch, Juan Antonio Llorente and Joseph Blanco White. "The image of Spain in which, for two hundred years, nobody thought, nobody wrote and nobody read, all because they lived in fear of the Inquisition, is so grotesque that the wonder is that anyone has seriously accepted it" (142).

8. Most famous are Isabel de la Cruz (arrested in 1519 and tried in 1524), Francesca Hernández (arrested in 1529), and Magdalena de la Cruz, who in 1543 confessed that her illuminations had come from Satan.

9. "[H]ombres de tomo, de letras y entendimiento." *Libro de la Vida*, ed. Dámaso Chicarro (Madrid: Cátedra, 2001), XI. 14: 197.

10. *The Life of Saint Teresa of Ávila by Herself*, trans. J.M. Cohen (London: Penguin, 1957), 95. These demurring remarks were likely directed to the Franciscan, Pedro de Alcántara. He had objected to her taking matters of inner life to the savants he presumed to be wholly out of their depth in addressing them.

11. From Chapter 18, she speaks of her unworthiness in being the receptacle of God's jewel-like mercies to her, "cosa tan ruin, tan baja, tan flaca y miserable" ["a thing so contemptible, so low, so weak and wretched"]; in Chapter 19, she speaks of her tears as God's gift sent into herself as a foul well, "parece que os hago pago de tantas traiciones, siempre haciendo males" ["it seems I am paying for so many betrayals, always doing evil"]; in Chapter 30, she condemns her own humility over evil-doing by saying that it was fake and demon-prompted, since true humility gives sweetness and light, not the darkness and aridity: "ni la escurece ni da sequedad," she felt, realizing no consolation even in the awareness that God is merciful; in Chapter 31, she is "esta hormiguilla que el Señor quiere que hable!" ["this wee little ant that God wishes to speak!"]

12. The groundbreaking work was Alison Weber's *Teresa of Avila and the Rhetoric of Femininity* (Princeton: Princeton University Press, 1990).

13. For an excellent review of recent criticism see Elena Carrera, *Teresa of Avila's Autobiography: Authority, Power and the Self in Mid-Sixteenth-Century Spain* (London: Legenda, 2005), 3–8.

14. *Vida*, Chapter 9.8. Augustine would have smiled at her presumption that the saints she read about, including him, had never suffered relapses, such as she remained subject to.

15. *Camino de Perfección*, ed. Maria Jesús Mancho Duque (Madrid: Espaca, 1997), 81. The italicized portion is from the Escurial Codex, the first version of this work, which was suppressed by the Inquisition and thus is the more valuable to us.

16. Chapter 40.8. In her many references to the churchmen who advised and in some instances befriended her, Teresa gives the impression that she got around the Church's gender racket by the sort of equity that intelligent persons find natural. She knew when to defer and often does so in her writing, but she never

17. Chapter 8.12.
18. See *The Third Spiritual Alphabet,* trans. Mary Giles (New York: Paulist Press, 1981), 494–514, esp. 497.
19. As her maternal grandmother and her mother were gentiles, no Jew would now say that Teresa was Jewish. Still, the story imposes: when the Church, in fear of inchoate Protestantism, decided to banish all non-Christians or to force them abroad, her Jewish grandfather chose to become one of the *conversos,* a term that subsumed both Jews and Muslims. The initiation into Christian life included a series of public humiliations: processions of whippings in robes after which the robes were hung as reminders in the parish church of the converted. The Inquisition was suspicious of *conversos* and imposed dire threats for any evidence of recidivism.

    A key question remains unanswerable: did Teresa herself know of her Jewish background? Does it matter that in describing herself negatively she often used the hebraism, *ruin*? The issue is not helped by ignoring it. Her Jewish background came to light by accidental discovery in an archive a few years after the Second World War and caused brief unrest. Then, like most disconcerting and apparently unpleasant facts, it underwent the usual denial, although some clerics rejoiced in the discovery, as though Teresa herself had been a Jewish convert. The most weighty of authorities on Teresa in the twentieth century, the Reformed Carmel friar, Elfren de la Madre de Dios, underplayed her Jewish lineage to the end.
20. The Index carried five sections, books in Latin, Spanish, German, Dutch, and what was called vulgar Portuguese. A facsimile of it was published by the Real Academia Española in 1952.
21. See Gillian Ahlgren, *Teresa of Avila and the Politics of Sanctity* (Ithaca, NY: Cornell University Press, 1996), 16–17.
22. "Cuando se quitaron muchos libros de romance, que no se leyesen, yo sentí mucho, porque algunas me daba recreación leerlos y yo no podía ya, por dejarlos en latin." *Libro de la Vida,* XXVI. 5: 323. Chicarro remarks in note 12 on that page that Teresa's transcriptions of Latin, although labored, suggest that she knew "aspectos concretos de la flexión."
23. John, 4:1–27. If Teresa was aware of her Jewish heritage, she knew this woman, like the Phoenician woman in Mark, 7: 24–30, was not only excluded from Jewish culture but, perhaps for that reason, able to engage with Jesus, to parry with him, and to be transformed by the experience.
24. She once said she didn't know why people called her the foundress, "pues que Dios, que no yo, es el que que ha fundado estas casas" ["as it is God, not I, that has founded these houses,"] *Dichos de Santa Teresa, Obras Completas,* III, eds.

Efren de la Madre de Dios and Otger Steggink (Madrid: BAC, 1959), 909, no. 302. In her history of the foundations of the Reform Carmel she repeatedly cites God as the real founder.
25. Marcelle Auclair, *Teresa of Ávila*, trans. Kathleen Pond (Garden City, NY: Image, 1959), 233. This book is a smooth read with an unremitting blandness. It's a bad start when Auclair sweeps past the by then established fact that Teresa's father and grandfather were Jews.
26. *Fundaciones*, XXVII: 229. "[P]orque deseaba fundase tantas como tengo cabellos en la cabeza."
27. With her necessarily unquestioning deference to male authority, she was helpless when one of its arbiters tacitly subverted another. She insisted it was by God's grace that she found generous and supportive men along the way, including the Discalced friar accompanying her, who abetted the divine enterprise when Teresa's strength and resolve sometimes slackened.
28. These were in Ávila, Medina del Campo, Malagón, Valladolid, Toledo, Pastrana, Salamanca, and Alba de Tormes.
29. "[Q]ue aunque hasta aquí he vivido y gouenado entre Descalças, sè bien, por la bondad de el Señor, como se han de gouernar las que no lo son.... Bien conozco nuestra flaqueza, que es grande; pero ya que aqui no hegamos con las obras, lleguemos con los deseos; que piadoso es el Señor, y harà que poco a poco las obras igualen con la intencion, y deseo." *Cartas de la Santa Madre Teresa de Jesus*, ed. Don Juan de Palafox y Mendoza (Madrid: Maria de Quínones, 1662), 556.
30. For a helpful summary of major points in the sanctification's depositions see Ahlgren, *Politics of Sanctity*, 148–156.
31. Luke 11:52 for the theft of the key and the not entering; on the kingdom of heaven within, Luke 17:21.
32. *Moradas*, II:1. "Sea varón y no de los que se echaban a beber de bruces, cuando iban a la batalla," a vivid image which I presume she borrowed from her brother, Lorenzo de Cepeda, who had fought for Spain in the Americas. Some of her keenest insights she imparted in letters to him as she became in effect his spiritual director and he is one of the four of her critics whom she addresses in her satiric *vejamen*, (Herráiz edition, 602–603). In the *Camino* VII: 8, she called on the sisters to be "varones fuertes."
33. In *St. Teresa of Avila: Author of a Heroic Life* (Berkeley: University of California Press, 1995), 112–113, Carol Slade suggests that Teresa's life implicitly follows the course of the *conquistador*, Hernando Cortez, whose letters from America were published by his father in the year of Teresa's birth, 1515. There is no evidence that she read these letters, but Slade suggests that Teresa's *fundaciones* around Spain constituted "a domestic new world chronicle" (111).
34. *Moradas*, VI:9. "[A]sí hay muchas personas santas que jamás superion qué cosa es recibir una de aquestas mercedes, y otras que las reciben, que no lo son." (Herráiz edition, 701).

35. *Camino*, IV: 4. "[A]mor unas con otras; desasimiento de todo lo criado; verdadera humildad, que, aunque la digo a la postre, es la principal y las abraza todas." Lowliness precedes and subsumes love for others because it is the precondition for seeking God.
36. At the end of the *Camino*, XLII, 4, she laments how different our wills are from God's; that God wills we seek truth but we seek falsehoods; God is eternal and we pursue what fails ("nos inclinamos a lo que se acaba"); God wills that we seek sublimities but we settle for the baseness of the earth. She remarks toward the end of the Escurial Codex that it would be erroneous to assume that we can ever be free of testings, imperfections, or even sins, and she admits of herself, "me veo rodeada de flojedad y tibieza y poca mortificación y otras muchas cosas."
37. *Camino*, XVI: 7, note 370, a citation from the Escurial Codex (see footnote 13). "[D]igo que no parecemos christianos, ni que leímos la Pasión en nuestra vida" ["I'm saying we do not seem to be Christians nor ever to have read in our lives of the Passion."]
38. *Camino*, IV, 7. "[Y] guárdense de estas particularidades, por amor del Señor, por santas que sean, que aun entre hermanos suele ser ponzona y ningun provecho en ello veo; y si son deudos, muy peor: es pestilencia."
39. *Camino*, IX, 2. "No sé yo qué es lo que dejamos del mundo las que decimos que todo lo dejamos por Dios, si non nos apartamos de lo principal, que son los parientes." See also her *Cuentas de Conciencia*, XXXV, on the Carmel's Constitutions forbidding close family ties: "Nos dicen que nos desviemos de deudos" ["They tell us to stay clear of relatives"], adding that dealing with her relatives "Me cansa y deshace" ["wears me out and does me in"] (Herráiz edition of *Obras Completas*: 952).
40. *Camino*, X, 2. "[S]er contra nosotros es recia cosa, porque estamos muy juntas y nos amamos mucho."
41. *Camino*, XIII, 7. "Esta casa es un cielo, si le puede haber en la tierra."
42. *Camino*, XXVIII, 10. "[H]ay otra cosa más preciosa, sin ninguna comparación, dentro de nosotras... tenemos tal huésped dentro de nosotras...."
43. *Camino*, XLI, 4. "[S]omos flacos y no hay que fiar de nosotros." When she shifts, as in that statement, to the masculine predicate, "somos flacos," it is a wry turn. It seems an inclusive view: all God's children are weak, but at the same time, she reminds her sisters to be manly.
44. *Camino*, XVIII, 7.
45. Matthew 9:13. Who were the righteous in Teresa's age but the official ecclesiasticals' voices?
46. "Aquí veréisla madre que os dio Dios, que hasta esta vanidad sabía." The chess metaphor opens Chapter 24 of the Escurial Codex and corresponds to the beginning of the revised (Valladolid) text at its Chapter 16. For a comparative edition see Herráiz, *Obras Completas* (Note 48).
47. This passage closes Chapter 68 of the Escurial Codex, which corresponds to the close of Chapter 39 of the Valladolid version.

48. Matthew 7:1–5.
49. *Camino*, XXXII, 7. On the gift of union by which Christ transforms those he loves into himself.
50. María Jesús Mancho Duque, in her introduction to the *Camino*: 9 (see Note 4).
51. "[T]odos los demonios" and "amistades forzosas" in letters to Ambrosio Mariano, 184 (BAC numbering), March 15, 1577; and 189, May 9, 1577. Herráiz numbers them 187 and 192.
52. "Oh desventurados tiempose y miserable vida en la que ahora vivemos…!" *Moradas:* VI.:6, 11, Herráiz. 683–684.
53. February 16, 1577, *Epistolario* III: 327. "[N]o tengo pena de nada, que cuando mejor parece que van las cosas suelo yo estar más descontenta que ahora estoy."
54. "[C]omo a quien le ha ocurrido un sabrosisimo suceso." Cited from Gracián's *Scholia* in the *Obras Completas* of Teresa, III: 881–882, no. 105.
55. "[Y] gríteme todo el mundo, cuánto más que estaré yo quizá muerta cuando se viniere a ver." *Moradas:* VII:1, 2 ; Herráiz, *Obras Completas:* 711.
56. "[E]n el mismo Dios—digo estando dentro en él—hacemos grandes maldades…" *Moradas:* VI: 10, 4, Herráiz: 703.
57. See Luce López-Baralt, "Santa Teresa de Jesús y el Islam," *Teresianum* 33 (1982), 629–678.

   A well-known *souvenir d'enfance* in Teresa's autobiography has her leaving home with her brother to seek martyrdom in their fantasy of an Islamic Spain. They were quickly apprehended. This capacious essay tells of a greater journey into Islam and what Teresa got from it, poaching from a storehouse of poetic symbols dating to the first generations of Sufi mysticism. The symbols are wine and ecstasy from its imbibing; the constriction and expansion of the soul: *apretura* and *anchura*; the garden of the soul; the mystical tree; the silkworm; and a castle's seven concentric rings.

   López-Baralt goes into the mythic recesses for these symbols, to the *Upanishads* and the *Bhagavad-Gita*. She draws upon secondary literature in mystical symbolism (Jung, Eliade, Massignon, Etchegoyen, Asíen Palacios), but it is the Islamic texts that matter in their close conjunction to Teresa's writings. The briefest instance: in *Moradas* Teresa cites the silkworm's construction of the house in which it is going to die (V, 2) and says the Carmel sisters can achieve the same end, laboring with God's help, "quitando nuestro amor proprio y nuestra voluntad" ["abandoning our love of self and our willfulness"]. Teresa admits she has never seen a silkworm at this work, only heard about it. And could it be that she knew of Rumi, Sufi mysticism's foremost poet? His *Divan-e-kabir* speaks of the silkworm in exactly Teresa's sense, with the twist that the silkworms of love have no leaves (worldly provisions) from which to make their precious silk. A brilliant match!

This essay has application to Thérèse. *Apretura*, the constriction of the soul into grief, has its opposite in *anchura*: the correspondent Arabic terms are *qabd* and *bast*. They are sometimes construed as a veiling and a revelation, but they might also be construed with Thérèse's tunnel of love, the table of sorrow on one hand, and on the other, her expansive mission to do good upon the earth. Does not the first remain as a precondition to the second? Didn't her mission begin with her prayer at the table?

58. "[U]na mariposica blanca muy graciosa...." *Moradas:* V:2, 2, Herráiz, *Obras Completas*, 639.
59. *Moradas:* VI: 4, 7. "[U]n gusano de tan limitado poder como nosotros que no ha de entender sus grandezas," and "con unos gusanos quiere así comunicarse y mostrarse," Herráiz, *Obras Completas*, 671, 652.
60. *Moradas:* VII: 2, 5; Herráiz, *Obras Completas*, 716.
61. I Kings, 6:7.
62. "[L]a menor de todas y esclava suya...poniendo piedras tan firmes que no se os caiga el castillo...." *Moradas:* VII: 4, 9 ; Herráiz, *Obras Completas*, 726–727.
63. LT 65 (October 20, 1888) and C 25 v. Cf. Matthew 6:3.
64. Teresa's poem is "Vivo sin vivir en mí" and the refrain, "muero porque no muero." For Thérèse, DE, August 2, no. 4; September 4, no. 7.
65. In the *Fundaciones:* XII, she celebrates Beatriz de la Encarnación as a model of perfection. This saintly woman died young. She used to say she would be willing to be cut into 1,000 pieces in order to save a soul. Madre Teresa tops that by saying she would be willing to die 1,000 deaths to the same end. But she also pays Beatriz the honor of quoting, a very rare practice in any of her writings. Beatriz said that "no tiene precio la cosa más pequeña que se hace, si va por amor de Dios" ["the smallest deed done is priceless, if it's for the love of God"], which anticipates one of Thérèse's favorite lines from Juan de la Cruz. Finally, Beatriz at her internment emitted "él grandíssimo y muy suave olor" the saintly fragrance, which became a superstition claimed for Teresa, and for Thérèse at her beatification hearings.
66. "[U]n muladar tan sucio y de mal olor...." *Vida*, 10.9.
67. *Vida*, 18.8. See Manuscript B, 4v-5r: Thérèse's little bird, hindered from flying by its little "méfaits" (misdeeds) and "bagatelles" (trifles), is assailed by storm clouds and vultures, but Teresa's little bird, wet by heavenly rain in the soul's garden, is put in a nest by God's own hand.
68. *Vida*, 4.7. "[E]l Señor me había dado don de lágrimas...." Of her novice years she says that her heart was so hard, she could have read the story of the Passion through without a tear. *Vida*, 5.3.
69. Chapter 14.9.
70. Chapter 15.7.
71. "[L]es étincelles de l'amour...à pleines mains dans nos âmes...." and "...mais du moins ne sommes-nous pas obligées d'y jeter de petites pailles?....Jésus

est content de nous y voir mettre un peu d'aliment..." in A48r and LT 143, respectively.
72. 71. As Teresa remarked in Prologo 3, in the Escurial version of the *Camino*, suppressed but preserved by the king (a copy for his library): "No diré cosa que en mí o en otras no la tenga por experiencia o dada en oración a entender por el Señor." These are astoundingly audacious words.
73. In DE, July 4, 1897, no. 4, she tells Pauline that Pichon treated her too much as a child!
74. "[S]ur les flots de la *confiance* et de l'*amour*..." (A80v) and "je veux aimer le bon Dieu autant que sainte Thérèse," PA, 159.
75. "[J]e peux bien aspirer á la sainteté, même à une sainteté plus élevée, si je le veux, que celle de Ste Thérèse, puisque Notre Seigneur a dit: 'Soyez parfaits comme votre Père céleste est parfait.'" Pauline's testimony, NPPA, Espérance, p. 2.
76. Matthew 5:48. On the failures of her spiritual sisters to believe the gospels wholly, Teresa complains that there's no use in breaking her head by repeating scripture. *Camino*, XXIII, 6.
77. Her phrase is "hecha la tierra cielo," *Camino*, XXXII, 2.
78. *Camino*, XXXI, 13. "[Q]ue hacéis mucho más con una palabra, de cuando en cuando, del *Paternoster*, que con decirle muchas veces apriesa." See Ms C, 25v, Thérèse in her dryness.
79. "[L]os pecados y conocimiento propio es el pan...," *Vida*, 13.15. She tempers these words by cautioning against excessive dwelling upon one's sins. Better to go from that bread to other dishes! However, in the *Camino*'s meditation on the *Our Father*, at 36.10, she says contemplatives want their sins known and delight in speaking of them. She refers to the sister's humbling herself by this delight before the community so it can reinforce her low self-estimate.
80. *Vida*, 22.4. "[N]o podía traerle [su retrato y imagen] tan esculpido en mi alma." For Thérèse's fancy of painting with her little brush the details of Gonzague's portraits of the other sisters of their Carmel, see "Final Charity."
81. *Camino*, XXXIII.4. She claims that devils are intimidated by determined souls. In Manuscript A, 10v, Thérèse writes with humor of how as a child she routed some little demons ("deux affreux petits diablotins") from washbasins in the family's backyard in Alençon.
82. *Vida*, XXIII, 4 and XXIV, 6. The latter passage: "[N]unca más yo he podido asentar en amistad ni tener consolacíon ni amor particular sino a personas que entiendo le tienen a Dios y le procuran a servir."
83. José-Carlos Gómez-Menor, "Linaje Judío de Escritores Religiosos y Místicos Españoles del Siglo XVI," in *Judíos. Sefarditas. Conversos. La expulsión de 1492 y sus consecuencias*, ed. Ángel Alcalá, 591 (Valladolid: Ámbito, 1995). He calls it "hipotético, pero probable...que su madre tuviera sangre morisca." See also Richard P. Hardy's hagiographical *John of the Cross: Man and Mystic* (Boston:

Pauline Books, 2004), Figure 15 in the inlay, an icon of Juan with his name in Arabic "to signify his Islamic roots."

84. See Luce Lopez-Baralt, *The Sufi Trobar Clus and Spanish Mysticism* (Lahore: Muhammed Suheyl Umar, 2000).

85. See Julio Valdeón Baruque, "Motivaciones Socioeconómicas de las Fricciones entre Viejocristianos, Judíos y Conversos," in *Judíos. Sefarditas. Conversos*, ed. Alcalá, 69–87.

86. See Charles Amiel, "El Criptojudaísmo Castellano en La Mancha a Finales del Siglo XVI.", in *Judíos. Sefarditas. Conversos*, ed. Alcalá, 503–512. In their testimony the captives revealed that they had believed they were the last remaining Jewish community in Spain (509).

87. Quoted by J. H. Elliott, *Imperial Spain: 1469–1716* (New York: New American Library, 1966), 50.

88. "[P]or medio de razones y la invitación y suave moción de la voluntad...." Quoted in Ángel Alcalá, "Tres Cuestiones en Busca de Respuesta: Invalidez del Bautismo Forzado, Conversion deJudios, Trato 'Cristiano' al Converso," in *Judíos. Sefarditas. Conversos*, ed. Alcalá, 527. Pope Gregory I, 540–604 (Gregory the Great, Doctor of the Church, creator of "Gregorian" chants, which drew on Jewish musical traditions) urged Christians to convert by benefactions and homilies, not by force.

89. "[P]recisa y absoluta...," *Judíos. Sefarditas. Conversos*, ed. Alcalá, 529.

90. See Luis Fernández Martin, SJ, "El Colegio de los Jesuitas de Medina del Campo en tiempo de Juan de Yepes," in *Juan de la Cruz, espiritu de llama: Estudios con ocasión del cuarto centenario de su muerte*, ed. Otgar Steggink, 41–61, esp. 52–53 (Kampen, The Netherlands: Kok Pharos, 1991):), 52-53, on Jesuit curriculum in Latin; 55, on beneficent reforms of Juan's instructor in Latin rhetoric, Juan Bonifacio; 57–58, on composition and performance of theatrical dialogues in Latin; 61, on Juan's mother's Islamic lineage as a factor in his not entering the Society of Jesus.

91. He may have attended lectures by the Jewish convert and Augustinian friar, Luis de León. Courses in Juan's last year at Salamanca were on the Prima Secundae portion of the *Summa*, including discussions of blessedness and its position in the practical and speculative reasoning (quaestio 6, articulus 4); also, on motivations in the exercise of the will (quaestio 9, articulus 4).

92. "[A]gilidad en los numerosos torneos dialécticos..." Vicente Muñoz Delgado, "Filosofía, teología y humanidades en la Universidad de Salamanca durante los estudios de San Juan de la Cruz," in *Juan de la Cruz, espiritu de llama*, ed. Steggink, 190.

93. "[F]ue la de los grandes proyectos de pacificación de Europa, de America, del hombre con Dios." Melquiades Andrés Martin, "La teologia en Salamanca durante los estudios de San Juan de la Cruz (1560-1570)," in *Juan de la Cruz, espiritu de llama*, ed. Steggink, 218.

94. "[L]e tienen por un santo, y en mi opinión lo es y ha sido toda su vida..." *Epistolario*, III: 380, no. 206.
95. Msgr. Guy Gaucher, *Jean et Thérèse* (Paris: CERF, 1996), 32, observes that the Carmel did not give her "un chemin d'épanouissement intérieur" ["a route of inner blossoming"] and Père Marie-Eugène de l'Enfant-Jésus, *Ton amour a grandi avec moi* (Lisieux: Edition du Carmel, 1987), 113, suggests that she needed Juan's experiential light in searching for her own.
96. See RP 5, 26; Ms A 83r; PN 18, strophe 35. In the latter, she specifies that in leaving her flock she is seeking "mon seul Agneau Nouveau" ["my sole New Lamb"], something Juan does *not* say. He leaves the flock in 28th strophe of his Canticle.
97. "Que ya sólo en amar es mi ejercicio" and "un poquito de este puro amor y más provecho hace a la Iglesia, aunque parece que no hace nada, que todas esas otras obras juntas." San Juan de la Cruz, *Obras Completas*, ed. Lucinio Ruano de la Iglesia (Madrid: Biblioteca de Autores Cristianos, 1982), 570 (verse), 687 (commentary). Translations of *Llama viva* and the *Cantico* Thérèse used are from 1875 (Paris: Ch. Douniol et Cie) and based on a 1702 Seville edition.
98. In the 54th of the *Cuentas*, from 1575 in Seville, Martha and Mary go together, "En fin, andan juntas Marta y María." Contemplative prayer and community are necessarily complementary.
99. "Le plus petit mouvement de pur amour est plus utile à l'Église que toutes les autres oeuvres réunies ensemble."
100. "Grande es el poder y la porfía del amor.... Dichosa el alma que ama, pues tiene a Dios por prisionero rendido a todo lo que ella quisiere." *Obras Completas*: 698.
101. "*Si loin* que nous soyons il nous transformera en flammes d'amour." LT 197.
102. "Mais le *pur amour* est-il bien dans mon coeur?"
103. On benefactions, Matthew 25:34–40; on fruits, Matthew 7:16,20; on rejection of those working in his name, Matthew 7:21–23.
104. *Obras Completas*: 607. "Pide...determinadamente le descubra y muestre su hermosura, que es su divina esencia; y que mate con esta vista, desatándole de la carne, pues en ella no puede verle y gozarle como desea."
105. "...porque el amor no se paga sino de sí mismo...."*Obras Completas*: 603. It is a commentary on the ninth strophe and the bride's question, why does the thievish lover not enjoy the plunder of her heart?
106. The evidence of this misreading comes in LT 85 (March 12, 1889) to Céline: "Jésus a fait des folies pour Céline.... Que Céline fasse des *folies* pour Jésus... L'amour ne se paie que par l'amour...." In her blazon for Manuscript A, she writes of the mutuality of love in the Trinity.
107. "[E]l amante no puede estar satisfecho si no siente que ama cuanto es amado," *Obras Completas:* 719. In the thirty-eighth strophe, the bride anticipates that her groom shall soon show her what her soul has been longing for all its way, viz. a perfected mutuality of love.

108. She uses it sixty-five times in her writing; twenty-two in Manuscript C. This drawing is a function of her lasting indebtedness, an inability to count upon her own works. As she told Pauline, DE, August 6, 1897, she could not imagine receiving the grace required to fulfill Juan's injunction to acquit all of one's debts. "On éprouve une si grande paix d'être absolument pauvre, de ne compter que sur le bon Dieu." This difference between her and Juan points to an elementary part of her spirituality, a calm, affirmative acceptance of her helplessness.

109. "[L]es peines de l'âme, les aridités, les angoisses, les froideurs apparentes." LT 94, to Céline. The verb, *purifier*, occurs only twelve times in all her writings; the noun, not once. That says enough about her response to the old-fashioned notion of sins to be purged.

110. "[T]oute ma vie sur la route obscure..." LT 112.

111. "Pour moi, je n'ai que des lumières pour voir mon petit néant. Cela me fait plus de bien que des lumières sur la foi" DE, August 13, 1897 (to Pauline); "Toutes ces images ne me font aucun bien, je ne puis me nourrir que de la vérité. C'est pour cela que je n'ai jamais désiré des visions." DE, August 5, 1897 (to Marie as reported by Pauline).

112. "L'Amour, j'en ai l'expérience/ Du bien, du mal qu'il trouve en moi/ Sait profiter (quelle puissance)...." Cited in the NEC edition of the *Poésies*; 438–439, from a note Marie de la Trinité dated November 8, 1942.

113. "Y toda deuda paga" and "tus pecados e imperfecciones, que son los hábitos malos," *Obras Completas*, 792.

114. "[Ô] Jésus s'il faut que la table souillée par eux [the unbelievers] soit purifiée par une âme qui vous aime, je veux bien y manger seule le pain de l'épreuve jusqu'à ce qu'il vous plaise de m'introduire dans votre lumineux royaume." C 6r.

115. *Noche Oscura*, I:3,3, in *Obras Completas*: 326.

116. "[E]lle est vraiment une fille de celui pour qui la foi est habituellement 'nuit' obscure et certaine." Guy Gaucher, *Flammes d'amour: Juan et Thérèse* (Paris: CERF, 1996), 113.

117. "Au Ciel, je verrai le bon Dieu, c'est vrai! Mais pour être avec lui, j'y suis déjà tout à fait sur la terre." DE, May 15, 1897, no. 5.

118. *Flammes d'amour*, 117. On p. 118, Gaucher takes Marie-Eugène's definition of contemplation, "regard lui-même," as "regard de foi" for Thérèse; I urge that it be her "regard d'amour."

119. "Pendant sa maladie, reduite à un amaigrissement effrayant elle conservait toujours le même calme et le mot pour rire était sur ses lèvres. Elle voyait arriver la mort sans aucune apprehension. Une de ses novices ayant tèmoigné sa frayeur personelle du Purgatoire, elle lui repondit: 'Ah! Que vous me faites de peine! Vous faites une grande injure au bon Dieu en croyant fatalement aller en purgatoire. Quand on aime d'amour pur il n'y a pas de purgatoire!'" NPPA, Céline, p. 29. In the writing, she lower-cases Purgatory when Thérèse

is quoted, a deft touch! In the manuscript this anecdote has an "X" through it. Not all the sisters, not even Pauline, could share Thérèse's affinity with Juan de la Cruz, and the thought of circumventing purgatory would have been outrageous for all cases save the most saintly. Juan says in the *Noche Oscura* II, 20:5, that those already purified by love, "ya por el amor purgadísimos," do not enter purgatory but he concedes these are few, "los pocos." Thérèse did not read this work, but its sense is hinted in the *Llama de Amor Viva*, I:21, which she did read. There, God is likened to a physician, "medicinando y curando al alma en sus muchas enfermedades para darle salud," the cure implicitly being salvation. But the soul itself, transformed into love's flame, is vouchsafed as a portal to eternal life in the passage Thérèse most often cited from the *Llama*, which is I:6.

CHAPTER 2

1. C 11v. "Il sait que le cœur de ses disciples brûle d'un plus ardent amour pour Lui."
2. Luke 24:13–35. Pseudo-Mark, 16:12–13 gives a terse encapsulation of this incident.
3. KJV translation.
4. Jean Grelier, "*La manuel du chrétien*": *Bible de Thérèse de Lisieux*, Archives du Carmel, p. 38.
5. CSG, p. 80. "Si j'avais été prêtre, me disait-elle, j'aurais étudié l'hébreu et le grec afin de pouvoir lire la parole de Dieu, telle qu'il daigne l'exprimer dans le langage humain."
6. For an extended discussion see the entries on Joseph Courtès's articles in my Selected Bibliography.
7. Isaiah she had from copies that Céline had made for her and brought with her to the Carmel in 1894. The translation was by Bourassé and Janvier. The *Song of Songs* Céline copied from Jean-Baptiste Glaire's four-volume, 1873 edition of the Bible, a translation that is still reprinted in France, most recently in 2002. It is a favorite, for its literalness, of the Christian right.
8. LT 145. "Pour trouver une chose cachée il faut se cacher soi-même, notre vie doit donc être un mystère, il nous faut ressembler à Jesus, à Jesus dont le visage était cachée."
9. It is interesting that she does not take inspiration and guidance from Jesus's silence before his adversaries when she was herself confronted with the demonic voices in C 6v, threatening her with nothingness. Instead, she says, she turns and runs off to Jesus and tells him she is ready to confess that there is a heaven.
10. Pri 12. "Notre unique désir est de charmer vos Yeux divins en cachant aussi notre visage afin qu'ici-bas, personne ne puisse nous reconnaître."
11. LD, July 3, 1893, CG II: 699. "[J]e fais si peu pour Dieu et vous, vous lui donnez tant. Je vous trouve si bonnes et moi je suis si mauvaise!..."

12. LT 142. "'Mes pensées ne sont pas vos pensées' (dit le Seigneur) Le mérite ne consiste pas à faire ni à donner beaucoup, mais plutôt à recevoir, à aimer beaucoup...."
13. In MsA 66v she recalls the monitory signs for women she saw during her trip to Rome in November 1887, threatening them with excommunication for minor infractions: "Ah! Les pauvres femmes, comme elles sont méprisées!" ["How despised women are!"], then she adds that the loyalty of women to Jesus during his Passion signified his sharing with them the scorn he had to endure, and in heaven they would not be last but first. This is a bold observation in an age not known for feminism.
14. Isaiah 58.10 is the only scriptural entry in her notebook, which included extracts from the letters of Théophile Vénard, a missionary martyred in Vietnam in 1861.
15. CSG, 96. "Quel mystère! Par nos petits vertus, notre charité pratiquée dans l'ombre, nous convertissons *au loin* des âmes."
16. CSG, 95. "[C]'est-à-dire avec coeur, avec amour, avec désintéressement, si vous consolez ceux qui souffrent, *vous recovrerez votre santé intérieure*, votre âme ne languira pas."
17. I quote from the facsimile of the 1599 edition, published by L.L. Brown, Ozark, Missouri, 1990. There is no pagination. The quotation comes from "The Argument" that prefaces "Salomons Song." The text immediately precedes Isaiah.
18. This cruel mockery of a woman's ardent and suffering love has numerous occasions in ancient myth; outstanding among them is the story of Demeter mourning in her search for Persephone, in Ovid's *Metamorphoses*, V. Simon's scorn of the woman anointing Jesus (Matthew 26: 6-13) could also be adduced.
19. LT 182. "Ne réveillez pas ma Bien-Aimée, laissez moi seul avec elle, car je ne saurais m'en séparer un seul instant."
20. See Marvin H. Pope's engaging, richly nuanced discussion, *Song of Songs* (New York: Doubleday, 1977), 385–388.
21. Santa Teresa de Jesús, *Obras Completas* (Madrid: Aquilar, 1957), 519 (the 4th chapter of her writing on the *Canticum*, "Conceptos del amor de dios.").
22. An exception occurs in LT 122, the earliest citation (October 14, 1890), when she dumps on the processional cult of the Sacred Heart and states her preference for the he-is-mine, I-am-his (2.16), with "la solitude de ce délicieux coeur à coeur en attendant de le contempler un jour face à face" ["the solitariness of this luscious heart to heart while awaiting one day a mutual contemplation"].
23. PO, 456. "Pendant mon oraison, Jésus m'a donnée la clef du mystère."
24. LT 230. "[C]e soir, je vous ai montré ma *vertu*, mes TRÉSORS de *patience!*... Et moi qui prêche si bien les autres!!!!!!!!!!!!!!.."
25. LT 230. "[C]ar je sens bien que je ne pourrais en supporter davantage, mon coeur se briserait étant impuissant a contenir tant de bonheur."

26. Some of her omissions are noteworthy. Why did she never have occasion to refer to Psalm 21 (22) which carries the script of the Passion?
27. She omits the *Manuel du chrétien*'s intermediate phrase, "dans ma vieillesse," ["in my old age"].
28. Ms C 3r. "Quel sera-t-il pour moi cet âge avancé? Il me semble que ce pourrait être maintenant."
29. C 3v. "[L]e Bon Dieu n'a besoin de personne (encore moins d'elle que des autres) pour faire du bien sur la terre." Cf. A 53r, which does not have this parenthesis and speaks of God's "œuvre" rather than "bien sur la terre."
30. Ms C 5r. "[R]éjouis-toi de la mort qui te donnera non ce que tu espères, mais une nuit plus profonde encore, la nuit du néant"
31. RP 3, 21v. "[V]ous êtes Hérétique, Relapse, Apostate, Idolâtre, vous avez par vos sorcelléries fait couronner un roi hérétique agitant au-dessus de sa tête pendant le sacre votre étendard enchanté... maintenant vous pouvez aller en paix, l'Eglise à laquelle vous avez refusé votre soumission ne peut plus vous défendre.... Toute branche morte doit être separée de la vigne et jetée au feu."
32. C 3r. "[R]ude escalier de la perfection."
33. C 5v. "Jésus m'a fait sentir qu'il y a véritablement des âmes qui n'ont pas la foi, qui par l'abus des grâces perdent ce précieux trésor, source des seules joies pures et véritables."
34. In Psalm 101 (102):9 the helpless soul eats ashes as though they were bread. It might be said that at Thérèse's table, bread is eaten as though it were ashes.
35. C 6r. "[E]lle vous demande pardon pour ses frères, elle accepte de manger aussi longtemps que vous le voudrez le pain de la douleur et ne veut point se lever de cette table replie d'amertume où mangent les pauvres pécheurs avant le jour que vous avez marqué...."
36. In the Carmel's constitution, it is prescribed that a sister who was not present on time in the refectory was obliged to prostrate herself until the prioress signaled her to rise.
37. C 5v. "Le Roi de la patrie au brilliant soleil est venu vivre 33 ans dans les pays des ténèbres, hélas! Les ténèbres n'ont point compris que ce Divin Roi était la lumiére du monde...."
38. At verse 33, the Hebrews' faithlessness is punished, according to the Septuagint and the Vulgate, thus: "Their days were spent out in vanity, and their years with haste." In the KJV and in Pope Pius XII's new Latin version, issued on March 24, 1945, it is God who causes this waste.
39. The notion of the deviant involves yet another fairy-tale trope, the isolation of the bereft woman. It can be found later in Apuleius's story of Psyche and, as he takes on the feminine role, of Dante in his dream autobiography and celebration of Beatrice, the *Vita Nuova*. I discuss the parable of the Prodigal Son in *Thérèse of Lisieux: God's Gentle Warrior* (New York: Oxford University Press, 2006), 318–319.

40. C 36v. "[M]ais surtout j'imite la conduite de Madeleine, son étonnante ou plutôt son amoureuse audace qui charme le Coeur de Jésus, séduit le mien."
41. It comes from a priest, Michel-Ange Marin, *Vies des Pères des Déserts d'Orient*, Vol. III (Paris: Lyon, 1824), Book IV, Chapter XVII.
42. "...sa penitence d'une heure a été plus agréable à Dieu que celle que d'autres font pendant longtemps parce qu'ils ne la font pas avec autant de ferveur qu'elle." Quoted in *Histoire d'une âme: Manuscrits autobiographiques* (Paris: Cerf, 1997), 285.
43. LT 224. *"toute" petite* et très imparfaite" (her emphasis) and "je sais qu'Il a fait en moi de grandes choses et je le chante chaque jour avec bonheur. Je me souviens que celui-là doit aimer davantage à qui l'on a plus remis aussi je tâche de faire que ma vie soit un acte d'amour et je ne m'inquiète plus d'être une *petite* âme...."
44. She savored the bracing oxymorons in *Llama de amor viva*: "Oh, cauterio suave! Oh, regalada llaga!" ["Oh, tender cautery! Oh, comforting wound!"] but her poetic imagination does not extend to this baroque fancy. See my discussion of her poetry in *Thérèse de Lisieux: God's Gentle Warrior*, pp. 220–247.
45. LC 186, June 7, 1897.
46. LT 247 "amoureuse audace" and "je sens que son coeur a compris les abîmes d'amour et de miséricorde *du Coeur de Jésus,* et que toute pécheresee qu'elle est ce Coeur d'amour est non seulement disposé à lui pardonner, mais encore à lui prodiguer les bienfaits de son intimité divine, à l'élever jusqu'aux plus hauts sommets de la contemplation"
47. The Greek text has the definite article that Glare ignores and that is only implicit in Jerome's Vulgate: "me the sinner," indicates that the publican is contrasting himself with the pharisee.
48. C 36v. "...au lieu de m'avancer avec le pharisien, je répète, remplie de confiance, l'humble prière du publicain."
49. NPPA, Pauline; cf. DE (August 12, 1897), 318: "Je me sentais comme le publicain, une grande pécheresse. Je trouvais le bon Dieu si miséricordieux!... Ah! Comme il est bien impossible de se donner à soi-même de tels sentiments! C'est le Saint-Esprit tout seul qui peut les produire dans l'âme."
50. LT of June 21, 1897. "[J]e suis la voie qu'Il me trace. Je tache de ne plus m'occuper de moi-mème en rien et ce que Jésus daigne opérer en mon âme je le lui abandonne, car je n'ai pas choisi une vie austère pour expier mes fautes, mais celles des autres." This is not an endorsement of the Sacred Heart. She entered the Carmel for priests and exited it for and with atheists.
51. This is one of only three instances when Thérèse uses the word *mystical*. The word is not even listed in the concordance. In Ms A 79r, she reminds Pauline that her dreams are usually not about God but the natural world—streams, meadows, woods—with happy children running about, a setting she enjoyed on holidays at Saint Ouen-le-Pin. "Vous voyez, ma Mère, que si mes rêves ont une

apparence poétique ils sont loin d'être mystiques." ["You see, my Mother, my dreams are a bit poetic but far from being mystical"]. In her last poem, "Pourque je t'aime, ô Marie!" she writes of the Virgin's words of love (the Magnificat) as "mystiques roses" (PN 54, 7:5) which shall give their fragrance to coming ages.

52. Pauline had composed a similar work for Thérèse's first Communion, July 8, 1884, which was also the day Pauline professed her vows at the Carmel of Lisieux.

53. RP 3, 21v. "[U]ne Vierge qui va au-devant de son époux...." Note her capitalization.

54. C 5v. "Jésus m'a fait sentir qu'il y a véritablement des âmes qui n'ont pas la foi.....Il permit que mon âme fût envahie des plus épaisses ténèbres...."

55. In A 20v the portent of Louis's affliction is noted in the mysterious veiled figure Thérèse saw stooping as he passed through the family's garden: "Comme la Face Adorable de Jésus qui fut voilée pendant sa Passion, ainsi la face de son fidèle serviteur devait être voilée aux jours de ses douleurs, afin de pouvoir rayonner dans la Céleste Patrie auprès de son Seigneur...." ["As the Adored Face of Jesus was veiled during his Passion, so the face of his loyal servant had to be veiled in the days of his sorrows, so as to be able to shine in the Celestial Country beside his Lord...."] This is the first time in Thérèse's autobiography that she refers to the Face that is within her own name. The connection it establishes between Jesus and her father is noteworthy, as is the fact that she does not once mention the Face in either B or C.

56. A reader could object that as the virgins were summoned to meet the groom and the servant was entrusted with a deposit, they all represent those who deny God's existence and heaven's "contre leur pensée" (C 5v), against their own awareness and better judgment; they are the recusants Thérèse originally identified as nonbelievers.

57. Teresa of Avila had paved the way of this boldness by assuming the right to teach her sisters about the *Song of Songs* in writing her meditations upon this text.

58. For all her sternness as a disciplinarian, Gonzague, no less than Thérèse's natural sisters, deferred respectfully to her intelligence and to what the sisters realized was a wisdom beyond their own means. The latitude she was given did not come from sentimental indulgence.

59. C 18v. "Ah! Que les enseignments de Jésus sont contraires aux sentiments de la nature, sans le secours de sa grâce il serait impossible non seulement de les mettre en pratique mais encore de les comprendre"

60. C 17v. "[C]e que Jésus m'a fait comprendre au sujet de la charité...." My emphasis.

61. C 10r. "[J]e ne sens pas la pauvreté n'ayant jamais manqué de rien" and "la douce et facile mission que vous m'avez confiée."

62. LT 201. "[E]n dehors de cette aimable *volonté* nous ne ferions *rien*, ni pour Jésus, ni pour les âmes."

63. Her one substantial deviation from the *Manuel* (and from Glaire) is that she speaks of "those" rather than he, celui-là, who shall do the will of God.
64. Exodus 21:24; Leviticus 24:20; Deuteronomy 19:21.
65. Her one concrete application of the command to love persecutors is recorded in the DE, July 30, 1897, when she was sitting in the sun outside the infirmary, tormented by flies. She said they were her only enemies but as God had commended forgiveness of enemies, she was happy to find an occasion to practice it.
66. C 16v. "Ah! Quelle paix inonde l'âme lorsqu'elle s'elève au-dessus des sentiments de la nature.... Non il n'est pas de joie comparable à celle que goûte le véritable pauvre d'esprit." And "Ma Mère chérie, je suis bien loin de pratiquer ce que je comprends et cependant le seul désir que j'en ai me donne la paix."
67. C 22v. "Ma Mère, depuis que j'ai compris qu'il m'était impossible de rien faire par moi-même, la tâche que vous m'avez imposée ne me parut plus difficile, j'ai senti que l'unique chose nécessaire était de m'unir de plus en plus à Jésus et que Le reste me serait donné par surcroît" This a striking variant upon what Jesus says on the Mount: "Seek first *the kingdom of God and his justice* and all these things shall be given you in addition" (Matthew 6:33). It is wholly characteristic of Thérèse that she opts for an immediate and intimate bond with another person, Jesus, rather than seeking a distant, Oz-like realm, one she could no longer believe in. But the matter cannot be left there: in the manuscript she capitalizes at a strategic point: "et que Le reste," "and then The rest," meaning heaven? Was her lost belief in it given back? No; the context indicates that "The rest" refers to the benefaction of helping her novice sisters to love God.
68. C 22v–23r. "[F]aire du bien c'est chose aussi impossible sans le secours de Dieu que de faire briller le soleil dans la nuit" and "il faut absolument oublier ses goûts, ses conceptions personnelles et guider les âmes par le chemin que Jésus leur a tracé, sans essayer de les faire marcher par sa propre voie."
69. A splendid example of how quickly Thérèse was advancing in maturity during her last weeks begins on July 17, 1897, when she remarks "ma mission de faire aimer le bon Dieu comme je l'aime, de donner ma petite voie aux âmes" ["my mission to make God loved as I love him, to give to souls my little way"] and just four days later this vital amendment: "Qu' est-ce que cela me fait que ce soit moi ou une autre qui donne cette voie aux âmes?" ["What difference is it to me whether it's I or someone else who gives this way to souls?"]
70. In all of her writings there are only three references to resurrection, two of which (LT 175 and RP 2) are capitalized as they concern Jesus's resurrection only. In her second play on Jeanne d'Arc, the heroine doubts a dead child's resurrection can be attributed to herself (RP 3, 15v).
71. Neither does she refer to the anonymous benefactors, apparently rare, for whom St. Paul draws a breath in Romans 2:10, amid fulminating blasts against sin of every stamp; nor John 5:29, where Jesus speaks of imminent judgment upon doers of good and doers of evil. These terrorizing passages she had a hard time

with, I believe, as a scarcely hidden vengefulness in apocalypticism was incongruent to her view of a benevolent, loving, merciful God.
72. A 83v. "Jamais je ne l'ai entendu parler, mais je sens qu'Il est en moi, à chaque instant, Il me guide, m'inspire ce que je dois dire ou faire."
73. C 18v. "Cela contenterait l'amour-propre car donner, c'est un acte plus généreux que de prêter."
74. In the Greek, Jesus says: *daneizetemedenelpizontes*, lit. credit without expecting to get back the interest or even the principal. A *danistes* was a money-lender such as we find in Luke 7:41–42, who does exactly as Jesus bids. Jesus is asking creditors to "forgive" loans, which in effect is a great giving, indeed, tantamount to giving one's money (fortune?) away. This is a capital instance to justify Thérèse's frustration in not knowing the Biblical languages.
75. *Why I am Not a Christian* (London: Allen and Unwin, 1957), 12.

CHAPTER 3

1. Portions of this chapter were delivered at the Colloque international pour le centenaire du procès de beatification de Thérèse de l'Enfant Jésus, Lisieux, September 4, 2010.
2. An end-of-life analogue might be found in the remark of St. Ignatius of Antioch, who, en route to being devoured by lions, wrote that he was now becoming a Christian.
3. See Céline's testimony, PO, 270, that Thérèse did not even have a spiritual director to help her towards entry into Carmel or effectively to discourage her from taking that route.
4. DE, June 6, 1897. "Monsieur Youf m'a dit pour mes tentations contre la foi: 'Ne vous arrêtez pas à cela, c'est très dangereux.' Ce n'est guère consolant à entendre, mais heureusement que je ne m'en impressione pas. Soyez tranquille, je ne vais pas casser ma 'petite' tête à me tourmenter. Monsieur Youf m'a dit encore: 'Etes-vous résignée à mourir?' Je lui ai répondu: 'Ah! Mon Père, je trouve qu'il n'y a besoin de résignation que pour vivre. Pour mourir, c'est de la joie que j'éprouve.'"
5. *Living Flame of Love*, Commentary on Stanza 3, para. 29–33 in *The Collected Works of St. John of the Cross*, ed. Kieran Kavanaugh, OCD, and Otilio Rodriquez, OCD, 620–622 (Washington, DC: Institute for Carmelite Studies, 1973). Juan speaks of three blind men: the soul needing guiidance, a "director," and Satan. Teresa, in her turn, must have puzzled Thérèse in urging her to consult pious but learned laymen, sorts she says in her autobiography she came to depend upon more and more (*Vida*, ch. 13) in her mature life. But Thérèse never had the company of a Salcedo.
6. *The Life of Saint Teresa of Ávila by Herself*, trans. J.M. Cohen (New York: Penguin, 1957), 94.

7. This is the image she is holding in her feverish hands in the last three photos Céline took of her before the infirmary period, all taken on June 7, 1897.
8. *Llama de amor viva* in San Juan de la Cruz, *Obras Completas*, ed. Lucinio Ruano de la Iglesia (Madrid: 1982), 767. "Y así la muerte de semejantes almas es muy suave y muy dulce; más que les fue la vida espiritual toda su vida; pues que mueren con más subidos impetus y encuentros sabrosos de amor, siendo ellas como el cisne, que canta más suavemente cuando se muere."
9. She had spent a lot of time reading him, beginning in her sixteenth year (her second in Carmel) as the correspondence attests, from LT 81, to Céline, January 23–25 (?), 1889.
10. Cantico B, Anotacion para Cancion 28 in *Obras Completas*: 687.
11. Pri 12. "[S]urtout des âmes d'apôtres et de martyrs afin que par elles nous embrasions de votre Amour la multitude des pauvres pécheurs."
12. Even the attributive "poor" is exceptional in her writing of sinners until the last year. The first instance comes in her prayer on the mystical flowers, November 1894; the second in her play, *La Fuite en Egypte*, in January 1896. It recurs twice in C, both times on the sixth folio.
13. DE, July 6, 1897. "Monsieur l'Abbé m'a dit: 'Vous aurez un grand sacrifice à faire en quittant vos soeurs.' Je lui ai répondu: 'Mais, mon Père, je trouve que je ne les quitterai pas; au contraire, je serai encore plus près d'elles après ma "mort."
14. DE, July 8, 1897. "Il me semble que je rêve!... Enfin, ils ne sont pas fous."
15. *Llama de amor viva* in *Obras Completas*: 838. "porque cada uno de éstos no puede en la imagen hacer más de lo que sabe, y si quisiere pasar adelante sería echarla a perder."
16. Besides, femininity, being without any rank within the Christian hierarchy, posed the risk of antinomianism. There were historic examples, such as Mme. de Guyon, whom Bossuet felt obliged to imprison. Two of the most influential enthusiasts of the late nineteenth century were the Russian Jewish theosophist, Elena Petrovna Blavatsky, and the founder of Christian Science, Mary Baker Eddy.
17. She had kept a folder of transcriptions from scriptural texts, first mentioned in LT 108 (July 18, 1890) to Céline. In that letter she quotes the song of the soul in *Subida del Monte Carmelo*, strophe 8: "My face upon my lover having laid / From all endeavor ceasing: / And all my cares releasing / Threw them amongst the lilies there to fade," (Roy Campbell's translation).
18. San Juan himself distinguished his poems from their commentaries by saying the former were as things living in comparison to the latter as things painted. See Allison Peers' translation, *Complete Works of Saint John of the Cross* (London: Burns, Oates and Washburne, 1953), 2:1–2.
19. C 20r. "[J]e suis un petit pinceau que Jésus a choisi pour peindre son image dans les âmes que vous m'avez confiées. Un artiste ne se sert pas que d'un pinceau, il lui en faut au moins deux, le premier est le plus utile, c'est avec lui qu'il donne

les teintes générales, qu'il couvre complètement la toile en très peu de temps, l'autre, plus petit, lui sert pour les détails. Ma Mère, c'est vous qui me représentez le précieux pinceau que la main de Jésus saisit avec amour lorsqu'Il veut faire un grand travail dans l'âme de vos enfants, et moi je suis le tout petit dont Il daigne se servir ensuite pour les moindres détails."

20. This image complements Juan's other reference to stone sculpting of his brethren. In his *Cuatro avisos a un religioso por alcanzar la perfeccion* he speaks of each brother having to be chiselled by others so that he can be put "como la piedra...en el edifico." *Obras Completas*: 63.

21. C 23v. "Avec certaines âmes, je sens qu'il faut me faire petite, ne point craindre de m'humilier en avouant mes combats, mes défaites; voyant que j'ai les mêmes faiblesses qu'elles, mes petites soeurs m'avouent à leur tour les fautes qu'elles se reprochent et se réjouissent que je les comprenne par experience."

22. For her usual formulation of *petitesse*, remaining little, see LT 141, 154, 242; PN 11, 13, 31, 45, 54; RP.1, 7; DE, April 18, May 27, August 6 & 7, September 25.

23. *Pensées sur la charge de Maîtresse des Novices dans l'Ordre de Notre-Dame du Mont-Carmel*, Aix: Nicot, 1873: 11. "Qu'elle ne compte ni sur ses efforts, ni sur ses talents; mais que toujours persuadée de son inutilité personelle, elle plante, elle arrose, et attende de Dieu seul."

24. *Pensées*, 11. "Il faut aussi se garder de croire que l'on connaît une novice tout de suite ou dans peu de temps, excepté certains caractères si pronouncés et si évidemment dangereux pour une maison religieuse."

25. "Archives de Famille: septembre-decembre 1890," VT 102 (April-June, 1986), 104. "Pour toi, ma chère petite soeur, ton rôle a été et sera toujours de te sacrifier." This letter is assigned by the archivists to late September 1890. In fact Marie at the crucial juncture years later opposed Céline's entering Carmel, even as she had opposed Thérèse's. 113, October 20, 1890: "Pour toi continuellement Jésus cueille des roses là-haut dans les jardins du Ciel. Il n'est pas une épine qui transperce ton coeur qu'Il ne change aussitôt en rose eternelle, en joie qui ne passera JAMAIS!"

26. "Archives de Famille: avril-septembre, 1891," VT 104 (October-December, 1986), 238. The letter is from April 26 or 27, 1891. "Ton coeur c'est une petite fleur consacrée, elle est maintenant à Jésus pour toujours!"

27. "Archives de Famille: janvier-avril, 1891," VT 103 (July-September, 1986), 180. "c'est le point de mire de Jésus, il dirige là toutes ses flèches. Mais comme la pierre frappée avec force jette des étincelles, ainsi ton coeur brisé deviendra toute flamme."

28. VT 104: 246. "O Céline! Et toi aussi tu ne seras pas du monde! Pas une de la famille ne contractera donc d'alliance ici-bas! Il me semble qu'au ciel notre Mère chérie doit être bien heureuse de voir ses voeux si complètement réalisés."

29. The best indication of how ripe that antagonism became is in a poem Thérèse wrote in October, 1895, fourteen months after Céline had applied for admission to Carmel: "Jésus, mon Bien-Aimé, rappelle-toi!" In it Thérèse confounded her

sister's request to have her sacrifices for Jesus appreciatively recorded. Instead, Thérèse wrote of all that Jesus had sacrificed for Céline.
30. LT 81, January 23–25 (?), 1889.
31. LT 82, February 28, 1889. "Quelle joie ineffable de porter nos croix FAIBLEMENT" and "noviciat de douleur." As early as LT 47, May 8, 1888, Thérèse had written of Céline being "Carmélite par le coeur" ["a Carmelite at heart"]. In LT 53, June 17, 1888, Thérèse makes the peremptory claim that Jesus had already put the mystical engagement ring upon Céline's finger, thus precluding any more marriage proposals beyond the one Céline had received on the evening of April 9, 1888, the day Thérèse entered the Carmel.
32. For the Feast of Madre Teresa de Jesús, October 15, 1888, Céline had bought and framed for her sister an engraving of the "Veronica cloth" in the "Tours" version of Charles Dupont, a widely popular image of reparationist cultism (offering oneself as victim to divine justice in atonement for the secular profanation of the sabbath, for blasphemies, etc.).
33. LT 57, July 23, 1888.
34. All of this comes in LT 65, October 20, 1888.
35. LT 81, January 23–25 (?), 1889. "[V]ite l'amour propre vient comme un fatal vent qui éteint tout!"
36. LT 109, July 27–29, 1890. "Remercie bien le bon Dieu de toutes les grâces qu'il te fait et ne sois assez ingrate pour ne pas les reconnaître"
37. For example, to Pauline in the summer of 1889 (LT 95), she writes of wishing to save souls and then "voler plus promptement vers sa Face chérie!" ["to fly the more readily toward his cherished Face!"].
38. LC 118, Fall, 1889. "c'est la souffrance, plus encore le sacrifice qui vous fera une grande sainte."
39. She expressly refers to descending in LT 137, October 19, 1892, telling Céline that like Zachaeus, they must both come down from their tree and make themselves a dwelling place for the homeless Christ. But that is not a subterranean movement.
40. LC 117, October 4, 1889. "Je vous défends au nom de Dieu de mettre en question votre état de grâce. Le démon en rit à gorge déployée. Je proteste contre cette vilaine défiance. Croyez obstinément que Jésus vous aime."
41. LT 92, May 30, 1889.
42. LT 94, July 14, 1889.
43. The most striking formulation of the nexus between tribulation and Jesus comes from an unlikely source, the neglected Martin sister, Léonie. In a letter to Céline dated November 13, 1890, she lets the cat out of the bag, remarking of life's dolors, "ne nous plaignons pas, nous sommes plus que les amies de Jésus, nous sommes ses épouses, voilà pourquoi il nous traite ainsi" ["let's not complain, we are more than the female friends of Jesus, we're his spouses, and that's why he's treating us this way"], as though marital life were a predictable and certain

misery. See Archives de Famille, septembre-decembre, 1890), VT 102 (April-June, 1986): 118.
44. LC 112, May, 1889. "[L]e martyre du cœur."
45. LT 91, May, 1889. "C'est le Seigneur qui a fait cela." Cf. C 5v: "Jésus m'a fait sentir..." and "Il permit que mon âme fût envahie...."
46. Her unsettling testimony is in LC 127, May 5, 1890.
47. This grotesque notion, hiding in Christ's face, derives from a common mistranslation of the admittedly slippery Hebrew. The text in question is Psalm 30 (31): 21. Glaire has: "Vous les cacherez dans le secret de votre face," which Thérèse rendered in the more intimate "dans le secret de ta Face." She is speaking not of the Jews' Iahweh but of Christ. She drew on this text repeatedly in her poems: PN5:6; PN 11.3; PN12:8; PN16:1. See also her prayer, Pr12, "Consécration à la Sainte Face," which dates from the summer of 1896 and is the last reference to Psalm 30. The Hebrew word for "face" has the broader sense of "presence," rightly caught in the KJV, "Thou shalt hide them in the secret of thy presence," and most modern translations so render it. NIV: "In the shelter of your presence, you hide them from the intrigues of men." The Hebrew-English Tanakh of the Jewish Publication Society (Philadelphia, 1999, 5759), 1446: "You grant them the protection of your presence against scheming men." See also William Osburn, Jr., *A Hebrew and English Lexicon to the Old Testament* (Grand Rapids, MI: Zondervan, 1981), 210–211, but for detailed references, including the Latin senses, coram te, in conspectu tuo, see Ludwig Koehler and Walter Baumgartner, *The Hebrew and Aramaic Lexicon of the Old Testament* (Leiden: E.J. Brill, 1996) III: 937–944.

Both the Septuagint and the Vulgate take the literal first entry, face.

In Thérèse's use of "face," which was all she had to go on, she replaces God the protective, sheltering father of Psalm 30 (31) with Jesus, who, as the *Sainte Face*, cannot protect her since he himself is subject to scourging and abuse. She goes even further in this conceit, so worthy of John Donne, in making Christ's face her homeland: "ma seule patrie...ma seule richesse" ["my only country...my only treasure..."] (PN20:1 & 3).

The ultimate position she assumes is stated in Pr16 (undated but likely 1897), in which she amazingly takes the "adorable" quality of the infant Jesus's face and ascribes it to the tortured *Sainte Face*. She prays that Christ will impress onto her own countenance his "Divine Ressemblance" so that he cannot look upon her soul without beholding himself. She might well have taken this idea from Juan de la Cruz, in whose *Cántico Espiritual* XXXVI, commentary on verse 5 (OC, 712) the soul asks to be transformed into Christ's beauty "que, siendo semejante en hermosura, nos veamos entrambos en tu hermosura" ["that, being similar in beauty, we may see one another in your beauty."] Thérèse does not seek nor presume such mutuality.

48. LT 95, July-August, 1889. "*[S]ur de ne plus pécher!*" Her emphasis.
49. It was a commonplace among the Carmelites to seek the maternal solicitude of Mary under her cloak.
50. Pri 2, September 8, 1890. "Jésus pardonne-moi si je dis des choses qu'il ne faut pas dire, je ne veux que te réjouir et te consoler" Her first recorded prayer is to the Virgin Mary and dates from her protracted illness in the spring of 1884.
51. LT 120, September 23, 1890.
52. This remark refers to one of her favorite childhood fictions, Mme. Woilliez's *L'Orpheline de Moscou ou la jeune institutrice,* discussed in my *Thérèse of Lisieux: God's Gentle Warrior* (New York: Oxford University Press, 2006), 36–37.
53. Cf. one of her few extant letters from this period, July 8, 1891, to her aunt and namesake, Mme. Guérin, where she quotes from *Oeuvres du Bienheureux Henri Suso, de l'Ordre des Frères Prêcheurs* the concern Suso had in having spent an entire month without suffering in mind or body: was that a proof that God had forgotten him? VT 104 (October-December, 1986): 244.
54. "Jésus est mon unique amour." I have been unable to determine what instrument she could have used for this singular act. Not her sewing scissors, surely. A refectory utensil? Rather more intriguing is the question, why did she make this carving?
55. LC 144, to Thérèse, late 1890 to early 1891. "Hélas! Notre nature nous rattache toujours à ce matériel de la vie."
56. In LT 137, October 19, 1892, however, Thérèse waxes over the marvel that she claims Jesus has wrought within the two sisters, "union de sentiments, unité d'âmes et de pensées,' ["a union of feelings, a unity of souls and thoughts"]. In her writings, "union" comes 35 times, "unity" occurs only 5, the last instance being happiest, LT 226, when she speaks of herself as a zero and her spiritual brother, Roulland, as a 1, which, placed beside her, gives her value.
57. LT 127, April 26, 1891. "[C]ar sans doute le même trône est réservé a celles qui sur la terre n'ont jamais été qu'une seule âme." "Those" is given in the feminine. In August 1885, when she was the only Martin at Camel, Pauline wrote to Marie "ne pouvons-nous point aimer le bon Dieu d'une manière unique avec ce coeur unique qu'il nous a donné?" ["can we not love the good Lord in a singular way with this single heart he's given us?"] Archives de Famille, Soeur Agnès de Jésus à Marie (1882–1886), VT 16 (October? 1976): 310.
58. *Souvenirs autobiographiques,* 95–99, Archives du Carmel. "Il raffole de toi!"
59. CS, 136. "[E]t toi, l'épouse de Jésus, tu veux bien pactiser avec le siècle, adorer l'idole du monde en te livrant à des plaisirs dangereux?"
60. Ibid. "Vois comme le Dieu a récompensé la fidélité de serviteurs et essaie de les imiter."
61. *Pensées,* 12. "[U]n zèle soutenu."
62. LD, October 8, 1893. "Laisse là le vain travail de la peinture" and "toi dont l'âme est comme un nuage...ne te dissipe pas, ne te mêle pas au souffle empoisonné

du monde..." and "le milieu où tu vis présente plus d'un mirage et parfois tu pourrais croire que c'est nous qui sommes dans les ténèbres."

63. LT 149, October 20, 1893. "[A]u moment d'être unie avec un jeune païen qui ne respire que l'amour profane il me semble que Céline aurait du trembler et pleurer." When it came to familial relations, Thérèse had to be tactful. There was no "pagan" within the Guérin family or among their cousins, the Maudelondes, with whom they had often played throughout their childhood. When Céline Maudelonde became engaged in the spring of 1894, leaving Céline Martin feeling more remote from domestic bliss, Thérèse urged that "si les tendresses des créatures ne sont pas concentrées sur elle (her sister), la tendresse de Jésus est tout entière CONCENTRÉE sur elle" ["if creaturely tendernesses are not concentrated upon you, the tenderness of Jesus is absolutely CONCENTRATED upon you"], LT 157, March or May 1894. Her letter to the Maudelonde girl, now Mme. Pottier, LT 166, July 16, 1894, contains joyful, uplifting words on marriage such as she never countenanced for her own sister: "Quelle grâce pour vous de vous sentir si bien comprise et surtout de savoir que votre union sera immortelle, qu'après la vie vous pourrez encore aimer l'époux qui vous est si cher! ...." ["What a grace for you to realize you are understood and to know that your union shall be everlasting, that after life you can still love the spouse who is so dear to you"]. Yet she knew full well that this cozy tableau is nullified by Jesus's teaching that in heaven there are no marriages.

64. Marie, the eldest, and Céline's adoptive mother after Mme. Martin's death, opposed Céline's entry into the Carmel. She had also opposed Léonie's hapless attempts at a religious vocation. The root of her opposition on both counts may well have been rooted in the fact that she herself had been rooked into the Carmel, under pressure from Pauline and Pichon. Marie had learned the hard way (her "heart's sacrifice") how costly conventual life could be without a firm inner conviction to propel one in the ardors of that direction. Thus, two of the four Martin Carmelites entered without a genuine calling from within themselves.

65. LC 149, August 17, 1892. "[U]ne série de néants ou plutôt un mysterieux néant...dans les ténèbres ....je ne pense à rien" and "appuyée sans aucune appui." Marie to Céline, April 28, 1891, asked "quelle est cette lumière divine qui t'éclaire ainsi sur le néant du monde si ce n'est pas la science de la croix" ["what is this divine light which is enlightening you thus about the nothingness of the world if it's not [Juan's] science of the cross."] Archives de Famille, avril-septembre, 1891," VT 104 (October-December, 1986): 239.

66. After Louis's return to Lisieux, Léonie began to prepare for another application to the Visitandine convent at Caen, which she entered in June of 1893. On Céline's feelings of being abandoned see LD, July 3, 1893, note b, CG II, 700.

67. The Carmel's superior, Delatroëtte, had made it clear after Thérèse's entry that there would be no more Martin sisters admissible.

68. LT 137.
69. Ibid. "Hélas! je sens que le mien n'est pas tout à fait vide de moi."
70. NPPA and quoted in CG II: 668."'Priez beaucoup pour moi,' me dit-elle d'un ton grave. 'La Sainte Vierge m'a inspiré d'éclairer Sr. Marthe. Je vais lui dire ce soir tout ce que je pense d'elle.' 'Mais vous risquez d'être trahie,' lui dis-je, 'alors Notre Mère ne pourra plus vous supporter, et vous serrez renvoyée dans un autre monastère.' 'Je le sais bien,' répliqua-t-elle, mais puisque je suis certaine maintenant que c'est mon devoir de parler, je ne dois pas regarder aux conséquences.'" This episode was not among Pauline's remarks at the apostolic hearing itself. See PA, 49–52 (paragraphs 155–170). In NPPA, 95, Pauline concedes that Thérèse herself had been attracted by "les éclairs de vertu, de générosité et de bon sens que Mère M. de G. [sic] dévoilait de temps en temps, joints à de réels charmes répandus dans toute sa personne" ["the flashes of virtue, generosity and good sense Mother Gonzague revealed occasionally, joined to the real charm she bestowed] but she adds that her sister "triompha toujours de cette tentation, quelquefois si violente qu'il lui fallait" ["always triumphed over this temptation, however violent it must have been for her some of the time"].
71. This assumption omits the fact, known to Marthe, that Thérèse's profession of vows had in fact been delayed by the superior, Delatroëtte, on the grounds of her exceptional age.
72. Geneviève Devergnnies, OCD, "Thérèse and Her Carmelite Community," in *Saint Thérèse of Lisieux: Her Life, Times, and Teaching*, ed. Conrad de Meester, (Washington: Institute for Carmelite Studies, 1997): 117. That view might be informed by Pauline's own negative testimony, that Marthe "ne se gênait pas d'humilier Sr. T. de l'E. J. [sic], de lui dire des paroles dures, de la traiter comme son inférieure, et pourtant se disait son amie" ["she didn't hold off from humiliating Sr. T. de l'E. J., from saying harsh words to her, from treating her as her inferior, and yet she called herself her friend"]. NPPA, p. 104. The Archives du Carmel hold two copies of Pauline's NPPA, one in her own hand and another transcribed far more legibly by Sr. Marie de la Trinité and Sr. Madeleine de St. Joseph. All citations come from the latter. Neither is dated.
73. In preparing her deposition for the apostolic hearings, Marthe recalls that when working in the kitchen she sometimes refused service to the other sisters or would become moody (*triste*) toward them and then they would summon Thérèse to straighten her out: "'Que vous me faite de peine,' me disait elle, 'de vous voir si peu vertueuse.'" ["'How you hurt me,' she said, 'seeing you so short of virtue.'"] NPPA, pp. 4–5, Sr. Marthe de Jésus.
74. In testimony she gave only eight months before her death (September 1916), Marthe de Jésus says that Thérèse told her that she would like to be a *converse*: "Votre vie est humble et cachée...." ["Your life is lowly and hidden."] PA, 417.
75. PO, 273. "[P]eu intelligente, sans vocation pour le Carmel, épuisait le zèle et les forces de la Servante de Dieu, apparemment en pure perte." She was

giving this testimony while Marthe was still alive; hence, the coyness behind the anonymity.

76. It may be that Pauline was a bit jealous of the attachment Marthe and Thérèse felt for one another from the start and that survived the bumpiness of Marthe's moods.

77. C 20v. "...caractère enfant faisait oublier la différence des années" and "aussi bientôt vous avez eu, ma Mère, la joie de voir vos deux petites postulantes s'entendre à merveille et devenir inséparables." HA, 180 says lamely, "Il s'établit entre nous une véritable intimité" ["A true intimacy developed between us."]

78. C 20v. "[P]etits entretiens spirituels." Gonzague seemed fearsomely jealous of any confidentialities of which she was not a part, even the one she had arranged for the two novices: "malgré cette permission nous étions obligées de nous cacher afin de n'être pas découverte, ce qui aurait occasionné de grandes scènes. Car cette bonne Mère était prise de jalousie sitôt qu'elle voyait qu'une soeur donnait sa confiance à une autre qu'elle" ["despite this permission we were obliged to hide ourselves so as not to be found out, which would have brought on big scenes. For this good Mother was seized with jealousy as soon as she saw a sister showing trust in someone other than herself."]. NPPA, p. 13, Marthe de Jésus.

79. PA, 412. "[P]our le profit de mon âme." Whereas Marthe admits to her early attachment to Thérèse, Ms C indicates mutuality.

80. NPPA, p. 8, Marthe de Jésus. "[E]lle paraissait touj [sic] heureuse de me recevoir, et me souriait aimablement ce que elle faisait certainement par vertu. Car quel plaisir pouvait elle trouver à s'entretenir avec une pauvre petite ignorante comme moi, qui naturellement devait plustôt [sic] l'ennuyer que l'intéresser." And "Que je voudrais être comme ma Sr Thérèse de l'Enfant [sic], elle parait si heureuse, si consolée. Elle sourit de ma confidence et me dit que son âme était comme la mienne dans la plus grand obscurité. Sa réponse me surprit persuadée que j'étais du contraire."

81. NPPA, p. 15, Marthe de Jésus. "Vous savez bien que si l'on vient à sortir je ne vous abandonnerai pas, vous viendrez avec moi? Mais que dirons vos soeurs, elles ne voudrons pas m'accepter en leur compagnie? Si elles ne veulent pas de vous, répondit-lle, je louerai une petite chambre et nous vivrons ensemble toutes les deux." Most of the reminiscences of Marthe, as of other testifiers, supply no dates of their occasion, so it is impossible to determine whether the supposed expulsion and plans for a rented room date from the time when the two women were under Marie des Anges as their *maîtresse*, i.e. before the election of February 20, 1893, or subsequently, when Thérèse became *compagne de novices* with Gonzague nominally *maîtresse*.

82. PO, 430. "[C]e qu'elle ne faisait jamais." Thérèse violated Carmel's proprieties not only by embracing Marthe but by inviting her into her cell. Primarily, however, Thérèse's unilateral action was objectionable, a covert operation behind the prioress's back.

83. C 21 v. "[A]vec des expressions si tendres, en lui temoignant une si grande affection que bientôt ses larmes se mêlèrent aux miennes." PA 412. On Thérèse's wishing to remain in the novitiate all her life, Marthe remarks "Aussi j'y demeurai moi-même parce que je ne voulais pas me séparer d'elle' ["I, too, wanted to stay there because I didn't want to be separated from her."] In that way, Thérèse as her novice-mistress would have seen Marthe each day. What would Teresa have said to that arrangement?

84. PO, 430. "[L]'affection que vous avez pour votre mère prieure est trop naturelle, elle fait beaucoup de mal à votre âme, parce-que vous l'aimez avec passion, et ces affections-là déplaisent au bon Dieu; elles sont un poison pour les âmes religieuses" ["your feelings for your mother prioress are too natural and are doing your soul much harm because you love her passionately, and such feelings as these displease God. They're a poison for religious souls."] becomes in PA, 418: "Vous faites beaucoup de peine au bon Dieu parce que vous vous recherchez trop avec notre mère: votre affection est trop naturelle, ce qui est non seulement un grand obstacle à votre perfection, mais met votre âme dans un grand danger" ["You're paining God because you're looking for too much favor with our mother; your feelings are too natural, and that's not only a great obstacle to your perfection but it puts your soul in great danger"].

85. NPPA, pp. 17–18, Marthe de Jésus. "[P]our les choses vraiment utiles et indispensables. Alors elle me confia les sacrifices qu'elle avait fait au début de sa vie religieuse. Mais n'étant pas contente de ses réflexions pourtant très juste, je lui répondit avec vivacité. Vous y allez bien pourquoi ne ferai-je pas comme vous?" And "il ne m'est plus nécessaire de me refuser cette consolation parce que mon coeur est affermi en Dieu."

86. An exception is Sr. Marie de la Trinité, whose testimony has been given book-length treatment.

87. PO, 227. "[C]'était une âme plus froide, moins enthousiaste; elle n'était pas tant femme. Il n'y avait pas d'exclamations dans son langage" and "une âme extraordinaire en fait de sainteté." The witness is the Scot, Thomas Nimmo-Taylor, strategically placed immediately after Pauline, the first witness at the hearings. The date was August 20, 1910.

88. NPPA, 128. "Ah! Voilà bien l'inconvénient d'avoir des soeurs! Vous désirez sans doute que votre soeur soit mise en avant, mais c'est autre chose que je dois faire. Elle est beaucoup plus orgueilleuse que vous ne pensez, elle a besoin d'être constamment humiliée et d'ailleurs c'est une personne qui semble être venue ici tout simplement pour vivre tranquille, elle ne fait pas rien et je ne suis pas la seule à la remarquer. Si c'est pour sa santé que vous venez m'implorer, laissez moi faire, ça ne vous regarde pas." John Beevers cites this unpublished passage in his hagiography, *Storm of Glory* (New York: Sheed and Ward, 1950): 101, but I have been unable to determine how he got hold of it.

There is an ironic turn in this story. It was Gonzague who took the first step toward Thérèse's beatification. In 1900, she requested of the presiding bishop, Mgr. Amette, the opening of Thérèse's cause, but Amette had read *L'histoire d'une âme* and did not like what Thérèse had written about priests of his diocese. The cause was instigated by Mgr Lemonnier six years later.

See the essay of Sr. Camille Bessette, ocd. "La préhistoire du process de beatification de Thérèse de l'Enfant Jésus de la Sainte Face," in *Actes du Colloque sur le centenaire du Procès de Béatification de Thérèse de l'Enfant Jésus de la Sainte Face* (forthcoming).

89. NPPA, 88. "[J]e la grondais quelquefois et très sévérement, quand j'étais de mauvaise humeur. Je lui prêtais tel ou tel sentiment d'orgueil ou de jalousie, je l'accusais d'une faute qu'elle n'avait pas commise. Plus tard, au Carmel, elle me dit que je m'étais trompée em bien des circonstances."

90. NPPA, 90. "[E]t plus elle pleurait, plus je l'accablais. Je refusais de lui pardonner, rien ne m'apaisait, et je restai ainsi fâchée assez longtemps. Je m'excusais moi-même en pensant qu'il fallait bien lui apprendre l'ordre.... Je la tourmentais pour sa prétendue lenteur et son manque de soin...."

91. LT 9, from November or December, 1882 and LT 190, June 29, 1896, which is the remarkable "Legend of the Very Little Lamb," a parable Thérèse composed to heal the wounding Gonzague felt for months after her bitterly contested re-election to the priorate.

92. CG II: 1175, in a series of short prose portraits of the community, "Feuille de Présence des Carmélites de Lisieux," written in 1893 but discovered 80 years later in the archives of the Visitandine convent at Le Mans.

93. The small volume of her delicate yet legible notes of blue ink are in the Archives du Carmel. Next to some of the entries someone put a series of short dashes in pencil. It is my surmise, given the pertinence of these entries to her emergent spirituality, that Thérèse is responsible for the dashes but the matter remains open.

94. As the information on Sr. Saint-Joseph comes at best third hand and without any clinical acuity exercised along the way, no certain conclusions can be made about what troubled her. She seems to have been close to the neighborhood of a borderline personality disorder (between neurosis and psychosis), as its syndrome of violent mood swings and the attendant difficulty in sustaining interpersonal relationships appear to be pertinent. However, the phenomenon known as IED, intermittent explosive disorder, would also have to be considered. What intrigues about this disorder is the commonly attested sense of regret (a kind of penance?) shown by the victims after their outbursts. According to the *Diagnostic and Statistical Manual of Mental Disorders, IV-TR* (Arlington, Virginia: American Psychological Association, 2000), 664, "the explosive behavior is preceded by a sense of tension or arousal and is followed immediately by a sense of relief. Later the individual may feel upset, remorseful, regretful, or embarrassed about the aggressive behavior."

95. NPPA, 97. "[L]a Mère Prieure jugeait avec raison qu'il n'était pas possible d'imposer à qui que ce soit un si épouvantable fardeau" and "...avec son pauvre esprit malade, elle fit endurer un vrai martyre à son héroïque conseillère...il fallait lutter, se fatiguer et subir des scènes terrible parfois...[Thérèse] savait bien que ses efforts étaient pour ainsi dire stériles." Thérèse herself remarked after one of Sr. St. Joseph's blow ups that she wondered how this poor woman kept from falling into despair: "je vous assure qu'elle souffre moralement et qu'elle est plus à plaindre qu'à blâmer" ["Let me assure you that she suffers morally and is more to be pitied than faulted"]. Quoted in NPPA, 134.
96. Manuscript B 4 affords no less than seven phrases about tossing flowers.
97. LT 194. "[U]n enfant missionaire et guerrier quelle merveille!"
98. LT 195. "Le martyre le plus douloureux, le plus AMOUREUX est le nôtre puisque Jésus le voit. Il ne sera jamais révélé aux créatures sur la terre mais lorsque l'Agneau ouvrira le livre de vie, quel étonnement pour la Cour Céleste d'entendre proclamer avec ceux des missionaires et des martyrs le nom de pauvres petits enfants qui n'auront jamais fait d'actions éclatantes...."
99. LT 200, tentatively dated in the NEC to the end of October, 1896: "un brave qui mérite des épaulettes d'or."
100. LT 217, tentatively dated to January, 1897: "moi comme une pauvre petit passereau je gémis dans mon coin." However, Manuscript B closes with its author huddled like a small bird in a storm, "sa petite tête se cache sous la petite aile" ["its little head hides under its little wing"] (5r). If we assume that similarities in wording justify proximity in dating, this *billet* may be closer to September 1896 than to the date suggested by the NEC.
101. She strategically implicates Jesus in these notes: Jesus will take the flowers Sr. Saint-Joseph throws to him (LT 194); Jesus sees her martyrdom (LT 195); she is to sleep upon his heart (LT 200 and LT 205).
102. They include a poem she wrote for Sr. Saint-Joseph, PN 28: "Le cantique éternel chanté dès l'exil," ["The everlasting song sung from exile"] composed for her feast day, March 21, 1896. It is not an inspired work but has the proleptic lines that suggest how Sr. Saint-Joseph might have come to feel about Thérèse: "Oubliant ma grande misère tu viens habiter en mon coeur."
103. See LC 153, Sr. Saint-Augustin to Thérèse (1893); also the chant that Sr. Marie des Anges composed for Thérèse for her profession, September 8, 1890: "Ah! Donnez tout à ce Dieu si jaloux! Restez toujours son humble favorite, Son Lys aimé, le Lys de son amour!" ["Oh, give everything to this jealous God! Remain ever his humble favorite, his beloved Lily, the Lily of his love!"]. "Poesies du Carmel de Lisieux," Archives du Carmel.
104. LT 141, April 25, 1893.
105. LC 152, April 28, 1893. "Chaque mot de ta lettre chérie est à mon coeur un monde...."

106. PO, 156, col. 2. "[E]lle fut éprouvé par des sécheresses presque continuelles durant son séjour au Carmel."
107. LT 143, July 18, 1893. "[Q]uand nous sommes dans les ténèbres, dans les sécheresses."
108. LT 144, July 23, 1893. "[L]a terre a disparu à ses yeux elle ne sait pas où elle va si elle avance ou recule."
109. Ibid. "Jamais Notre Seigneur ne m'a encore refusé de t'inspirer ce que je L'avais prié de te dire. Toujours Il nous fait les mêmes grâces ensemble."
110. Ibid. "La nuit deviendrait plus claire que le jour."
111. LC 155, quoted by Céline to Thérèse, July 27, 1893.
112. LT 145, August 2, 1893. "[L]a foule des Juifs" and "soyons avares pour les autres mais prodigues pour Lui." This letter is unusual in that it remained unsigned and may be unfinished.
113. LC 180, May 30, 1897. "[U]ne veritable abime d'amertume" and "faiblesse maternelle." This letter marks the beginning of a reversal of roles. During her visit to Rome, ten years before, Thérèse had written, "Oh! Pauline, continue à me protéger. Je suis si loin de toi...." ["Oh, Pauline, keep protecting me. I'm so far from you...."] (LT 36). Now, Pauline was in that station of need before her receding sister. The solution came from the co-editing of Thérèse's writings and the DE project, already begun in April 1897, whereby, to whatever extent she could, Pauline incorporated her sister. In Proust, the narrator's mother overcomes her grief at the loss of her mother by trying to become her mother.
114. LC 180, May 30, 1897. "[E]lle lui appendra d'en-haut à maitriser ses impressions si désolantes."
115. During Pauline's priorate, 1893–1896, Thérèse wrote only 46 letters, all addressed to the family. Under Gonzague, beginning in March, 1896, Thérèse wrote 81 letters, only half of them to family members. Much of what she wrote within house amounted to only a few lines (LT 187, 188, 203, 209, 210, 214, 219, 222, 223, 233, 235, 236, 237, 238, 239, 246, 248, 252, 256, 262, 264, 265, 266), but they are still denominated as Letters, and a few of them have some very weighty remarks. Far more substantial, by obvious contrast, are the lengthy exchanges with her foreign correspondents, the spiritual brothers, Bellière and Roulland, to all of which Gonzague was privy.
116. LC 182, May 31, 1897. "[S]i vous priez pour moi je vais vraiment commencer une vie nouvelle" and "je ne sentirai pas autre chose qu'une attraction plus puissante vers le Ciel" and "J'ai pourtant été bien infidèle dans ma petite vie religieuse mais je vais commencer à me convertir, à vous ressembler; le bon Dieu voyant cela me pardonnera, j'espère, mes petites péchés" and "au-dessus des nuages Vous jouant avec paix dans les prairies des Cieux."
117. RP 8: 6r. The play was performed on February 8, 1897. Thérèse was not strong enough to perform the leading part or any other; Gonzague may have forbidden her to do so.

118. DE, July 17, 1897. "Je veux passer mon Ciel à faire du bien sur la terre."
119. Pauline understood well enough the centrality of suffering but not any present joy, hidden as it were, within it. See LD, November 8, 1887, addressed to her two little sisters en route to Rome, wherein she describes the sequences of suffering without and then within the Carmel. Thérèse's joy came from her intuitive awareness of Jesus's complicity in her suffering, that he was guiding her in unknown directions and putting her out of her familiar depths.
120. LT 258, July 18, 1897, just one day after she stated anew her option for doing good upon the earth, DE, July 17, 1897. To Bellière she says the thought of heavenly happiness causes her no joy, because suffering is inextricably bound with her performance of God's will. In RP 8, 6r her St. Stanislaus speaks to the Virgin of his desire to work in Paradise to save souls, and makes it clear that without that occupation he wouldn't be happy.
121. LT 253, July 13, 1897. "Jésus m'a toujours fait désirer ce qu'Il voulait me donner."
122. LT 244, June 9, 1897. "Je ne meurs pas, j'entre dans la vie."
123. RP3, *Jeanne d'Arc accomplissant sa mission*, performed on January 21, 1895, with Thérèse in the title role. "J'entre dans l'éternelle vie!... Je vois... les anges, les élus...."
124. LT 245, dated in the NEC edition to approximately June 1897. "Un jour nous nous retrouverons dans le Paradis."
125. PO, 273. "[S]i difficile à former qu'elle ne dut rester au Carmel qu'à la patience de notre jeune maîtresse" The same, it would seem, could have been remarked of Céline herself.
126. LT 242, June 6, 1897. "Vous voulez savoir si j'ai de la joie d'aller au Paradis? J'en aurais beaucoup *si j'y allais* mais...." The italics are hers.
127. Reported to her by Pauline, LC 185, June 4 (?), 1897.
128. LT 108; LT 119; Pri 4 and Pri 6 (Offrande).
129. Pri 15, "[D]'oublier les ingratitudes des âmes qui vous sont consacrées et de pardonner aux pauvres pécheurs." This prayer has been tentatively dated in the NEC to the retreat of September 1896, but as the anguished egotism of sisters came to the fore with the clear signs of her impending death, I would suggest that Pri 15 belongs to the following June or thereabouts. Pri 16, with its request that her soul be consumed rapidly in divine love, echoes LT 242 (June 6, 1897), while her asking Jesus to impress his image upon her so that he sees himself when he looks at her charmingly calls up C 20r, which was written in mid-June, 1897.
130. LT 246, June 13, 1897. "[L]'ingratitude des âmes qui ne l'aiment pas assez " My italics.
131. RP7, 3v. "[S]uggérez-leur surtout de s'occuper d'elles-mêmes; l'amour propre est le faible de tous les humains, il se trouve aussi dans les communautés cloîtrées et je vous le confie à vous, mes amis, c'est mon arme la plus sûre pour ralentir l'amour d'Adonaï dans les coeurs de toutes ses nonnes...."
132. A 2r. "[D]issiperait mon coeur en l'occupant de lui-même"

133. LT 247, June 21, 1897. "Je tache de ne plus m'occuper de moi-même."
134. LT 211, Christmas, 1896. "Il aime mieux te voir heurter dans la nuit les pierres du chemin que marcher en plein jour sur une route émaillée de fleurs qui pourraient retarder ta marche."
135. Communication from the Carmel of Lisieux.
136. A, 82r. "La seule chose que je ne pouvais accepter, c'était qu'elle ne soit pas l'épouse de Jésus, car l'aimant autant que moi-même, il m'était impossible de la voir donner son coeur à un mortel. J'avais déjà beaucoup souffert en la sachant exposée dans le monde à des dangers qui m'avaient été inconnus." Just as Céline had kept her sisters in the dark about Pichon's Canadian venture (he had sworn her to secrecy), so she kept them ignorant of her close relations with Maudelonde. Her explanation to Pauline, dated June 23, 1905, about why she said nothing to Thérèse at the time, seems disingenuous, at best: "Je la croyais trop jeune pour écouter de telles horreurs et je craignais de ternir sa belle petite âme." ["I believed she was too young to listen to such horrors and I was afraid of tarnishing her beautiful little soul."] Cited in the NEC edition of the Manuscrits autobiographiques: 262, note on 82r, 5. Nonsense.
137. Souvenirs autobiographiques, quoted in the NEC edition of Manuscrits autobiographiques: 281, note on 82r, 5. "Je n'aurais eu qu'un mot à dire, qu'un regard! Quand j'y songe, je suis saisie d'épouvante, ma vocation a été si près de sombrer! Il me semble que cela ne tenait qu'à un fil."
138. Pauline, NPPA. "Prudence" : "mais s'édifiaient en même temps de la conduite et des conseils de leur prudente maîtresse qui restait calme."
139. Pauline, NPPA. Humbles sentiments de soi-même, p. 5. "Alors une émotion parut sur le visage de Sr. Thérèse de l'Enfant Jésus, et le soir elle m'écrivit ces lignes."
140. LT 230, May 28, 1897. "Ah, ce soir, je vous ai montré ma vertu, mes TRÉSORS de patience!.. Et moi qui prêche si bien les autres!!!!!!!!!!!!!!.. Je suis contente que vous avez vu mon imperfection."
141. C 17 r-v. "[C]roit me distraire en me faisant un peu la causette" and "croyant peut-être m'inspirer des idées poétiques" and "...je ne sais pas si j'ai pu écrire dix lignes sans être dérangée....[C]ependant pour l'amour du Bon Dieu et des mes soeurs (si charitables envers moi) je tâche d'avoir l'air contente et surtout de l'être."
142. C 15r. "[M]aintenant je ne m'étonne plus de rien, je ne me fais pas de peine en voyant que je suis la faiblesse même, au contraire c'est en elle que je me glorifie et je m'attends chaque jour à découvrir en moi de nouvelles imperfections."
143. LT 107, May 19–20, 1890.
144. LT 243, June 7, 1897. "Oui il suffit de s'humilier de supporter avec douceur ses imperfections. Voilà la vraie sainteté!"
145. Pri 12. "[I]l nous faut...surtout *des âmes d'apôtres et de martyrs* afin que par elles nous *embrasions de votre Amour* la multitude des pauvres pécheurs." Thérèse wrote the italicized words in red ink.
146. To me the most intriguing instance comes in her last play, *Saint Stanislaus Kostka*, performed on February 8, 1897. In its third scene, the Jesuit general,

Francesco di Borgia, calls upon young Stanislaus to confess his sins. Stanislaus has just spoken vaguely, much like Maurice Bellière, of his derelictions. Even if he could perform miracles, "le souvenir de ma vie passée ne saurait s'effacer de ma mémoire. Ah! Je suis un misérable indigne des grâces du Bon Dieu!" ["the memory of my past life wouldn't efface itself.... Oh, I'm a wretch unworthy of the Good Lord's mercies"] but all he confesses is his resistance for 18 months after he had experienced a divine calling. Borgia forgives him this "faute." In short, it is hard to get any real sense of sin in this youth. Kostka's sense of unworthiness had clearly kept him from fulfilling the call; he did not see that it was that sense of unworthiness which may have prompted the call. As to resisting a divine command, what of Gethsemani?

147. LC 183, Pauline to Thérèse, June 2, 1897. "[S]es délires de scrupules."
148. Carnet Rouge of Sr. Marie de la Trinité, published in VT (January 1980): 59. "Quel saint canonisé a jamais parlé ainsi: 'Nous autres, me disait-elle, nous ne sommes pas des saints qui pleurons nos péchés, nous nous réjouissons de ce qu'ils servent à glorifier la miséricorde du bon Dieu."

CHAPTER 4

1. See my *Thérèse of Lisieux: God's Gentle Warrior* (New York: Oxford University Press, 2006).
2. Communication from the Carmel of Lisieux.
3. "Mon Chant d'Aujourd'hui," "Et je pourrai t'offrir une grappe dorée Seigneur, dès aujourd'hui."
4. Hyacinthe Loyson, *My Last Will and Testament*, trans. Fabian Ware (London: Cassell, 1895), 26.
5. Flaubert, *Correspondance*, September 2–3, 1868.
6. Loyson, *My Last Will*, 31.
7. Ibid., 44.
8. George Sand, *Impressions et Souvenirs*, (Paris: Librairie Nouvelle, 1873), 277. "les funestes et les honteuses conséquences du célibat des prêtres."
9. Ibid., 47.
10. LT 129. "[U]ne âme qui semble à jamais perdue.... Les détails m'ont bien intéressée, tout en me faisant battre le coeur bien fort."
11. Ms. A, 69 v. "pour sauver les âmes et surtout afin de prier pour les prêtres"
12. See George Sand's scathing letter of September 13, 1868, to Sylvanie Arnould-Plessy, an actress and one-time mistress of Prince Napoléon (cousin of Napoléon III). Sylvanie had been converted to Catholicism by Loyson in January of that year.
13. LT 129. "[C]'est bien triste de voir ainsi souffrir ceux que l'on aime" and "le malheureux prodigue" and "il est facile de voir que le *remords* le ronge, il parcourt les églises avec un grand crucifix et il semble faire de grandes adorations...."

14. Ibid. "[P]lus coupable peut-être que ne l'a jamais été un pécheur qui se soit converti" and "pauvres petites épouses...de ramener au bercail cette pauvre brebis égarée."
15. In Matthew 9:27–31, two blind men are healed by their own faith, and Jesus then charges them to say nothing but they spread his fame throughout the land. In Mark 10:46–52, only one blind man, Bartimaeus, presents himself to be healed, and he, too, is cured by his own faith. He remains as a follower of Jesus. Thérèse's sanguine remarks on Loyson suggest a conflation of these stories. Significantly, she passes over the matter of Loyson's marriage, saying nothing whatever of the infamous American wife.
16. LT 129. "[U]n jour viendra où il lui ouvrira les yeux et alors qui sait si la France ne sera pas parcourue par lui dans un tout autre but que celui qu'il se propose."
17. *La Croix du Calvados*, July 9–16, 1891. "...religieux défroqué et marié, protégé des francs-maçons et des impies partout où vous passez." I have quoted from Thérèse's invaluable clippings. The municipal library in Lisieux unfortunately has no collection of *La Croix du Calvados*, and the other local newspapers of that time have no record of Loyson's itinerary.
18. *La Croix du Calvados*, July 23–30, 1891. "[S]i l'Eglise lui prouve qu'il est en défaut, *il veut bien reconnaître son erreur, et reprendre humblement sa place dans l'unité chrétienne.*"
19. Since the Loyson incident coincided with the beatification hearings for Thérèse, one might uncharitably suppose that the Carmel had a vested interest in trying to get Loyson back into the Church. It would be a coup for Thérèse if she could be credited with a recantation from such a black sheepish celebrity. But Pauline's correspondence indicates that was not the procedure or intent. In a letter of January 13, 1910 she tells Msgr. Teil that a priest, Abbé Rivain, had asked the Carmel to entreat Thérèse "pour la conversion du malheureux Père Hyacinthe." Pauline notes that a zealous person had asked Msgr. Amette for permission to send Loyson a copy of *Histoire*, "mais ce miracle [the recantation] Sr. Thérèse l'avait déjà tant demandé de son vivant!" [...but Sister Therese had already so many times asked that while she was alive!]. "Archives du Carmel."
20. Hyacinthe Loyson to Mère Agnes, February 5, 1911, Archives du Carmel. "[C]ette belle âme avait offert à Dieu ses prières et ses souffrances pour ce qu'elle appellait ma "conversion,' c'est-à-dire ma soumission aux enseignements imposés par le Pape aux consciences qui abdiquent entre ses mains."
21. "The lack of this knowledge is the guilt of the Church, a lack which is worldwide and age-long. For who possesses true knowledge? Whom does it not always elude? Who does not enter his name as a competitor in those races?" Karl Barth, *The Epistle to the Romans,* trans. Edwyn Hoskins (1933; rpt. New York : Oxford University Press, 1968), 372.
22. Ibid., 373.
23. Hyacinthe Loyson to Mère Agnes, February 5, 1911, Archives du Carmel. "Je peux me tromper, ma Révérende Mère, je me suis trompé plus d'une fois dans ma

longue vie, mais je suis persuadé que ce que Dieu condamne dans l'homme, ce n'est pas erreur, quand elle est sincère, c'est l'égoïsme, l'orgueil et la haine. Je crois pouvoir dire devant la mort et devant Dieu que tels n'ont jamais été les mobiles de ma pensée et de ma vie."

24. Soeur Geneviève, *Conseils et Souvenirs* (Paris: Cerf, 1996), 186. "C'est incroyable comme, à la fin, tout ce que l'on pouvait me dire n'effleurait même pas mon âme, parce que j'avais compris le peu solidité des jugements humains."

25. *Procès Ordinaire*, 145. "[T]oute, toute petite et sans vertu."

26. LT 259. "Je ne puis être brisée, éprouvée que par des justes, puisque toutes mes soeurs sont agréables à Dieu. C'est moins amer d'être brisé par un pécheur que par un juste, mais par compassion pour les pécheurs pour obtenir leur conversion je vous demande ô mon Dieu d'être brisée pour eux par les âmes justes qui m'entourent."

27. A word carefully chosen as it informs the Carmel's motto "Zelo zelatus sum."

28. C 11r. "[E]lles n'ont pas à craindre de se tromper même s'il leur paraît certain que les supérieurs se trompent" and "leur unique boussole," and "Mais lorsqu'on cesse de regarder la boussole infaillible, lorsqu'on s'écarte de la voie qu'elle dit de suivre sous prétexte de faire la volonté de Dieu qui n'eclaire pas bien ceux qui pourtant tiennent sa place, aussitôt l'âme s'égare dans des chemins arides où l'eau de la grâce lui manque bientôt."

29. C 11r. "[V]ivant en votre âme et me communiquant par vous sa volonté."

30. This is the point of Céline's objection, posed to Loyson in a letter of February 11, 1911, in which she addresses him in the third person: "Hélas! Celui qui a cru il croit encore J.C. infaillible refuse d'y reconnaître son successeur." ["Alas, he who has believed he still believes Jesus infallible refuses to recognize that in his successor."] After that letter, with its sometimes hectoring tone, came six months of silence. On July 21, 1911, Loyson wrote to Céline that the renunciations she asked of him, of his apostasy and his marriage, would be a grave sin against the truth. Besides, he reported, when he had met with Leo XIII early in the 1880s, the pope had offered to recognize Loyson's marriage in return for his recognition of papal infallibility.

"Vous êtes charitable, ma très honorée Soeur, mais vous n'êtes peut-être pas assez humble, et vous jugez les autres sans vous dire que Dieu a peut-être sur les âmes, sur l'Eglise et sur le monde des voies que vous ne connaissez pas." ["You're charitable, my very honored Sister, but maybe not humble enough, and you judge others without saying that God maybe has paths you don't know about for souls, for the Church and for the world."]

Her second and last letter sustained a supplicating tone. Thérèse's maternal watch over him had undoubtedly brought him many graces—had he been faithful to them? And how could his Carmelite sisters ever consent to be separated from him forever: "...et vous ne mépriserez pas l'ameçon doré qu'elles vous tendent." ["...and you'll not scorn the golden bait they're extending to you."] By that she meant the *Histoire*, but it required a single word in response, *Erravimus*, or "I've been mistaken." With just that he would be reconciled to the Church and the Carmel, and snuggled under the Virgin's mantle, a favorite image of that day.

If all that seems a bit wheedling, there is one passage which sounds like Thérèse herself, an appeal to Loyson's humility: "Une grande personne calcule, mais un petit enfant ne sait pas raisonner et d'un seul bond il franchit des obstacles." ["A grownup calculates but a little child does not know how to rationalize and in a single bound he gets past obstacles."]

Loyson at nearly 85 proved too old a dog for any tricks and died in his apostasy the following January. On the 26th, Céline wrote to Léonie of how pained she was, since Thérèse had so desired his conversion. "Enfin, tous nous avons échoué. Ah! Que c'est triste l'orgueil." ["In the end, we all botched it. Oh, how sad pride is."] "Archives du Carmel."

31. In fairness to Loyson, I cite from A 83r her only other reference to a compass, there identified as *abandon*, that unqualified yielding of self to the will of God: "Je ne puis plus rien demander avec ardeur excepté l'accomplissement parfait de la volonté du Bon Dieu sur mon âme sans que les créatures puissent y mettre obstacle." ["I can ask nothing with greater ardor than the fulfillment of the Good Lord's will in my soul without other people putting any obstacle there."] What else would Loyson have said?

The difference between A 83 and C 11 is not only 18 months, January 1896 to June 1897, but Thérèse's profound maturing over that time through the twofold suffering of a spiritual void and tubercular mortification.

32. Breviaire Romain, II: 614. "Il ne passa pas de jour sans donner quelque preuve éclatante de sa foi, sa piété et de sa sainteté."

33. After Loyson's death, Pauline inquired about his fate in worlds beyond. On August 6, 1912, she heard from a cleric of the parish of St. Denys de la Chapelle, Paris: "Pour ce qui regarde le P. Hyacinthe par révélation particulière, il serait sauvé, mais condamné à rester en purgatoire jusqu'à la fin du monde." ["As to Father Hyacinth, by special revelation, he'll be saved but condemned to stay in purgatory until the world's end."] "Archives du Carmel."

34. Quoted in Eugen Weber, *Satan franc-maçon* (Paris: Julliard, 1964), 174. "Ce bateau du Palladisme a été un vrai cuirassé auprès du remorquer que je fis, pour mes débuts, envoyer à la chasse aux requins dans la rade de Marseille."

35. Weber, 113. "[C]hiamata dalle profonde tenebre alla luce di Dio, preparata dalla divina providenza, e armata di scienza e di esperienza personale, si volta al servizio della Chiesa, è inesauribile di preziose publicazioni, che non hanno pari in esattezza e in utilità. La Massoneria ne è costernata, e per riparo ai gran colpi della fiera viragine, fa spargere che essa non esiste, ed è un semplice mito."

36. Weber, 115. "L'hostilité envers l'Eglise, poussée jusqu'à l'abstention de la liqueur des Chartreux, voilà qui est typique." And "Aujourd'hui, Miss Vaughan est une fervente catholique, combattent le bon combat en véritable champion de la foi."

37. Ms A 32r. "[L]a même inspiration Céleste" The capitalization is Thérèse's.

38. Ms A 27r. "La maladie dont je fus atteinte venait certainement du démon.... Je crois que le *démon* avait reçu un pouvoir exterieur sur moi."
39. Ms A 76r. "[J]e trouvais la vie du Carmel bien belle, mais le démon m'inspirait l'*assurance* qu'elle n'était faite pour moi, que je tromperais les supérieures en avançant dans une voie où je n'étais pas appelée.... Mes ténèbres étaient si grandes que je ne voyais ni ne comprenais qu'une chose: Je n'avais pas la *vocation!*"
40. In the Carmel's *chauffoir*, the recreational room where the plays were performed, a folding screen kept the "demons" out of sight. Only the Carmel's pitchforks were visibly projected. Chains were rattled to further effect.
41. RP 7, 3r. "[D]'une manière lamentable pour notre cause."
42. It is altogether possible, however, that as Diana Vaughan had become a sensation within the Catholic press, other Carmelite sisters could have received publications on or about her from their relatives. Vaughan's memoirs were even being read in monastic refectories. It is not now known what happened to the Vaughan literature that was then circulating within the Lisieux Carmel. Communication from the Carmel of Lisieux.
43. PO, 166. "Ce n'est pas possible que cela vienne du bon Dieu."
44. Two weeks later this same kind of apparatus precipitated the famous Charity Bazaar fire, which killed more than 125 Parisians.
45. This work had its genesis in France, in a satire published in 1864, Maurice Joly's *Dialogues aux enfers entre Machiavel et Montesquieu*. The *Protocols*, which were published as such in Russia in 1905 by the Czar's secret police, came as an appendix to a book on the coming Anti-Christ.
46. PO, 166. "Elle avait pour les moindres mensonges, même joyeux, une véritable horreur. C'était la droiture personifiée."
47. Ms A 30v. "Hélas! Comme je l'avais senti, mon bonheur allait disparaître et se changer en amertume.... Toutes ces questions me troublèrent et me firent de la peine.... [J]e me figurai *avoir menti....*"48 PN 50. "Le cruel étranger t'abreuva de douleurs."

CHAPTER 5

1. This is one of the self-amusing engagements she had long been making up, starting with little Jesus and his toy ball; she and her sisters indulged in them when she was struggling to enter the Carmel. What is strikingly different here is that now she imagines Jesus speaking, asking her where she wishes to go.
2. LT 110, August 30–31, 1890. "Alors Jésus m'a prise par la main, et Il m'a fait entrer dans un souterrain où il ne fait ni froid ni chaud, ou le soleil ne luit pas et que la pluie ni le vent ne visitent pas, un souterrain où je ne vois rien qu'une clarté à demi voilée, la clarté que répandent autour d'eux les yeux baissés de la face de mon Fiancé!..."

3. Ibid. "Je ne vois pas que nous avancions vers le terme de la montagne puisque notre voyage se fait sous terre, mais pourtant il me semble que nous en approchons sans savoir comment. La route que je suis n'est d'aucune consolation pour moi et pourtant elle m'apporte toutes les consolations puisque c'est Jésus qui l'a choisie, et que je désire le consoler tout seul, tout seul!..." The "all alone"—"tout seul, tout seul"—makes clear that it is Jesus who is all alone, but one can infer that Thérèse for her part is or wishes to be alone, as well—with him.

4. The *Abandon* can be seen in the exhibition case of the girls' bedroom at Les Buissonnets, along with other vestiges of Thérèse's childhood, including her confirmation gown, books, and games.

5. As in LT 122, October 14, 1890, to Céline: "faisons de notre coeur un petit parterre de délices ou [sic] Jésus vienne se reposer...ne plantons que des Lys dans notre jardin...des Lys il n'y a que les vierges qui peuvent en donner a [sic] Jésus." ["Let's make of our heart a little parterre of delights where Jesus may come to rest...let's plant only lilies in our garden...only the virgins can give lilies to Jesus"].

6. Five months after her profession of vows Pichon congratulated her "pour votre voyage de noces au Calvaire!" ["on your honeymoon to Calvary!"] LC 146, February 16, 1891.

7. *Song of Songs*, 5:4. "[M]y beloved put in his hand...and my bowels were moved for him." Madre Teresa de Jesús in her commentary on the *Song* knew when to pass by.

8. See CG, II: 616–619.

9. LC 143. "[E]lle ne cherche que la croix de son bien aimé, qui a été abandonné à tous...." In the NEC text this letter is given a wide berth for dates, "end of 1890 to summer of 1891."

10. Ibid. "Tantôt le bien aimé nous conduit au Thabor mais plus souvent au calvaire [sic], c'est là qu'Il nous a donné pour enfant à sa Mère."

11. I Kings, 19:10, III Kings.19:10 in the Douai version. Odd, that it was not altered to "Zelo zelata sum" for the Carmel's sisters.

12. A 76r. "[L]'aridité la plus absolue" and "ma grande retraite de l'éternité."

13. Pri 2, September 8, 1890. "[S]i je dis des choses qu'il ne faut pas dire" and "oubliée comme un petit grain de sable à toi, Jésus."

14. LT 114. "[L]e petit grain de sable" and C 2v "le grain de sable obscur foulé sous les pieds des passants."

15. A 86. "Notre grande richesse—12 fevrier 1889."

16. The remark from Céline occurs in her CS, 76 "ses retraites du mois lui étaient un supplice"; those from Pauline, PA, 467. "Il lui semblait si difficile à elle d'offenser Dieu quand on l'aime! Pendant tout le temps de ces exercices, je la voyais pâle et défaite, elle ne pouvait plus manger ni dormir et serait tombée malade si cela avait duré."

17. Beatrice Didier, *L'Écriture femme* (Paris: Presses Universitaires de France, 1991), 19 : "...les revanches de l'imaginaire autorisaient...leur 'moi' à forger un univers qui échappait à toute contrainte" and 20: "le merveilleux où le nouement entre le réel et le surnaturel se fait sans heurt, où le merveilleux s'immisce dans la vie la plus quotidienne."
18. She wonders, as though to herself, whether this dream marked the tenth anniversary of the Virgin Mary's smiling upon her in her illness.
19. B 2v. "[J]e *croyais*, je *sentais* qu'il y a un Ciel et que ce Ciel est peuplé d'âmes qui me chérissent, qui me regardant comme leur enfant."
20. B 2v. "[D]'accomplir pour toi Jésus toutes les oeuvres les plus héroïques." Didier: 53 notes that for Teresa of Avila a childhood spent reading chivalric tales as well as saints lives meant that "comme pour beaucoup d'enfants le lecture se fait mime, mimique, mimétique. Il ne suffit pas de lire, il faut vivre la vie de ses héros." ["as with many children, reading becomes a mime, mimicking and mimetic. It's not enough to read one's heroes' lives, they have to be lived."]
21. B 3r. "[M]es *petits désirs enfantins*" and "autres *désirs* plus *grands* que l'univers" (her emphases); B 3v "ma place dans l'Église."
22. B 3v. "[J]e m'elevai si haut que je pus atteindre mon but." "je m'elevai" could be rendered as either "I raised myself..." or "I was raised...."
23. See Leviticus 22: 18–25. Thérèse has missed (or ignored) one of the antitheses. Looking to perfection and imperfection, she cannot accept impurity as the opposite of the purity she herself has posited under the Old Testament sacrifices. Instead, she substitutes weakness, as though the earlier sacrifices were themselves mighty for their all-powerful God.
24. San Juan de la Cruz, *Obras Completas*, 466. "[E]l cual [amor] no se paga sino de sí mismo" (BAC edition).
25. Ibid., 555. "[E]l amante no puede estar satisfecho si no siente que ama cuanto es amado" ["the lover cannot be satisfied unless he loves as much as he is loved"].
26. B 4r. "[Ô] Bienheureux habitants du Ciel, je vous supplie de *m'adopter pour enfant*."
27. B 4v. "[C]es riens te feront plaisir."
28. San Juan de la Cruz, *Obras Completas*, 687. "[E]s más precioso delante de Dios y del alma un poquito de este amor puro y más provecho hace a la Iglesia, aunque parece que no hace nada, que todas esas otras obras juntas." Thérèse does not in this instance cite the crucial players in this Juanist drama, God, the soul, and the Church, all delighted and benefitted by Mary's contemplative love. In LT 221 to Roulland and LT 245 to her three natural sisters in Carmel, Thérèse adds Juan's "provecho," rendered "utile," useful to the Church, but with no reference to God or the soul.
29. Ronald Knox, in his famous translation, *Autobiography of a Saint* (London: Collins, 1958), 188, editorializes this pure love as "disinterested love," which it might be, but Thérèse is very sparing of "disinterested," using it only twice: A13, C27.

30. B 4v. "[A]près avoir aspiré vers les régions les plus élevées de l'Amour, s'il me faut ne pas les atteindre un jour, j'aurai goûté plus de *douceur dans mon martyre, dans ma folie,* que je n'en goûterai au sein des *joies de la patrie...*" (her emphasis).
31. B 5r. "[T]ous ses méfaits" and "cette souffrance méritée."
32. B 5r. "[H]eureux d'être *faible* et *petit*" (her emphasis). In underscoring her weakness, she answers the Breviary's citation (BR II: 32) of Augustine's commentary on Psalm 90 (91), verse 4. The trusting soul is like a bird that shall be freed from the fowler by a bird mightier than any snare: "He shall cover thee with his feathers and under his wings shalt thou trust." Augustine adds "pourvu que tu reconnaisses ta faiblesse" ["provided you acknowledge your weakness"]. Thérèse needed no effort to do so. The imagery was commonplace. For another weak little bird tested by God, see her cousin Marie's letter to Céline, August 1–2, 1892 (four years before B), "mes ailes sont encore bien petites et bien faibles, mais sans doute qu'elles ont assez de force pour supporter cette épreuve" ["my wings are quite little and feeble yet surely they're strong enough to bear this testing"]. But Marie refers to a week's separation from Céline! Archives de Famille (July 1892–January 1893), *VT* 109 (January–March, 1988): 49.
33. B 5v. "[C]aché sous l'apparence d'une blanche hostie." This bird episode becomes a splendid little drama that could be recast as a *récréation pieuse* for a solo performer in contemplation of Jesus, her "office d'*amour*" ["office of *love*"]. She draws that phrase from San Juan de la Cruz, *Cantico,* strophe 28: "ya no guardo ganado ni ya tengo otro oficio, que ya sólo en amar es mi ejercicio" ["now I tend no flock nor hold another office, for now only in love is my practice"], *Obras Completas:* 683.
34. B 4v. "Je cherche la verité.
35. B 2v. "[L]e prélude de grâces plus grandes dont tu voulais me combler."
36. B 2v. "[L]a sublime dignité du Sacerdoce" and "j'admire et j'envie l'humilité de St. François"
37. *Imitatio Christi* III. 24.2. She does cite this monition, but only once, in A 56r. The jubilee pilgrimage to Rome provided the context. Amid the Norman nobility en route, Thérèse felt a bourgeois unease about titles, which she got over by biblical reminders: God has names to hand out to His elect (Isaiah 65:15); on the Latter Day, each Christian soul shall receive a name known only to the recipient (Revelation 2:17).
38. B 3v. "[A]insi je serai tout.... [A]insi mon rêve sera réalisé!!!" and A 10r "je choisis tout."
39. B4r. "[J]e craindrais de me trouver accablée sous le poids de mes désirs audacieux."
40. DE, August 20, 1897, no. 15. "Je voudrais être sure qu'elle m'*aime,* la Sainte Vierge."
41. NPPA, Céline, p. 10. "Oh! Si vous passiez seulement cinq minutes par les épreuves où je subis!" and "Est-ce qu'il y a un ciel?... parlez-moi du ciel..." and

"le plus souvent il fallait changer de sujet, car mes paroles semblaient augmenter ses tortures... je compris alors l'horrible état des damnés qui vivent sans foi et sans espérance." CS: 147–148 has "tentations que je subis" instead of "épreuves que je subis" and "sa torture" instead of the plural.

42. C 4v. "[V]otre priorat beni."
43. PO, 146–147; PA, 201.
44. Archives de Famille, fevrier–avril, 1893, VT 115 (July–September, 1989): 167. "Heureusement elle [Pauline] aura la Mère M. de G. pour la guider."
45. Ibid., 180–181. "Elle me parlait hier soir comme une personne mourante, j'étais brisée, je pleurais! Elle me disait que le bon Dieu m'aiderait, qu'elle ne m'était plus nécessaire, que la Mère Geneviève serait avec moi, etc.... et me donnait ses dernières recommandations... juge de ma peine!"
46. For an extended discussion of these two women's management of the Carmel at Lisieux see my *Thérèse of Lisieux: God's Gentle Warrior* (New York: Oxford University Press, 2006), 122–126.
47. Claude Langlois (see Bibliography) argues that Pauline urged the resumption of Thérèse's writing as a means of overcoming her own "violent crisis of jealousy" (*Lettres:* 39, 40). "She already saw Therese in heaven and herself organizing the cult: she explained that to Therese with a curious mix of sincerity, naivete, and brutality, thinking that her affection for her sister justified everything she told her and everything she made her do...[her] motivation is a bit troubling, not to say sordid: to know everything written and oral of what she did not know about her sister. There's a gently inquisitorial side to her, a way of using her sister while there is still time, a melange of manipulative cynicism and of sincere affectivity, of gnawing disarray and sickly possessiveness."
48. LT 190. "[E]t comme si l'agneau eut été son égal, la Bergère, lui confiait ses peines et parfois pleurait avec lui...."
49. Ibid. "Pour s'élever, il faut *poser* son *pied* sur les *dégrés* des créatures et ne s'attacher qu'à moi seul...."
50. LT 190. "[C]ar, s'éloigner des créatures ne servirait qu'à une chose, *marcher* et s'égarer dans les sentiers de la terre...."
51. PO, 147–148; PA, 173. "Car j'ai reçu trop grandes lumières à ce sujet, je ne veux pas les garder pour moi seule; je vous assure que la charité n'est pas comprise sur la terre, et pourtant, c'est la principale des vertus."
52. See the 144th of her *Lettres spirituelles*, Pierre Serouet, ed. (Paris: Desclée de Brouwer, 1965): 142, on why she preferred adoration to thanksgiving: "parce qu'il est plus étendu et qu'il nous expose moins au danger de nous occuper trop de nous mêmes sous pretexte de remercier Dieu des biens qu'il nous a faits, surtout quand ils nous sont particuliers" ["because it is more expansive and exposes us less to the danger of excessive occupation with ourselves under the pretext of thanking God for good things he's done for us, especially when they are particular to us."]

53. Some vestige of the French notion might subsist in our expressions of appreciation couched in the phrase "in recognition of services rendered."
54. CG, I:75, n. 66: the two extant letters are LT 9 and LT 190 (the shepherdess parable). The NEC edition says that to judge from the number of responses from Gonzague, Thérèse's lost messages figure at an undoubtedly higher number than fifteen.
55. C 7v. "[S]atisfaction naturelle dans le désir que j'avais du Ciel.... [C]ar je n'ai plus de grands désirs si ce n'est celui d'aimer jusqu'à mourir d'amour...."
56. LT 244. "O mon cher petit frère, que je suis heureuse de mourir!... parce que je sens bien que telle est la volonté du Bon Dieu.... [M]ais je ne meurs pas, j'entre dans la vie et tout ce que je ne puis vous dire ici-bas, je vous le ferai comprendre du haut des Cieux...."
57. It's a minor deception, though, to speak of a full circle, as if she had consciously, deliberately reached an end. She tells Gonzague that she intends to speak of her missionary brothers, Bellière and Roulland, but never gets around to doing so. That inconclusiveness may in part be due to her debilitation under the condensed milk that the Carmel physician, Cornière, had been imposing on her. As she was lactose intolerant, this fare was nauseating in the extreme.
58. C IV. "[L]'education *forte* et maternelle" and "l'eau vivifiante de l'humilation" (my emphasis). Thérèse writes only "sa petite fleur." The closure with "life giving waters of humiliation" strikingly alters Christ's message to the Samarian woman at the well, on vivifying water: John 4:10–14.
59. The negative press on Gonzague begins at the beatification proceedings. The youngest of the novices, Sr. Marie de la Trinité, who felt little warmth toward Gonzague, whom she called "the wolf," has harsh words about the prioress's treatment of Thérèse, PO, 462. Cf. PA, 494, below.
60. C 2r. "[L]'eau si fade des compliments." What might Gonzague have said at the hearings? Sr. Marie de la Trinité claims that the prioress told her she would have chosen Thérèse as her successor because she was "parfaite en tout; son seul défaut est d'avoir ses trois soeurs avec elle" ["perfect in everything; her only defect is in having her three sisters with her"], PA, 494. That is not a slight upon any of the Martin sisters per se. Gonzague means, I believe, that their familial presence had retarding effects upon Thérèse's spiritual formation. And yet Gonzague had been responsible for bringing each of them into the Carmel, and Thérèse would not likely have entered the Carmel, had Pauline not preceded her.
61. C 5r. "[J]'étais intimement persuadée que Jésus au jour anniversaire de sa mort voulait me faire *entendre un premier appel*" (my emphasis). *Persuader* comes seldom to her pen, but in a couple of telling instances, it suggests a profound inner conviction, as when in A 78r she writes of being "persuadée" that the venerable Mère Geneviève upon her death went directly to heaven, and in LT 176 (April 28, 1895) she was "intimement persuadée" that her sister Léonie's true vocation had at last been found, as a Visitandine sister in Caen.

62. C 5v. "Jésus m'a fait sentir qu'il y a véritablemnt des âmes qui n'ont pas la foi, qui par l'abus des grâces perdent ce précieux trésor, source des seules joies pures et véritables."

63. It occurs fifty-five times in C, proportionately much greater than the eighty-four in A, but nearly equivalent to the 19 in B. The letters after her retreat of September 1896 offer thirty-two instances.

64. She had entered the Carmel at thirty-five (the usual age was twenty) but left after one year when her mother was dying. The prioress, Mère Geneviève, told her she would have to wait for nine years before re-entering. She did. The *circulaire* that Pauline composed for her, in 1924, portrays an unusually self-effacing sister, one of Madre Teresa's saintly simple souls. Even so, she criticized Thérèse's predisposition to an early death, her own mother's having cost her dearly.

65. In Pri 5, the seventh couplet, which dates from November 1894, she prays (on behalf of Sr. Marie-Madeleine) that the guardian angel will keep her from ever offending Jesus, but for herself, Thérèse would always prefer to address such a prayer to Jesus or to God directly, as in C 6r.

66. PN 46. "Je veux pendant ma courte vie / Sauver mes frères les pécheurs" Guardian angels have been on watch since the time of Hammurabi, a good two thousand years' distance from Tiberius and Christ. For Catholicism and its Tradition, the guardian angel has served to protect the entrusted soul from demonic harm, including the physical, and to convey God's will. For over three centuries the Church has observed October 2 as the guardians' feast day, one day after Thérèse's own.

67. PN 54. "[F]rères pécheurs." See Romans 8:29.

68. C 65. "[N]e peut-elle pas dire en son nom, au nom de ses frères: Ayez pitié de nous Seigneur, car nous sommes de pauvres pécheurs."

69. Luke 18:13. In DE, August 12, 1897, she remarked to Pauline that at the confession during communion she had felt "comme le publicain, une grande pécheresse' ["like the publican, a great sinner"]. At that time she had, she says, shed tears of a perfect contrition but adds: "Ah! Comme il est bien impossible de se donner soi-même de tels sentiments! C'est le Saint-Esprit qui les donne, lui qui 'souffle où il veut.'" ["Oh, how really impossible it is to give such feelings to oneself! It's the Holy Spirit who does so, he that 'blows where he wishes.'"]

70. In her Constitution for the Carmels of Spain, Madre Teresa stipulated life imprisonment for any sister found guilty of apostasy.

71. A 45v. "[J]e résolus de me tenir en esprit au pied de [la] Croix pour recevoir la Divine rosée qui en découlait, comprenant qu'il me faudrait ensuite la répandre sur les âmes...." These words informed the statuary Thérèse for generations, save that instead of the "dew" she has been dispensing rose petals. It is curious that the otherwise thorough NEC editors do not connect this passage with Hebrews 12:24, in which Jesus is identified as mediator by the sprinkling of his blood. In A 45v, Thérèse is clearly assuming a median, i.e., priestly position

between the Cross and "souls" by sprinkling the blood she has gathered from the Cross.

72. C 6r. "[E]lle accepte de manger aussi longtemps que vous le voudrez le pain de la douleur et ne veut point se lever de cette table remplie d'amertume où mangent les pauvres pécheurs avant le jour que vous avez marqué...."
73. C 7r. "[P]auvres incrédules" and PA, 151 "les pires matérialistes."
74. C 6v. "'Tu rêves la lumière, une patrie embaumée des plus suaves perfums, tu rêves la possession *éternelle* du Créateur de toutes ces merveilles, tu crois sortir un jour des brouillards qui t'environnent, avance, avance, réjouis-toi de la mort qui te donnera non ce que tu espères, mais une nuit plus profonde encore, la nuit du néant.'"
75. RP 4, 4r. "[F]lambeau de la Foi" and C 12r "flambeau de la charité."
76. C 7r. "[L]a jouissance de la Foi" and "A chaque nouvelle occasion de combat, lorsque mes ennemis viennent me provoquer, je me conduis en brave, sachant que c'est une lâcheté de se battre en duel, je tourne le dos à mes adversaires sans daigner les regarder en face, mais je cours vers mon Jésus, je Lui dis être prête à verser jusqu'à la dernière goutte de mon sang pour confesser qu'il y a un Ciel." *Jouissance* denotes both the pleasure of something and its *possession*. Thérèse chooses her words carefully. The word *combat* occurs five times in A, never in B, and fourteen times in C.
77. A 51r. "[C]ontraire à la prudence humaine."
78. A 75v. "La *prudence humaine* au contraire tremble à chaque pas et n'ose pour ainsi poser le pied..." a remark inspired by *Imitatio Christi* III, 5:4. She concludes, however that even God made use of prudence by testing her when Uncle Isidore confounded Céline's proposal that Louis, incarcerated in the sanatorium in Caen, be allowed to attend Thérèse's profession of vows in September, 1890.
79. One of them is Pri 19, which was found marginal to a letter from about the time of C, "Mon Dieu, avec le secours de votre grâce je suis prête à verser tout mon sang pour affirmer ma foi." ["My God, with the help of your grace I am ready to shed all my blood to affirm my faith."]
80. Romans 4:18.
81. Galatians 2:20; cf. A 36r; PN 24, 29.
82. PO, 362. "[I]l ne faut pas juger du fond des âmes, que ces gens-là avaient reçu bien moins de grâces que nous, et qu'ils étaient plus malheureux que coupables." The testimony is dated December 12, 1910.
83. Pri 4. "Les blasphèmes des pécheurs ont retenti douloureusement à nos oreilles" The prayer is entitled "Hommage à la Très Sainte Trinité" and dates from February, 1894.
84. PN 17. "[C]'est essuyer ta Face / C'est obtenir des pécheurs le pardon / O Dieu d'Amour! Qu'ils rentrent dans ta grâce / Et qu'à jamais ils bénissent ton Nom.... Jusqu'à mon coeur retentit le blasphème / Pour l'effacer, je veux chanter toujours Ton Nom Sacré, je l'adore..."

85. *Fundaciones*, ed. Victor García de la Concha, (Madrid: Austral, 1991), 55: "esta miserable entre estas almas de ángeles."
86. Matthew 22:1–10 specifies that the host is a king whose son is getting married, so it is a royal wedding feast, but Luke 14:16–24 makes no mention of a wedding. The guests who decline to come are usually construed to be the Jews who refused Christ's ministry and summons. In Matthew, the quondam guests kill the servants sent to invite them, and the king orders soldiers out to kill the recusants. In Luke, there is no such violence, but the people brought in off the street are the abandoned: the poor, the lame, the blind.
87. C 7r. "[E]st-il une *joie* plus grande que celle de souffrir pour votre amour" and "pour l'éternité aux pauvres incrédules."
88. Such is the view of one of her most authoritative scholars, Claude Langlois, *Lettres à ma Mère bien-aimée*: 107. (See the bibliographical essay on this important text.)
89. These were the very words delivered at the Gregorian in Rome, November, 2003, on the fifth anniversary of Thérèse's elevation as doctor of the Church. The speaker characterized her childlike side as a "Tinkerbell." These remarks afford the most grotesque and distorted view of her on record.
90. There is a biblical sanction, in Luke 16:10, when Jesus warns, "He that is unjust in the least is unjust also in much."
91. Matthew 25:34–40.
92. Eventually she was too crippled to be ambulatory. She died in November 1895. The facts of her debilitation and her acute pain make the bizarrely comic dance closing this scene in the film by De Filippis astoundingly tasteless. (See Bibliography, Film.)
93. C 29r. "[J]e me mis à l'oeuvre et j'avais tant de bonne volonté que je réussis parfaitement."
94. Matthew 6:3, to which she had just alluded.
95. C 29v. "[U]n salon bien éclairé, tout brillant de dorures, des jeunes filles élégamment vêtues se faisant mutuellement des compliments" and 30r "le Seigneur l'illumina des rayons de la vérité qui surpassèrent tellement l'éclat ténébreux des fêtes de la terre que.je ne pouvais croire à mon bonheur."
96. C 14v. "[A]nimé d'un saint zèle."
97. "Celle qui sera accusée se garde bien d'en accuser une autre pour le seul soupçon qu'elle aura d'elle." ["She who shall be accused is to keep from accusing another sister out of the mere suspicion she has of her."], *RPC*: 200.
98. C 15r. "[]a *faiblesse* même...c'est en elle que je me glorifie et m'attends chaque jour à découvrir en moi de nouvelles imperfections."
99. Ibid. "[D]es fruits de ma victoire" and "laissant la soeur continuer son discours qui ressemblait aux imprécations de Camille contre Rome."
100. LT 147: "[D]épouille complètement les âmes qui Lui sont les plus chères. En se voyant dans une aussi grande pauvreté ces pauvres petites âmes ont peur il leur

semble qu'elles ne sont bonnes à rien puisqu'elles reçoivent tout des autres et ne peuvent rien donner, mais il n'en est pas ainsi l'*essence* de leur *être* travaille en secret *Jésus* forme en elles le germe qui doit se développer là haut dans les célestes jardins des Cieux" and "des instruments les plus *vils* afin de leur montrer que c'est bien Lui seul qui travaille."

101. CSG: 159.
102. Romans, chapter 6, passim; Ephesians: 4:21–24.
103. The Greek *ptokoi*, often translated "poor in spirit," should be rendered "beggars in spirit."
104. Godefroy Madelaine, however, testified at the apostolic hearing (August 31, 1917) that Thérèse believed herself damned and that was why she multiplied her acts of faith. PA, 559. She nowhere writes of her damnation nor can it be inferred from her words on a final nothingness, which is not the same thing.
105. C 6r. "[N]e veut point se lever de cette table avant de jour que vous avez marquee...."

APPENDIX 2

1. The first reference comes in LT 82, written in February 1889, to Céline. In that month their father was committed to the sanatorium in Caen, and Gonzague was re-elected prioress. Céline and Léonie had just moved to Caen to be near their father, but they were allowed to visit him for only thirty minutes each week. LT 82 is consolatory; the nightmare that all the Martin sisters were going through gave special force to Thérèse's words. The second reference came in LT 130, July 23, 1891, the day Céline declined a marriage proposal from a cousin, Henri de Maudelonde. Thérèse tactfully omits Teresa's dismissal of all those who are "greedy for their own pleasures" ("codiciosa de sus gustos") and lose everything of true worth for the sake of some wretched thing in front of them ("lo pierden todo por gozar de aquella miseria que ven presente").
2. For a helpful contrast of Augustine's conversion and Teresa's divine call, see Carol Slade, *St. Theresa of Avila: Author of a Heroic Life* (Berkeley: University of California Press, 1995), 34–38.
3. *Obras Completas*, ed. Maximiliano Herráiz (Salamanca: Sigueme, 1997), 1029: "puesta en cárcel tan penosa como esta mortalidad" ["set in so painful a cell as this mortality"]. All citations of the *Exclamaciones* are from this edition.
4. *Obras Completas*, 1044. "[L]a herida que habéis dado" and "tan bien empleado."
5. *Obras Completas*: on separation from God, 1030: "Cómo podré yo saber cierto que no estoy apartada de Vos?" and on the ending of divine favor to her, 1032: "Por ventura, Señor, tienen término vuestras grandezas o vuestras magnificas obras?"
6. *Obras Completas*, 1042. "[V]uestro divino rostro airado contra mí."
7. *Obras Completas*, 1035. "Pues, qué menester es mi amor?"
8. *Obras Completas*, 1031. "[C]uán olvidados se olvidan de sí."

9. *Obras Completas*: 1030. "Y así sus gozos se templan en ver que no gozan todos de aquel bien."
10. *Obras Completas*, 1038. "Oh, dureza de corazones humanos!"
11. *Obras Completas*, 1030. "Oh, Jesús mio! Cuán grande es el amor que tenéis a los hijos de los hombres, que el major servicio que se os puede hacer es dejaros a Vos por su amor y ganancia." It is odd that Teresa does not mention Jesus's identification of himself in the hungry, the sick, the imprisoned, Matthew 25: 35–40. In their spirits all nonbelievers are sick, hungry, and imprisoned.
12. Luke 10:40. This passage is among the few from the New Testament that Teresa expressly cites three times. In the *Camino* 15:7, she notes that Jesus defended Mary against both Simon the Pharisee and against Martha. (Teresa was victim to the long held notion that the sister of Martha and Lazarus was also Mary of Magdala and that Mary of Magdala was also the unnamed woman whose love Christ recognized when she anointed him for burial. This confusion played havoc for centuries, even beyond Thérèse's time.) In the *Moradas*, 7:1, 11 Teresa fantastically divides the Christian self into two, the suffering sensibility, which must put up with many daily travails and distractions ("tantos trabajos y ocupaciones"), and the soul itself, which in the last of the dwelling places of the interior castle can enjoy a singularly wonderful companionship with God. She says the suffering part of the self complains of the soul's bliss, as Martha complained of Mary.In one of her *Cuentas de conciencia*, however, she speaks of the soul's will being in union with God while the other faculties are freely working in God's service. "En fin, andan juntas Marta y María." This is the fifty-fourth of the *cuentas* according to the most recent redaction, which is by Maximilano Herráiz (see Chapter 1, Note 1). The BAC edition lists it as 58a. It dates from Sevilla, in the first months of 1576. This allusion amounts to a fourth reference to Martha and Mary.
13. It is odd that she never once alludes to Jesus's questioning and injunction to Peter, John 21:15ff., that if Peter loves him, he should feed Jesus's lambkins.
14. For a discussion of recent psychological interpretations, chiefly by Luce Irigaray and Julia Kristeva, see Carol Slade: 133–144.

A Selective Bibliography

I have chosen the entries of this bibliography chiefly for their pertinence to the theme of this book, Thérèse's life in Carmel as she passed deeper into the darkness of doubt. Some of the works listed omit or suppress the evidence of that doubt, and I have criticized them accordingly. Others illuminate it in imaginative or otherwise unexpected ways. This listing complements the selective bibliographical essays in my previous book, *Thérèse of Lisieux: God's Gentle Warrior*.

Biographical Studies

De Meester, Conrad, ed. *Saint Thérèse of Lisieux: Her Life, Times and Teaching*. Washington: Institute of Carmelite Studies, 1997.

The volume, sumptuously illustrated with color photographs of sites associated with Thérèse and including rare scenes within the Lisieux Carmel, abounds in invaluable data about Thérèse, both before and in Carmel. Brief, illuminating essays on her life and spirituality come from Carmelite scholar friars. Documentation about the Carmel includes brief portraits of all the sisters Thérèse knew in her nine conventual years, the daily regimen, and the informing Spanish tradition. Thérèse's writings, prosaic and poetic, are generously cited. A first-rate introduction to the Carmel and its most beloved saint, even though her darkness and her solidarity with atheists is underplayed.

Furlong, Monica. *Thérèse of Lisieux*, 1987; rpt., London: Darton, Longman and Todd, 2001.

This brief, smoothly written study bristles with objections to a life lived and sacrificed for an institution alleged to be unworthy of its victims: women. Furlong analogizes Catholic women to ante-bellum blacks: they understand Christian suffering far better than the masters purveying it. Following the lead of van der Meersch and Robo, and the psychologizing of Ida Görres (Louis is repeatedly called a depressive),

Furlong is especially critical of Gonzague for an apparently gratuitous cruelty toward Thérèse, and of the Martin sisters for infantilizing Thérèse for their own sake, even though they programmed her into a saint. Thérèse herself comes in for hard knocks: priggish, pompous, deluded, pathetic in her selfish extremism. Her ploys to get Céline to enter Carmel reveal Thérèse's "extraordinary egotism buried in the claims of self-abandonment.... The self-deception of this—the hidden will to power—is distasteful" (p. 94).

Furlong hauls in Nietzsche's notion of *ressentiment,* seeing Thérèse's working toward selflessness as only a coy inversion, the trick of heralding littleness and inconsequence as supreme values.

So vehement a book as this epitomizes a plaintiff not likely to leave court, a modern, professional woman who bitterly assails the negation of self required of women by an oppressive male hierarchism. It indicts the priestly establishment's approval of submissive, self-humbling figures like Thérèse, exemplary for playing this old game. Saintliness becomes collaborationism, the self-victim an eager partner to the oppressor. Yet Furlong hails Thérèse's ambition and her ability in making the most of her very little and inconsequent life within the Carmel's confines.

Furlong neglects completely the most substantial part of Thérèse's life, where her very real audacity was transmuted in the darkness of her last eighteen months. Thérèse's profound spiritual struggle, her discovery of Christianity as charity, her explicit solidarity with a wretched "secular" world—all of this remains absent from the discussion.

St. Thérèse of Lisieux by Those Who Knew Her. Edited and translated by Christopher O'Mahony. Dublin: Veritas, 1995.

First published in 1975, this volume selects testimony on Thérèse offered at the Procès informatif ordinaire. The PO was issued in a modern edition by the Teresianum in Rome, 1973. Of the forty-four witnesses, O'Mahony has chosen fifteen: her natural sisters, her novices, people from her school days, Godefroy Madelaine (co-editor of the *Histoire d'une âme*) and a few others. Beyond hallowing remarks on Thérèse's life, words, and character, some lively details make this book a curious read: Pauline on the correspondence of the first cultists, published annually as "Pluie de roses," and the sales records of the *Histoire*; Marie's claim to have been first to speak of "la petite voie" (Thérèse first speaks of it on June 4, 1897); Céline's portrayal, turning Thérèse into a wind-up doll; many disparagements of Gonzague (pp. 31, 54, 75, 119, 142, 159, 163, 195); the sparagmos of secondary relics. And the enthusiast Céline quotes (p. 164) in explaining Thérèse's exceptional appeal: at last, a truly likable saint, imitable, not ascetic, not forbidding.

This volume is instructive in a negative way: the testimonies cheat Thérèse's darkness and thus give a misleading view of the depth that her spirituality attained. One of the PO's witnesses, not included here, Sr. Thérèse de Saint-Augustine, later wrote that Thérèse confessed her non-belief to her.

Scallan, Dorothy. *The Whole World Will Love Me: The Life of St. Thérèse of the Child Jesus and of the Holy Face (1873–1897)*. Rockford, IL: Tan Books, 2005.

A reprint of a 1954 study, this book presents the Sacred Heart view of Thérèse as filtered, fictively, through Pauline and especially Marie du Sacre-Coeur. The centerpiece of this effort lies on pp. 240–250, in which these two sisters discuss Pauline's election as prioress. Pauline relates Jesus's speaking to her from the Holy Face in vituperative accents, a model of vengefulness: "For, you see, this singular tragedy of being thrown over and discarded while the mediocre and faulty and envious triumphing over Me were preferred above Me, was my bitter lot in life" (p. 248).

What appalls in this atrabilious attempt at a biography is its new life fifty years on: there is still a readership for the *Histoire d'une âme*, the doctored version of which did not give us Thérèse in her own words. The undoctored texts finally came to light just two years later, in 1956, but the re-issue of this book means that for some, the real Thérèse might just as well have stayed hidden.

Contrary to what this book asserts, nowhere does Thérèse speak of entering Carmel in order to do penance; she entered Carmel out of love for Jesus and in order to pray for priests. Yet on pages 304–305 we find this grotesque distortion of Thérèse's prayer at the table of sinners in C 6r: "she asks pardon for her unbelieving brothers.... in the name of her guilty brethren." These misleading phrases are straight out of the *Histoire*. Pauline was attributing to Thérèse the old model of condescension, that of the Christian looking down in solicitous pity upon souls in darkness. That position is exactly the one Thérèse does *not* assume.

Reparationism, the vault key of Sacred Heart ideology in those days, is altogether foreign to "the little way" of a trusting love for a merciful God. The title derives from a quote of dubious authenticity from the *Novissima Verba*, that on rereading her manuscript Thérèse sighed, "Ah! Je le sais bien, tout le monde m'aimera..." This outburst, perhaps meant ironically, comports ill with other remarks on herself, even at her most feverish.

The Bible

La Bible avec Thérèse de Lisieux. Paris: Editions du Cerf, 1979.

This book, edited by an archivist in the Carmel of Lisieux, Sr. Cécile, is intended as a book of meditation and reference. It identifies by title, chapter, verse and within canonical sequence all of the passages from both Old and New Testaments that Thérèse quoted (often from memory) or alluded to in her writings. Under each entry is the pertinent passage and an indication of its source. The citations are unadorned, but there is a helpful introduction by Msgr. Guy Gaucher, who establishes the nexus between Thérèse's understanding of the Bible, her taking it for meditation and as nourishment, and her sense of a universal mission through it.

A book-length study of Thérèse and the Bible remains one of the chief desiderata of Theresian scholarship. *La Bible avec Thérèse* provides the indispensable first step toward understanding Thérèse as a writer. Unfortunately, handy as such a book as this proves, it is unlikely to receive an English translation.

Courtès, Joseph. "Les citations bibliques dans la Correspondance de Thérèse de Lisieux." Revue d'ascetique et de mystique 44 (1968): 63–85.

Courtès reviews each gospel's frequency (low for Mark, high for John) and notes what Thérèse conspicuously omits: miracles Jesus performs and parables he gives. The conclusion from the absence of miracles, that Thérèse's spirituality is not one of the extraordinary but of the daily, seems dubious: how, then, to explain the peculiar slighting of the parables, which are drawn precisely from daily life? Also, it cannot be assumed that texts Thérèse does not cite were of little or no importance to her; silence might cue further probing, a door ajar rather than closed, as I have indicated in this study.

Of certain interest to any reader of Thérèse is her frequent transposition, recasting a biblical line so as to implicate her reader, as in John 14:3, "Jesus has gone ahead to prepare a place for us." All of Thérèse's readings of scripture hold this appropriative force; for her the Bible, so far as she knew it (very little, as was the case in her time), was consistently a living source, far more a kind of dramatic script than an occasion for study or even meditation, as my book but not this essay reveals.

Courtès, Joseph. "Les citations scripturaires dans les Manuscrits Autobiographiques de Thérèse de Lisieux." Revue d'ascetique et de mystique 44 (1968): 217–231.

Complementing the study cited above, this one comes to many of the same conclusions: Thérèse drew most of her New Testament citations from the *Manuel du chrétien* and those of the Old Testament from the Maistre de Sacy; she called upon memory for short passages, often cited in several instances, and transcribed longer ones directly from the texts; she lacks references to such central matters as the workings of the Holy Spirit, the miracles, even the Virgin; she had no apparent interest in Israelite history, in the messianic hope of Jews, in eschatology.

Most pertinent to the present study is the discussion of C and how from God's love and the sinful, suffering condition of humanity, fraternal love emerges with resounding point. The frequency of this theme substantiates her claim to have discovered what charity means. In tandem with it comes an attention to prayer, its source, its effects and Christ's exemplifications of it. What matters finally is his instruction to her (and us), so the gospels have immediate bearing in present life. As Courtès notes at the close, it was not her intent to "know" the scriptures but to live them.

Grellier, Jean. *Manuel du chrétien: Bible de Thérèse de Lisieux*, 2001. Unpublished document in the Archives du Carmel, Lisieux.

This meticulous forty-one page effort lists biblical citations by Thérèse in parallel with the translations of the Hebrew and Greek in the *Manuel du chrétien*, in the 1864 edition that Thérèse used, a volume she had with her daily. Grellier provides succinct analytical summaries, including statistical tables. We learn, for example, that Céline received the overwhelming number of biblical citations: ninety in thirty-three of the sixty-one letters to her.

Grellier delves into Thérèse's motivations for altering the texts. One instance: John 15:13, "to give one's life for one's friends" becomes "to give one's life for those one loves." She knew, remarks Grellier, that friendship means reciprocity, but Jesus died as well for those who did not love him. That is an essential point for understanding the importance of Ms C.

Finally, he discusses the *Manuel*'s inclusion of the *Imitatio Christi*, a work Thérèse had memorized from the translation by Lamennais before she entered the Carmel. In at least twenty instances she drew upon her memory rather than upon the text to hand. Thus as a writer she enjoyed the use of substantial internal reference.

Special Aids

Les Cahiers d'école de Thérèse de Lisieux 1877–1888. Paris: Cerf, 2008.

With an introduction and notes by Guy Gaucher, this hefty volume of 655 pages gives us a complete collection of Thérèse's school writings: her exercises in calligraphy, arithmetical calculations, cartography, dictations, and creative writing. Her prose is gratifyingly abundant in misspellings and accentual faults, all left intact in the printing. Here, we find not a saint but a robust and industriously ordinary girl.

This book is invaluable in its own right as a documentation of how a Catholic girl in France would have been prepared (for domesticity) during the first generation of the Third Republic. This is a gold mine for anyone interested in the history of primary education. Gaucher provides a twenty-two page survey of Thérèse's Abbaye Notre-Dame-du-Pré, the Benedictine school that she attended from October 1881 to March 1886 and her subsequent private tutelage under Mme. Papinau. There is substantial testimony from participants at the beatification hearings and Carmel scholars on those trying years of timidity and withdrawal, the secret lot of a very young life. The anxieties that brought Thérèse to face her doubt began here.

In sum, this is an extraordinary archival rescue of permanent value.

Manuscrits Autobiographiques. Lisieux: Office Central de Lisieux, 1956.

This facsimile edition of the three manuscripts affords an invaluable opportunity to study Thérèse literally at first hand. Her writing, mercifully, is most of the time calligraphic, accessible, and attractive, and all the more amazing in that she wrote late in the Carmelite evening and only from 8 to 9 P.M., seated on a very low stool and bent over her *écritoire*. She was able to marshal her thoughts and guide her narrative, tired though as she was at day's end, chilled in the dark months of every year, and exhausted by fever in the time of C. The facsimile of B is much harder to read as Thérèse wrote on note paper supplied for her in retreat; the script is small and cramped.

Her emphases, occasional rewriting (the original dedication of Manuscript A was to Marie de Gonzague, not to Pauline), phrasing squeezed at a line's end, tantalizing erasures, italicization of biblical quotes by slanting characters to the right, carets—all are worth scrutiny. Accompanying the facsimile is a volume of excellent, detailed notes by one of her foremost enthusiasts of the last century, Père François de Sainte-Marie.

The Archives du Carmel at Lisieux have photocopies of all of Thérèse's writings, ample testaments to my claims for her standing as a writer.

Les Mots de Sainte Thérèse de l'Enfant-Jésus et de la Sainte-Face: Concordance générale. Paris: Éditions du CERF, 1996.

To approach Thérèse with any seriousness, one must have a good working access to her in her own language. One indispensable route is this 960-page concordance, a marvel unto itself that can be read with pleasure and instruction. Each word's entry is listed according to its precisely cited occurrence in the autobiographical works, letters, poems, plays, and prayers. There is a supplementary concordance for the *Derniers Entretiens*. At the end of extensively recurrent words comes a numerical summary, with distributions among the different works. We learn that Thérèse refers to God 895 times; to Jesus nearly twice that number: 1,616. But in the *Entretiens*, she speaks to Pauline of Jesus only 25 times; of God, mostly *le bon Dieu*, 228 times. Key words unfold like archaeological strata: *caché* with 212; *joie* at 311 beats out *bonheur* at 238; *souffrir* with 228 but 704 for *aimer*. *Hating* occurs only thrice: once in a biblical quotation and twice from the devils in Thérèse's seventh play.

To the extent that our word frequencies, written and spoken, say much about who we are, this massive volume provides one of the best and truly reliable portraits of Thérèse. It has been a consistently valuable and instructive aid to this study.

The Photo Album of St. Thérèse of Lisieux. Allen, Texas: Christian Classics, 1997.

This work first appeared from the Office Central de Lisieux in 1961, with a commentary and an insightful, informative introduction by François de Sainte-Marie. The translation comes from another Carmel friar, Peter-Thomas Rohrbach.

Here is an invaluable opportunity to look upon the Thérèse not provided in the hallowing painted portraits, which the photographer herself, Céline, began shortly after her sister's death. A painting was long assumed to capture through artistry the genuine self masked by the ordinary one. But I argue that it is the ordinary Thérèse who counts, as these photographs register subtle differences in mood and occasion. There are the collective scenes of virtually the entire community (absent the terribly shy Sr. St. Jean de la Croix), scenes of the natural sisters with or without Gonzague, gatherings with the novices, sometimes huddled together in the communal whole, and solos. The last summer's photos include the three striking poses of June 7, 1897, and the very last picture of Thérèse alive, recumbent in her father's *voiture* just outside of the Carmel's infirmary. Most haunting of all is the photo of Thérèse in her signature role, scattering flower petals by the cross that stands in the cloister's courtyard. It is blurred, and her closed eyes give her face the aspect of a death mask. It seems the very emblem of her darkness. (See Chapter 5, Fig. 5.4.)

The sisters were not allowed to have any photographs in their cells but could consult the Carmel's holdings during recreations. How very much more fortunate are we in being able to have at leisure these documentary glances into the Carmel's well tended silences. And what a mercy that Pauline, then prioress, allowed her sister to violate a cardinal rule of the order by bringing with her in that autumn of 1894 the vanity of a quite private piece of property.

For anyone seriously interested in Thérèse and in the Carmel of her time, this book should be considered invaluable.

Pluie de Roses: Interventions de Sr Thérèse de l'Enfant Jésus pendant la guerre. Lisieux: 1920.

This curious and rare little volume of 235 pages says much about Thérèse's populist appeal. It came in a series of annually published testimonies about her miraculous effects upon ordinary people's lives: sudden healings and cures, conversions of the impious, apparitions. These accounts were gathered at the Carmel of Lisieux. *Pluie de Roses* had been serving as a chronicle of an upsurgent folk Catholicism and tacitly as its makeshift propaganda on behalf of Thérèse's beatification and canonization.

Interventions was a special issue of the *Pluies*, composed of letters from soldiers, officers, and their relatives, and a few religious, within the crucible of the First World War. The Carmel included disclaimers: first, that the correspondents' use of words such as *miracle, sainte, vision* were printed "without the intention of advancing or prejudicing the decision of the Church," which was then reviewing the testimonies of the apostolic hearings (March 1915 to August 1917); second, that the narratives had not been confirmed "scientifically or canonically," yet served to show "how general is the trust *(confiance)* of the faithful in the intercession" of Thérèse.

Thérèse is always denominated by half, Soeur Thérèse de l'Enfant Jésus, as though Christ's unmitigated suffering under the greatest military machine of antiquity, a suffering for which *la Sainte-Face* was emblem, somehow did not register on the pious wartime consciousness.

Amid pious effusions one might feel churlish in weighing in the other scale the ongoing barbarity of martial violence; the unbridled, shameless profiteering of a few at the bloody expense of many; the total absence in these pages of any genuinely Christian response via Thérèse to the grand obscenity of arrogant chauvinism that finds ways in every generation to open its maw and bellow against the appeal of charity, which is the real heart and pulse of her spirituality. Let's put it simply: what did "the little way" have to do with despising and killing "the bosch"?

Prières au Carmel de Lisieux au temps de soeur Thérèse, VT 131 (July–September, 1993): 191–205.

This collection of three "annexes," originally meant for inclusion with the prayers of Thérèse published in 1988, offers an invaluable inventory of *feuillets* or leaflets of prayers by various hands, all known to Thérèse during her nine years at the Carmel. She makes it clear in her autobiography (C, 25r) that the abundance of such prayers caused her head to ache; besides, she preferred to improvise her own, orally and in writing. Nonetheless, such texts as the prayer misattributed to Thomas Aquinas and the eucharistic prayer of Thérèse Durnerin, both printed here in full, intriguingly anticipate some of Thérèse's rhetoric.

This review also includes the "rhythms" of daily prayers at the Carmel in her time, a kind of anatomy of each day, from the rising and dressing attended by a sequence of prayers set out in the *Direction spirituelle* to the ninth hour in the evening, when each sister examined her conscience over the course of the day. A third section identifies the prayers for various occasions: for the deceased, for processions, for the renewal of vows, even to such particulars as the *Ave Maria*, which a sister recited whenever she was called to the *parloir* to receive, veiled and through the grill, a visitor from the world. Last, a list of her father's collection of books in which Thérèse could find prayers: of the eleven cited, only one was published before she was born. One was home-made, the flower book Pauline composed for her little sister's daily use in preparing for First Communion.

Ancillary as these works might seem, they serve to frame the lexical and semantic world in which she grew up. A conscientious biographer of Thérèse will find an abundance of texts for a thorough rummaging, an undoubtedly helpful and possibly revelatory avenue toward his subject or hers.

Sainte Thérèse de Lisieux: La vie en images. Paris: Éditions du CERF, 1995.

This 500-page collection of devotional cards, compiled with accompanying texts by Pierre Descouvement and Helmuth Nils Loose, reflects acutely well the temper of Catholicism in the last generation of nineteenth-century France. The cards represent a period art, which seems in some instances sickly, if not repellent. But while its aesthetic value is debatable, each card meant something to its recipient, Thérèse. Many were given to her by her natural and spiritual sisters, clearly self-identified on the backs; others, by fellow Benedictine school girls.

Many confections by Thérèse herself are included, such as her paintings (and statues she painted at Carmel), her charming early sketches when she was on holiday, and tableaux by Céline. I for one find Thérèse's attempts at painting l'Enfant Jésus and angelic hosts a ghastly business. The same holds for Céline's disastrous portraits of her sister made after 1897, any and all of which are confounded by her own photographic efforts. Why bother with paint and plaster when the photos bring us, if only in the fraction of a minute, to the insuperable varieties of fact?

The Carmel and the Church

Caprioli, Mario. "I Papi del Secolo XX e S. Teresa di Lisieux." Teresianum 46, no.2 (1995): 323–362.

Appearing three years before Thérèse was proclaimed Doctor of the Church (October 1998), this essay seems to be preparing for the event, but Caprioli was duly vague about the prospects. The mathematics more than adds up, however, as he reviews with documentary precision the response of each pope after Leo XIII to Thérèse's transcultural status. More appealing than the colloquies and other formal occasions for hailing "l'infanzia spirituale" are the personal responses that individuate each of the pontiffs. It is well known that Pius XI regarded the canonization as the gem of his seventeen-year papacy, but less well known that he privately invoked "la mia piccola santa" when in a dispute with Mussolini's regime. John XXIII, when a nuncio in Paris, made two official visits to Lisieux and three more incognito. John Paul I remembered her valor in facing tuberculosis, a disease which afflicted his adolescence with fear.

The popes' formal appreciations are not mere repetitions of each other. Benedict XV's promulgation of the decree on her heroism, August 2, 1921, is exemplary; he augurs that her saintliness shall be hidden from no one, a nice turn. Pius XI supplies one of the hidden motivations for her canonization, that her simplicity and purity were antidotes to an epoch of "tanta impurità di vita, di tanta insolenza di sensualità" (p. 330). And Pius XII makes a surprising defense of "spiritual infancy," showing that it could be misconstrued as a kind of reverse elitism, closed off to those who have the burdens of prudence and responsibility. (The term has since been deemed anachronistic.) For this pope it was a valuable post-war alternative to "the harm of 'activism'" (il danno dell' "attivismo").

Gaucher, Guy. *Jean et Thérèse: Flammes d'Amour.* Paris: Cerf, 1996.

This closely drawn, modest yet precise study reviews all of the passages of Juan de la Cruz to which Thérèse alludes. It underscores by documentation this central influence upon her spiritual development: although her study of Juan was intense in her early years at Carmel, it continued to the end of her life, despite her claim that only the gospels mattered to her by then. Her debt to Juan's *Llama de amor viva* and his *Cantico* informed her instruction of fellow novices.

Gaucher includes translations of Juan's maxims, another work to which she had access. He observes that in their many references to faith they provide a theology of this virtue. Is there some irony in this special attention, given that Juan's conception of love, the greatest of the theological virtues, was what really mattered to Thérèse? He also gives a chapter to hope as a complement to poverty: one who has all is no longer hoping. True: hope, like faith, is an anticipatory virtue, but was not Thérèse already rock-solid in her trust in God's love? In the end, as this book shows, it was love that counted for her.

Paul-Marie of the Cross, OCD. *Carmelite Spirituality in the Teresian Tradition.* Washington, DC: 1959; rpt. Institute of Carmelite Studies, 1997.

This brief, lucid introduction to the spirituality of Carmel is especially helpful in drawing implicitly the contrast between, on one hand, the high-flying Hispanic mystics of the sixteenth century, Teresa and Juan, and on the other, the unaccomplished

Thérèse of Lisieux. Outwardly, they share the postulates of a "a dark faith," that truth can be apprehended only in shadows, as well as of a hope that does not and cannot possess its object (else it would not be hope), but for the Hispanic masters such darkness means the void of all images and representations; they are not commensurate with the tunnel, vault, fog that Thérèse writes of. Indeed, when Fr. Paul-Marie comes round to her, he resorts to a fragrant, flowery rhetoric about her, "truly universal because her spirit is truly Catholic" (p. 68). He says nothing about her definitive *épreuve*.

Fr. Paul-Marie's discussion of "infused contemplation," a stage higher than the intellectuality of meditation, indicates the staggering athleticism of noneffort that is required for God's work upon the soul. The very language seems to belong to a realm far distant from the piteous, distracted world that Thérèse discovered as the terminus of her darkness. Yet Fr. Paul-Marie has assimilated convincingly the mystical sensibility of five hundred years ago.

Williams, Rowan. *Teresa of Avila*, Harrisburg, PA: Morehouse Publishing Co., 1991.

This brief, dense study by the Lady Margaret Professor of Theology at Oxford at the time of this writing and currently Archbishop of Canterbury, abounds in insights and caveats. On the *Vida*: "it is brilliant and clear as individual phenomenology; strained and muddled as a structural map of Christian growth" (p. 69). The *Camino* he finds mischievous and almost conspiratorial in its wit as Teresa has moved past the certification of orthodoxy for the male authorities.

Williams warns readers off of tendentious readings of feminism and other modern agendas for approaching Teresa's writings. Yet he fairly acknowledges her audacities, as in her taking the Lord's Prayer as a prayer for death. And there is her bold claim of authority in teaching the Bible when she meditates on *The Song of Songs*. But Williams also iterates Teresa's many cautions on contemplative life, the hazards of private religiosities and the self-absorptions passing as raptures. As to her foes in the faith, he frankly states that she had no real grasp of the Reformation. He acknowledges her marginal due as a Jew.

Perhaps most valuable is Williams' steady walk through the brilliantly devious and confusing maze of the *Castillo*, mansion by mansion: the challenges of self-regard, the intensification of conflicts and fears within oneself, the false zeal for improving others, the restless awareness of the ordinary life and its duties, the distress over worldly rejections of God—Christ himself longed to be free of the sinful world—and, not least, the Christian's "persistent vulnerability to conflict, trial and pain" (p. 137).

Some may find more profit in his discussion of mysticism and its gnarls. If it is "the whole movement of the soul toward Christlikeness" (p. 147), we need not follow what Williams felicitously calls "a schema of psychic adventure" (p. 148). Besides, Teresa teaches that the divine love we seek inevitably sends us back into the world and to our place in Christian community, even as Thérèse's love took her into the world's darkness.

Darkness and the Temptation Against Love

Cesbron, Gilbert. *Briser la Statue*. Paris: Robert Laffont, 1952.

This three-act play was premiered in Paris on December 19, 1947. Cesbron, a prolific author of prize-winning novels and plays, was only thirty-four years old. The first and third acts draw substantially on Thérèse's writings and testimony about her. The titular "breaking of the statue" is the intent of this drama, to reveal Thérèse in her human lineaments and in unexpected ways.

The play begins with a priest sparring gently with a couple of "intellectuals" sickened by what Claudel called "the Thérèse industry." The priest brings them to the autobiography, then available only in Pauline's palimpsest. "What was thought to be syrup was blood," he says.

Two intriguing scenes: Thérèse is tempted by a double of herself, a complacent "fulfilled" Madame Thérèse who has settled into a comfortable bourgeois ambiance, married and bringing a child with her. She charges Sr. Thérèse with futility and vanity for choosing the Carmel. Then a phantom Louis reproaches her for deserting him, but Thérèse identifies all the false notes he sounds; a phantom Céline reproaches her with ignorance of how much the novices truly suffer without her knowing it.

About the table of *douleur* and her understanding that there are those who suffer without faith and hope, Cesbron's Thérèse adds these luminous words: "But what does *understand* mean? I had to *live* their life." She parries with Satan, embarrassing him with the question, If there's no eternal life, why are you here? The devil's last ploy is to accuse her of imposture toward the novices, of posing as one for whom the veil of faith is all but rent when in fact she is up against a vault sealing her off from heaven.

A thoughtful cinematic production could be very effective in portraying the plaintiff as well as defendant views of this saint.

Fitzgerald, Constance. "Impasse and Dark Night." In *Living with Apocalypse*. Edited by Telden Edwards, 93–116. New York: Harper and Row, 1984.

The author, a Carmelite sister, provides an anatomy of spiritual darkness according to San Juan de la Cruz. She notes that the impasse of total helplessness that deprives one's life of joy and purpose can also consume its victim by a defensive apathy. But if one can accept "the sorrow of finitude" (p. 96) and give up the fetish of control, that is, preoccupations of self, then with a willing surrender to "the unknown, the uncontrolled and unpredictable paths of life," the soul can reach "affective redemption," by which Sister Constance means the ripening of love's vulnerability. She means a love that is unstintingly serving God and others, an expending that, as Thérèse once put it, is not concerned with bank balances. In challenging the desire to project one's own notions of God onto divine mystery, Sister Constance underscores the transfiguring power latent in being powerless and broken. In place of comforting re-assurances and affirmations, one must accept weakness and aloneness. Job had to do so and so did Thérèse.

Sister Constance carries the dark night from the personal to the cultural. All of her strictures regarding the selfish concerns of control and dominance have painful relevance. The antidotes she prescribes are prayer and contemplation, but she asks, "Do we really expect anything at all of the contemplative process of prayer in our world today?" (p. 107).

The concluding portion of this essay, "Feminine Impasse," complements the other two: experiencing God in one's impasse may allow a transformation of the heretofore overwhelmingly masculine language and imaging by which we conceive of God, not to serve feminist ideologies but to hand over to the divine spirit the powerlessness that women in most cultures have suffered. What would Thérèse have said to that?

Guillet, Louis. *Gethsémani: Sainte Thérèse, l'amour crucifiée*. Lisieux: Office Central de Lisieux, 1979.

The first part of this book discusses the gospel texts on Christ's agony in the Garden. The second is devoted to themes in Thérèse's writings establishing that her temptation against faith was a kind of agony, an imitation of Christ. Guillet marshals an imposing number of references from the letters and manuscripts into a lifelong progression toward the final darkness.

He poses a problem between Thérèse and Juan de la Cruz, based upon Juan's view that Christ even in the Garden, isolated and menaced, "enjoyed the *délices* of the Holy Trinity" (*délice* denotes voluptuousness). He acknowledges that Thérèse's *joie* in the midst of suffering, both physical and spiritual, had no such *délice*, but he argues that her eerie calm and equanimity were transcendent. Unfortunately, Guillet does not cite Juan's texts and their numbered passages, only page numbers from a French translation. As to the *joie* itself, we are up against two mysteries: first is the perspective afforded only to a dying person, someone learning detachment from banal and selfish concerns; second is the peace Christ offers, "not as the world gives."

One cavil is that Guillet isolates Thérèse from her community; to the end she was attentive to the world she was leaving. Further, she had always fought valiantly against the subtleties of self and would have recoiled from what is at the center of Jesus's agony, the contest between his own will to flee from an imminent death and God's will that he face it. Thérèse's agony sets her between her lifelong love of God and the temptation to give in to an engulfing darkness of meaninglessness. She knew she was perilously close to blaspheming. Guillet cheats us and her of these terrible moments.

Langlois, Claude. *Lettres à ma Mère bien-aimée, juin 1897: Lecture du Manuscrit C de Thérèse de Lisieux*, Paris: Cerf, 2007.

The distinguished historian of modern French Catholicism and the author of three other books on Thérèse resumes his nimble sleuthing in a 400-page inquiry into C, 60 pages of which reproduce its entire text. Langlois is not providing a commentary, a task sufficiently mediated by the NEC editors, but rendering the text problematic. He poses many questions, often leaving them in the air but only after drawing them out from the ambiguities of Thérèse's writing. As the title indicates, he conveniently apportions the manuscript into a series of "letters," each sent daily to Gonzague, with a total of twenty-seven between June 3 and July 1, 1897. Within those dates he identifies the major topics as the new way of saintliness; the temptation against faith; foreign missions; brotherly love; the directing of the novices; and divine mercies. He gives substantial attention to the unhappy politics of Gonzague and Pauline, arguing that the elderly prioress had informed perceptions of Thérèse's maturity, as Pauline did not.

Drily procedural as this presentation may seem, Langlois surprises repeatedly with fresh angles and insights. He does not hesitate to criticize Thérèse, as in what he finds the pharisaism of her vaunting over her sisters in need and even at the table of sorrow. He is consistently attentive to Thérèse's tones and tactics as a writer, her coyness, her evasiveness, her peremptory way of what he calls "auto-legitimation," her adroitness in writing what she herself may not wholly have believed. She emerges as a far more complex and engaging figure than any hagiography could afford, and that is a genuine service to her and no less to her cultists. This is an indispensable book for specialists but even "general" readers will find it engrossing.

Martini, Carlo Maria. *Nel Dramma della Incredulità con Teresa di Lisieux*. Milan: Ancora, 1997.

The Milanese cardinal took 150 priests from his diocese to Lisieux in February, 1997, there to confront unbelief, especially as it besets Christians, including priests. Martini addresses "l'offuscamento della speranza nella vita eterna" (p. 37), "the obscuring of hope in eternal life" as the key issue of modern Christianity. The present age is not strictly atheistic but bewildered and confused. Believers prefer not to talk of an afterlife, as though biological limits suffice to define the good life and its aspirations. Pressed, even clerics speak only of the need to trust in God.

Martini discusses Thérèse's "little way" in two aspects: (1) the *pars destruens* goes beyond trust in human efficacy, including the presumption in merits as a way to attain heaven; Martini uses the delightful word, "smantellamento" (p. 39) a dismantling of glorious certainties and observed pieties, the steady diet of faith and hope; (2) the *pars construens* signifies that the way of love lies in fragility and weakness, in an absolute trust in God (Martini uses the Lutheran term, *fiducia*, rather than the credal *assensus*), a forgetting of self, and a loving of God that seeks to make God loved. This is the Theresian mission.

Martini dwells on the paradox that out of negativity comes a great positive. His two examples: first, from Thérèse's testing, her night, her suffering came "l'irradiazione della fede stessa" (p. 73), the astounding mass movement in response to her, a loving that persisted through and despite a century of spiritual indifference. Then, from Mark

6:1–6, the incredulity, resistance, and prejudice Jesus faces in his own homeland does not lead him to despair. He marveled at the lack of faith reflected in the suspicious and punitive questions put to him but he went on and preached in other villages. Martini reads the Christmas "conversion" of Thérèse in comparable terms: she met the weary disdain her father expressed and made from it a positive change in her life. At the close he prays, Let us ask for the grace to accept and live with contrariety.

Poupard, Paul. "Sainte Thérèse de l'Enfant-Jésus, docteur de l'Amour et le monde de l'incroyance." VT 122 (April-June, 1991): 69–83.

As president of the Pontifical Council for dialogue with nonbelievers, Cardinal Poupard addresses Thérèse's contribution to that effort, which he identifies as a sacrificial love extended to the many moderns indifferent to divinity or denying God altogether. He claims that people are more desperate than ever to find reasons for living. Does Thérèse speak to them?

Reviewing her late poems and the *entretiens* of 1897, he quotes generously. However, he falls into the common practice of making inferences with language that Thérèse herself does not use. For instance, her love for Jesus "sustains her hope and makes it invincible" (p. 75). Disbelief prompted in her "an interrogation, not a destruction of her faith" (p.79). Her famous last words to God, when the tubercular toxins were terminal, he glosses thus: "Thérèse passed the decisive stage (*étape*), that of faith vivified by love, which crowns hope." This is pre-emptive triumphalism, padding the love she herself says was all that was left her, with the very things that the darkness took, else it would not have been darkness. Better to admit the groping toward mystery, that Thérèse's perspective, her experience remains elusive.

The cardinal celebrates her as God's chosen to face the most radical degree of *incroyance*, she an insignificant creature far from the ideological and cultural whirls of her day and yet made to confront their negations of God. He may be right to claim that only love can break down the walls of atheism, a love crucified and immolated. He echoes Balthasar's point, that only love is worthy of our trust. It does not follow that such a message will resound with the weary or cynical, the dyspeptic or indifferent to whom it is addressed.

Valabek, Redento Maria. "Desiderare la sofferenza: La 'piccola via' di Teresa di Lisieux," Roseti del Carmelo 31, no, 3 (September-December, 1978): 65–75.

This essay on the darkness is refreshingly free of cosmetics or extenuations. The phrasing is stark from the first. Fr. Valabek, a Carmelite, asks how can we, in an age preoccupied with the elimination of every kind of suffering, consider as other than mentally deranged someone who believed a life free of suffering would be insupportable? Like every saint, Thérèse teaches that a Christian's participation in the paschal mystery of Christ means participation in his passion and death.

He cites the roles of Pichon and Sr. Marie des Anges in enforcing upon Thérèse the coherence of loving and suffering, but stresses that what they meant was a suffering that comes from God, not from below. Even so, "people of our time might identify themselves with this young woman, immersed on her death bed in the thickest spiritual darkness, unheard in her prayers, and to whom everything seemed to run contrary to what she had desired" (p. 68). Could they accept as she did that a wholly dark night, "the spiritual void" (*vuoto*) she experienced was in fact a manifestation of divine grace? That is what she realized and that is why she embraced it.

Vasciaveo, Chiara. "Contemplativi per la condivisione: Teresa di Lisieux." Presenza del Carmelo 55 (September-December, 1991): 79–84.

As bracing as the preceding essay, this one poses the darkness in Pascalian terms. At the table, Thérèse was between doubt and the wager (*scommesa*) on the reality of faith, its promise, and its logic. Vasciaveo contends that contrary to all mysticism, the Theresian journey brought her to the threshold of despair but also to a far greater vision than anything she had experienced before, namely that "To love God means to discover the beloved, which means that nothing and no one can be excluded from such love, be it even by the scandal of the cross, of sin, of indifference, of suffering, of death" (p. 83). To complement such a sweeping view, this superb little essay notes what usually goes unsaid, that at her life's end Thérèse's view of sinners changed, that she no longer wished to become a saint in order to save them. It sufficed her to realize that she was their poor sister, that she was "fascinated amid her brethren by the lowly prayer of the publican and the example of Mary Magdalene" (p. 84).

Thérèse, Theologian and Doctor

Bro, Bernard. "De L'Histoire d'une âme au Doctorat," VT 155 (July-September, 1999): 22–68.

The eminent Dominican writer on Thérèse here undertakes to lay out a theological understanding of her. He carefully reviews the strata of different ways of reading her (historico-critical, sociological and psychological, contextual—the latter including feminism); next, these readings vis-à-vis major theological developments of the twentieth century; then, her originality relative to the other Doctors of the Church; last, a listing of agenda, issues concerning her that need further exploration and development.

Bro insists that she counts as more than a guide for "second-class Christians" wary of theology. Like Pope John Paul II, he sees the theology of Juan de la Cruz as accessible to every Christian, and his interweaving of Thérèse's texts with those of Juan and especially of Thomas Aquinas does substantial service toward this democratization of the great teachers. As Thérèse has become a Doctor of the Church, why should not the formidably mediaeval Doctors be as approachable as she is?

Bro says she conjoins the three tasks of theology: "the purification of ideas, symbols and concepts so that they be worthy of God and yet not diminish mystery; the demonstration of connections among the mysteries; the introduction of a new order of existence which implicates the sharing of divine life" (p. 47). Daunting as all that may sound, he weighs much upon Thérèse's simplicity, yet "she has the power of an Augustine, the analytical acuity of an Aquinas, the linguistic genius of a François de Sales, but a simplicity sustained by the synthetic intuition of a feminine grace" (p. 51).

DeMeester, Conrad. "Thérèse de Lisieux et son désir de 'Faire du bien.'" Teresianum 49, no. 1 (1998): 3–50.

This look at Thérèse's self-appointed mission post mortem privileges Ms B, perhaps unduly. There can be no doubt that the begetting of souls, *enfanter*, was at the heart of Thérèse's mission as she conceived it in September 1896. But as she had identified well before that time the role of one's *suffering* in that begetting, was she not more apt for the role when she was locating herself with atheists at the table of sorrow, in June 1897? There she is no longer a mother of souls but a sister, demoted to a final helplessness. Only a suppliant prayer is left for her to make.

De Meester does not venture that far. Instead he uses Ms B as the framework for her posthumous benefaction. In B, she felt, he says "very much one with Jesus and Heaven's inhabitants" (p. 13) but what of her solidarity, to use Pope John Paul II's favored word, with the unredeemed, the "materialists"? Ms B may reveal what De Meester calls "her strong convictions that one day, when she'll be in Heaven at last, she'll be able to intervene actively beside God" (p. 14), but why, then, did she speak of spending *her* heaven (*passer mon Ciel*, as though it were time, not residence) doing good on earth? Why so singular an enterprise?

The giveaway comes in claiming "she will live this desire and this conviction in faith and hope"; that is, in obedience to Christ she will realize her mission from heaven. This language seems a bit gratuitous, if not forced. One might well infer that faith and hope were present, but what do they have to do with the absence of either when she is in the tunnel, under the fog, at the table of sorrow? What of her concern about blaspheming? Of her telling Sr. St. Augustine that she did not believe in heaven? Did her total helplessness at the table inform the blurriness of her language? She does not speak of begetting souls, a vivid image, but of doing good, which sounds vague. Is it not there that she is truly empty-handed, void of choreographic presumptions?

It is not in the flower power of B but at the table of helplessness in C that her littleness and her weakness reached their apogee. It is there that she becomes a ruse of the Holy Spirit.

Gennari, Giovanni. "S. Teresa di Lisieux: Un' Eco del Cuore di Dio" Teresianum 19, no. 1 (1968): 81–192.

Given what he calls the razor's edge between divine initiative and human freedom, Gennari reads Thérèse's life as a harmonic convergence of human disposition and divine reality. She knows that Jesus is love even when she feels nothing. Good, so what is novel here? This: Gennari's putdown of the "spiritual infancy" tag as "an enormous impoverishment of the wealth in her lexicon" (p. 128). This abstraction is ruinous, for in it Thérèse is lost to unbelieving, desperate souls, all those tormented by doubts. "Spiritual infancy" divides humanity into an elite, which believes it understands her and those distracted sinners who will say, "How can I, an insignificant and culpable person, dream of living as a child of God?" Gennari says that we must see that God takes the initiative through love. A charitable, pastoral insight and a caveat about glibness.

Gennari's most extravagant reading is of B, where Thérèse aims to become Love. He interprets this outlandishness as the Holy Spirit's transformation of her into itself, which seems to be putting it backwards. Did not the *offrande* signify the cessation of self claims? No, says Gennari, for in it Love is every minute purifying and renewing her soul. Thérèse *did* say (to Pauline in the *entretiens*) that she had renewed the *offrande* many times.

This is a high-flying pneumatology of Theresian spirituality. Should she be regarded more seriously as a trinitarian theologian?

Grelier, Jean. "Deux docteurs de l'amour." VT 147 (July-September 1997): 39–71

Thérèse became familiar with François de Sales in *Petites Fleurs*, the inspirational texts she was reading just before she entered Carmel. She heard about him in retreats given by Fr. Pichon and followed his prayer sequences in the *Direction spirituelle*. Grelier's citation from the *Introduction to the Devout Life* and the *Treatise on God's Love* is substantial, showing that much of François became vintage Thérèse: as François says we do not know what loving God means, so Thérèse claimed toward her life's end that charity was misunderstood—and she would set us right.

Do these urgings point to the immediate audiences of these saints? Both spent great effort addressing the spiritual needs of anxious women. The attention François gives to little daily acts done with love (*Treatise*, XII, ch. 6) and to the lowly way that agrees best with our insufficiency and littleness (*Introduction*, III, ch. 2)—this is Thérèse writing and counseling. We prefer sweets, says François, but the bitterness of the spiritual void is in every instance more fruitful. That could be his commentary on her darkness.

Grison, Michel. "Amour et Paix chez Thérèse de Lisieux." VT 106 (April-June, 1987): 45–58.

This Saint-Sulpicien pastor canvasses the many instances of peace as Thérèse understood and used the word, from her early letters through her darkness's temptation against love. It makes an intriguing register, as some instances arguing her spiritual advancement also suggest the pharisaism of complacency. Grison does not make this allegation, but he gives chapter and verse to pursue the question.

The truly helpful instances of *paix* that he trots out have an undertow: peace in the midst of suffering comes when one wants what Jesus wants (LT 87); peace coming always at the bottom of the bitter chalice (A 77r); in C 17r, peace coming in the desire to practice what she knows and admits she is far from practicing. In short, Thérèse subtracts from herself what might turn peace into flab and smugness. Perhaps the best citation in this vein occurs in the *entretiens* when she claims "such a great peace in being completely impoverished," empty-handed, inadequate, helpless, all the hiddenness in which there *might* be something salvific.

Hausman, Noëlle, *Nietzsche et Thérèse de Lisieux: Deux poétiques de la modernité*, Paris: Beauchesne, 1984.

Hausman's thorough bibliographical review of Nietzsche studies in France evinces her respect for this titanic figure, and she quotes him generously, but the contest between two such markedly antipodal figures as her title announces has already been decided within these pages. Nietzsche's influence shadowed the twentieth century and modern secularism owes enormously to his impetus, but here it is Thérèse who comes off triumphant. Nietzsche emerges as a Goliath of modern nihilism—he, its self-announced opponent!—and she, an obscure David.

Hausman dwells upon *Also sprach Zarathustra* as the key text. She finds it a Christ-haunted work of someone who achieved the "pure solipsism" of becoming a god. The pivotal image from *Zarathustra* is, however, the innocent child. She finds Nietzsche's innocence fatally flawed by its curious lovelessness, which she locates as a kind of pathic specimen, within the fact that Nietzsche could acknowledge nothing and no one beyond the claims of a rigorously autonomous self. That self was too protean to contain. Nietzsche's insistence on the play of words only in themselves and without ulterior import (here interpretation by Derrida and other derelicts is evident) reflects his inability to assume the chief task of suffering by and for others.

Hausman means Christian suffering, obviously. One wonders how Nietzsche himself, ripe in his sense of a lone mission, a Promethean challenge to vanquish all theism (Christianity) would have faced this charge. As it is, Thérèse's love via suffering for both God and an unredeemed humanity, the chief message of C and the table of suffering, provides the antidote.

Hausman, Noëlle, *Thérèse de Lisieux, docteur de l'Église: Entrer dans son oeuvre*. Paris: Desclée de Brouwer, 2007.

A sister of Saint-Coeur de Marie, Hausman sets out an economical progression through the genres of Thérèse's writings. She maintains that the "theological fecundity" there teaches that Thérèse has yet to be discovered. That is a helpful insight, one that precludes the symmetries of convenient theological rationales. Thérèse, after nearly a century at the hands of expository churchmen, remains elusive.

The freshness of approach in this study extends beyond structures and themes. Hausman provides insightful, even provocative remarks: Thérèse read the Bible only because she found there "the personages of her own development" (191); by her frequent biblical citations and allusions Thérèse is indicating that they can be substituted for her own writings (202); the silence of love in C had hidden her from her own eyes (247).

Lethel, François-Marie. "Le Jésus de l'Amour: Le christocentrisme de Thérèse de Lisieux à la Lumière de la Théologie des Saints." VT 144 (October-December 1996): 7–49.

The infinite totality of love, a mystical response to God, is, Fr. Lethel maintains, chiefly the province of female saints. Thomas Aquinas and Juan de la Cruz wrote tracts, without word of themselves; Teresa and Thérèse wrote theological narratives in the vulnerable first person. Such subjective valorisation of human limits is beautiful and modern. As Lethel notes, Thérèse understood that God's love for all of us through Jesus must be experienced by each of us uniquely.

He observes that Thérèse's devotion to the littleness and poverty of Jesus marks her predilection for him, this side of the Resurrection. That is, she opts for suffering, not glory. But Lethel could go further: Thérèse also opts for the intimate now of a love that makes faith and hope seem otiose. Put otherwise, faith and hope are like promissory notes, but love cashes in. It is immediate, an intensely personal loving of Jesus such as males (unless homosexual?) are not able to match. The old legerdemain by which men get to have souls that are feminine does not count much. It is unconvincing. Women have the far greater share, "the better part." Is that why the disciples prove dismal failures in the gospels, while the women as friends of Jesus come off so much better? Small wonder that the Church declines to invest women with priestly powers. For anyone interested in studying the christology of Thérèse, this essay is perhaps the best place to start the trench work of secondary reading.

Louf, Andre. "Saint Bernard et sainte Thérèse de Lisieux" Carmel, no. 3 (1997): 3–18.

The saints form one great family of tacit connectedness, one to every other. This brief, inspired glance at the affinity between the foremost of mediaeval Cistercians and Thérèse might seem artificial, but the points are weighty. Here are a few: Bernard on the soul's ascent by grace and then its lowering to other souls who in turn seek grace could be a gloss on Thérèse's maturation from Manuscript B to C. (It is of ancient pedigree, found in Plato's metaphor of the cave and in the traditions of the *boddhisattva*.) Second, another pertinence to C's table of sinners and Thérèse's place among them, that God's favored are humbled, as the stories of Moses, of David, and of the woman in Solomon's *Song of Songs* (the occasion for many of Bernard's sermons) attest. Third, a true love for God is not given for a payoff. Fourth: mystical union is offered to every soul, even that of the most miserable sinner, which is to note that Thérèse's democratic spirituality has its antecedence in the twelfth century. "Every soul," cries one of those sermons, "even one burdened with sins, entangled in vice, snared by seductions, captive in exile, imprisoned in a body, sunk in slime, already putrefying with the dead and turned out with those who are in hell, every soul, I say, even one damned and prey to despair can find in itself not only hope of compassion but can even dare to aspire to wedding with the Word (Christ) and not fear to bear with the King of angels the sweet yoke of love."

Hard to beat that.

Pope John Paul I. "La Gioia, Carità Squisita." In his *Illustrissimi: Lettere ai grandi del passato* (Padua: Edizioni Messaggero Padova, 1996), 200–207.

Written when he was Albino Cardinal Luciani, this celebration of Thérèse came in a series of newspaper columns he published between 1971 and 1975. The luminaries, each addressed as by letter, included Saints Luke, Bonaventura, and François de Sales, not to mention Goethe, Manzoni, Dickens, Péguy, and even the Barber of Seville. The letter to Thérèse begins with a reminiscence of when a serious illness consigned the adolescent Albino to a sanatorium and, frightened, he recalled reading of Thérèse's fearlessness in facing death at only twenty-four.

This "letter" arrives quickly at what became essential in Thérèse's life shortly before its end: "seeking the face of Christ in the face of another provides the only criterion that guarantees a genuine love for everyone, surpassing antipathies, ideologies, and even philanthropies" (204–205). Such is one of the cardinal teachings of Manuscript C.

This pope, whose papacy lasted only one month, deserves special mention as a Theresian sort of man. With the *audace* of humility, he was the first pontiff in over a thousand years to decline to wear the papal tiara upon his installation. He preferred to be known as the bishop of Rome. In the midst of high church officials he was observed talking with page boys about school. And one of his letters is addressed to Pinocchio.

Pope John Paul II. "Lettre Apostolique pour la proclamation de Sainte Thérèse de l'Enfant-Jésus et de la Sainte-Face Docteur de l'Église universelle." Vie thérèsienne 149 (January-March, 1998): 8–22.

This statement remains the best and most succinct exposition of Thérèse's life and writing for what they have contributed to the life of the Church throughout the twentieth century. Pope John Paul II comments upon the significance of each genre of her writings (he gives more space to C than to A and B combined), including her plays, which must have had a particular appeal to him, a fellow playwright. He reviews her importance to the developing thought of the Church in the Second Vatican Council and its *Dei Verbum,* to the magisterium, and to the *Catechism of the Catholic Church* (see Nos. 127, 826, 956, 1011, 2011, 2558).

Having referred to her "doctrine" (pp. 10,15), the Pope writes that "even if Therese does not strictly speaking have a doctrine, *veritable flashes of doctrine* come from her writings, as by a charism of the Holy Spirit" (p. 15). This helpful distinction points to the pneumatological importance of the Theresian witnessing, especially at the table of sinners. The Pope also refers to the singular charism of wisdom in her, which makes her all the more vital to an age athirst for "living and essential words, heroic and credible testimonies" (p. 20).

Finally and not least is the Pope's recognition that Thérèse is the youngest and most modern of the Church's Doctors. Aptly, he had first announced her doctorate to the World Youth Conference (the 12th) in Paris, on August 24, 1997, two months prior to the formal proclamation.

Simon, Bruno-Marie. "Sainte-Thérèse de l'Enfant-Jésus et la Théologie de la Rédemption." VT 126 (April-June, 1992): 333–348; and VT 127 (July-September, 1992): 407–428.

Embedded deep here in a forest of scholastic regards upon the redemption, the little flower barely receives any light. Simon tells us of Anselm's view, that the redemption was an appeasement of God's honor. As sin meant not giving God his due, Christ's death was a chastisement by a God bent upon justice. According to Thomas Aquinas, however, the offense of sin could be overcome only by love: Christ's death reconciles humanity with God, obtaining for us the divine intimacy God wants us to want. "He thirsts for our thirst," says a prayer from Gregory of Nazianzus (415).

Thérèse, Simon notes, grew up with Anselm's orientation and cast it aside in favor of God's compassionate love. Fine; but that does not help his claims that Thérèse "never failed to quake at the divine justice punishing sin" (408) and that her *confiance* in God's love "rests on the certitude of the real danger one runs of damning himself" (409). Such off-the-mark claims cheat her unshakeable view that God is a loving father who needs only a show of trust from his children.

Sleiman, Msgr. Jean Benjamin, o.c.m., "Maternité spirituelle dans la perspective thérésienne." VT 174 (2004): 45–64.

With her elevation as Doctor of the Church, Thérèse has been moved up from *l'esprit d'enfance* to spiritual maternity. In Sleiman's words, she becomes trans-substantiated and "christified," herself nourishment and communion, a universal spiritual mother of and for the Church (51, 53). From there he takes us to the darkness of C: Thérèse descended into hell (not her word for the darkness) and, sinless (not what she says of herself), she became sin in order to redeem all the prodigals and impious. Sleiman, having thus given her a Christological profile, sees here the culmination of her maternal spirituality.

While her itinerary culminating at the table of sorrow undoubtedly gave her the wisdom befitting a mother, it remains unclear why Sleiman does not see Thérèse simply as an older sister in a relationship of tacit equality with, first of all, her fellow novices. She identifies herself as sister to her brother sinners at the table. Sleiman ignores the salient fact that she is as helpless as they are *save that her love for God allows her to pray*, both for them and for herself. She wants a new spiritual light for herself as well as for them.

Sleiman cites *Evangelium Vitae*, John Paul II's encyclical urging keen sensitivity to the personhood of others, but the solidarity and openness to "the other" is there based on one's sense of the other as equal, not as offspring. Is the spiritual sorority of

Thérèse, underscored in her perception of her own littleness and inadequacy, worthy of theological pondering? This essay has raised that issue. Do priests regard their spiritual sisters as truly their equals?

Thérèse Beyond Catholicism

Boulet, Jean. "Thérèse de Lisieux ou la réforme intérieure." VT 97 (January, 1985): 27–38.

An evangelical pastor underscores Thérèse's turning to scripture and to self as a Protestant itinerary, inward and experimental, as it was for Luther. He claims she was tacitly reformist in her strict observance of the Carmel's Rule, but that does not make her extraordinary. Truly singular was her work with her fellow novices, a task Boulet reads as evidence of "spiritual realism." He does not press the crucial fact that by remaining in the novitiate, Thérèse stayed on a threshold to the end of her life. This marginality contributed substantially to the audacity of her insights. That does not make her a Protestant but does indicate the voluntarism associated with its heresies. All the better, that her working to train her fellow novices was exceptional and anomalous, that she throve in a limbo without fixed roles. Appointing her was a stroke of genius on Gonzague's part.

Her community settled for admiration and then veneration of her, an attitude of stasis, side-tracking her into what Boulet styles a packaging (*emballage*) foreign to her and occlusive of her "genuine evangelical message." The positive aspect of this treatment is that it has kept her memory going so that now an authentic witnessing can begin. Boulet commends Vatican II for passing from a protectionism that kept saints in plaster, but Pope John Paul's appointment of Thérèse to the doctorate of the Church marked an even more auspicious advance. Yet her implicit Protestantism goes only so far: she interpreted the Bible for herself and she acknowledged only Jesus as her spiritual director. Two giant strides, to be sure.

Fontaine, Dominique. "Thérèse, la Mission de France et l'Incroyance." VT 113 (January-March, 1989): 17–27.

In 1942, with France's fortunes at lowest ebb, Cardinal Suard inaugurated from Lisieux the Mission de France. The intent was to reach those distant from a belief in God. As France was then under Nazi occupation, those distant were all but next-door neighbors to Christians in France.

A priest in charge of formation of MDF religious, Père Dominique casts light where many Theresian scholars see only darkness, the table setting Thérèse presents as the centerpiece in her temptation. He argues that the nonbelief she finds there offers a spiritual pathway to God, one that Thérèse learned to take in solidarity with nonbelievers, aware as she was that they, too, are loved by God. He claims that to remain in the shadow of Christ crucified is to begin a journey into darkness. It means taking up the cross of the nonbelievers' indifference and becoming their companion on a march through spiritual night. One experiences God by loving a world where God has been set aside and forgotten.

This bracing insight deserves pondering. It is a substantial variant upon the well-established model of condescension, where one prays distantly for and down to sinners but does not engage their world. Thérèse, ordered by a confessor not to probe the darkness she was in, went her audacious way, living out the interrogatives of her temptation as a gift from God, with a profound sympathy for people the Church had never fully acknowledged and considered immoral. Père Dominique ascribes to her the discovery of perpetual combat within the self, between trust and distrust, and suggests we borrow her itinerary along this daily terrain.

Leclerq, Jacques. *J'aime les lointains.* Paris: Desclée de Brouwer, 1998.

This priest from the Mission de France spent several years incognito, working as an agronomist in China. His insights into the challenging "alterity" of a people who have never known nor even heard of Christ recast for our time what this exilic task imposes.

Thérèse wanted to join one of the daughter Carmels in Vietnam. Her illness precluded the possibility, but Leclerq's account of China complements to a degree her own at the table of sinners in C; that is, what he calls a mystical solidarity with those of no faith. China, he says, affords not only uncertainty and anxiety to a Christian but also a cross or dark night that exists only in expectation. He says the Church truly encounters itself in mission, in other people God has given the Christian to acknowledge, love, and serve—a formidable task among people wholly unaware of forgiveness.

Of the table Leclerq claims that Thérèse knew that the non-believers seated there with her were bearers of grace. (Recall Bernanos's claim that the invisible Church is composed of heretics and non-believers as well as the pious faithful.) Some incendiary remarks: "It's as if China had been given to the Church so it would not forget that God is different" and "The night's blindness is the very hunger of the Chinese people which becomes our hunger." His cautions on the Church's "strategy" in approaching China as a fertile ground for mission are sobering, deeply informed by experience and hard-earned respect for the Chinese people. One senses his learning would have been Thérèse's, had she made her way to the Far East.

Pagans don't need a missionary so much as he needs them.

Only love can be the very name of God, as only love for others makes one live.

An English translation has been in the works.

McNamee, John. *Diary of a City Priest.* Franklin, WI: Sheed and Ward, 1993.

Readers who stoutly elect rosewater and consolations over and against the cross they have been told to carry would do well to avoid Thérèse. They would also do well to avoid this book, an account which does not spare its author. Fr. McNamee, retired at the time of this writing, spent over twenty-five years serving the Church and a neighborhood of the hopeless and forgotten in a terrain of trashy vacant lots, abandoned houses, and crossfire. Mostly black (Muslim) and Hispanic, the poor of North Philadelphia subsist on methadone, car thefts, wine in paper bags, and handouts from official and unofficial charities, including the priest's wallet.

Fr. McNamee's chronicle of one year, at age fifty-eight, early on leaves the reader wondering how he managed to keep going solo: the incessant importunities of addicts and petty criminals at the Church's door, the accompanying to and from hospitals and courts, and the acute aloneness, the crescent hopelessness he feels and struggles against. "Well," one might say, "he chose to be a priest, did he not?" Of course, and he entered the priesthood in a time when priests were still revered as their communities' pillars. But he did not anticipate Vatican II nor his arrival at a war zone cluster of people who were not, for the greater part, his parishioners but became his flock: goats, not sheep. Extra ecclesiam nulla salus? He never raises the question.

The chief merit of this unadorned and relentlessly unsentimental narrative is that it gives a grim, contemporary, urban equivalent of Thérèse's table of suffering, the setting which she did not choose but to which she knew that Jesus had sent her—allowing it to happen, as she tactfully puts it. There, she found the priesthood she had pointlessly desired. Jesus paid back her desire with interest. North Philadelphia shows us the sordid concreteness in that payback.

Revealing the cost of Christian discipleship, this vivid, gritty book has permanent value.

Films and Recordings

La correspondance intégrale de Sainte Thérèse de Lisieux et de l'Abbé Maurice Bellière. Studio SM Atelieir JADE, 1, square Puccini, 78150 Le Chesnay, 1992.

This two-CD set includes a reading of all the letters between Thérèse and Bellière, an exchange co-terminous with her darkness at the table. Brigitte Fossey, well-known to the French from her young child role in *Les jeux interdits*, gives a splendid rendition of Thérèse. Though some might find her voice too polished and mature to suggest a 24-year-old, the listener is likely to settle in quickly and agreeably. David Clair's Bellière matches her with an ardent, almost pleading tone, an altogether convincing way to conjure up a young would-be missionary, earnest and anxious, needful of a guardian angel.

Defilippis, Leonard. *Thérèse*, Xenon Pictures and Luke Films, 2004.

This is the first film about Thérèse without French language and culture, an American stylization of her with a message of comfort. It was clearly made for a piously unreflective audience expecting a soothing version of this saint at the expense of the real dynamics of her life and death. Her ongoing darkness in the nine years at Carmel is not to be guessed.

Defilippis, who doubles as director and Louis in his forties, is to be commended for taking on episodes ignored in other films: the ten-year-old girl's hallucinatory illness linked to Pauline's departure into Carmel, the Pranzini episode, the antagonism Thérèse faced as a teacher's pet. Within the convent, the episode of Thérèse escorting the arthritic Sr. St. Pierre as partying music is heard from beyond the convent's walls is played well for its humor but then falsified grotesquely by Thérèse forcibly dancing with her charge. For all her saintliness, this girl was just as vulgar and fun-loving as the rest of us? This warping cheats Thérèse's point, that she would not have traded her time with old St. Pierre for a lifetime of parties.

Too much else is slighted or glossed over. Gonzague is all but absent. Sr. St. Augustin, unidentified but apparently meant, plays the "heavy" with her bossiness. Carmel itself, like Les Buissonnets, is more plantation than confining space, with broad never-never land vistas, a bourgeois idyll at a reassuring distance from the austerities of Teresa's house of prayer.

Wanted: a film director who will take the time for thorough immersion in Thérèse's life via all its documentation, portray it in the full justice of its chiaroscuro, cast credible, skilled, and un-pretty actors, avoid the sickening cream of hagiographic whitewashing and all traces of sentimentality, limit music to sources or enlist a composer who knows what Dante would call the teeth and bonds of love's suffering. As the latter participant, Krystof Penderecki? SofiaGubaidulina?

Gröning, Philip. *Die grosse Stille*, Zeitgeist Films, 2005.
At a Carthusian monastery in the French Alps a photograph of Thérèse hangs on the wall of a small room that some friars enter in the midst of this rare and exhausting film. She is the only woman there.

An un-narrated succession of scenes in their lives includes the offices, the weekly gathering at the refectory, daily chores, and an open-air discussion of the proprieties of hand-washing. In their chapel's vast darkness, the chants bear a sublimity that only sacrificed lives could attain, as though in proof that the human voice can be distilled of all impurities and become one with the ancient harmony of the spheres. An established harmony comes within juxtapositions of monastic interiors with Alpine environs, the mountainous majesty and diminutive botanies of meadows almost conspiratorial with the Carthusians' rugged simplicity. When, in the *Benedicite*, the friars call upon heat and cold, dew and clouds to bless God, we of the secular life are invited to gauge our "worldly" distance from nature itself.

Gröning, several months in their midst, called upon each friar to look solo and silent into his camera for fifteen seconds, a singular gesture none would ever have anticipated as part of Carthusian life. Their dispassionate acceptance of him and his lens conveys the gentle but resolute Christian way of facing an unhappy, confused, inimical world. Only one friar, bent with age and blind, speaks at length toward the film's end, reflecting upon the ways of grace, thanking God for his blindness (a Theresian note!), and voicing sadness for the modern abandonment of God. The friars look out from the abbey and see *us* at the table of sorrow.

A caveat: this film *must* be faced within the cavernous darkness of a theater. (I was lucky to view it with an audience of about a dozen amid some 300 seats.) The DVD version is bound to forfeit the engaging power of a theater viewing, scaling down and trivializing the experience. Best to feel trapped in a great, dark, silent space.

Index

Acedia, defined, xvi, 212n1
   See also Dryness
Alcántara, Pedro de, Fr., 7, 8, 15, 81, 213n10
Alumbradismo, 5–6, 7, 8, 12, 13, 14
Aña de Jesús, Madre, 154, 158, 160, 163
Aquinas, Thomas, Saint. *See* Thomism
Augustine of Hippo, Saint, 213n14
   Confessions of, 7
   mystical exaltation of, 90
   Order of, 9, 12

Balthasar, Hans Urs von, Cardinal, 73–76
Bellière, Maurice, Fr. 58, 60, 67, 105, 106, 113, 114–15, 124, 174
Bible, 38–77 *passim*
   Book of Job in, 17, 62, 64, 75
   Gospel of Luke in, 54–56, 58–60
   Isaiah's Suffering Servant in, 40–44
   Psalms of, 38, 48–54
   Song of Songs in, 18, 23, 38, 44–48
   See also Thérèse de l'Enfant-Jésus de la Sainte-Face, Sr.
Blino, Laurent, Fr., 21
Bloy, Léon, on sainthood, 161

Carmel, Discalced Order of
   circulaires of, 102, 167
   ethos of perfection in, 151
   foundational history of, 2–18, 23–30
   as house of prayer, 160
   imitatio Christi in, 96
   Jesus as heart of, 37

   in Vietnam, 105, 170, 171, 182
   See also Juan de la Cruz, San; Teresa de Jesús, Madre
Cisneros, Ximénez, Cardinal, 4, 25
Claudel, Paul, on the Thérèse industry, 164
Confiance, 21, 62, 93, 158, 179, 184
Conversos, Muslims as, 25
   Jews as, 25–26, 28–29
   Teresa's relatives as, 8
   See also Jews; Muslims
Cornière, Alexandre de, Dr., 84, 169
Crashaw, Richard, 2

Dante, 121, 177
   compared to Thérèse, 182–83
Day, Dorothy, xvii, 126
Didier, Beatrice, 153–54
Dostoevsky, Fyodor, xviii, 128, 194, 195
Dryness
   defined, xv–xvi
   See also Acedia

Erasmus, Desiderius, 4, 5, 34

Fénelon, François, Bishop, 96, 126
Feuerbach, Ludwig, xviii
Flaubert, Gustave, on Loyson, 124, 126
France, republican anticlericalism of, 68–69, 72, 128, 136, 138
   Freemasonry in, 136–38
   Gallicanism in, 127–28
   See also Loyson, Hyacinthe, Fr.; Taxil, Léo

Francis of Assisi, Saint, 160–61
Gaucher, Guy, Msgr. 36, 66
Gonzague, Marie de, Mère, 14, 49, 51, 66, 67, 69, 80, 85, 94, 97, 102, 112, 118, 131, 134
　advising Thérèse, 92, 97, 150, 198
　composing *Histoire d'une âme*, 165–67
　criticisms of, 168–70
　in Manuscript C, 166–73
　and Marthe de Jésus, 98–102
　painting with Thérèse, 86–87, 172–73, 187
　Thérèse's parable for, 169–71
Gracián, Jerónimo, Fr. 2, 13, 16, 29, 35, 81
Guérin, Isidore (uncle), 93, 97, 123, 130, 181
Guérin, Jeanne (cousin), 88, 95
Guérin, Marie (cousin), 92, 98, 105

Hus, Jan, 5
Huse, Marcelline, in testimony on Thérèse, 181

Illuminism, 6, 71, 174
　See also *Alumbradismo*; Mysticism
Inquisition, Spanish, 5, 10, 12
　See also Spain
Islam. See Muslims

Jeanne d'Arc, Sainte 19, 115, 133, 154, 160, 166
　and Diana Vaughan, 137–38, 140–42
　Thérèse's writings on, 50, 64, 145–46
Jesus, as center of Carmel spirituality, xvii, 10, 12–13, 14
　as fairytale beloved of Thérèse, 110, 149, 150, 155
　hiddenness of, 41, 80, 109, 158
　as instructor of Thérèse, 66–67
　as painter of Carmelites, 86–87
　as Suffering Servant. 40–44
　thirst for souls in, 33, 73
　wrath of, 74–75
　See also Thérèse de l'Enfant-Jésus de la Sainte-Face, Sr.

Jews
　as bureaucrats in Spain, 95
　despising Samarians, 48
　in family of Juan de la Cruz, 23
　in family of Teresa de Jesús, 8–9, 214n19, 215n25
　Jesus's silence before, 41, 110
　in polemics with Church, 44
　in psalms, 48–54
　Spanish persecutions of, 4–5, 44
　Sephardics in Spain, 24
Joan of Arc, Saint. See Jeanne d'Arc, Sainte
John of the Cross. See Juan de la Cruz, San
Juan de la Cruz, San [Juan de Yepes y Álvarez], 22, 81
　asceticism of, 30, 182
　Cantico Espiritual of, 29, 31, 34, 84, 155–56
　childhood of, 23
　compared to Teresa, 30
　death of, 30
　Dichos de luz y amor of, 29, 34
　family ties of, 30, 94
　imprisonment of, 16, 28, 166
　indebted to Islam, 24, 28
　Llama de Amor Viva of, 29, 34, 83, 86
　Noche Oscura of, 29, 86
　on pure love, 31, 194
　purification in, 35, 85–86
　science of the Cross in, 75
　and *Song of Songs*, 31–33
　Subida del Monte Carmelo of, 29, 86, 92
Judaism. See Jews

Kierkegaard, Soren, 37, 75

Le Bon, Gustave, 138
Leo XIII, Pope, 137–38
Loyson, Hyacinthe, Fr.
　apostasy of, 123–35 *passim*
　career of, 125–26
　Catholic press on, 131–32
　as counter to Louis Martin, 131, 142
　founds Gallican Church, 127–28

in letters to Carmel, 133, 246n30
on marriage of priests, 127, 128
marries, 126, 130
opposes papal infallibility, 126
Thérèse on, 131, 134, 135, 178, 245n15, 245n19
on universal charity, 129–30
Luther, Martin, 4, 5, 34, 129, 179

Maria de San José, Madre, 12, 29
Mariano, Ambrosio, 13, 16, 29, 35
Marie de la Trinité, Sr., 34, 35, 46, 115–16, 117, 121
Marie de Saint-Joseph, Sr., 102–07
and intermittent eruption disorder, 239n94
Marie des Anges, Mère, 92, 97, 98, 104, 106, 107, 116, 167
darkness of, 100, 141
Marthe de Jésus, Sr., 121, 181, 186–87
contending with Thérèse, 98–102
Martin, Céline (sister), 20, 82, 85, 108, 164
as antagonist to Thérèse, 90–91, 96–97
in correspondence with Loyson, 246n30
courting of, 118
on Marie de la Trinité, 115–16
on Marthe de Jésus, 99
and Pauline, 88–89, 96
sacrifices for her father, 42, 92
on Thérèse and purgatory, 36
Thérèse's struggles with, 88–98, 108–09
understanding Juan de la Cruz, 94, 97
understanding *Song of Songs*, 46
without vocation to Carmel, 118
Martin, Louis (father), x, 88, 92, 130, 142, 148, 171, 172, 192, 227n55
affliction of, 62
in sanatorium, 91, 93, 152
as Thérèse's first spiritual director, 181
Martin, Marie (sister), 34, 66, 88, 89, 93, 125, 235n64
Martin, Pauline (sister), 66, 80
apprehensions of, 93, 110–15
composing *entretiens*, 85

in crisis over Marthe de Jésus, 98–99, 100
as editor, 165–66
as first cultist of Thérèse, 113, 187
on Léo Taxil, 144
on Marie de Saint-Joseph, 104
on Mère Gonzague, 103, 168–70
in testimony on Thérèse, xvi, 47, 74, 118
Martin, Zélie (mother), 98, 111–12, 126–27
affliction of, 62–63
Maudelonde, Henry (cousin)
courting Céline, 118
Merton, Thomas, xvi
Montalembert, Charles de, on Loyson, 126
Muslims
compulsory baptism of, 25
in family of Juan de la Cruz, 23
silk industry of, 17, 25
Spanish persecution of, 4
and Teresa de Jesús, 217n57
Mysticism
of Carmel, 17–18, 145
dangers of, 29, 86
as quietism, 6
See also Alumbradismo; Illuminism; Juan de la Cruz, San; Teresa de Jesús, Madre

Newman, John Henry, Cardinal, on Loyson, 126

Osuna, Francesco de
Tercer Abecedario of, 8, 19, 20

Paul, Saint, xvii, 10, 54, 58, 72, 92, 132, 176
on hope against hope, 180
and new man in Christ, 85
on Pentecostal gifts, 155
on redemption, 189
regarding women, 11
Philip II, King of Spain, 2, 11, 25, 29
Pichon, Almire, Fr. 21, 81, 82, 92–93, 97, 104, 126, 132, 142, 150, 163, 173, 192
See also Taxil, Léo

Pius IX, Pope, 126, 127, 132
  "secret amours" of, 136
Pranzini, Henri, 130–32, 178

Renan, Ernest, 38, 130
Roulland, Adolphe, Fr., 32, 43, 67, 106, 124, 132
Russell, Bertrand, on anger of Jesus, 73

Saint-Jean-Baptiste, Sr., 46–47, 118–19
Saint-Pièrre de Sainte-Thérèse, Sr., 185–86
Sand, George [Amantine Lucile AuroreDupin]
  on Loyson, 126, 129, 132, 153
Spain
  publication in, 4, 10
  religious persecution in, 4–5, 10, 11, 16, 22, 213n7
  university education in, 27
  See also Juan de la Cruz, San; Teresa de Jesús, Madre

Taxil, Léo [Gabriel-Antoine Jogand-Pages], 123, 124, 135, 144, 192
  Catholic education of, 136
  as counter to Almire Pichon, 142
  and Freemasonry. 136
  as guide to Thérèse, 145–46, 177
  at Paris press conference, 143
  See also Vaughan, Diana
Teresa de Ávila, Santa. *See* Teresa de Jesús, Madre
Teresa de Jesús, Madre [Teresa de Cepeda y Alhumada]
  affective way of, 20–21
  Camino de Perfección of, 2, 7, 12, 13, 15–16, 18, 21, 22, 36, 80, 117, 120, 191
  Castillo Interior of, 2, 6, 12, 13, 16–17
  on Christian suffering, 15, 17
  compared to Thérèse, 2, 8, 18–22, 77, 81–82
  correspondence of, 2, 16
  Cuentos de conciencia of, 2
  darkness of, 205–09
  in diplomacy with Church, 6, 13
  dryness of, 19
  educated childhood of, 8–9
  on entrance into Carmel, 9
  Exclamaciones del alma a Dios of, 205–09
  on family ties, 14
  as founder of Reformed Carmel, 2, 10
  and Franciscans, 5, 8, 9
  Fundaciones of, 2, 3, 12, 123
  humility of, 8, 14, 15
  at Incarnation Carmel, 9, 11–12
  Libro de Vida of, 6, 9, 10, 12, 18, 19, 22, 175
  metaphors of, 15, 17, 19, 43, 88
  morbid fears of, 8, 9
  mysticism of, 6, 7, 12, 45, 171, 209, 217n57
  in politics with God, 8, 13
  reform measures of, 10–12, 13
  self-deprecations of, 7, 8, 16, 19, 213n11
  and self-estimate as woman, 7–8, 12
  on sin, 17
  and *Song of Songs*, 2, 3, 18, 227n57
  Thérèse's references to writings of, 18–19
  unitive prayer of, 8, 10, 13
  vejamen of, 30, 31
  visitations of, 3, 10
  on women as Christians, 12–13, 14, 17–18, 134, 182
  as writer, 19, 22
Thérèse de l'Enfant-Jésus de la Sainte-Face, Sr.
  abandon of, 172, 247n31
  in admissions to Pauline, 34
  appeal of paradox to, 41, 43, 57
  audace of, 40, 56, 57, 66, 68, 98–99, 102–07, 111, 114, 162–63, 179, 194
  attending to the marginal, 43, 102–07
  compared to Teresa de Jesús, 2, 8, 197–98, 208
  cult appeal in, 47–48, 149, 164

darkness of, 34, 49, 85, 92, 114–15, 145–46, 150, 157–58, 164, 173–74, 194–95, 197
distant from Sacred Heart cult, 224n22, 226n50
doubt in, 22, 93, 151, 163, 194
dryness of, 19, 108
on dying and death, 80, 82, 84
Easter conversion of, 150, 152–53, 154
elevator image of, 51–52, 81, 117, 170
épreuve de l'amour de la confiance in, 178
and family ties, 14, 88–98, 108–09
as friend to Marthe de Jésus, 98–102, 121, 181, 186–87
in *Histoire d'une âme*, 164–66
in ignorance of Biblical languages, 37–38, 40, 41, 45, 71–72, 229n74
imitatio Christi in, 20, 56, 96, 109, 124, 179
imperfectability of, 46–47, 118–21, 173
importance of Saint Luke to, 54–56, 58–60, 70, 98, 158, 162, 176, 197
indifferent to Jesus's miracles, 61–62
influence of Juan de la Cruz on, 30–36, 83, 84
on Isaiah's Suffering Servant, 40–44, 73
Jesus as fairytale lover of, 149–50
on love of enemies, 67–69, 71–72
as *maîtresse auxiliaire de novices*, 87, 98–99, 102, 107, 173
in Manuscript B, 153–64, 188–90, 194
in Manuscript C, 166–95
as a New Testament figure, 37–77 *passim*, 160, 194

offrande of, 20, 32–33, 38, 77, 83, 152, 158, 162, 173–74, 194
pastoral praxis of, 80–122
in prayers, 83, 93–94, 151, 154, 156, 158, 171, 173, 174, 176, 179, 180, 182, 187, 193, 194
on psalms, 38, 48–54
reading Juan de la Cruz, 18, 40
reading Teresa de Jesús, 2–3, 18, 21
reconnaissance frequent in, 172
and shepherdess story for Gonzague, 169–71
at table of sorrow, 20–22, 52–53, 65, 70–73, 80, 84, 88–98, 108–09
in training of Céline, 88–98, 108–09
tunnel and vault imagery in, 147, 148, 164, 165, 177, 180, 193
weakness as strategy of, 154–56
as writer, xvi, 22, 83, 85
See also Jesus; Juan de la Cruz, San; Teresa de Jesús, Madre
Thomism, 13, 26
education of Juan de la Cruz in, 27–28

Vaughan, Diana, 124, 137, 138, 143, 248n42
Catholic press in support of, 137, 139, 140
lesson of, 146, 179
Thérèse's enthusiasm for, 140–42, 144
See also Taxil, Léo

Williams, Rowan, xvi

Youf, Louis, Abbé, 82, 84